Pan Africanism in the African Diaspora

Pan Africanism in the African Diaspora

An Analysis of Modern Afrocentric Political Movements

Ronald W. Walters

Wayne State University Press   Detroit

African American Life Series

A complete listing of the books in this series can be found at the back of this volume.

General Editors

Toni Cade Bambara
Author and Filmmaker

Geneva Smitherman
Michigan State University

Wilbur C. Rich
Wellesley College

Ronald W. Walters
Howard University

Library of Congress Cataloging-in-Publication Data
Walters, Ronald W.
    Pan Africanism in the African diaspora: an analysis of modern Afrocentric political movements / Ronald W. Walters.
      p. cm.—(African-American life series)
    Includes bibliographical references and index.
    ISBN 0-8143-2184-4 (alk. paper)
    1. Africans—Politics and government. 2. Blacks—Politics and government. 3. Pan-Africanism. 4. African diaspora. 5. Black nationalism. I. Title. II. Series.
DT16.5.W35 1993
320.5'49'096—dc20   92-30256

Designer: Mary Primeau

This work is dedicated to
mom and dad,
Maxine C. Walters and the late
Gilmar L. Walters,
and the Walters family

Contents

Preface

My first awareness of Pan Africanism, and perhaps the beginning of this book, occurred in 1963 when, as a senior at Fisk University, I wrote an essay entitled "The Blacks," which won a *Readers Digest* national essay contest. The essay was constructed as a mythical discussion taking place on a ship between two long-lost descendants of Africa, one an African and the other an African American. Although the ship was sailing from America to Africa, it didn't matter where the boat was going; the important thing was that it was a neutral site for such a discussion. The prize included a trip to New York City and a meeting with writers such as John Williams, Bloke Modisane, a South African, and William Melvin Kelly; they only deepened my thirst fully to understand what I had written. That dialogue between "The Blacks," reflecting more than a century of the unresolved tensions of what came before and after the Middle Passage of slavery, is still a subject deep in the recesses of my mind and, I think, of the Black mind in general, shaping such fundamental concepts as that of total allegiance to and identity with America.

In the 1960s, my association with the Pan African movement

in the United States and with a cadre of dedicated Pan Africanist activists and scholars taught me much about the African dimension of my own identity and about the quality of obligation that this identity implied. And therefore, I owe a great debt to the leaders of the Pan African movement, most especially to Howard Fuller (Owusu Sadauki), Jimmy Garrett, Courtland Cox, Amiri Baraka, Maulana Karenga, Stokely Carmichael and William Strickland. Just as important are the members of my "extended family," the African Heritage Studies Association, whose brilliant intellects and camaraderie was fundamental in sharpening my appreciation of the need to conceptualize aspects of this subject. I owe a fraternal debt to professors James Turner, John Henrik Clarke, Ofuatey Kodjoe, Barbara Wheeler, Leonard Jeffries, Charshee McIntyre, Nancy Arnez, Wilfred Cartey, Molefi Asante, Barbara Sizemore, Doc Ben and others.

I would also like to express my thanks to the Abraham Sachar International Fund at Brandeis University for travel to England to carry out research in connection with this work in 1971; the Howard University Faculty Research Fund for research assistance on this project in 1980 and 1981; Dr. Charles Harris, distinguished professor of history at Howard University and scholar of the African Diaspora, for his invitation to me to be a part of the African Diaspora Studies Institute series of conferences examining the African Diaspora in 1979 and for his invitation to present a paper from this work at an African Diaspora Conference in Naibori in 1981. During this entire period of work on the manuscript, I benefitted greatly from the inestimable assistance of the staffs at both the Moorland-Spingarn Research Center at Howard University and the Schomberg Library in Harlem, New York City. I appreciated also the opportunity to travel under the auspices of the United Nations for more than a decade as a consultant to the Center Against Apartheid, travel which enabled me to make contact with Africans living in various parts of Europe and the Caribbean. And I was fortunate to be able to make a tour of Brazil as a visiting scholar in 1990 under the sponsorship of the United States Information Agency. I also owe a profound debt of gratitude to Dr. St. Clair Drake for his initial guidance given me during a long discussion at Stanford and to Professor Willard Johnson for several readings of the manuscript and for invaluable suggestions. However, the faults of the manuscript are essentially my own.

I had originally conceived of this work as a tightly drawn study of comparable white-dominant social systems such as England and South Africa. It, therefore, appeared necessary to analyze the comparative aspects of the white dominance against which the politics of pan African communities was directed, utilizing the analytical approach suggested here. I considered this important because many studies of Black people in the African diaspora have been conducted without a proper analysis of the context within which they live as an important ingredient that shapes the content of pan African relations. The next step was to examine the relations between the Black communities within each of the countries. This approach was responsible for the three chapter sequences for both the British and South African case studies.

As the study progressed, however, two points became clearer. The first was that the African-American experience was the critical dynamic around which all of the cases revolved. This accounts for the placement near the book's beginning of the chapters on African-American pan Africanism both within and beyond the United States. Finally, I decided that the study would not be complete without addressing the Caribbean and Latin America, but that the concept of white dominance was not a satisfactory device for examining Pan Africanism in these areas. Therefore, consistent with the analytical approach, the Brazilian case is largely concerned with comparative politics of Brazilian and American Black communities, and the Caribbean chapter is an examination of the interactive involvement of Black people there and in the United States in the Pan African Movement of the 1960s.

Finally, the individual chapters should be considered to belong to small sets, addressing the same case study or illustrating a different approach to the analysis of Pan Africanism. For example, the focus of chapters 2 and 3 is African-American Pan Africanism both inside and outside of the United States; chapters 4, 5, and 6 are concerned with African Americans and Blacks in Britain; chapters 7, 8, and 9 examine the linkage between African Americans and Blacks in South Africa; then chapters 10 and 11 cover the Latin American (Brazil) and Caribbean area respectively, with the former using the Comparative approach and the latter using the Pan African approach. With respect to the time frame involved, all of these case studies are concerned with

political movements that are set within definite periods of recent history. And most cover the time-span of the past three decades. However, the controlling feature in the selection of all
the case studies was the extent to which and the period in
which pan African relationships constituted a critical dimension. Therefore, the virtual absence of a Pan African movement in the United States and the severely diminished impact
of such politics upon the African Diaspora after the mid-1970s
set natural time limitations on the analysis of cases included in
this work.

I would like to thank my colleagues in the African American
Life Series of the Wayne State University Press, in particular Geneva Smitherman, for encouraging me to submit this work, and
for their editorial guidance Lee Schreiner and subsequently
Kathryn Wildfong in this effort, as well as Robin Rhodes and
Yvonne Carter for their technical support in the preparation of
the manuscript.

Stylistic note

The term "Pan African" is used throughout
when referring to aspects of the formal movement being analyzed. On the other hand, the term "pan African" or "pan Africanism" refers to the phenomenon itself in the generic sense of
its usage. Similarly, the capitalized concept Black Power refers to
the formal movement while Black power is the more objective
use of the concept.

African, Black, African American, peoples of African descent,
and African-origin peoples are referred to interchangeably, but
with due deference to the context involved. The context often
involves such factors as parsimony of language as well as the
attempt to achieve clarity when discussing peoples of African
descent in different countries. The term Black is capitalized
when referring to a group such as Black Americans or as a qual-
ifying adjective to other subjects such as Black education, Black
politics, etc. The author prefers this usage in order to conceptually indicate that insofar as the term "Black" refers to a unique
people and their culture, and not simply a color, it should be
capitalized throughout, with reference to Blacks in Britain and
South Africa as well. In this sense, it carries the same connotation as Irish, Italian, or other such cultural appellations.

1
A Theory and
Method of the
Relationship

One of the modern realities of world affairs is the movement of peoples outward from their ancestral homes to establish new groupings in other places. Thus, for example, recent wars have uprooted thousands of Asians, depositing them in foreign lands; civil repression has affected the migration of Haitians, Jews, Poles, Latinos, and others; some, such as migrants from the Indian subcontinent and the Middle East, are settling elsewhere to practice newly acquired industrial skills.

Similarly, African peoples are continuing to expand their areas of residence, primarily in the countries of Western Europe. There they have faced the virulence of racist practices on the part of the white indigene as they attempt to establish themselves.

These happenings are evidence of the continuing struggle of African-origin people to survive by following the availability of gainful employment, jobs to which they feel they have a right because of centuries of expropriation of their land, labor and other resources, especially by Western Europeans. As a result, while there are approximately 350 million peoples on the African continent, there are nearly 100 million African-origin people outside of it. This is a substantial diaspora, and its existence raises questions concerning the tensions and harmonies of relationships among African peoples in the world.

The continuing relationships among African peoples are rendered more complex by the multiplicity of places of residence and the nature of the problems faced especially by those outside of the African continent, and how they have come to identify themselves in relation to continental African peoples. For example, anyone who has followed the tortuous course of American history and the saga of the struggle between Africans and Europeans can foretell what similarly lies in store for Black Britians, Black Australians, Black Canadians, Black Brazilians, and so on. Thus, the possibility of similar styles of development also may establish an identity among these communities of African-origin peoples marked by their similar relationship to whites in these societies as well as by their similar origin. This calls for a description of the "process" by which the African Diaspora is created—the methods involved, the community that is subsequently established, and the strategies utilized to maintain the community and achieve shared objectives in the new place of residence.

The essence of the problem becomes: What forces drive African-origin peoples to continue identifying with the source of their cultural origin? And how do these forces affect the quality of relationship both among Africans in the Diaspora and between them and Africans on the continent. We begin this search for "forces" and their effect by a discussion of the factors which created the diaspora, the formation of African-origin communities in the Diaspora, their survival, and the method of analyzing Pan African relations.

Creation of the Diaspora

To many, considering the world impact of the slave trade, the method by which the African Diaspora was formed is an obvious fact of history. Professor Oruno Lara broadly conceives of the Diaspora as having been created by slavery and the slave trade and by the factors within the system of imperialism and colonialism that forced Africans to leave their continent.[1] However, the dispersal of any group of peoples over centuries is a complex phenomenon that yields itself to more than one or two methods, even allowing for the preponderant impact of slavery. Other aspects of this process which we will consider below are commerce, war and migration, and although all of these factors may be considered to have taken place simultaneously in the process of European imperialism, still there is a certain logical course of events which makes possible an historical description in our case. We will then, consider slavery, commerce, war and immigration in that order, not in an effort thoroughly to analyze each but to make a commentary on their essential contribution to the creation of the African Diaspora.

Slavery

No one knows how many Black men, women and children were taken from Africa during the slave trade, for few accurate records were kept and many of the scholarly estimates proceed from different assumptions. For example, one author says that conservative estimates consider that the numbers involved in the slave trade increased substantially in each century, from nine hundred thousand in the sixteenth century to 2.8 million in the seventeenth century, reaching the apogee of 7 million in the eighteenth century and falling to 4 million in the late nineteenth century at its end.[2] Two things should be noted, and they refer to the fact that approximately fifteen million slaves were delivered to the "New World"—the Americas—as a total and that slave trading companies in Europe and America were responsible for the shipping process. First, if one assumes that perhaps thirty million Africans were taken from the continent and that fifteen million were delivered to the Americas, then the loss rate (50 percent) is certainly within the projected average loss rates reported in the eighteenth century; such figures, therefore, have a strong hint of accuracy.[3]

But if it is difficult to say accurately how many slaves were actually shipped to the Americas, then it is also difficult to know how they were divided, beyond some rough estimate, among the various regions. However, census figures indicate that by the middle of the nineteenth century there were roughly four million Blacks in Brazil alone.[4] W. E. B. DuBois reports that about this same time (1850) there were 3,638,808 Negroes in the United States.[5] The slave population of Canada is insignificant in comparison, there having been something more than 1,100 slaves in New France in 1759 and about 7,000 in 1789. Further movement to Canada from the United States was stimulated by the imposition of such laws as the Black Codes and the Fugitive Slave Act,[6] and by the middle of the nineteenth century, the total number of Blacks in Canada probably reached twenty-five thousand.

The remainder of the African population in the New World was located in the Caribbean; figures show that in the middle of the nineteenth century Cuba had approximately six hundred thousand Africans and Puerto Rico forty-two thousand.[7] Shortly before Haiti gained independence there were roughly one-half million slaves in that island country and a similar number in Jamaica, and perhaps another half million blacks on the other islands down to the end of the nineteenth century.[8] All in all, it would be difficult to place more than two-and-one-half million Africans in the Americas at the end of the nineteenth century. Assuming the fifteen million total noted above, this leaves over four million Africans to be accounted for. If one considers seriously the estimate of Sir Henry Johnston that in 1911 some twenty-four million Africans lived in the New World, then the problem is even larger.[9]

If one takes the most conservative estimate of Frank Tannenbaum, one finds that approximately half of the total population of African slaves was distributed between North America and South America, with the lion's share of those in North America going to the United States and most of those in South America rather equally divided between the Caribbean and Latin America.[10] This constitutes a rough approximation of the distribution of African people in the New World through the end of the slave trade, the overwhelming method by which the Diaspora communities were created.

Commerce

During the slave trade and especially for a period thereafter, Africans, renowned for their skills as seamen, played a role in the expanding world commerce fueled by the industrial revolution. These skills were ancient. In the words of two experts on the Black maritime tradition: "Africans have a long, distinguished maritime heritage. The Black pharaohs of Egypt are known to have sailed wooden plank ships 170 feet long on the Mediterranean and are believed to have reached American shores in the eighth century B.C."[11] In the nineteenth century, freed Africans were able to gain employment and make their home port in seaport towns such as Liverpool, Cardiff, Nantes and Marseilles. They married local women or imported African brides, beginning the process by which permanent communities of African peoples were formed.

One noteworthy example was Olaudah Equiano, an African taken from his homeland in the late eighteenth century and "seasoned" in the West Indies where he became a valuable ship-hand and earned his freedom. He lived in England for some time before moving to Sierra Leone.[12] It is important to note that the story of his life was first narrated by the subject himself and published in 1789. Eighteenth-century records also tell of James Forten, a seventeen-year-old freed Black who worked as a seaman in order to get to England. He lived for three years (1783–1786) in Liverpool and London and then returned to the United States; there, having learned the skill of sail-making, he soon became prosperous and was the captain of his own ship. Later, he was to play an important role in the American Colonization Society, a movement to resettle blacks on the coast of West Africa.[13]

After slavery, Africans served as seamen on all sorts of ships—privateers, whalers, merchant vessels, U.S. warships. Indeed, they helped man the first whaler in the United States. American ship owners particularly sought Cape Verdean sailors. One account says that since the late eighteenth century, whalers from New England frequently stopped at the Cape Verde Archipelago and brought its renowned seamen to America to work in their cranberry bogs and factories. Cape Verdeans thus were encouraged to come to America, bringing friends and family, by whatever means were at their disposal.[14]

As late as 1970, the practice of Cape Verde seamen sailing between New England and Africa was still continuing.

I had the opportunity to interview several elderly Black merchant seamen living in Syracuse, New York who spoke of the continuing role Black seamen played in the process of creating the Diaspora. Some had served on non-American–flag ships and in the navies of other colonial powers. The sailors described the social world of various members of the African Diaspora—Americans, West Indians, Africans, in various seaport towns around the world. The major comments centered on the nature of communities in which Black seamen were forced to marry local women, with the result that some sailors had wives in several ports. They also pointed to the unity displayed by these groups in the face of white racism.[15]

Given the role of African seamen in the process of creating and maintaining the Diaspora, the lack of scholarly attention to his story is a major shortcoming in the documentation of the dynamics of the ways in which Diaspora communities are formed.

War

The function of the African soldier is as old as civilization, the prowess of Nubian warriors down to the early exploits of Hannibal well recorded, and black soldiers played a role in the Moorish conquest of Spain, in the armies of Southern India and the expansion of the great kingdoms of the Sahara Desert. These activities in turn played a part in the extention of African civilization and influence both inside and outside the African continent. That the Civil War was fought largely over slavery reminds us that the Black community in America was created in large part as a result of a war.

In modern European wars, massive numbers of Africans were put into uniform by the American and European powers and suffered heavy casualties. Nevertheless, this military service often facilitated the establishment of new Diaspora African communities. This fact should lead scholars to examine the roles of war and of the African soldier in the creation of the Diaspora.

In World War I the Germans mobilized 1,168 African soldiers in East Africa and the British mobilized nearly 63,000 African soldiers and 190,000 porters. Although thousands of German and British African troops were lost, only the French African soldiers fought on the continent of Europe. On this point, it is reported that 215,000 Africans enlisted in the French Army, of which 156,000 participated in campaigns in France, in the Near East or in Gallipoli, with 30,000 being killed in action.[16]

In the Second World War, France fell so suddenly that there was no opportunity to employ large numbers of African soldiers in its defense. However, African soldiers under British command were active in repulsing the Italians on the African continent so that "by May, 1945, the total number of Africans serving in the regular British military units and in the employ of the Italians, combatants as well as ancillary, amounted to about 374,000."[17]

Where African soldiers are concerned, it was often just as important that they were mobilized as that they were able to fight in Europe or elsewhere outside Africa. Mobilization for war brought them into contact with European languages and military systems and, not incidentally, resulted in the acquisition of a range of new skills.

For example, one observer notes that: "The askaris became proficient in using bazookas, light mortars and Bren guns, as well as rifles. Many also learned new civilian skills as clerks or as truck drivers, and thereby advanced into semi-skilled military occupations. In addition, black soldiers travelled widely, to India, Burma, Palestine and other countries from which they often returned with new ideas and a broader outlook."[18] Of course, many of these soldiers never returned home once they were mustered out of military service. This was especially true of those who had fought on the battlefields of Europe and had come to believe they had developed a stake in the metropole not only as colonial subjects but as citizens with a new claim on human rights.

In America, Black men have fought in every war since the founding of the nation, including foreign wars, in an effort to prove thereby that they were entitled to the benefits of first-class citizenship.

There were Black soldiers in the Spanish-American War in

1898 who saw action at San Juan and Santiago.[19] Of the 2,290,529 Black men mobilized during World War I, two hundred thousand were stationed in France, forty-two thousand serving as combat troops.[20] These numbers were to increase sharply in the Second World War when three million Black men registered for service, nearly one million served, and five hundred thousand Black men and women served overseas in one capacity or another.[21] Though the Korean and Vietnam conflicts in Asia were clearly lesser in scale, each saw substantial Black participation of perhaps twenty-five thousand.[22]

Although we have cast the foreign service of Black men and women in terms of war activities, it is important to note that the United States occupies a unique status as a world military power. As a result, this nation maintains extensive military bases in foreign lands in times of peace. Consequently, thousands of Black men and women have been serving all over the world as a part of the armed forces and no doubt have made their contribution to expanding the African Diaspora in several ways.

Immigration

The modern history of Africa unfortunately began with its peoples colonized and, thus, the movement of these people severely controlled. Historians of the African Diaspora are just beginning to compile the record of the travels of people out of Africa and back to the continent on the "return." It is very difficult to obtain data on the extra-continental movements of African people after the advent of European slavery and colonialism in the seventeenth century. Rather, intra-continental migration becomes the dominant pattern recorded.[23] For our purposes, it is sufficient to note that external migration did occur, stimulated not only by military service but also by the need for education, employment, and political asylum.

Educational institutions in America and in Europe accommodated Africans in the eighteenth and nineteenth centuries, but it was not until the twentieth century that Africans in significant numbers left the continent to obtain an education. This practice had to wait until the loosening of colonialism and substantially until its death. Nevertheless, in the nineteenth century, some Africans were educated in England, France and the Americas. Kenneth Little says that the first Africans to come to England for this purpose were "The sons of chiefs and notables of African tribes in the neighbourhood of British mercantile settlements on the African Coast. The earliest record of their arrival is at the beginning of the 18th century. Some of them were sent over by missionaries to be educated, but most came at the expense of the traders, more particularly the Africa Company, or were proteges of the commanders of ships."[24]

Similarly, the record in France dates back at least to the 1790s when the revolutionaries encouraged Africans to study in France.[25] Among those to benefit from this brief policy were the sons of Toussaint L'Overture and Christophe of Haiti in the early 1800s. Because of lack of direct United States ties with African colonial territories, the practice of Africans coming to this country for an education was not common until the twentieth century. Still, studies show that Africans from the West Indies did enroll in such institutions as Howard, Lincoln and Hampton Universities and Meharry Medical School by the end of the nineteenth century.[26]

A number of colonial Africans began to come to the United States for an education early in the twentieth century, but increased by the 1930s and 1940s. The names of some, such as Kwame Nkrumah, are familiar, but there are others, such as Jacob Notsi, from Botswana in South Africa, who came to America in 1944 to Wilberforce University, proceeded to Atlanta University, and then became a Washington, D.C. resident.[27] His 46-year stay in the United States would certainly qualify him as one who has contributed to creating an African Diaspora. Many such individuals became professionals and found employment in the country where they received their academic training; by 1965 there were 287 professors and nearly seven thousand students in the United States alone from the African continent.[28]

The acquisition of a Western education often leads Africans to stay in the country where it was obtained because, for one reason or another, the acquired skill cannot be practiced—utilizing Western technology—in the mother country. In any case, the individual might not be able to earn as much money there as in the

Western country. This economic motive for immigration is relatively common both among the highly educated and the less
well educated alike. As we shall see, in the case of Caribbean
immigration to Britain, the movement toward Britain takes place
largely to satisfy economic need, causing immigrants to come in
search of employment both skilled and nonskilled. But once the
British government had satisfied its objective to utilize Afro-
Caribbean labor to assist in post-war reconstruction, it found
that it had established a relationship which could not be suddenly shut off, even though attempts to do so were made. African and Afro-Caribbean immigration constitutes the largest
source of the creation of the modern Diaspora in Europe.

Finally, political conflict remains a significant element in the
creation of the Diaspora, as was demonstrated by the immigration stimulated by the struggle against continued colonialism in
Southern Africa, and by civil conflict in Uganda, Ethiopia or Liberia which turned thousands of refugees into exiles in Europe,
America or elsewhere. After the ouster of Emperor Haile Selassie of Ethiopia, as many as forty thousand Ethiopians are estimated to have resettled in the United States.[29] In Washington,
D.C. this new element of the Diaspora is illustrated by the
growth of Ethiopian restaurants and the fact that nearly twenty
thousand Ethiopians had jobs in the taxi industry by 1985. Similarly, the small South African refugee community was increased
by a substantial movement of Black youths in 1976 as a result of
the rebellions and the harshly violent police retaliation. The
young Africans fled first to Botswana; then many found their
way to other African countries and finally to America and England. The pattern was repeated by refugees from Namibia
when the guerilla war was fought to establish a genuinely independent Black state.

The way in which various groups enter a society has a profound impact upon their social status and, consequently, their
social psychology. In America, slavery was the dominant way
African-origin peoples entered this society and, thus, slavery
has had a profound effect upon succeeding Black generations.
The impact cannot fairly be compared to that experienced by immigrants who were not socialized and "seasoned" against their
own cultural patrimony. Black communities in Europe have
been created largely by modern immigration and hence their

patterns of acculturation, their perceptions of the surrounding society, access to the opportunity structure and the like will be different from those of freed slaves in nineteenth-century America. What they have in common with slave-origin Black communities is that they face similar patterns of competition and cooperation with white majorities as they seek to fulfill their vision of community.

Having discussed four methods by which the African Diaspora was created, we will proceed next to comment on the question of the nature of the Diaspora community and the struggle to create that community and maintain it under varying circumstances.

The Social Function of the African Diaspora: Community Development and Survival

Development

The second process we encounter in the dispersal of Africans around the world is the creation of a way of life under new circumstances—or the creation of community. This term "community" should be construed broadly here to include the diverse types of living situations which the African developed in conflict with his various masters and competitors. Such an expansive definition might include types of structures ranging from independent nation states to autonomous communities within independent states. Here, my ideas have been heavily influenced by Professor E. Franklin Frazier, who wrote that cultural heritage is the substance of the adjustment which results in community, that the conflict between groups of different cultural backgrounds is resolved physically and biologically in terms of which has superior technology, and that this, in turn, affects both their "spatial relations" and the "sub-social charac-

ter of the competition between them."[30] Frazier aptly points out
that man's first impulse in a new environment is to re-create his
old environment and that this matter is always settled in terms
of his "cultural heritage." Thus, in the conflict posed between
the African and the European in the Western environment, Africans have sought to re-create their cultural heritage. But as Frazier also suggests, the degree of re-creation achieved has been
determined by the opposing forces, acting from a superior position of power and generally demanding that the African conform to their ways and purposes.[31]

Still, it is possible to argue that assimilation is incomplete,
owing not only to the recency of Black urbanization in the West,
even in America, but, more importantly, to the continued pressure of social, economic and political forces amounting to a racial oppression that prohibits access to the total cultures of the
West. Additionally, it may be that the deceptive appearance of
the assimilated *form* of cultural patterns and traits being substi-
tuted for substance results in overstatement of the degree of real
assimilation in any evaluation of this complex problem. Some
support for this observation comes from the experience of Professor Melville Herskovits, who went to Harlem in the mid-
1920s to make an assessment of the degree of cultural adaptation
of the Negro. His conclusion was: "What there is today in Harlem distinct from the white culture which surrounds it, is, as far
as I am able to see, merely a remnant from the peasant days in
the South. Of the African culture, not a trace."[32] But by 1940,
after years of research on African cultural retentions in the
Caribbean and similar research in the American South, and even
after making meticulous measurings of the physical features of
American Blacks, Herskovits came to a different conclusion. He
noted that the adaptation of African cultural patterns such as
"mutual selfhelp in matters such as death, . . . [to] Euro-
American conventions such as lodges and funerals," and including the reinterpretation of song and dance were, in the process,
all subjected to "slightly modified African sanctions supporting
forms of a given institution that were almost entirely European."[33] Since only fifteen years elapsed between the first and
the second set of observations, we are led to believe that his first
conclusions were in error. Even today, we are only two generation since Herskovits' discovery of the extent of African surviv-

als in the New World. There has not been enough time for Blacks in America to have assimilated to such a degree as to move entirely away from the baseline of African culture, except among a highly acculturated and significant, though small, segment of the black middle class.

Yet we are concerned with form in another way, a way that gives us some indication of the ecology of residence of Africans in the Diaspora, since it is the combination of the cultural and spatial elements that will make it possible for us to determine what objectives are sought in the social realm, and consequently what is the nature of political conflict. A novel paradigm is presented by Professor Robert Hill, who has suggested that the patterns of residence of Africans in the New World could be found to be based on the dominant spatial frames of reference provided by the concepts of "bush," "plantation," and "ghetto."[34]

When one thinks of Africans living in the "bush," one automatically thinks of the rural or tropical areas of Africa without realizing or recalling that millions of African-origin peoples are living in types of "bush" in the Caribbean and Latin America and even Asia. Many of these so-called "Bush" Africans developed communities in isolation as a result of successful wars with European colonialists leading to the establishment of "liberated" zones. This revolutionary process often formed the basis of distinct nation states, as in the case of Haiti or Surinam, or districts such as Palmares in Brazil.[35]

Today the existence of the Bush African culture in the New World, although perceived as a backwater in the social development of people and unimportant in relation to industrializing societies, is nonetheless highly important as the historical baseline of the attempt of African people to recreate their culture outside of Africa. It is important that Yoruba culture in Brazil and that Ashanti culture in Surinam exist today, little changed from their original setting, because this fact strikingly establishes possibilities of linkages among Africans and African Americans (as in Brazil and Surinam) who possess a similar baseline of culture.

In fact, such a linkage took place in 1970 when the government of Surinam made it possible for Paramount Chiefs of several "Bush Negro" groups to travel to West Africa. Once in Ghana, they and their hosts experienced repeated surprises, because of the evidences of cultural familiarity which flowed between them. For example, on arriving and being received by Ghanian Prime Minister Busia, both the Surinam and Ghanian leaders poured libations and said prayers, and after a chief from Surinam gave his blessing, an observer noted: "He invoked God's blessing over the land, and concluded with a prayer in 'Kromanti,' a sacred language [of the Bush Negro] in which the Almighty, Nana Kediapon, is invoked. This caused great emotions, for the same supreme Ruler is invoked in Ghana."[36]

Another kind of contact which often takes place in Africa today between more Westernized Africans and those more closely associated with the traditional baseline of African culture has also occurred in the Americas. Two Black Harvard University professors, S. Alan Counter, a neuro-biologist at the Medical School, and an associate, David Evans, an electrical engineer and senior admissions officer, traveled to Surinam in June of 1972 and made contact with one of the African groups referred to above, living in the bush. Counter tells of a fascinating dialogue which occurred at their initial meeting.

His ancestors having never been slaves, the Surinam Bush African chief asked the natural question: ". . . are you still the white man's slaves?" To that, Counter and Evans replied: "We are not slaves in our land. Well, not really in the true sense of the word."[37] His people having fought for their freedom and won, the chief asked another profound question: "Well, have you won your fight?" To that, they responded: "The battle is still being fought." Most poignant of all, the Bush Africans were supremely aware of having been taken from Africa and, therefore, of being in a different place from that where they had originated. So, they asked Counter and Evans about their origins, and the professors explained that they also were from the same people taken from Africa: "Well, have you found the road home?" Counter and Evans had to admit that they were still searching. The encounter, a Pan African story of deep emotion and discovery, ended with the Bush Surinamese acknowledging Counter and Evans as brothers who had long been lost and were found.

Perhaps the answers to the questions posed are incomprehensible to those asking them, since between questioner and respondent stood an expanse of more than two-hundred years of differences in global, regional movements of people, changes in the uses of technology, and other factors complicating commu-

nication. Nevertheless, the answers might also provide an illuminating context for the evaluation of the history of African
peoples in the Americas.

Thus, to have such a powerful dimension of traditional Africa
available in the Western Hemisphere is crucial to cultural synthesis, once modalities of contact and linkages are accomplished
with some scope and regularity. To find among the people of
Surinam and similar places the concept of the "Big Bush" (Africa) as a reference to the place from which they were taken may
provide them with a continuing motivation for renewal of such
contacts.

Africans throughout the Americas have extensive experience
with the plantation community as the basic form of their ancestors' residence under slavery. One should not forget that more
often than not it was from the plantation that the "Bush Negro"
escaped. The system of European imperialism created the plantation as an economic unit and as a system to be utilized in the
exploitation of the natural resources of those areas where the
sovereignty of Europe was extended following the lead of industrial capitalists, traders and adventurers.[38] In the Caribbean and
the South of the United States, it was cotton and sugar which
were the main crops cultivated and harvested by Black slave labor and sold by the Europeans. Communities similar to those of
the slaves in the U.S. South developed elsewhere in the Americas out of the similarity of the local plantation. The plantations
in South America were different not in their economic operation
but in the specific culture of the dominant imperialist group.
One observer has noted that there was no functional economic
difference within a global slave system which employed Africans in America and Africans in Brazil, such that the explanation
of the differences between them must be sought in the cultural,
rather than the social or economic, realm.[39] As such, the institutions which develop within the slave community, be they religious, fraternal or educational, are all structured to serve the
community and support its members in their function as members of the plantation system.

John Blassingame's masterful portrayal of the American plantation system from the perspective of the slave suggests that
generally the form of the plantation was not so oppressive that
it did not yield, at critical points, to the development of some

semblance of African autonomy, even if the area of development was relatively small. The reasons for this reside first in the suggestion that the agrarian nature of African culture facilitated the Africans' adjustment to the harsh conditions of systematic labor in the field; also, cultural difference between the slave and the master created some areas where the master was not competent to control the behavior of the slave; and the apparent behavioral adaptation of the slave to the social requirements of the master provided a screen for real attitudes and, often, behavior. This situation led to a social structure which promoted the slave quarters as a "primary environment" where ethical rules were provided for fostering mutual cooperation, assistance and solidarity. The work environment, then, was regarded as a secondary environment and the two, often in severe conflict with each other, provided the nexus out of which emerged the social objectives of slave life. Such objectives included staying alive, keeping the family together, using the system to prosper, and escaping the system altogether.[40]

Just as the rural ecology of the African in the Diaspora of the Americas was controlled by the dominant economic activity, the transfer of residence from rural to urban settings was often determined by the same factors. Frazier, for example, says that with respect to both the rural and urban residence of Blacks, economics was the determining factor. Because of their lesser economic resources, Blacks settled in the "vulnerable" areas of the city, expanding as the city expanded and coming into conflict with whites when that expansion contradicted the residential objectives of the more economically powerful group.[41] The situation Frazier describes was accurate during slavery, when cities were centers of commerce in the South as well as the North, and after slavery as well.

Richard C. Wade uses data from cities, mainly in the South, during the period 1820–1860 to show that the basic pattern of slave holding in cities contributed to the institution of slavery in vital ways. He concludes that from one-third to two-thirds of the cities under review had slave-holding populations (usually designated by heads of households) but that the largest percentage of such slave-holders had only a minimal number of slaves (usually from one to two).[42] This is wholly understandable in view of the ecology of cities and their greater mobility in comparison with rural areas. Still, there was a small percentage of slave-holders who had large numbers of slaves in the city, but these were usually industrialists of one variety or another.

This pattern of slave-holding made possible even greater measures of social control. For example, wide-spread coopera-tion among individuals and institutions of the city were often responsible for recapturing runaway slaves.

As the capital of urban Black America, Harlem was born in the period 1907–1914, when real estate speculators in the area over-committed themselves and found it necessary to sell off cheap to Blacks hungry for decent housing. When Blacks be-gan to move in (whites called it an "invasion") to a well-to-do neighborhood, tensions were unleased between the races as Blacks struggled to establish community institutions and whites struggled to prevent that. There were restrictive housing cove-nants designed to prevent Blacks from further home purchases or rentals; there were fights to prevent Black churches from moving into certain areas; there were efforts on the part of whites to prevent Blacks from obtaining leisure-time facilities such as movie theaters, even though Blacks could only sit in the balcony at the existing theater.[43] By 1913, it had become clear that Blacks were winning this struggle to establish a community with the attendant institutions in Harlem; the white resistance began crumbling as a result of a lack of support on the part of both white and Black landlords as well as real estate brokers who had profitted from the Black "invasion."

This example of the rise of Black ghettoes in urban New York, however, was not unique. As George Edmund Hayes, director of the National Urban League, noted in 1913, "There is growing up in America a distinct Negro World [neighborhoods which are] isolated from many of the impulses of the common life and little understood by the white world . . ."[44] Actually, this pattern had been noticed much earlier by W. E. B. DuBois, who in 1900 had observed: "Here then, in a world of itself, [is the Black com-munity] closed in from the outer world and almost unknown to it, with churches, clubs, hotels, saloons, and charities; with its own social distinctions, amusements, and ambitions."[45]

More recently, the process of urbanization has proceeded to the point that it can be safely said to be the dominant ecological pattern of living for most Black Americans and, indeed, to be more highly developed than among any group of African-origin peoples in the world. We remember Frazier's thought that this pattern of living has expanded as the city itself in America has grown, and this latter development has been made possible by the growth of America as a major industrial power with the city as its basic unit of social organization.[46] Thus, the labor power of Blacks was drawn into the cities as part of the process of industrialization. I agree with one observer who concludes: "The ecological transformation of Black society within the context of an industrializating American society has led to increasing social differentiation within Black America, with domestic and communal institutional forms associated with status distinctions."[47] Nevertheless, the basis of such differentiation is as much owed to racial as to economic factors.

By 1970, the Black American population was 81 percent urban, 18 percent rural and 2 percent on the farm.[48] This very high percentage of urban residency provides one explanation for the trends cited above, but another must be found in the growth of the Black middle class. For example, in 1970, 84.3 percent of Black families had an average income below $12,500; by 1980, the average had fallen to 49.5 percent, while those in the over-$15,000 category of income had risen from 9.6 to 42.8 percent.[49]

Similarly, the urban Black population of Europe has grown. In Belgium, Portugal, Britain, and France, small African populations have existed for hundreds of years as a result of the slave trade; the Africans lived largely in seaport towns and capital cities. England, for example, had a small Black population in the 19th century, mainly in London and in the seaport towns of Bristol and Cardiff, but vigorous repatriation in the 1870s made Britain virtually an all-white nation again.[50] Also, as we will see below, the great waves of modern migration of African-origin peoples to Britain came essentially after the Second World War, when the African and Afro-Caribbean population grew from 21,000 in 1951 to 304,000 by 1966.[51] That "race relations" in these European countries can be compared with those in America is confirmed by one observer who finds that the phenomenon of Black industrial workers arriving from the colonies in the cities of Great Britain, Holland, France, Belgium, Portugal and others and presenting racial problems was not dissimilar to the problem of descendants of Negro slaves immigrating from the South to the urban cities of the North.[52]

There were perhaps 1,000 Africans in France at the time of the revolution of 1789, but the number had grown to at least 50,000 after the Second World War, spurred on by the independence of former French colonies and the slow migration to France by "citizens" from Guadelope and Martinique.[53] Today, the African-origin French population is estimated at 1 percent and, as in the case of Britain and other colonial metropoles, such residence is nearly all urban and has mostly taken on the form of the American-styled ghettoization.[54]

What remains important about the ecology of these Africans in the European Diaspora is not that they are urbanized, but that they face the dilemma of Black Americans who, in their trek to the Northern urban centers, sought to recreate African culture with all of the attendant supporting social institutions. The European Africans face a struggle to establish community in the face of tremendous ambiguities between their original culture and the dominant culture of the urban, industrial, technological European matrix of factors exercising a powerful and constant force upon their existence. Indeed, exercise of power by those who originally colonized them evokes respect and awe in the colonized to such an extent that many seek the source of its attraction in the culture of the colonizer. This phenomenon was thoroughly explicated by Frantz Fanon in his book, *The Wretched of The Earth*. The resulting syncretism of culture has some of the characteristics of both of its antecedents, but within a broader context is substantially a new creation.

This attempt to recreate and (in the Herskovitsian sense) reinterpret African culture in the new place of residence and the resulting variations of African culture have created a dilemma—to what extent may the communities be regarded as "African"? I have used the term "African-origin" in this work as an objective reference to such communities. However, I firmly reject, for example, Roger Bastide's dichotomy that the distinction is between African cultural communities and "Negro" cultural communities.[55] "Negro" is a political and economic category and a designation created by imperialists, colonizers and slave masters; it provides no information about the ethnological content of the variation from the original African culture. As such, it was a convenient category of subordination. Secondly, the early analysts of this problem have overlooked the primary cultural variation which exists on the African continent itself and the now accelerating secondary variation created as a result of the impact of Westernization, urbanization and industrialization on the continent. Therefore, the perspective of this work is that the African-origin communities existing outside of the continent are but another variety of African community that should be identified by their specific ethnolography—Afro-Brazilian, African Brazilian, Afro-American, African American and so on.

Survival

African communities in the Diaspora are living, breathing, dynamic entities, made such by the very environment in which they are forced to exist and by their very struggle to survive. Because of their unique characteristics— skin color, history, and others—the establishment of a Black community anywhere in the world outside of Africa has usually been a gigantic task and a constant signal to whites to oppose its formation. This has been so both because of political and economic motivations compounded by cultural differences that have carried race prejudice all over the globe, and because of the objective factor that the incoming group brought with it the possible threat to the position and resources of the dominant groups, especially to those nearest the lower-stratum class position of the Blacks. The result has been a pattern of stratification worldwide, with the African-origin community at the bottom of the social ladder in most societies. Thus, regardless of the longevity of existence of Black communities in some countries and territories, this pattern persists because of the constant effort by whites to dominate them.

The community is important as an entity to struggle for because it is intimately connected with the survival of individuals and their families and other secondary and tertiary racial groups. The community becomes a resource in the adaptation of individuals and groups to the new environment, an internal protector, a transmission belt of information about social mobility, a nurturer from the wounds of the external society, and a reference point to anchor the social activities of the in-comers. Most important, the idea of community—of the social psychology of the cohesiveness of its members—is shaped by the historical experiences of its members and the way in which they enter the broader society. That is why slavery has made the immigrant group approach to an understanding of the problems of African Americans in America largely irrelevant. The resulting perception of community by African Americans thus, is not only unique, but also constitutes a distinct prism through which modern issues are viewed, a difference that is often the source of conflict with the larger society.

I should point out, however, that the survival needs of individuals and groups within the community form the basis for the process of social differentiation of functions into institutions. Frazier notes three types of such institutions: (1) those that have their roots entirely in the Black community, such as the church and other cultural and social institutions, (2) those that have their roots in both the Black and white communities, such as the schools, and (3) those that have their entire roots in the white community, such as places of employment.[56] In the newly established African community, especially in the urban setting, the walls of segregation have been so strict that many of all these types of institutions have been duplicated. Still, it is within the first type of institutional setting that the greatest degree of differentiation of a strictly racial character has occurred. The Black barbershop, the Black store, the Black social club, the Black recreation areas, the Black theaters, the Black church, the Black businesses, the Black newspapers, and other units of the infrastructure are established. The struggle to establish them is part of the political struggle to compose the entire community and to secure its base of strength.

Conflict occurs, therefore, in this process of attempting to establish a community—to find the sites for living, to set up operation and to practice the values of the Black community. This conflict is often of a serious nature and occurs between Black and white institutions, with means utilized conforming to the prevailing stratification of power between the two social groups. For example, large numbers of people are effected in the Black community by decisions made in the white community by key decision-making institutions such as banks through mortgage rates, real estate dealers who set a racial boundary, social service agencies which fix the amount of welfare allowances, educational agencies which settle upon certain textbooks or make decisions about the kind of teachers available to Black schools, plants which set quotas on the hiring of certain numbers of Blacks, and so on.

It is the natural instinct of those effected in the Black community to oppose this type of behavior by the dominant group because it effects their ability to survive. While the essence of the political environment, then, is determined by the nature of this kind of conflict, in actuality the daily lives of those involved in the community swings from conflict with oppressive institutions and their by-products in the black community to cooperation with other dominant institutions determining the quality of existence. The intensity of the political conflict is determined by the nature of the issues faced and the degree of oppression perceived by the aggrieved group seeking redress or by the dominant group seeking to maintain its control.

What I am suggesting is that, in agreement with the views of other observers, the essential relations between the African-origin and European communities as they exist within nation states go beyond the simple fact of racial stratification in a white dominant-subordinant Black pattern, but that the function of the institutions in the European community strongly constitutes an *internal colonial* pattern. And although many observers have described this relationship, it should be noted that its chief product is the fostering of a climate of oppression and opposition as the dominant characteristic of relations in a culture of conflict. This "culture of conflict" runs along the entire spectrum of possible race contacts and turns every possible situation into a "political" event fraught with possible winners and losers because, while the immediate stakes may be viewed as individual or collective, they ultimately are perceived to be related to the ultimate strength and viability of each community.

The forms of oppression coming from the dominant European group include race prejudice and discrimination leading to the physical exclusion of Blacks, the physical confrontation with and anniliation of Blacks, and negative social policy and manipulation. These factors form the targets of opportunity to which political strategies must be tailored by leaders of the Black community in its mobilization of resources. Mobilization, therefore, takes place around such issues as the right of the community to reside in certain areas and the right of community members to exercise full citizenship. It is often based on the grounds that ". . . the colonized were brought to the 'mother' country to be enslaved and exploited. Internal colonialism thus involved the conquest and subjugation of a people and their physical removal to the ruling state. The command of the resources of the captive people (their labor power) followed."[57] The political strategies, therefore, are designed to resist the attempt of the state to eject the immigrants after the state has finished exploiting their labor power. The African-origin community asserts the right of compensation for the systematic theft of its resources during colonialism; it can do so because in the process of contributing its labor, the community has gained the right to some of the entitlements the state has to offer. The community also attempts to resist the more dehumanizing processes of capitalism by joining the organized segment of the working class in coalition with other workers.

The community's members are often denied decent housing because it is the location and quality of housing that determines where the community will reside. The African has even moved into hovels in a concentrated area and has attempted to live with a semblance of dignity in such conditions. But political strategies have also been formulated that have seen the African population protest housing discrimination barriers, lack of adequate services and high rents by means of mass demonstrations, rent strikes and court action. One observer says, "One tactic available to officials is to give token satisfaction . . . to blunt protest drives, they [the bureaucracy] may also change their internal procedures and organization."[58] Also, it has been noted that some integration of facilities and housing will be tolerated by the dominant group so long as the law of dominance holds, that is, "as long as they were sure that the white group concerned would remain in the majority in those facilities or areas."[59] Where the dominance of the whites becomes doubtful, a likelihood arises of "spatial-racial confrontation."[60] Such a situation would lead to neighborhood racial violence initiated by whites and designed to contain the African population and prevent it from growing. Ultimately, government officials would propose a policy of spatial dispersal to blunt the African community's base of strength, a base that makes possible Blacks' exercise of such political strategies.[61] Hence, both containment and dispersal are serious options for policy planners both in England and America.

The education of Black children coming into the schools of the dominant European group causes conflict, whether in Brazil, Boston or Birmingham, England because it threatens cultural hegemony. Without exception, the culture of the African is assigned an inferior status, and the African is made to receive education within the cultural framework of the dominant European group—even though that may involve using materials that assert or assume the innate inferiority of the African school child. The political strategy used by the African group in response has been to struggle to have its history and culture included within the educational system's curriculum as "Black studies" and to struggle to control as much of the educational process as possible by securing employment as teachers, principals, headmasters, members of school boards.

These brief examples and the potentiality for political conflict should suggest to the reader why some observers feel that the relations between Black and white are often marked by "rancorous conflict in community politics." It has been noted that "Rancorous conflicts are characterized by the belief that norms about the waging of political conflict in American communities have been violated. In such conflicts, actions occur which produce a shared belief that tactics used to influence the outcome are 'dirty,' 'underhanded,' 'vicious' and so forth."[62] I say that the communities in which such conflict occur are characterized by such factors as high emotional strains, low integration and the solidarity of affected groups, a definition that fits the alienation felt so deeply by Blacks in the urban setting. One political strategy, as we will see below, is the strategy of expressive violence or rebellion. Those social scientists who have searched for the seeds of rebellion in the Black community find that the violence of the dominant society against the Black community was enough cause to produce the shared belief among Blacks that such tactics were unjustly visited upon it. Also, incidents such as the killing of Dr. Martin Luther King produced the same symbolic response and led to expressive violent outbursts as a strategy for redressing grievances. For, whereas most political strategies are within the perview of the civil procedures of the society, the need to move beyond these procedures to an extreme degree of hostility marks the deep belief of the African community that institutional solutions controlled by the dominant group are ultimately unable to provide a just pattern of race relations.

In all of the foregoing strategies, I have suggested that the community provides both rationale and resources, since it is both the reason for struggle and the provider of materials for struggle. Therefore, the nature of the community's goals as embedded in its ideology is important, as are its leadership and organizational structure.

Then, while it is important to recognize that the utilization of these strategies based on community resources will be engaged in a hierarchical battle with the dominant institutions, the community must recognize the resources available in its struggle, resources that emanate from the *Pan* African linkages with other similar African-origin communities in the Diaspora and on the African continent. Indeed, the foregoing discussion has assumed that a similar pattern of social dynamics may be found in the relations between the African-origin communities and the dominant groups in the societies where they exist. In this process an explicit cross-national consciousness and a series of Pan African relationships have developed historically to such an extent that the resource base of these African communities in the Diaspora has been expanded theoretically and practically.

I am attempting here to de-emphasize the time-bound historical aspects and the purely romantic ethnocentric aspects of Pan Africanism in order to show the functional qualities of the concept as a natural part of the lives of African-origin peoples. Two empirical factors are involved. First, given what we have said above, it is obvious we are able to show that the patterns of life in the Black community and the relations between Black and white have a similar quality across cultures and nations. Secondly, we will also be able to show that because of the similarity of problems encountered, similar strategies have been employed for their amelioration. Understanding that such similar strategies could be employed in each African-origin community autonomously, I will also endeavor to show that there have been interactive occasions where survival strategies were shared. It remains for us to expand upon the methodological rationale for this approach in the section immediately following.

Analyzing the Relationships among African-Origin Peoples

Concept

The task of conceptualizing both the African Diaspora and Pan Africanism was initially that of W.E.B. Du-Bois. For although even DuBois himself generally credits H. Sylvester Williams with putting the word "Pan African" in the pages of history at least three years earlier, DuBois presented a scholarly paper, "The Conservation of Races," at the March 1897 meeting of the American Negro Academy, in which he said, ". . . the advance guard of the Negro people—the eight million people of Negro blood in the United States of America—must soon come to realize that if they are to take their just place in the van of *Pan-Negroism* [my emphasis], then their destiny is *not* absorption by the white Americans." [63] This statement illustrates that DuBois had a view or concept of the African world that was comprehensive even then and rested upon a "developmental" perspective that presumed group advancement through the leadership of African Americans. This conclusion was natural for DuBois, since he had earlier been a close student of the process by which the Diaspora was created in his work *The Suppression of the African Slave-Trade to the United States of America, 1838–1870*, published in 1896 as the first volume in the Harvard Historical Studies series. Even in this work, where he endeavored to make a "contribution to the scientific study of slavery and the American Negro," he established a frame of reference for the study and analysis of the Diaspora by looking at such matters as the legal approach to slavery and the significance of Toussaint L'Ouverture.[64] George Shepperson, in his introduction to DuBois' work *The Negro* (1915), chronicles other aspects of the DuBois pioneering role in conceptualizing the study of Africa and especially African history. But he also points to the fact that *The Negro* opens up the study of Africa for a line of distinguished Black historians such as Rayford Logan, William Hansberry, Carter Woodson, and John Henrik Clarke.[65]

Thus, with the historical framework for the study of the African Diaspora established, Shepperson himself attempts an explicit rendering of this phenomenon as a field of historical study. Writing of the function of migration as a methodology in the creation of the Diaspora, he notes, "But it must be emphasized that not all migration from Africa comes within the bounds of *the concept of the African diaspora which is the study of a series of reactions to coercion, to the imposition of the economic and political rule of alien peoples in Africa,* to slavery and imperialism" (my emphasis).[66] Now, if one compared this definition with those describing "Pan Africanism," it would most surely be regarded as an apt characterization, especially for what might be regarded as "political" or "revolutionary" Pan Africanism. Vincent Bakpetu Thompson, for example, says that "the Pan-African Movement up to the present has been dominated by the struggle against western European colonialism and many Africans believe that this can only be achieved through unity of action."[67]

Nevertheless, the line of demarcation in this definition connects the concept of the Diaspora to an early period in the history of the contact of Africans with European imperialism. The definition thereby further re-emphasizes the African slave trade as the era and the method in the creation of the Diaspora and, thus, makes the concept time-bound. But what of the later migrations, such as the sizeable Afro-West Indian migration to Britain after World War II? Why should this not fall within the definition of the Diaspora? I assert that it does, inasmuch as it helps to establish the African community in Britain as a viable part of the African world. This essentially means that the concept of the Diaspora is dynamic, inasmuch as in this recent period it is responding to forces of postindustrial capitalism, as well as to questions of cultural identity and problems attendant to the formation and maintenance of modern nation states.

Next, Shepperson gives us five themes in the study of the African Diaspora: the question of Black inferiority raised by slavery and culture contact, the impact of the African slave trade, the existence and value of African survivals in the New World, the influence of New World Negroes on African nationalism, and the historic quest for African unity under "Pan Africanism."[68] But this listing, which is primarily subjective, again confuses the concept of the Diaspora with the concept of Pan Africanism, especially in the inclusion of the last two subjects. Certainly, the attempt of so-called New World Negroes to influence African nationalism as an explicit objective begins at the turn of this century and is further developed and continued through the Pan African movement in the period from 1900 to 1945.

The principal dilemma presented by this listing, however, lies in the failure conceptually to separate the Diaspora from Pan Africanism. I would argue, as I have above, that the concept of the African Diaspora must be based upon the idea of the nature and function of the African community—*the struggle to achieve it, the struggle to maintain it, and the struggle to utilize its resources in order to achieve social, political and economic objectives in society and in the world.* The objective processes which form the Diaspora, such as slavery trade, commerce, military service, and natural migration, continue throughout history to affect the distribution of the children of Africa according to the dictates of powerful world forces such as imperialism, world war, national liberation movements, capitalism, internal struggles for political legitimacy, and other such forces.

The focus of some historians on "contacts" and "linkages" in the Diaspora, thus, often appears anecdotal, first because these historians focus on individuals, and secondly because their focus has little contextual foundation. What we find is that many of the individual contacts among Africans in the dispersal process occurred as interesting manifestations of their time and place in certain unique situations, but others are clear linkages to movements—stronger, more basic currents supplying the will of Africans to find ways to utilize the survival strategies created by each other to combat oppression. It is, thus, *very often the movement behind the contact which is important, but for the clearest context, the movement must be seen within the various stages of the struggle for community.* Only then is it possible to assess the importance of the various "contacts" and "linkages" unearthed and described. Those "contacts" and "linkages" designed to regain or enhance unity or identity or for some other political, cultural, or economic objective we regard as varieties of Pan Africanism. Therefore, the individual or collective relations among Africans in the Diaspora, among African-origin communities outside the African continent or between them and those on the continent are important varieties of Pan Africanism.

Methodology

Figure 1 illustrates what might be called the "African World" or Diaspora. It is represented as a process of outmigration of peoples from the central African core existence to various places in the world. From this simple rendering, three basic concepts might be delineated: (1) outward movement, (2) the return, and (3) the movement among communities in the Diaspora. Each of these has a significance in terms of the original creation of the modern Diaspora as well. There is in the concept of the Diaspora as it has been developed the implication of a dynamic in that peoples are studied in terms of the extent to which they have migrated or located in one place or another. The concept of the African World implies more of a finality to the act of dispersal in that one studies the global communities of African peoples as a *settled phenomenon*. Thus, one studies Pan Africanism based on the *relationships between peoples and nation states* without emphasizing travels or movements.

Utilizing this scheme, therefore, it is possible to study five types of Pan African relationships: (A) among African states; (B) among African states and African-origin states in the Diaspora, as in the Caribbean; (C) among African states and African-origin peoples (communities) in the Diaspora; (D) among African-origin states in the Diaspora and African-origin communities in the Diaspora, and (E) among African-origin communities in the Diaspora.

It is this objective rendering of a typology of the kinds of relations available among states in the African Diaspora that begins to complement the value-laden concept of the African Diaspora offered by Shepperson or Oruna Lara, who says, ". . . for

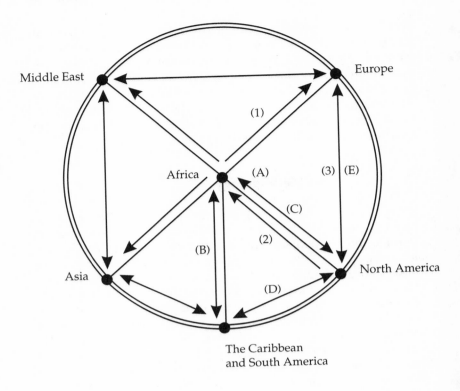

Figure 1. The African Diaspora

the African Diaspora to exist, it must resist against capitalist power, colonial power, [and] dictatorial power of the bourgeoise." [69] It is possible to agree with Lara and to recognize at the same time that he has defined the Diaspora in terms of its Pan African activity. Indeed, St. Clair Drake makes a distinction between two kinds of Pan Africanism: pan Africanism with a lower-case p, ". . . has ends that are not political and is part of a people-to-people approach to trans-Atlantic relations among black people," and Pan Africanism with a capital P, or political movements and other such relationships. [70] From this, we understand that Drake believes that Pan African cultural relations best describe the normal range of activities within the Diaspora, but that political relations are unique and deserving of special recognition as Pan African in nature. I make no such distinction because both cultural and political relations exist, on an equal plane, within each of the five categories listed above.

Moreover, St. Clair Drake appears to confirm this conclusion when he makes a distinction between traditional (or racial) Pan Africanism and the new (or continental) form of Pan Africanism. Traditional Pan Africanism, to him, emphasizes "fostering solidarity between all black people everywhere. Both cultural and political activity have always been present, with the former reinforcing the latter."[71] Drake perceptively suggests (and I will show) that the advent of continental Pan Africanism placed racial Pan Africanism in a "defensive posture," that "they are not always compatible" and that the "constant dialectical interplay between them sometimes results in contradictions which must be resolved."[72] But as suggested above, racial (or traditional) Pan Africanism is potentially the dominant form among the variety of forms of Pan Africanism in existence, especially with the creation of the African World, while continental Pan Africanism is dominant in terms of the issues which form a continuing cultural and political attraction to all African groups outside the continent.

Now from this point, it should be profoundly understood that the nature of the African Diaspora is so diverse and the varieties of Pan Africanism so limitless that an infinite number of topics and methods of analysis may be employed. I have chosen in this work to deal substantially with Pan African relations of a *political* nature and, thus, to select the tools and insights most closely related to this discipline. But in selecting those tools I begin with an important suggestion from St. Clair Drake who is responsible for helping to shape the approach I utilize here. In a lecture given in 1968 at Columbia University he said:

> I begin with a political concept developed by men of action not scholars, by a group of American Negroes and West Indians between 1900 and 1945—"Pan Africanism"—the idea that Africans and peoples of African descent in the New World should develop racial solidarity for the purpose of abolishing discrimination, enforced segregation, and political and economic exploitation of Negroes through the world. Viewed sociologically, without value judgments and using values only as data, one can define "The Pan-African Aggregate," that is, all of the potential members of

whatever voluntary associations and political units arise among Negroes with the goal of uniting them for Pan-African ends. The efforts of intellectuals and organizational leaders to raise the level of "black consciousness" within the "Pan-African Aggregate" can be described and analyzed as well as their attempts to develop "race pride" and "race solidarity" and to direct them toward specific ends. A research scholar could then devise means for measuring and assessing the extent to which goals set by Pan-African leaders have or have not been achieved at any given point in time without committing himself as to whether he feels that the goals are desirable or not.[73]

As much as possible of the complete idea has been included here in an effort to help the reader understand the complexity of the challenge St. Clair Drake has posed, a challenge that I decided could not be met by the use of one methodology alone.

First, in looking at the problem posed, it is clear that several of the relationships noted above fall into the category of studies of cross-national analysis, usually addressed by the approach of comparative politics, defined by one author as follows: "*Comparative*—laying bare the crucial aspects of political systems, noting uniformities as well as differences from one system to the next, searching for laws about the relationship of variables, and attempting to account for such similarities, differences, and relationships by means of systematic and integrated theory."[74] This definition, focusing on political systems and their variables and upon the need to account for similarities and differences, will allow us to assess important aspects of "political culture" in the study. For example, in the United States, Britain and South Africa the system which produces most of the conflict is structured by the dominant position of the white community and its activities relative to the subordinate Black community. Given that fact, we regard this dominant-subordinate system as the "environment" within which community objectives are developed. One other aspect of the study of this political "environment" is the comparative analysis of British and American approaches to their African-origin communities or "race-relations," given the similar nature of their societies in structure and culture. Also, comparative aspects of the structure of the African-origin or "Black" communities in both the United States and Britain will be examined in an effort to assess the possibility for developing similar racial goals for the communities within their respective environments.

The use of the comparative framework of analysis assumes, in this case, that the *content* of the racial dynamics in such societies have evolved in a very similar way regardless of the fact that in the United States the African-origin community is much older than its British sibling and has had longer experience inside a Western state. Between older and younger African communities, Pan African relations could be most fertile because of the potential of sharing political strategies and other approaches to the survival of the community.

Secondly, while the comparative method will yield important data, by itself it is inadequate to render comprehensive meaning to the Pan African phenomenon. And so, we must fashion an approach based on the phenomenon itself, an approach we will call *the Pan African Method* of analysis. The first feature of the method is its *interactive* nature, a feature that is unmistakably intended in the following statement by DuBois. "To help bear the burden of Africa does not mean any lessening of effort in our own problem at home. Rather it means increased interest. For any ebullition of action and feeling that results in an amelioration of the lot of Africa tends to ameliorate the condition of colored peoples throughout the world. And no man liveth to himself."[75] By positing the dual responsibility of African Americans toward themselves and Africa and the collective destiny of all African peoples, DuBois shows the implicit necessity for mutual exchange of influence among African communities. The nature of this exchange may be through individuals, groups or even ideas, as we shall show below.

The other feature of the Pan African Method is deduced from the previous statement by Drake, who says that after we have identified the units of the Pan African "Aggregates" that are in contact with each other, as well as the objectives of the contacts, we should seek to evaluate *the degree to which these contacts have accomplished the goal of racial unity* implicit in the relationship.[76] This criterion we will call the "ideological criterion of African unity." The tools we will use to evaluate the degree to which the criterion has been achieved will be subjective, seeking to determine what political event or movement was initiated as a result of the contact, consonant with the overall objectives of the community. It is this ideological criterion of African unity that gives to the method a Pan African character, that informs the phenomenology of these events by a specific cultural objective.

Conclusion

This study, therefore, will replicate aspects of other studies that have attempted to compare the political dynamic which emerges from the *vertical* relations between the dominant white and the subordinate Black communities within the framework of separate nation states. We have asserted, however, that the Pan African analytical approach is most useful in determining the degree of functional interaction between communities within the nation states, or with the *horizontal* relations of transnational African communities as a resource for each other's competition with the dominant systems of society in each state. I conclude, then, that *the Pan African analytical approach is an associated Black studies methodology in that it recognizes the dominant influence of the racial variable within the context of domestic relations, while the Pan African method recognizes the dominant influence of African identity, history and culture in the transactional relations of African-origin peoples in the Diaspora.*

A strong motivation for this study of the subject of Pan Africanism was my observation that the academic approaches used to analyze the subject were time-bound and consequently the application of the concept to modern problems was dormant. The academic texts treating this topic were largely produced by historians who have been concerned with an explication of the Pan African movement as defined by the nineteenth-century movements and personalities in the African Diaspora and the Pan African conferences from 1900 to 1945, culminating with an examination of the Organization of African Unity. Other studies in the field have largely been concerned with special biographies of organizations such as the Council on African Affairs or with individual Pan Africanists such as Edward Wilmot Blyden, Henry Sylvester Williams, W. E. B. DuBois, James Padmore, and Kwame Nkrumah. More current studies have emerged that are dedicated to examining the cultural basis of Pan Africanism known as "Afro-centrism," a subject that might be called the American version of the concept of Négritude.

This study was born out of an awareness that just as the political legacy of the subject of Pan Africanism is vast, so its utility as a modern tool for the study of African civilization is valuable, as I have attempted to suggest in the concluding chapter of this work. The study has various geographical theaters to consider, various political, cultural, economic and other combinations of problems to examine, and various historical eras are involved. What has been missing is an approach to this vast datum of Africana other than the historical approach that has been the initial gift of those interested in examining discrete aspects of the African Diaspora. Thus, this work sets out to "modernize" the study of peoples of African descent in the world by suggesting that existing social science methods might be modified to be utilized in the study of specific subjects in the African Diaspora. It is important, then, to note that the emphasis in all of the case studies included here take place within the past three decades. This work, then, is also narrowly constructed in that it addresses only the political dimension of a few modern case studies involving African-American linkages. Therefore, to break with the orthodoxy in the treatment of this subject and to construct a new approach has been my objective as much as the rendering of previously unpresented case studies of important Pan African events.

At the outset, therefore, it is also necessary to say that the study challenges the attitude of some historians regarding the definition of this phenomenon. It is, of course, difficult to move on without a sense of "settled history"—a sense that one stands upon a firm foundation of historiography where concepts and events have provided stability to the field. Yet it is possible to find scholars using the concept of Pan Africanism with a welter of confusing meanings, as noted by W. Ofuatey Kodjoe and others.[77] P. Olisanwuche Esedebe would agree with Kodjoe as to the variety of usages: ". . . there is still no agreement on what it is all about. Explanations that some African scholars and politicians give often differ from those suggested by African descendants abroad. Sometimes the continental Africans themselves advance conflicting interpretations."[78] Esedebe goes on to demonstrate the existing confusion and to craft his own substantive definition as follows: "Pan Africanism is a political and cultural phenomenon which regards Africa, Africans and African descendants abroad as a unit. It seeks to regenerate and unify Africa and promote a feeling of oneness among the people of the African world. It glorifies the African past and inculcates pride in African values."[79] I accept this formulation for the purpose of discussion, but there is still the question of why we should accept it in the absence of a systematic approach.

The most important discussion of the definition of Pan Africanism thus far is by Professor W. Ofuatey-Kodjoe, cited above.[80] He suggests that Pan Africanism existed as a body of ideas that led to the formation of a political movement containing many different organizations. He, nevertheless, derives from these different organizations two common characteristics: "the acceptance of a oneness of all African people and a commitment to the betterment of all people of African descent."[81] He defines the ideology of Pan Africanism as essentially "nationalist" and then proceeds to discuss the common elements of that nationalism as they relate to the definition.

I am in general agreement with Kodjoe's rendition of these elements, but the problem is that unless one has a sense of how they cohere into a logic of the definition, all of them may stand as separate parts. My suggestion, then, is that there is a logic to the definition of this term that is inherent in the very term itself. There are what we might term *core values* and *transitory values* that comprise the comprehensive definition of the term. (In fact, the two common characteristics Kodjoe identifies are included below within one core value.) The two "core values" are contained in the very term itself.

1. *First of all there is "Pan,"* a term which Webster's dictionary says applies to all members of a specific group and which also implies a belief in the unity or commonality of the members of that group. This definition raises questions about the location of "all" of that group. In the first instance, we agree with Kodjoe that it is unity in the abstract, of whatever location, based on common descent. Then, there is the political form of that unity, centered as it is on the notion of nation states, as suggested by Esedebe, and communities, as we have suggested. Thus, we have determined that the term applies to those on the African continent as well as those descended from the African continent

in the Diaspora. So, the inclusiveness of the term is one value in that it applies to all, but it also suggests an additional value of *unity* among the members. But there is an additional general value which scholars have used to express the notion that the members of the group seek to exist in certain states, in a condition of "liberation," "victory," and so on, that is to say, the members of this collective seek to exist not only in a state of theoretical—or neutral—unity, but in a state of well-being.

2. *Secondly, there is the term "African,"* which identifies the specific group that is referred to. It is first a term of identity and as such raises questions about what one means by "African." If we agree with Ali Mazrui, then we are held to the view that the so-called "triple heritage" is the substance of the continental African identity. However, in the Diaspora, we are dealing with the hyphenated identities in the various nation states that are bound to Africa by heritage. The theory of Afro-centrism states that the ontology of Africaness or African identity—or African descendant identity—presupposes the centrality of Africa; then, according to whatever identity one has developed in the Diaspora, it also implies a sense of *obligation* that makes it necessary to operationalize one's identity with these dual elements in tension.

The "transitory values" are those that both divide the general subject of Pan Africanism into separate categories and change according to the challenges of each age. In the first instance, we believe that the nationalist character of the term Pan Africanism need not imply that Pan Africanism is inherently political, because it identifies a specific people that the term itself did not call into existence or into unity; the people existed before the term as a distinct culture. I regard the objective fact of the existence of African people in the world and, therefore, of Pan Africanism as a baseline proposition.

Beyond this, the struggle of African peoples to exist may be divided into many subject areas, such as political, cultural, economic, and so on. Thus, when John Henrik Clarke says that Pan Africanism began when the first European set foot on African soil and began the long pean of African resistance to oppression, or that the military nature of that resistance was "Pan African" in character, he is suggesting a categorical (or specific) definition of the term that is highly political. In another sense, Négritude may be regarded as a cultural project of Pan Africanism along with its sister concept, Afro-centricity. Marcus Garvey's economic vision may be regarded as Pan Africanist because it was in support of his plan for the redemption of Africa and of African peoples. Without a discussion of these features, at the risk of endangering the paradigm we are describing, it should be noted that these categories may contain the many projects and events which occur in the history of Pan Africanism.

This leads us to the last feature of the "transitory values," or their *historical* nature. If within the category of political Pan Africanism, we define the term as meaning opposition to European oppression, it is, ipso facto, the case that the specific quality of that oppression to be opposed in one age changes to another feature in another era of history. So that, just as a Pan African project to use the conferences to build a platform from which to sensitize Europeans to the evils of colonialism was legitimate pan African work in one age, it was equally Pan African to press a revolutionary strategy in another, both of these strategies being *political* in nature.

This study asserts that, far from having died, when the ethic of African unity and liberation as the definition of Pan Africanism moved onto the African continent, simultaneously, the original concept continued and, indeed, grew in power and commitment in the Diaspora. Thus, I reject the notion that the only Pan Africanism is that which is involved with the affairs of African states and resurrect the complementing DuBoisian notion of a Pan Africanism consisting of the Diaspora's obligation to Africa, adding the modern notion of the linkages of unity, regarding strategies of liberation in the Diaspora. I, therefore, consider to be false a statement made by one author that "the first phase of Pan-Africanism, between 1900 and 1945, remained in the realm of ideas"[82] since that writer undoubtedly means that the concept of unity among African states was not realized until after 1945. What, then, had been occurring all along? This is the question to which I mean to provide an answer as it applies to current events. Has modern Pan Africanism in the Diaspora existed only as "ideas" or in action?

Now if we return to the definition given by Esedebe, it is possible to dissect its essential parts according to the supporting concepts of core values and transitory values. In his definition,

the transitory values are first and the core values second. Nevertheless, we recognize their function in any order. Equally important, it is now possible to make sense of any definition that is
used according to what core value it represents, to what category of transitory value it belongs and how those issues have
changed over time.

There is one final discussion to be broached at this point, that
is, the way in which the term Pan Africanism originated. This is
important because, while some scholars claim that there is little
evidence as to how the term was born, in fact, we know differently. Kodjoe, previously, refers to an idea also put forth by Esedebe, the fact that Pan Africanism existed first as a "body of
ideas" that later stimulated the formation of a movement. I believe this to be substantially correct with a few minor modifica-
tions.

It is important to say that Pan Africanism existed in *practice* as
the first stage of its existence. It was natural for people, who
were enslaved in the Americas, Africans in every sense of the
word and regarded as such by their captors, to want to go back
home. For a long time after their capture in Africa, it was likely
that they thought of going back to their village by name—or to
the specificity of their location and culture. But as their roots
grew in the Americas, the longing was for going back to "Africa." Since many did return, but to places other than their original homes, this movement popularized the linkage between
America and the African *landmass* in practice. As practice, African emigration was important in the early stages because it provided the manpower for colonies such as Liberia and Sierra
Leone, and such individuals as Paul Cuffee and Martin Delaney
will be remembered as examples of those who actually tried a
systematic approach to the return. However, as will be shown
here, this phenomenon of African emigration continued well up
to the 1960s.

As Professors James Turner, Hollis Lynch, Floyd Miller and
others have shown, from the turn of the nineteenth century to
the turn of the twentieth century, there was an evolution of concepts that resulted in the articulation of the Pan Africanist idea.[83]
In this period Edward Wilmot Blyden, Alexander Crummel,
Henry Highland Garnett, Bishop Henry McNeal Turner, and
others spoke of the integrity of African civilization and its re-

demption, and in 1861 Martin Delaney coined the phrase, "Africa for the Africans."

The next stage was the codification of the *term* itself; rudimentary forms of the term Pan Africanism began to appear after 1895. The term "Pan African Conference" was used first by a Black newspaper, *Advance,* describing a conference on Africa in Chicago in 1893.[84] Then, in March of 1897, a Black organization, the American Negro Academy, was founded. At its opening session DuBois delivered a paper in which he said: ". . . the [Negro people] must soon come to realize that if they are to take their just place in the van of Pan Negroism, *then their destiny is not absorption by the white Americans"*(my emphasis).[85] Next, we know that in September of 1897 the preparatory meeting for the 1900 Pan African Conference was held in London, but the Pan African Conference as such was not called until 1900 and was popularized thereafter by the journal *The Pan African,* and the formation of the Pan African Association.

The last phase in this sequence of events was the founding of the *Pan African Movement,* initiated by the Paris Conference of 1919 organized by DuBois. Thus, it is possible to say that Pan Africanism was born in a definite sequence of events which went from *practice* to *concept* to the *term* to the *movement.* This logical sequence in the formation of the concept of Pan Africanism provides us not only with a methodology for its historical definition but also with an approach to understanding how it came into being in concrete terms.

To remove the tentativeness at the core of the concepts that guide one to an understanding of the Pan African world experience is an important liberating factor in that it gives integrity to the subject. History would not have played such a powerful role in supporting American culture if it was generally accepted that no one knew where America originated, when the movement toward the revolution originated or when America became a nation. In fact, institutionalized history, often comprising myths, is important to its transmission and to the socialization of people to its belief. Scholars constantly challenge aspects of settled American or European history, but when they do, they are put on the defensive and considered to be "revisionists." In this context, the intellectual tentativeness in the history of African Americans is both a derivative and an extention of the phenomenon of racial oppression itself. Surely it must be confronted if there is to evolve an adequate tool utilized to provide the most illuminating analyses of the presence of African-origin people in the Diaspora.

2
The Pan African Movement in the United States

Examining the force of Pan Africanism as it exists in the African Diaspora, one understands that the African-American community has been a dynamic element in generating movement toward a world-wide African unity. With the rise of African nationalism and its driving force, ridding the continent of colonialism and establishing new nation states, an inevitable tension developed regarding the definition and function of the new Pan Africanism. Was it meant only for those in African states? Did it extend only to Black Africans?

What exacerbated the attempt of those on the continent to define Pan Africanism in terms of the quest for *intra*continental unity based on nations was the rejuvenation of what St. Clair Drake calls "racial Pan Africanism" in the United States and around the world through the Black Power movement. In this chapter, these developments will be discussed in order to explore relevant aspects of Pan Africanism as they exist in a non-African country and within an African-origin community. We will try to discover the tensions that have been produced and the models utilized to resolve these tensions in pursuit of a functional Pan Africanism that can relate to the African continent.

It is, therefore, obvious that my approach to this subject, as I examine the history of this problem, will be through the Pan African method. Therefore, I will examine the rejuvenation of "racial Pan Africanism" and its attempt to achieve the criterion of unity with "continental Pan Africanism."

The Renewal of Racial Pan Africanism

In 1963, it appeared that simultaneously an era had passed and another was being born as the Organization of African Unity came into existence and W. E. B. DuBois died in Ghana and was buried on September 29. Ironically, in this same period, 250,000 people had gathered in Washington in the famous "March on Washington" to protest the lack of jobs and justice for Blacks. But with the founding of the OAU and the settling-in of continental Pan Africanism, St. Clair Drake could justly write that "obviously feelings of racial Pan-Africanism are not dead." Rather, he continued, as Black Americans adopted new roles and African societies modernized, both Africans and Black Americans were "groping for new fixed patterns of relationships with one another."[1] These sentiments were unmistakably true, and the leading edge of this phenomenon was the fact that younger American Blacks were breaking away from the moorings of a more conservative past toward Africa and the strategies of Black survival in America. And partly because this change was fueled by the African independence movement itself, there was among the younger American Blacks a re-examination of old attitudes toward the "Blackness" of their identity, a re-examination that simultaneously raised the question of the African source of their cultural heritage.[2] Eventually, there was a pride in this heritage which was expressed as Black pride, then as Pan African pride.

In the early 1960s, these two proud groups of people—Africans and African Americans —attempted the "groping" of which St. Clair Drake spoke, a process that was made even more complicated by virtue of the fact that, although different, they were also the same people and were beginning to intersect at important points in each other's history. This was a different phenomenon than had occurred earlier when the intersection was only that fostered by elites; this new development was the intersection of the masses and thus, a more profound phenomenon, fraught with guilt, unanswerable questions, false arrogance, and much sheer misunderstanding.

Somewhat typical of this "groping" was a public conversation between a Nigerian, Thomas O. Echewa, and the African-American novelist, John A. Williams, in the pages of *Negro Digest* in September of 1965, contained in an exchange of open letters responding to Echewa's article of the previous January, "Africans vs. Afro-Americans."

> There was an act of deception. It went like this: Whites called Negroes blacks. Negroes agreed they were blacks, no matter the amount of black and white pigmentation in their skin. Whites said Negroes came from Africa. Negroes agreed that they came from Africa. The Negro's fate thus placed in my hand, I, in my African humanitarianess, have welcomed him. But the Negro is merely my Nephew and cousin. Most of the mothers were my sisters, a few of the fathers were my brothers. But the greater number of the fathers were my 'brothers-in-law'—the white man in America. Old man, it was too bad you sowed your wild oats. You must now take care of my nephews and cousins running about in your compound, as I have taken care of the descendants of African slaves resulting from the internal slave trade.[3]

To this, John A. Williams retorted, "There is nothing like a trip to Africa to make an American Negro realize just how American he is."[4] Commenting extensively on perspectives of both writers, novelist John O. Killens posited that their petty quarreling was superceded by the fact that they were also bound up in a "Brotherhood of Blackness," whether or not they knew it, understood it or honored it.[5]

Ralph Ellison, an African-American novelist, illustrated a

more conservative Black attitude toward African politics but an approving attitude toward African culture when, in response to an interviewer's question on "religion in the present Negro societies," he said, "I am unacquainted with the religious movements in the societies to which you refer. If the Mau Mau is one of these, then I must say that for all my disgust for those who provoked the natives to such obscene extremes, I feel it to be regressive indeed."[6] And elsewhere he said, "I know little of the current work in sculpture by Africans, but that which I have seen appears to possess little of that high artistic excellent characteristic of ancient African arts."[7] To say flatly that these sentiments were "typical" would be a serious mistake. However, the depth of the conflict in cultural attitudes between Africans and African Americans that then existed should not be underestimated, the enlightened opinion holders in both communities constituting a rank minority.

A factor which helped to cut through the confusion and tension produced by the "groping" to understand these intersecting histories was the clarity of Malcolm X. In the Spring of 1964, Malcolm X went to Mecca and on his way back to the United States stopped in several African countries, among them Nigeria and Ghana. His remarks at Ibadan University in Nigeria showed that Malcolm possessed an advanced conceptualization of Pan Africanism, not only in its philosophical dimension, but in a political sense as well.

> I urged that Africa's independent nations needed to see the necessity of helping to bring the Afro-American's case before the United Nations. I said that just as the American Jew is in political, economic, and cultural harmony with world Jewry, I was convinced that it was time for all Afro-Americans to join the world's Pan-Africanists. I said that physically we Afro-Americans might remain in America, fighting for our Constitutional rights, but that philosophically and culturally we Afro-Americans badly needed to 'return' to Africa—and to develop a working unity in the framework of Pan Africanism.[8]

Malcolm, then, had a plan to get the message of the Black American before the court of world opinion and would ask the assistance of the African family of states. However, his emphasis on

Pan African unity as the framework for the Black American's freedom struggle was an advanced form of politics, the parallel of the attempt by DuBois to internationalize the race question through his Pan African conferences and through the League of Nations and the United Nations. Indeed, it was significant that Malcolm X was the first Black American of national stature to visit West Africa since Ghana's independence.

This visit was to have an important impact upon Malcolm as he sought to strengthen the Organization of Afro-American Unity in the United States, Africa and Europe. It was to add a revolutionary content to his international perspective, a content that also suffused his aspirations for the OAAU. For example, there is some evidence that his well-known phrase, that Black people should achieve freedom "by any means necessary," might have been inspired by the African independence movement. Malcolm X said that the determination of those who created the OAU was a model for African Americans to accomplish the same objective of gaining freedom and independence for peoples of African descent, first in the United States and ultimately in the entire Western Hemisphere, "and bring about the freedom of these people by any means necessary."[9] At another point, he says: "That's our motto. We want freedom by any means necessary."[10] The OAAU, then, was to become part of Malcolm X's legacy to Pan Africanism, as much in concept as by its brief operations in America and in the other places where it was established.

Malcolm made a return journey to Africa in July of that year and appeared before the OAU in Cairo to deliver a message of solidarity between Africans and Afro-Americans and to tell the assembled heads of state that "our problems are your problems" and that "you will never be recognized as free human beings until and unless we are also recognized and treated as human beings."[11] In terms of concrete results, Malcolm did secure a resolution from this meeting that, although cautiously worded, praised the United States for passing the Civil Rights Act, but noted the continuing evidence of racial discrimination as well.[12] This philosophy, molded by his insights on the continent of Africa, would influence his intended approach to organizing in America as well.

Black Power to Pan Africanism

The Student Non-Violent Coordinating Com-
mittee (SNCC) was one of the vanguard groups which led the
break from the older, more conservative civil rights organizations in ideology and tactics of struggle. To be sure, there were
some organizations concerned with Africa at this time, such as
The American Society for African Culture (AMSAC) in the late
1950s and, in the mid-1960s, the American Negro Leadership
Conference on Africa (ANLCA) was founded.[13] AMSAC was an
intellectual group of an interracial character but largely Black,
while ANLCA was founded by a coalition of civil rights organizations led by the NAACP.

On the other hand, responding to the unavoidable impact of
the Vietnam War, most Black activist youth organizations were
internationalist to some extent. For example, in 1967 SNCC sent
a delegation to Hanoi and in a position statement attributed the
causes of American involvement in Vietnam to the same factor
that prompted U.S. involvement in South Africa and Rhodesia,
the collusion between America and other Western colonialist
powers.[14] Nevertheless, the emphasis was on Africa, and as
early as 1965 Bob Moses and his wife, leaders in the SNCC organization, attended an OAU meeting. But James Forman, a key
internationalist in SNCC and its executive director, had gone to
Africa first in 1964, and again attended a United Nations Seminar on Apartheid, "Racism and Colonialism," in July of 1967.

Forman explicitly mentions the influence of Malcolm X's
thoughts and activities upon him and the rest of the SNCC
cadre. However, it is also important that Dr. St. Clair Drake, former adviser to Nkrumah, an adviser to SNCC and Forman's former professor at Roosevelt University, helped him with the
SNCC position statement for the UN Conference. Forman's activities in 1967 were critical in linking the activists in SNCC with
the African leaders, who included both the heads of state and,
more importantly, the radical leaders of the liberation movements. Forman not only became a spokesman before the Fourth
Committee of the UN, presenting the increasingly radical position of SNCC on the burning questions of African liberation—
South African Apartheid, Rhodesia, the Congo, and so on; he

also visited the OAU meeting in Kinshasa that year in an effort to acquire international support for H. Rap. Brown. Brown, the new head of SNCC, had come under pressure from the police authorities for his outspoken support of the Black rebellions occurring around the country and had eventually been incarcerated.[15]

SNCC's position and that of the newly formed Black Panther Party were anti-imperialist, and their growing analysis of world events illustrated this outlook. They attempted to link the support of the United States for Western European imperialism and colonialism to conditions in the Third World, while supporting the quest of Third World peoples and countries for independence. But while Forman was more internationalist, SNCC's Stokely Carmichael emphasized the African dimension of SNCC activities and his own personal activities in developing a Pan Africanist ideology. For example, in a 1967 speech that evinced a maturing Pan Africanism, he said that the white man only wanted Blacks to relate to Africa culturally, but not politically or economically, "because in that lies his death."[16]

This statement shows not only that Carmichael possessed a Pan African consciousness, but that at an early stage in the debate over the character of Pan Africanism, he had attempted to put forth the thesis that it should be comprehensive in nature and basically revolutionary in focus. As his analysis of Black Power will show, Carmichael also had accepted the relevance of the colonial model to the Black American condition, believing that "the struggle for Black Power in the United States is the struggle to free these *colonies* (my emphasis) from external domination" and that ". . . the struggle to free these *internal colonies* relates to the struggles of imperialism around the world."[17] But his vision of the necessity of Pan Africanism was not unconnected to the global sweep of independence, as he said in another place: "Black Power, to us, means that Black people see themselves as a part of a new force, sometimes called the Third World; that we see our struggle as closely related to liberation struggles around the world. We must hook up with these struggles."[18]

In the late 1960s, SNCC and other radical organizations were being influenced by these sentiments, and the influences were derived from a pantheon of revolutionary theorists, from Che

Guevara to Mao Tse Tung, but there was the unmistakable fact, as Forman was to say, that "my studies of Frantz Fanon were of particular help in this."[19] Charmichael confirms this influence and, for example, in one of his speeches he prefaced a long quote from Fanon with the statement that Fanon's work, *The Wretched of the Earth*, clearly contained the reasons for the relationship between the concept of Black Power and the new force of Third World liberation.[20]

Although Fanon's ideas were pivotal, it should also be explained that these were but the leading edge of the powerful penetration into Black American consciousness of the ideas of a series of continental African revolutionaries, spread partly by their activities in Africa, but also through their actual contact with their younger American "brothers and sisters" during visits to this country.

Illustrative of this group was Eduardo Mondlane, head of FRELIMO (Front for the Liberation of Mozambique), who came to the United States in November of 1963. Mondlane was a Methodist who had been educated in the United States, served on the faculty of Syracuse University and married an American. So it was natural for him to think that Americans would be sympathetic to the struggle in Mozambique. Some Americans were sympathetic, but government officials were unresponsive to his requests for various forms of assistance to FRELIMO, and it was, thus, instructive to hear him speak of this problem frankly with younger people, many of whom were Black and involved in the Black Power movement at that time.[21]

However, it was perhaps the visits and the ideas of Amilcar Cabral, leader of the PAIGC or African Party for the Independence of Guinea-Bissau and Cape Verde, a small colonial possession of the Portuguese in West Africa, that were the most important in this respect. Cabral had come to the United States first in 1962 to speak at the United Nations and ask for assistance for his people's struggle to liberate themselves from Portuguese colonialism. He returned in 1970 to deliver a lecture at Syracuse University honoring Eduardo Mondlane, who had been assassinated in February 1969. This speech on "National Liberation and Culture" was to make an indelible impression upon all who heard it because it came at a time when there was considerable debate within the Pan Africanist community on the aims of Pan

Africanism and the relative emphasis placed on culture versus politics in definition and practice.[22]

Cabral explained that in his experience a *cultural renaissance preceded and signaled revolutionary activity,* that the affirmation of the cultural personality of the oppressed was preparation for the act of rejecting the personality imposed by the oppressor, and that culture carried the seed of revolt because it was the foundation of the history of a people in its unfolding and its reaction to events. He proclaimed that the aim of revolution was to achieve the liberation of a people and that the first step in this process was the achievement of political independence, but that "national liberation takes place only when national productive forces are completely free of all kinds of foreign domination" (because only then can the authentic development of the people be facilitated).[23] At that point, he argued, people could return to the "upward path of their own culture" that had been aborted by the interference of imperialism. For him, culture becomes important because of the need for new values by people involved in change to move to an authentic expression of political independence. He said that the analysis of cultural values is important as a necessary step in developing strong organization through which to mobilize people "to face colonial violence"— that is, to resort to violence themselves, through "the armed struggle for national liberation," in the cause of their own freedom.[24]

Therefore, the culture of which Cabral speaks is a revolutionary culture able both to prosecute the struggle against colonialism and imperialism and then to recognize when true independence has indeed been achieved. These ideas would have meaning for African Americans in their understanding of aspects of the process of the African independence struggle (such as the rationale for armed struggle in particular) and in their decision to support the kind of movements represented by PAIGC in general.

In October 1972, Cabral returned to the United States to speak to the United Nations Fourth Committee and to receive an honorary doctorate from Lincoln University, a Black college in Pennsylvania. Many representatives of the Pan African movement in the United States traveled to Lincoln to hear Cabral's address and to meet with him afterward. On this occasion, he dwelled upon the theme of the "marginality" of the "petite bourgeoisie" and the frustration that produced conflicts stemming from its class situation, poised as it was between the colonial elite and the native masses.[25] Therefore, he said, in the need to reject marginality, the petite bourgeoisie rediscovered their original identity and "return[ed] to the source."

Cabral felt that marginality was a by-product of the frustration which African-descendant peoples developed as a result of the racism they experienced living in the colonial metropole. For him, then, it was "no surprise that the theories of Pan African-ism and Négritude [two pertinent expressions arising mainly from the assumption that all Black Africans have a common cultural identity] were propounded outside black Africa."[26] The strengthening of these movements, he felt, was clearly related to the emerging African independence movement. Cabral, therefore, says that the "return to the source" is not a voluntary step, but the only route through which the alienated petite bourgeoisie can enter the struggle to change their class situation. Clearly, this analysis, which blends the powerful logic of Frantz Fanon with the logic of Marx, Nkrumah, and others, was persuasive to some African-American Pan Africanists, and Cabral sought a more informal atmosphere to communicate these views by calling for a meeting of representatives of the Black community in New York shortly after this speech.

That meeting was organized a few days later by the African Information Services, headed by Robert Van Lierop, a leading Pan Africanist, who was also an attorney and producer of several significant films about the Mozambiqican revolution, such as "A Luta Continua." Representatives of some thirty African-American organizations met with Cabral, and the significant aspects of that discussion began with his rejection of the colonial model as a description of the American Black community, a model he had encountered in a discussion with Eldridge Cleaver of the Black Panther party.[27] Perhaps Cleaver had not clearly articulated the fact that "internal colonialism" as practiced in the United States was not, in fact, classic colonialism, but that both had strikingly similar sources and functions. Cabral had countered that colonialism implies foreign control over the continuous territory of a subjugated people. But although American internal colonialism may be described in roughly the same manner, Cabral had hit upon the essential difference.[28]

Secondly, he had sought to make a distinction between the African continental conception of Pan Africanism and Diaspora Pan Africanism in America and to point to the lack of feasibility of both if taken out of the context of the problems involved. In answer to one question, he said: "You see, my sister, you here in the United States, we understand you. You are for Pan-Africanism and you want it today. Pan-Africanism now! We are in Africa; don't confuse this reaction against Pan-Africanism with the situation of the OAU."[29] Cabral continued, suggesting that while DuBois was the father of the idea of Pan-Africanism, Nkrumah would have approached it differently had he another chance.[30] The reason for Nkrumah's re-evaluation of tactics might be said to have appeared in his *Class Struggle in Africa*, which had been published in 1970 and which ended with an analysis of the process of socialist revolution. This theme would be expanded in a later work, complete with a methodology for achieving socialist revolution.[31]

Lastly, Cabral wanted to make the point that if the end product of Pan Africanism only resulted in the establishment of a "cultural brotherhood" as the level of the relation of African Americans to the African liberation struggle, then Pan Africanism (and, therefore, African "brotherhood") was not valuable to the needs of Africa. But if it went beyond this to embrace revolutionary camaraderie as the basis of the relations, then Pan Africanism would have a foundation which could be functional to the process of national liberation in Guinea-Bissau and Cape Verde and in others places where Africans were struggling for their freedom. For his part, Cabral made clear that he preferred the concept of *comrades*.[32]

One of the most persistent influences from Africa, although he did not spend very much time in the United States, was Mwalimu Julius Nyerere, who during the decade of the 1960s maintained his Pan Africanist principles as head of the government of Tanzania, long after Nkrumah had passed from the scene in Ghana and after the The Pan African Movement of East and Central Africa (PAFMECA) experiment had failed. To Black American Pan Africanists he was a beacon of light in Africa, and when his government in 1967 released a *Declaration on Self-Reliance* at Arusha (known as the "Arusha Declaration") and its companion statement on education, *Education for Self-Reliance,* the effect was instant and pervasive.[33] The first document set out essentially a socialist direction that would govern those active in the party and especially those who would assume positions of leadership in the government of Tanzania. It focused on the amount of wealth which could be owned allowing, for example, government officials to own only one house or car and prohibiting them from land or property speculation, from becoming absentee landlords or engaging in other forms of capitalist endeavor. It also counseled them to invest their money in national saving institutions that work for the benefit of all the people and themselves as well.

The second document, *Education for Self-Reliance,* was equally ground-breaking because it tackled the basic question of the purposes of a national education system and the kind of system needed to conform to the principles of the *Declaration on Self-Reliance.*[34] It attacked the fact that the educational system inherited by Tanzanians was designed to force people to fit into the system of colonialism and, as such, minimized the kinds of skills required for young people to aspire to govern or to contribute to nation-building in the many professional tasks associated with a modern society. Likewise, it addressed the fact that the educational system produced individuals who, for most purposes, were carbon copies of the colonialist exploiters and that for self-reliance to work, new values would be needed as the basis of a *Tanzanian* education in a country which was largely agricultural, culturally Swahili, and poor.

From this understanding of the need for self-reliance was to come the Ujamaa village scheme, a system of collectivized agricultural development that has evolved since the late 1960s into a series of cooperative rural settlements. As a model of economic development, this idea stirred considerable interest internationally because it marked the first time since 1960, when Guinea had said "non!" to joining the French community of nations, that an African country had seemed to turn its back on Western models of development or predicated its development on concepts which did not presuppose the infusion of large amounts of Western economic aid.

The impact of the Arusha Declaration in the United States was electric because of the growing ideological trend toward the Africanization of the Black community but also because the declaration provided theoretical concepts relevant to the Black struggle. For example, it was not unnoticed that the concept of self-reliance was closely associated with the idea of Black self-determination stemming from the Black Power movement. Indeed, the first "Black Power Conference" was held in 1967, the same year the Arusha Declaration was issued, and accompanied the thrust of the Black Power philosophy into American education; students and such professors as Dr. Nathan Hare at Howard University began to challenge the structure and content of American education for Blacks and its lack of Black and African content.[35]

The attraction of the Tanzanian experiment in African socialism was irresistible to many African Americans, and in a short time, a small but significant number of them had established a community in Tanzania. Some of the members of this group of "pioneers" were intellectuals, some were former SNCC activists, some were just curious, and others were assorted ideologues and voyeurists. The mixture did not make for a harmonious Black community, and very often the Tanzanian government did not know what to make of the objectives of various segments of the group. Here, the comparative experiences of the Ghana and Tanzania Afro-American community (or "Afros," as they were often called) would prove fascinating and instructive, and we will address the story of a similar community in Ghana in chapter 3.[36]

The impact of the personage of Nyerere and the country of Tanzania resulted in the growth of a mythical following in the American Black community as a great locus of Pan African thought and practice in Africa, especially after the downfall of Nkrumah. Just as important, the cultural content of the Pan African movement in the United States took on a decidedly Tanzanian (or Swahili) cast. Symbolic of this fact was the scene one day in 1968 during the second Black Power Conference in Philadelphia, when Maulana Ron Karenga, head of United Slaves (US), and Imamu Amiri Baraka, head of the Congress of African People, and their entourages met in the hallway. After the preliminary greetings of "Hujambo" answered by "Sijambo," the principals proceeded to conduct a discussion for nearly thirty minutes completely in the Swahili language before an awe-struck and admiring audience.[37] As a consequence, Swahili language training became a must for many African and Afro-American studies programs newly developing on American college campuses. Similarly, the State Department invested considerable resources in the codification of Swahili and in the training of diplomats in that language.

The effect of this substantial baptism of Black American activists by leading African revolutionaries and their ideas was to further radicalize the movement for Pan Africanism in America. By 1968, however, the former leader of this movement, Stokely Carmichael, was a frequent visitor in the revolutionary country of Guinea, where President Ahmed Sékou Touré had given sanctuary to Kwame Nkrumah after the 1966 coup which had deposed him from the presidency of Ghana. Carmichael began to spend an extended period of time in Guinea, studying Pan Africanism with Nkrumah. Nkrumah had published a pamphlet in 1969 entitled "The Spectre of Black Power," which had communicated his approval—the approval of one of the world's eminent African activists and thinkers—to this new movement.[38] In this work, Nkrumah defined Black Power as "part of the vanguard of world revolution against capitalism, imperialism, and neocolonialism which have enslaved, exploited, and oppressed peoples everywhere, and against which the masses of the world are now revolting." Confirming Carmichael's earlier interpretation, he continued:

> Black power is part of the world rebellion of the oppressed against the oppressor, of the exploited against the exploiter. It operates throughout the African continent, in North and South America, the Caribbean, where Africans and people of African descent live. It is linked with the Pan African struggle for unity *on the African continent* (my emphasis), and with all those who strive to establish a socialist society.[39]

Nkrumah, then, defines Black Power as a force operating in the African Diaspora which linked peoples of African descent to the struggle for continental Pan Africanism, making it part of the world Pan African movement. But he also related it to the struggle to achieve scientific socialism, an element which begins to appear in Carmichael's speeches with increasing force in the early 1970s.

The Pan African movement in the American Black community was a part of and proceeded, as a logical extension, from the movement for Black Power. Indeed, within the Black Power conferences of 1967 and 1968, African issues were discussed, among them the civil war in Nigeria, perhaps in 1968 the most contentious issue. Here, the debate ended with a Pan Africanist resolution, opting for the unification of Nigeria as a strategy for fighting forces of imperialism that would rather have divided up the country in order to have access to its material riches.[40] Also, by the end of the 1960s, important organizational centers of Pan African activity had arisen in the United States, but there is no more important indication of the influence of the Pan African movement than the initiative taken by Black nationalists/Pan Africanists in calling the Congress of African People.

This meeting in Atlanta in September 1970 was notable, first, for the sheer diversity of Black leadership it attracted, representing varying ideologies and professions, most espousing some form of identity with the goals of Black nationalism or Pan Africanism. They ranged from Whitney Young, executive director of the National Urban League, to Democratic party politicians such as Richard Hatcher and John Cashin; leaders of SCLC such as Rev. Ralph Abernathy and Rev. Jesse Jackson; representatives of the Diaspora such as Roosevelt Douglas of Dominica (then in Montreal) and Minister Louis Farrakhan of the Nation of Islam.[41] It was, nevertheless, clear that the leadership of this meeting resided with Pan Africanists Hayward Henry (aka Mtangulizi Sanyika), Imamu Amiri Baraka, Rosie Douglas and Howard Fuller.

Howard Fuller (Owusu Sadaukai) read a letter from Carmichael, who had recently married South African singer Miriam Makeba and moved to Guinea. The letter struck his now familiar theme that "Pan Africanism is the highest political expression of Black Power," marrying it with the new theme that "the ideology of Pan Africanism must seek a land base."[42] Sadaukai appeared to agree with this "land base" concept of Diaspora Pan Africanism which made continental Africa the seat of the most legitimate expression of the theory. However, another definition emerged from the political liberation workshop of the Congress which, while acknowledging that "Pan Africanism is the global expression of Black Nationalism," declared that, while recognizing the "central importance of the African Continent to Black struggles for National Liberation," it was also necessary for African descendants to build a functional collective political and economic base outside of the continent in order to become a "functional ally" in African and Third World struggles. And then he continued: "Although it is absolutely necessary to have a unified and independent Africa, we must simultaneously move to design viable institutional alternatives wherever we are in which a meaningful (non-romantic) Pan-Africanism can be practiced."[43]

This partial rejection and important clarification of Carmichael's "land base" theory was a collective expression of the need to found Pan Africanism upon a more realistic basis, taking into consideration the link between Black struggle and the Third World and the new reality of the maturing political dynamic in the Diaspora of Europe and the New World.

Also associated with the above sentiment was the partial rejection of Carmichael's absentee leadership of the Pan African movement in the United States and the arrival of new voices. There were new grassroots voices now involved in the Pan African movement in such places as the Nairobi School experiment in Palo Alto, in the Institute for Positive Thought led by Don Lee (Haki Madhubuti), Zimbabwean Ruwa Chiri and Professor Anderson Thompson in Chicago, in the Pan African Congress and Secretariat led by Kwadwo Akpan in Detroit, in the Pan African Skills Project led by Irving Davis, in the Patrice Lumumba Coalition led by Irving Davis and Elombe Brath in New York, in the Center for Black Education in Washington, led by Jimmy Garrett, in Malcolm X Liberation University and the Student Organization for Black Unity in Greensboro, N.C., led by Owusu Sadaukai, Tim Thomas, and Mark Smith, and in the various chapters of the Black United Front (BUF) and the Congress of African People all over the country, with activists such as Rev. Douglas Moore of Washington, head of the D.C. BUF, Muhammad Ahmed of the African Peoples Party and many others.

As suggested, one central project in the early 1970s came to be the observance of African Liberation Day. It was first initiated by Kwame Nkrumah upon Ghana's independence, and later the Organization of African Unity officially adopted May 25 of each year as African Liberation Day. Observances in the United States started in 1971 when a delegation of individuals from the listing above, including Jimmy Garrett and Owusu Sadaukai, traveled to Mozambique, met with the FRELIMO guerillas and observed first-hand the progress of the armed liberation struggle. A major result of that visit is contained in the following excerpt of a message dated February 17, 1972, from Sadaukai to fellow Pan Africanists in the United States:

Dear Brothers and Sisters:

The African Liberation Day Co-ordinating Committee (ALDCC), an ad hoc national group, has been established to marshall support of Black people in the Americas for the valiant liberation struggles now being waged by our brothers and sisters on the African continent, particularly in South Africa, Angola, Mozambique, and Zimbabwe (Rhodesia).

As a beginning we are attempting to do the following things: 1) help make the masses of African (black) people in the United States, the Caribbean, and Canada aware of the political conditions in Southern Africa and the armed struggles being carried out by the brothers and sisters there; 2) to educate African (black) people in these countries about the relationship between what is happening to our people in Africa and what is happening to us in the United States and other places; and 3) to organize a national protest demonstration against the United States foreign policy which supports European colonialist rule in Southern Africa. This planned action is a result of meetings with liberation movement leaders in Mozambique during a prolonged trip to the continent last fall, during which I was able to witness the hard daily struggle our brothers and sisters are waging to regain control of their land. When asked how the masses of our people in the United States could best support them, I was advised that the most useful thing we can do *at this stage* is to provide them with strong moral support by showing the world our concern through massive Black protest and demonstration against U.S. involvement in Southern Africa.

The Organization of African Unity (OAU) has designated May 25th as the Worldwide Day of Solidarity with the People of Africa. In carrying out the three above objectives mentioned, the practically-formed national committee (including Julian Bond, Imamu

Baraka, Richard Hatcher, Betty Shabazz, and others) will focus its activities on May 27, 1972, when we hope to bring Black people from around the country to Washington, D.C. for a peaceful demonstration. All Black people, irrespective of political ideology, party affiliation, occupation, or social status, will be urged and encouraged to participate.[44]

Clearly, the message shows the direct influence of the continental movement for African liberation on the African-American Diaspora. The initial result of the call contained in this letter was the formation of the African Liberation Support Committee (ALSC), a coalition of Pan Africanist, Black nationalist and moderate Black organizations participating in the simple act of observing African Liberation Day in unity with Africans on the continent.

The first such meeting was a rather small event held in Washington, sponsored by the Black United Front, but the ALSC-sponsored event in 1972 drew an estimated 50,000–plus people to Washington. The line of march went from Malcolm X Park (Meridian Hill Park) on Sixteenth Street past the South African Embassy and the State Department to the Washington Monument grounds in one of the longest processions ever witnessed in the capital city. On the speaker's platform were representatives of the Pan African movement and Black elected officials, including Congressmen Charles Diggs, Jr. and Walter Fauntroy. Along the line of march and between the speeches the incessant chant was heard, "We are an African people!"[45]

The year 1972 was extraordinary in the history of Black America because, in addition to the African Liberation Day march/demonstration/rally, there was a major African policy conference held at Howard University, "The African-American National Conference on Africa," sponsored by the Congressional Black Caucus, and the National Black Political Convention drew some 10,000 people to Gary, Indiana.[46] In many ways, that year represented the climax of the Black Power/Pan Africanist movement and its influence over a significant spectrum of Black politics in America.

It also represented the ascending influence of the institutional Black politics movement in the form of a challenge to Pan Africanism, brought about by the newly organized Black elected officials in Congress and in the urban areas of the country. For many of these fledgling politicians, the ability of the Black Nationalist/Pan Africanists to bring a modicum of unity to Black political behavior was a welcome ingredient to their aspirations for political office and would be discarded when it no longer suited their purposes or when the mood of their constituents changed.

By 1974, another challenge to the nationalist formulation of Pan Africanism had matured. Actually, the potent division in the ranks had been growing since the late 1960s if we are to believe Baraka, who says: "The last part of the sixties saw perhaps the divisive spirit among young and old Africans caused in no small part by attempts to reassert so-called 'radical' European [Marxist] definitions into the African struggle. This cannot be done, with any benefit to Africans."[47] In any case, this division surfaced at the meeting of the executive committee of ALSC at Frogmore, S.C. in April of 1974 when Abdul Alkalimat (Gerald McWhorter), an activist professor, then at Fisk University, presented a Marxist-Leninist analysis of the goals of ALSC which was adopted by the committee. The analysis included a call for those in the coalition to adopt the principles of scientific socialism. Immediately, dissension raged within the organized Pan African community between the Black Nationalist and the Black Marxist interpretations of Pan Africanism in ALSC, and members of the coalition began to disaffiliate.

This dispute became even more public and intense as African Liberation Day neared; it dominated the public forum held the day before ALD at Howard University.[48] The most important signal was the unmistakable shift in the ideological tone of the speech by Owusu Sadaukai, but the most acrimonious set of remarks were in the presentation by Abdul Alkalimat (Gerald McWhorter) and the rebuttal by Stokely Carmichael (who had changed his name to Kwame Touré), then visiting the country. While Alkalimat made an analysis of the Pan African movement and its purpose suggesting that the movement should be oriented toward the working class and revolutionary in content, Touré chided him for a lack of personal involvement in the movement and posited that any theory of liberation in America had to treat white racism as its primary problem. But judging from the division of sentiments in the conference hall, the resolution of the debate saw no clear victory for either side.

Later in 1974, *The Black Scholar* magazine carried a representative debate initiated by Pan Africanist poet Haki Madhubuti, who suggested that the Black Nationalist and closely associated Pan Africanist movements in the Black community had come under "attack" by the "white left," but that major organizations such as the African Liberation Support Committee and the Congress of African People had been infiltrated by the more dangerous Black Marxists who were attempting to coopt them.[49] Madhubuti pointed to the chaos and disruption in these movements caused by the ideological conflict which ensued from the introduction of an alien European social ideology.[50] Madhubuti went on to mine the historical roots of white supremacy as an ideology and concluded that since it predated capitalism and imperialism, white supremacy is a basic force in world history and in the United States quite without regard to the economic structure of the state. Articles in the magazine's following issue took various sides of this argument in support or opposition to the views of Madhubuti.[51]

The transformation of the views of key leaders such as Imamu Amiri Baraka and Owusu Sadaukai from Black Nationalism to scientific socialism was complete by 1974, as indicated. Earlier in the year, Baraka had published a new position paper representing the views of the Congress of Afrikan People which indicated that "First of all many more of us now understand that our main enemy, the main obstruction to our complete liberation, is the system of monopoly capitalism and imperialism. It took some time for many of us, certainly the Congress of Afrikan People, to understand and acknowledge this, for a number of reasons . . . ."[52] Baraka went on to develop a sophisticated analysis of the historical forces shaping the Black Liberation movement and its relationship to the international struggle against capitalism and imperialism.

Without a detailed analysis of the substance of this ideological debate, suffice it to say, first, that what we see at this level is the Pan African side of a deeper ideological conflict taking place at the roots of Black Nationalism itself. It is a perennial conflict within the Black Diaspora which surfaces each time there is a political movement of substance. This recent conflict had its genesis with the rise of the Black Panther party as a self-professed Marxist formation within the context of the Black Power movement. It continued, gaining force with the workers revolutionary movements in Detroit such as DRUM (Dodge Revolutionary Union Movement), and surfaced in the Pan African movement, as we have suggested.[53]

However, there is no doubt that a potent source of the change of ideology came through the liberation movements in Southern Africa and Guinea-Bissau, with American Pan Africanist leaders seeking to unify the movement in America ideologically with the continental African movement. For example, despite his earlier view that Marxist definitions of the African struggle would not suffice, Baraka was among those who had changed his outlook. In an article entitled, "Why I Changed My Ideology," he asserts that a proper understanding of the revolutionary theory of Amilcar Cabral held that if there was to be a "national" Black culture which sustained the revolutionary impulses flowing within the Black community, it had to reflect such elements as the Black working class, both urban and rural, and the urban petite bourgeoisie.[54] Thus formulated, Baraka declared, his organization had become "revolutionary communist," a decision made in 1974 and one that intensified the existence in the Black community of what he called a "two-line struggle" between Marxism-Leninism and Black Nationalism.

This same "two-line struggle," however, was taking place in Africa itself. This struggle was manifested among the revolutionary movements contesting for power against European colonialists such as the Portuguese in Angola. In 1974, there had been a coup d'etat in Portugal, precipitated mostly by the victories of the liberation movements in the Portuguese African territories, victories that convinced a group of young Portuguese military officers of the futility of continuing the struggle and eventually of the injustice of colonialism itself.

The new Portuguese government fashioned a temporary governing council of the opposing liberation movements in Angola—MPLA (Popular Movement for the Liberation of Angola), UNITA (National Union for the Total Independence of Angola) and FNLA (Front for the National Liberation of Angola). MPLA, which had captured the capital city of Luanda and held most of the country, was a Marxist-Leninist political party, while the other main force, UNITA, operating in the southern part of the country, was Marxist-Black Nationalist.[55]

Any inference of a color problem in Angola might appear an

anomaly were it not for the existence of a mestizo (mulatto) class of Africans poised between the African masses and the Portuguese colonialists, a class produced by the assimilationist policy of the Portuguese. This class, on the other hand, even at the time DuBois organized the 1923 Pan African Conference in Lisbon, formed the embryo of the national liberation leadership. Predictably, Black Nationalists in America identified in this period more with UNITA than with MPLA, while Black Marxists were more comfortable with MPLA. The political positions within the American Black community, on this basis, were irreconcilable, as confirmed by the fact that a national conference on U.S. policy in Angola, held at Howard University in June of 1975, split and ended in disarray.[56]

The continental African level of the two-line struggle occurred between *independent states* as close together as Senegal and Guinea, perhaps the leading protagonists representing respectively the ideologies of Négritude and scientific socialism. In an excellent article entitled "Négritude or Black Cultural Nationalism," Abiola Irele points out that the word Négritude was used for the first time in 1939 in an article by Aimé Césaire, but that the concept was inspired by the Harlem Renaissance writers such as Claude McKay, Langston Hughes and Sterling Brown and was shaped into a cultural philosophy in Paris by Aimé Césaire, Léon Damas (an Afro-West Indian) and, of course, Léopold Sédar Senghor.[57]

What came to be a cultural world view, that peoples of African descent shared a similar culture or "way of being" because of common experiences of African cultural origin and white domination, was immediately attacked by Marxists. Although this debate over Négritude reached its highest point perhaps at the 1959 Rome Conference of Negro Writers, it became identified in the French African context with the personality of Senghor. By 1971, at a colloquium on Négritude in Dakar, Senghor presented an expansive intellectual defense of Négritude which included the charge that the real ideological conflict was not that between Arabism and Négritude, but that between the both of these concepts and Marxism-Leninism currently powerful in both Europe and Asia. His example was that within the colloquium, Guinea and Congo-Brazzaville, both strongly supported by the Soviet Union, were the most vociferous critics of Négritude.[58] Senghor's attitude, then, is reflective of the prevailing atmosphere on the continent created by the tension between Négritude and Marxism-Leninism in the early 1970s.

Also in this period, when the first issue of the new journal, *The Black Scholar*, appeared, it contained an article by Sékou Touré charging that "Holy Négritude" was a product of the colonial Black bourgeoisie. Commenting upon the controversial distinction Senghor had previously made between the European penchant for reason and the African for emotion, he said: "The Master transforms his slave into a Negro whom he defines as a being without reason, subhuman and the embittered slave then protest: as you are Reason, I am Emotion and I take this upon myself. This is how we loop the loops." Touré charged that the concept of Négritude was convenient, inferring that because it appeared to confirm the intellectual superiority of Europeans it was thus widely disseminated by the press. At the same time, no doubt referring to the support for this concept among Black Americans, he said that it constituted a "mystifying anesthetic for Negroes who had been whipped too long and too severely, whipped to a point where they have lost all reason and become purely emotional."[59] Senghor counters, however, that those who claim that Négritude only describes the emotional quality of African peoples take him out of context, that his distinction is based on the difference between emotion as *intuitive reasoning* and the *discursive reasoning* of European culture. He locates the challenges of the Marxists to the concept of Négritude in their "contempt for their national culture."[60]

Such was the charged atmosphere when the Sixth Pan African Congress was held in Dar es Salaam in 1974. This congress was reportedly conceived in June 1969 at a Black Power meeting in Bermuda on the initiative of Roosevelt Browne, a former member of the Bermuda Parliament. He had received encouragement from Kwame Nkrumah, who had written him a letter from Guinea, read at the meeting, stating: "I agree with the idea for a Sixth Pan African Congress. Go ahead and begin your work, and I will do what I can from this end."[61] Three years later, after much traveling by a group which included Browne, Jimmy Garrett, Courtland Cox, C.L.R. James, Liz Gant, and Winston Wiltshire (the latter became, temporarily, the conference secretary general) and encouragement by the Tanzanian government which had wanted to host the meeting, a document entitled *The Call* was issued on February 5, 1972.[62]

This document touched on the historical origins of the Pan African Congress idea as a political strategy, suggesting that the "Sixth Pan African Congress must draw a line of steel against those, Africans included, who hide behind the slogan and paraphernalia of national independence while allowing finance capital to dominate and direct their economic and social life."[63] Touching on the additional themes of self-reliance, support for liberation struggles and the humanization of technology, it presented the idea of a Pan African center of science and technology as a concrete objective of the congress.

Despite *The Call,* however, the travels of the dedicated cadre of congress organizers had surfaced important questions about its goals that were to be a persistent problem in the formation of the various delegations in Europe, Africa, the Caribbean and Latin America, and most certainly in the United States. The presence of C.L.R. James did much to help this small group overcome problems of dealing with heads of state and to rally progressive peoples of African descent in the Diaspora to the idea. His elaboration on *The Call* in the form of an interview was widely published and helped to answer some of the questions, but others remained.[64]

Garrett, for example, says that a meeting at Kent State University in May 1973 saw the beginning of the North American delegation's formation and that questions surfaced in the following vein: "Many people thought that the organizers did not really have the backing of Tanzania. Some felt that SIX-PAC was outside a historical context—that it was either too early or (more likely) too late. This was also one of the first times in five years that a strong Marxist force was felt in nationalist circles."[65] Baraka reports that at this same meeting Owusu Sadaukai asked whether or not neocolonialism had any use for Pan Africanism and a Nigerian delegate quickly suggested that Africa didn't have much use for such "opinions and that we'd best keep them over here in the U.S."[66]

Apparently, Sadaukai was not satisfied with the responses to his queries at this meeting, so in a letter in October 1973 to Courtland Cox, former SNCC leader who had become secretary general of the Congress, questions were raised regarding

(1) heads of state who might exploit the Congress for domestic purposes, (2) financial problems limiting the scope of delegations from the Caribbean, (3) the overall political position of the Congress re "progressive" issues, (4) the structure of the congress and its continuing apparatus, and finally, (5) the composition of the North American delegation.[67] Cox, by letter two days later, made a clear and detailed eight-page, single-spaced, point-by-point response to the questions raised by Sadaukai.[68]

Again, by early 1974, requests were made by Sadaukai and Baraka for "clarification" of these same essential questions. Therefore, Professor James Turner, the then director of the Africana Studies Research Center at Cornell University, who had taken over some of the logistical leadership of organizing the North American delegation, in a meeting with Baraka and Sadaukai, composed the following set of questions:

> 1. Will opposition parties and organizations of independent Afrikan countries and Caribbean countries be allowed to participate in the Sixth Pan Afrikan Congress as Official Delegates?
> 2. Will Liberation Movements that are not recognized by the OAU be allowed to participate in the Congress as delegates: We feel that the exclusion of U.N.I.T.A. based on the fact that "U.N.I.T.A. is not recognized by O.A.U." represents a serious weakening of the Sixth Pan Afrikan Congress, especially in light of the position taken to invite all of the Afrikan governments no matter how reactionary and its energetic role in the National Liberation Struggle in Angola cannot be slighted.
> 3. Will presentations be allowed that are in opposition to official State Positions that are scheduled to be presented at the Congress?
> 4. Will there be any move to stifle constructive criticism of social conditions and policies that are not in the interest of the peasants and workers of the Afrikan continent and the Caribbean?
> 5. Will the struggle of black people in the U.S., The Caribbean and Canada be treated as serious questions by the Congress?[69]

Admittedly, this relatively detailed account of the steps leading up to the Sixth Pan African Congress was not crucial to the result, except for the fact that the attempt to organize was itself a lesson in discovering the existence of a political process within African-origin communities. For example, given considerable hindsight, the questions listed above, which were sent to President Nyerere, appear to exhibit serious naïveté, but were more realistically intended to elicit either honest answers or politically embarrassing admissions. No conference where the head of state is host, and where other heads of state are providing funding, will either deny the principle of representation by governments or relinquish the right to decide upon the character of the delegation representing the individual state. Then, the attempt to achieve a negotiated agreement on the access of "progressive" issues to the agenda of the Congress, while laudible, was somewhat successful not because of the questions posed in this fashion, but because of the stature of the individuals seeking access—the primacy of politics.[70]

Nevertheless, because of the work of an augmented leadership group in the North American zone, which included Dr. Fletcher Robinson, Dr. Sylvia Hill, Dr. James Turner, Owusu Sadaukai, Amiri Baraka, Oba T'Shaka and Lerone Bennett, the meeting was held in June 1974, in Dar es Salaam.[71] However, the two-line struggle kept the American delegation from becoming united and, thus, it became impossible for the delegation to communicate a unified set of objectives. The American group was similarly unable to command the attention of the Congress, though not because of the ideological struggle but rather because of the control of the parliamentary apparatus by state representatives and members of liberation movements accustomed to international parliamentary politics who had been installed in strategic positions in the Congress machinery. Still, the speeches of both Owusu Sadaukai and Amiri Baraka stirred the American delegation with their substance and "left" ideological stance. One seasoned observer was led to say, "The tension between the Marxists and the Nationalists is palpable. It is sad. It seems we are going to have a replay of that tired and destructive drama. Why do we have to do through this in every generation?"[72]

Likewise, the "two-line struggle" among the representatives of continental African states was firmly engaged when the message sent by President Sékou Touré of Guinea attacked Négritude as "a kind of racism" and as "fatal to Pan Africanism," arguing instead that Pan Africanism must have a revolutionary content based among the working classes of all progressive peoples.[73] On the other hand, the Senegalese noted the attack, but it was reported that "Senegal's undauntable Alioune Sene took in stride Ahmed Sékou Touré's attack on Négritude . . ."[74] This was all the more important inasmuch as the African state representatives controlled the Congress machinery and, therefore, the destiny of the various proposals and resolutions being adopted and implemented.

In the prevailing atmosphere, the proposal for a Center for Science and Technology was attacked on the grounds that it represented "bourgeois science" and was improperly understood by the collective delegation of representatives. In any case, this most promising of projects did elicit some useful resolutions concerned with (1) the mobilization of skilled scientific manpower, (2) the development of African natural resources for the benefit of the common heritage, and (3) the extention of health care benefits to the people and the rejection of ill-advised health practices.[75] In the end, the general declaration of the Sixth Pan African Congress, which in effect defined the utility of Pan Africanism, was written to reflect the position of the dominant "progressives" in the Congress, and a raceless "revolutionary Pan Africanism" came to be the narrowly defined view of the concept. Tracing the history of the Pan African movement, the declaration argued that the new stage of Pan Africanism "must essentially be a dynamic force for liberation of the colonized peoples as well as for the liberation of the oppressed peoples and classes, and liberation necessarily means eradicating the systems of exploitation and building societies based on the power of the exploited working masses."[76] And also, "Pan Africanism must consider the most radical methods of putting an end to foreign domination, and liquidate the foundations of imperialism, colonialism, neocolonialism, apartheid and zionism, by the common actions of the peoples of Africa, peoples of African descent and all people of the world."[77] This hard-line definition of Pan Africanism was to alienate both the Black Nationalists in the American delegation and the Négritudists and African Socialists among the African state delegations represented. With such an outcome, the overall aim of promoting Pan Africanism, ironically, was diminished. Secretary General Courtland Cox was, thus, reduced to a closing statement that

amounted to the observation that the opportunity for the delegates to meet and discuss diverse ideologies, proposals and
hopes for the future was in itself a positive outcome and that
perhaps the Sixth PAC may have initiated a new dialogue and
dynamic in the direction of some *future* unity.[78]

A second very important meeting in the 1970s was the Second
World Festival of Black and African Art and Culture (FESTAC),
which took place in Lagos, January 14 to February 12, 1977. This
meeting was, in a crucial way, a cultural manifestation of Pan
Africanism just as the Sixth PAC had been in a political sense.
Without describing FESTAC in detail here, in the political discussion and other aspects of the meeting there were a few items
which relate to our analysis.[79]

What we saw in the Sixth Pan African Congress was an attempt by the Diaspora movement to express itself more and
more *within* the context of African continental politics; there it
confronted the tensions already existing among various political
ideologies championed by one state or another. FESTAC was yet
another occasion where some of these dynamics were apparent,
and for this reason we present a brief analysis of major themes
of the meeting rather than a lengthy description. In doing so,
we will briefly discuss the problem of defining FESTAC, the basis of its delegate representation and the product.

One of the early problems was, what to call the meeting.
Would it be a festival of *African* art and culture? Did the sponsors
mean just *Black* African art and culture, or would non-Black African cultures be invited? At a prelude symposium held in
Dakar, under the sponsorship of the government of Senegal, it
became clear that the organizers saw the meeting as an exposition of "Negro" or Black African art and culture, involving delegations of peoples of African (Black) origin from all over the
world.[80] But both Guinea and the North African countries countered that it should be a continental African cultural festival; this
dilemma was put to the Nigerian government, the host of the
meeting. The dilemma was resolved by making the gathering
the Second World Festival of Black *and* African Art and Culture,
creating a compromise, though a somewhat illogical resolution
to the two-line struggle over the question of who constitutes an
African. Certainly, the Diaspora delegations were invited. The

total African-American delegation numbered nearly 500 people, much larger than the delegation that attended the Sixth PAC in 1974.

The number of African Americans may appear to be very large, but as it affected their involvement in the colloquium where political discussions were conducted, the participation was indeed very small. For, whereas most of the Sixth PAC delegation was involved in political discussions either on the floor or in the caucuses, fewer than fifty were involved in the entire FESTAC colloquium and fewer than ten were directly involved in the section dealing with politics and government.

A major problem arose, similar to that at the Sixth PAC, from the fact that there was a mixture of delegations of varying status. There were delegations from the continent, delegations from Black states in the Caribbean, and delegations representing Black communities in the Diaspora. What quickly became obvious through the debate in the colloquium was that state delegations were accorded a higher status than nonstate delegations and those from Africa were given a higher status than Diaspora delegations. This meant that, for example, originally no main speaker from outside Africa had been scheduled, that Diaspora delegates had difficulty getting simple things done in order to participate in the deliberations and that, at all times, Diaspora delegates had to fight mightily for recognition from the chair to speak!

A second problem was the substance of the arguments presented at the colloquium. The fact that various cabinet ministers and official delegates were representing states meant that the initial quality of the debate was polite and that it did not deal with controversial issues. When the American delegation, represented by Drs. Abdul Alkalimat, Ronald Walters, and Maulana Karenga, chair of the delegation, made its presentation, that opened up for the colloquium the subjects of imperialism, capitalism, and racism which had hitherto been neglected by other speakers. But the Americans also had to defend the Diaspora interpretation of Pan Africanism in two important ways.

First, they had to make the point that although they did not represent governments, they nevertheless should have an equal voice in African affairs where issues of global Pan Africanism were concerned. Second, they had to suggest that the definition of Pan Africanism did *not* mean what Garvey had intended, that Blacks either would or should return en masse to Africa, but that instead there was a mutual agenda of support to which communities in the Diaspora could contribute, linking them to the continent in various ways. This point was also argued forcefully by Karenga in his major presentation to the entire colloquium. However, in my opinion, Karenga had made the case more powerfully in an interview given to *Black Books Bulletin* in 1976. "Speaking practically, continental Pan-Africanism is the *principal task* of Africans on the continent and the Black solidarity expressed in the thrust of global Pan Africanism must ultimately and essentially be translated into the struggle we as Black people wage to free ourselves right here." Karenga went on to indicate the absurdity of abandoning the struggle for freedom within the United States, "a key country" whose corporations held a substantial portion of Africa's wealth. He pointed out that the complementary nature of African-American support for African progress lay in the extent to which African Americans were successful within their own state. With this standard in mind, he felt it unwise to propose to Africans an "abstract unity," the content of which only sustained "an overabundance of impractical and emotional ideas," and "grandiose proposals."[81]

This view of Pan Africanism projected at FESTAC gave the African delegations the sense that some progress had indeed been made in advancing the definition and practice of Pan Africanism. Still, it was necessary to organize a Diaspora caucus composed of Australia, Brazil[82], Britain, Canada, Trinidad and the United States in order to mount a collective push for these ideas. Further proof of the rationality of the above statement is that no concrete product emerged from this meeting either, even though a proposal for a Pan African university or institute, to be sponsored by the OAU, had been put forward as a vehicle for the shaping of Pan African values, education and projects.

The late 1970s was not a period of political activism, and as the dynamism of other movements in the Black community subsided, so too did the Pan African movement. Nevertheless, there has been a noticeable diffusion of pan African practices and thinking (see the Postscript) as a result of the movement, even though the term is not always formally attached to these social activities and, as a result, has lost much of its currency. The question of the African identity of Black Americans is much less an object of challenge—among Blacks; African culture is more widely accepted in the Black community in the form of dance troupes (African continental and American), art exhibits, and so on. Kwanza, developed by Maulana Karenga as an annual commemoration of positive values of a pan African origin practiced both as a supplement and an alternative to Christmas, has spread widely; travel to Africa is an accepted fact and has increased among Blacks; and, overall, there is less of the tension of the early 1960s between Africans and African Americans and more of a base of knowledge and understanding in the Black community in the 1990s than had previously existed.

At the same time, the responsibility for the diffusion of pan African knowledge and practice has rested on a few activists and institutions such as cultural organizations or African independent schools. With respect to the establishment of strong centers of African culture with a pan African perspective within American institutions, little progress has been made and, perhaps, little should be expected. As a result, many in the younger generation, especially those in integrated educational and social situations, have little awareness or appreciation for pan African culture or practice. Yet the interest is evident in the many young people wearing African cultural symbols to an extent much greater than in the previous decade.

The major feature of the persisting Pan African movement of the past is the annual observance of African Liberation Day. After the demise of the original African Liberation Support Committee, this event was briefly taken over by a coalition of assorted Marxist organizations in 1975 and 1976, and a separate group, the All African Peoples Revolutionary Party (AAPRP), headed by Kwame Touré, rose to compete with them. The movement had become so fractious that in May of 1975 and 1976, in the city of Washington, there were actually three different ALD marches going on at the same time![83] One of these was conducted, as stated, by AAPRP, claimants to the Pan Africanist mantle. Another was led by Abdul Alkalimat, who had attracted a series of organizations to the remnant of the African Liberation Support Committee under the Socialist Workers Party framework. The third faction was that led by Baraka, which proclaimed a revolutionary communist line, following "Marxist-Leninist-Mao-tse-Tung Thought." Eventually, AAPRP drew bigger crowds and the two other factions disappeared, leaving AAPRP the sole sponsor of African Liberation Day each year.

AAPRP was first mentioned in the *Handbook of Revolutionary Warfare* by Nkrumah as the instrument or party which should be formed to bring about the socialist revolution in Africa and complete the process of African liberation, a process which was eventually to provide the most conducive environment for Pan Africanism to flourish.[84] However, while Touré is the apparent leader (despite pretensions to be just another party worker), his role as an itinerant lecturer in the United States while living in Guinea has seriously hampered the ability of this party to become much of a force. In addition, AAPRP has based its activity on some college campuses on the assumption that "students are the spark of revolution." This is, however, a highly questionable assumption when economic conditions in America are creating real alienation among the masses of Blacks and college students are becoming more conservative as a result of the same forces. At the same time, Touré preaches a doctrine tantamount to a Garveyist variety of Pan Africanism which requires African Americans to consider Africa as their land-base and, thus, eventually to make transition to Africa their primary objective. The potential of AAPRP, therefore, is lost in an outmoded "land-base" strategy, as well as an incorrect view of the process of political organization. Its version of Pan Africanism has misdirected its activities away from the daily struggle of Black peoples and, thus, its overall effect has been minimal.

Conclusion

What appears, then, in the almost linear course of the development of Pan Africanism by African Americans in the last three decades is the feeling that, indeed, the high-point in the strategy flowing from the formal movement has been reached. There was an attempt to develop a style of

Pan African practice that was highly interactive with Africa and that consequently demanded a high degree of ideological and institutional congruence with continental African actors and organizations. Some conclusions about this style of Pan Africanism will be discussed below.

First, as we have seen, there are different cultural and material realities to be confronted in Africa and the Diaspora that shape differing aspects of the problem of *interactivity*.[85] For example, it should be remembered that the American Diaspora is capitalist, Western, rich, urban, and technological, while the typical African environment is capitalist (neocolonized), African, poor, rural, and possessing an agrarian technology for the most part. In addition, there is the difference between the nation state in the African context and the nonstate environment in the Diaspora context, in North America, the Caribbean and Latin America. Then there is the difference between the classic colonial and the internal colonial relationships to European civilization and its continuing power.

In their dialogues with the leaders of the American Pan African movement, Amilcar Cabral and others attempted to have their audiences understand the differences in the political, cultural and economic environments and the different requirements of Africans in the Diaspora as opposed to those on the continent. The Pan Africanist leadership in the United States, while attempting to identify with Black Africa as closely as possible ideologically, failed to temper the experiment with the requirements of *realistic practice*. In order for Blacks truly to adopt a revolutionary ideology of the African Liberation movement and participate directly—or interactively—with that phenomenon, they would have to have far more control over American national resources than exists at present. Indeed, the irony is that the Irish Republican Army has been successful in obtaining revolutionary resources from America because of the presence of an Irish middle class that provides financial support, access to political power, information and protection for the IRA's American activities.

In Africa, direct interactivity with the liberation struggle meant the possibility of becoming a revolutionary comrade; in America, one could also be a comrade, but only in the context of the possibilities of the American system. Indeed, one might have to support the liberation struggle through non-revolutionary or even sometimes reactionary-appearing methods, individuals or organizations in order finally to achieve the desired result. This is the meaning of Garrett's acquired understanding that during the organizing of the Sixth PAC Tanzanian leaders did not want to deal with representatives of the unknown Black American masses as delegates, but "*did* want to deal with the [Mayor Richard] Hatchers, [Congressman Charles] Diggs and [Amiri] Barakas"; it was the essence of the charge ostensibly made by African officials of the FESTAC that the American delegation was *not* "prestigeous" enough.[86]

The formulation above by Karenga, then, would appear to be the most logical, that the most realistic foundation for interactivity exists within each country in the Diaspora. In the past, it had proven unproductive for Diaspora Africans to attempt directly to interject their political notions about the legitimacy of the existing African regimes into continental questions because they were without the means or status to make the question of legitimacy a functional issue within the Pan African context. However, from their own bases in the Diaspora, such as America, it was possible to entertain political questions of the legitimacy of various regimes and their value to the Pan African process occurring locally and how that process might affect Pan African relations. On the other hand, I consider it to be a perversion of Pan Africanism to raise the question of African political legitimacy outside the context of the objectives of the African-American community and outside a Pan African context.

I, nevertheless, do make an argument not for the exclusion of ideology or the raising of political questions, but for Pan Africanists to recognize the limitations of interactivity and those factors which shape the most effective projects in their quest for interactivity. That is why Pan African projects, such as those conducted by the Southern African Support project (SASP) of Washington, have been relatively more successful in raising funds for humanitarian projects in Southern Africa and in involving the grassroots community in the process.[87]

The basic finding here was that the ultimate price of a style of interactivity which demands a high degree of ideological and institutional congruence between continental African and Diaspora African movements has the potential of constantly polarizing the Diaspora itself. In this respect, it should not go unnoticed that participation in African Liberation Day was most successful in 1972 when ALSC was a coalition organization, but as the requirements for ideological and institutional unity increased, the organization and the event fell into disarray.

Finally, we should recognize that many of the political questions raised by Sadaukai and Baraka concerning the participation of Africans from the Diaspora in Africa-based conferences—such as the kinds of access allowed, the kinds of delegations allowed, the specific discussion of Diaspora questions—all dramatized the important problem of the uneven status among peoples in the Pan African world created by the nation state and its activities. Just as Nkrumah found the creation of political independence via state formations an impediment to the idea of continental African unity, so the idea of a functional continental Pan Africanism was complicated. This has created the problem of uneven status among delegates at Pan African forums such as the Sixth PAC or FESTAC. Progress would appear to lie in the direction of discovering how the state system in Africa and the Caribbean could facilitate Pan Africanism in the Diaspora, or how the state system might be circumvented altogether.

3
Black American
Pan Africanism in
Africa: Going Home
to Ghana

As we explored the phenomenon of Pan Africanism in the United States in the previous chapter, the conclusion became obvious that African-American activists attempted to achieve as much of a symbiotic relationship with Africans on the continent as possible. One of the relatively unexamined dimensions of this attempted symbiosis, however, was the extent to which African Americans actually went to reside on the continent and to join in the daily living of African culture, especially in periods of high Pan Africanist movement. As a result of this activity, African-American communities developed within several African states, and I will undertake a brief survey of the African-American community in Ghana because it provides an important contrasting view of the dynamics of the concept.

Thus, an interesting twist in the methodology takes place wherein the Pan African method will be employed; in the first instance, as expatriates African Americans seek to establish community among themselves and, since they live within a host African state, will attempt to establish relationships with the surrounding community. Therefore, the emphasis of our methodology must change, for while in the white-host context African-origin peoples sought to establish normal community relationships both internally and externally, in this context, we might expect that the motivations for entering Ghana might control African-American expectations of cultural, political and social synthesis. The effect is to diminish the force of the "challenge to subjugation" types of relationships between the African-American community and the host. In this study, our concentration will center on the essence of the community the African Americans established in Ghana and the movements made possible by their attempt to become a part of the "African symbiosis." Thus, I will seek to understand not only the motivating factors which initiated the community, but the nature of the community leadership, its goals and its relationship to the host community and to other continental Africans.

There is nothing unique about the existence of an expatriate community within a host country, even where the immigrants claim the same history and cultural origins but have grown to be different from the host because of their modern culture. Examples of this are the white Americans resident in England, the French Canadians in France, the recent Soviet Jewish immigrants to Israel and so on. It is, thus, a fascinating subject to seek to understand the degree of the "symbiosis" (or the extent to which the immigrants can become reintegrated into the culture and politics of the host country and participate successfully in its ritual.)

Discussing the "dialectic" between the African Diaspora and the homeland, Professor Elliot Skinner explains that one of the characteristic behaviors of exiles toward their ancestral homelands is that, for any number of reasons, they often want to return. These motivations, often formed in the Diaspora, shape expectations and behavior as the individual re-enters the host country and, thus, gives some indication of what to review in the "expectation-reception" interaction between African Americans and the host African community.[1]

In Skinner's excellent discussion of the factors which have historically motivated peoples to create a diaspora, he writes that "an important aspect of the dialectic between peoples in diasporas and their homelands is the difficulty arising whenever a sizeable group of the exiles returned home."[2] He notes that "the continental Africans have not always been happy with the returnees from the diaspora."[3] On the other hand, the returnees have not always been satisfied with their reception either, for a number of reasons. I intend, therefore, to utilize Skinner's explicit thesis regarding the dialectic, not only with respect to the reasons why exiles want to return to the homeland, but also in terms of the fact that there will inevitably be levels of conflict in the process of reintegration. The resolution of that conflict, I hypothesize, must take place within the framework of the overarching goals and activities of the host community.

The Regeneration of Africa

With respect to the return to Africa, the motivating factor might comprise the well-known "push-pull" model. On the one hand, the "push" factor might be explained by Edward Wilmot Blyden: "America, to which our fathers were carried by violence, where we lived and still live by sufferance as unwelcomed strangers, is not the rock whence we were hewn. Our residence there was and is transitional, like that of the Hebrews in Egypt, or Babylon, looking to an exodus."[4] Blyden was one of the strongest of the early Black Nationalist emigrationists who believed that the rightful place of the Black man was in Africa. How difficult it might have been for his spiritual brothers such as Rev. Henry Highland Garnett to have made this claim if it had not been for the fact of their oppressive subjugation by whites. In any case, this factor enabled Garnett to take a position typical of this group: "It is time for the colored people to look at things for themselves through their own spectacles. While we hate Slavery with intense abhorrence, and intend to fight it to the last, no man should deprive me of my love for Africa, the land of my ancestors."[5]

The existence of slavery as a hated institution that degraded Black humanity and the wish to escape it was, then, the most immediate cause of immigration to Africa. At the turn of the century, however, the new movement was based on the racial prejudice, violence and various forms of institutional subordination that Blacks suffered. In response, many returned to Africa. Among these, the first African-American returnees to Ghana were the few whom Alfred Charles Sam, who claimed to be an Ashanti Chief, was able to transport from camps in Weleetka, Oklahoma to a town in the interior of Ghana, Akim Swerdru, in 1914. Chief Sam, who was actually raised in a nearby small town, Kibi, was unsuccessful in establishing this settlement and, although a few of those who accompanied him managed return passage, most remained scattered in the Gold Coast territory, assimilating into the culture.[6]

The new "back-to-Africa" movement, however, would be fueled by different dynamics. The new movement represented the triumph of the first stage of the Pan African movement, the liberation of the African continent from colonialism. Thus, Pan Africanism was a tool to accomplish this; all those who would be supporters of this movement worked for this objective. And, as the objective came to be directed toward the continent, the concept of Pan Africanism became continental.

St. Clair Drake, who served as chair of the department of sociology at the University of Ghana (1959–1961), argued that the concept of *racial Pan Africanism—the liberation of Africans everywhere from oppression and colonialism—emerged at the height of the colonial period and was the basis of a "back-to-Africa" movement for Diaspora Africans at the turn of the century. Once the African independence movement had begun to produce independent states such as Ghana, the definition of Pan Africanism changed to one focused on the liberation of the African continent. He says,* "The implication was that at best now, New World Negroes were auxiliary forces in the struggle to 'liberate Africa.' *Continental* Pan Africanism not *racial* Pan Africanism was emerging as a significant force, and was the major interest of African leaders."[7] The last point in the above statement, however, is very important, for Professor Drake reflects the fact that the trend in the Diaspora toward the African continent was growing. "At the same time, however, the interest of Negro Americans in the new Africa was increasing."[8] This new Africa was significant to all African-origin peoples in the Diaspora because it called for a regeneration of the African personality.

In a statement that helps to give some perspective on the concept of continental Pan Africanism, Nkrumah also felt that: ". . . at last Pan-Africanism had moved to the African Continent where it really belonged. It was an historic occasion. Free Africans were actually meeting together, *in Africa,* to examine and consider African affairs."[9] The fact that the African independence movement had come home, however, was probably a powerful catalyst to Diaspora Africans to examine critically the cultural context within which they lived. Essentially, the contradiction was now clearly posed between that living environment that might offer the African in the world a possibility of full personhood and that environment that would continue to pose severe barriers to this achievement so long as the African remained outside Africa.

Fighting Racism

In the United States, in the period between 1957 and 1960, the historical process of acquiring a more Afrocentric political consciousness was developing as a product of both the evolution of a more militant phase of the freedom movement and the independence movement in Africa. As a result of the promise of equal educational opportunity contained in the 1954 Supreme Court Brown vs. Board of Education decision, there were attempts to achieve integrated schooling, and the rabid white resistance touched off the dramatic spectacle of the marching feet of Blacks in Montgomery, Alabama who defeated segregation under the leadership of Martin Luther King, Jr. Then there was the picture of courageous children marching against racist whites in Little Rock to enter Central High School; there was the murder of Emmett Till in the South for "ogling a white woman"; there was the breaking out of the armed self-defense movement in Monroe, North Carolina, and there was the growing prominence of the Black Muslims whose message of Black pride and white evil had begun to permeate the northern urban ghettoes.

All of this stirred a restless generation of Black youth and, as

Louis Lomax was to put it, a feeling that something had to be done. Their answer was the sit-in movement which broke out in the Midwest and then in the deep South. Black students wanted all Black people to be free; the chant "Freedom Now!" arose as a slogan. But to obtain this freedom, they also knew that there had to be a massive changing of attitudes, as was indicated in their song, "That old Negro, he ain't what he used to be." [10]

In the "massive resistance" of whites to the new demands of Blacks for freedom, racism appeared more boldly, more nakedly than ever before. And while a few Blacks had begun to react out of the optimism that through struggle equality might be won, others—perhaps possessed of a more keen political consciousness—concluded that it was time to leave the country, that America would not change. Many of these individuals left America for Europe because of the preception—and the fact—that social life there was much less overtly racist than in America. This expatriate tradition had been established especially by post–World War II Black artists, writers, visual artists, performers, jazz musicians. One such writer was Hoyt Fuller.

> I had left the United States in 1957 because quite literally, I no longer could live there. That was the year of Little Rock, the hope-shattering spectacle of a powerful nation writhing willingly, like a sick and pathetic cur, in the throes of a self-induced malignancy. But more than that: daily, across the nation, racists of every conceivable description were demonstrating their utter contempt for Black citizens and for the laws ostensibly designed to protect them. "Law and Order" was a charade. The incessant assault upon Black humanity was terrible to bear. [11]

While Fuller ultimately ended up in Guinea, his statement quoted above went on to say that the independence of Ghana both excited him and fulfilled him with the long desire for "rootedness" as an antidote to the racism he had experienced in America. [12]

The civil rights movement, however, was just beginning and, simultaneously, this movement was connected to Africa by the momentous independence of Ghana, celebrated by many African Americans, the French struggle against Algerian freedom-

fighters, and the combined Belgian/U.S./United Nations movement against Patrice Lumumba's Congo. Louis Lomax said:
"Then there is the matter of Africa: hardly a week passes that
the awakening giant's cries for 'Freedom' don't ring out over the
radio and television into the ears of American Negroes—
ashamed, as they most certainly are, that they are still oppressed."[13] In fact, on February 15, 1961, there was a riotous out-
burst (described by Richard B. Moore as "white hot indigna-
tion") by Blacks in the visitors gallery of the United Nations
General Assembly, denouncing the failure of the UN to move
with dispatch to deal with the murder of Lumumba and the intervention in the Congo.[14]

Ghana: Continental Pan Africanism

In other works on Pan Africanism, it has been
well explicated that the 1945 Pan African Conference in Manchester, England differed from previous such conferences held
between 1900 and 1927 in that it brought to the fore a serious
generation of African nationalist leaders, among them F. Kwame
Nkrumah, Peter Abrahams, Jomo Kenyatta, George Padmore
and C. L. R. James.[15] Many of these individuals who made African independence the theme of the post–World War II conference were later able to play a role in having the philosophy of
Pan Africanism transferred to the African continent by initiating
positive-action nationalist movements.

After the independence of Ghana in 1957, Nkrumah called for
George Padmore to come and help shape continental Pan Africanism, setting up a special bureau, the African Affairs Center,
for this purpose.[16] Nkrumah believed that the independence of
Ghana was meaningless unless it was related to the liberation of
the entire African continent.

The first such project was the sponsorship of the Conference
of Independent African States which met in Accra in April 1958.
At that time, there were eight independent states on the conti-

nent: Egypt, Ghana, Sudan, Libya, Tunisia, Morocco, Liberia, and Ethiopia. The purpose of this conference was to devise additional strategies for the liberation of the remaining areas of the continent, and harmonize the policies of the independent states in other areas.

Nkrumah had made a signal theoretical statement crucial to the vitality of the Pan African doctrine—that Africa as the center of the African world and the root of the Diaspora should be the focal point of Pan African unity. It remained only for the form of that unity to be debated.

Understanding that the nationalist movement included more than simply the independent states, and wanting to provide a Pan African frame of reference for the political movements stirring in the colonized territories, Nkrumah sponsored the first All African Peoples Conference. And whereas the eight independent African states were represented in the CIAS conference earlier in the year, representatives of 62 African political organizations came to Accra for this meeting held in December of 1958.[17]

These meetings set the tone for a series of others. For example, the All African Trade Union Federation met in November of 1958, the Conference on Positive Action and Security in Africa met in April of 1960, and the Conference of Independent States met again in June of that year, with the Conference of All African Peoples meeting again in early 1961.[18]

Far less written about is the second model of continental Pan Africanism pioneered by Nkrumah, the Conference of All African Peoples. While the first idea as the basis of Pan Africanism takes into consideration the nature of state-to-state relationships, the latter considers those who exist outside of the boundaries of states. And while Nkrumah saw this initially as a device for organizing solidarity among representatives of political parties existing in territories that were not yet independent, the concept has a much wider potential. In fact, it was assumed that once all the territories on the continent were independent, there would be no need to have a forum for "All African Peoples." Nkrumah envisioned that over time, these meetings of all African peoples in political, economic, social spheres would grow and become more effective to the point that "when full political unity has been achieved . . . we will be able to declare the triumphant end of the Pan African struggle and the African liberation movement." [19]

In other words, to the extent that Kwame Nkrumah's vision of the functional utility of continental Pan Africanism was the prosecution and completion of the liberation struggle, it was limited in scope at this point. What helped to widen the conception, ironically, was the interest in the process of African independence stimulated by the independence of Ghana and by Nkrumah's activities as well. This would have an impact on Africans of every description on the continent, but most important, it initiated an African revitalization movement in the Diaspora.

Return to Ghana: The Call

The second manifestation of the political significance of Ghanian independence was that, simultaneously, African Americans were being attracted to come to Ghana out of many motives. Perhaps the most important reason besides the sheer drama of independence was the perception by many that Nkrumah was a kindred soul, having been in the United States, studied the works of DuBois, Garvey and other Black intellectuals, studied the condition of the Black community itself, and shared the pain of American racism.[20] African Americans were, therefore, doubly receptive to Nkrumah's own call for them to come "home" to help in the development of Ghana. His call actually began with an invitation to Black leaders to come to Ghana for the independence celebration. The delegation included Rev. Martin Luther King, Jr., Congressman Adam Clayton Powell, Dr. Ralph Bunche, A. Philip Randolph, Norman Manley from Jamaica, and Mrs. Louis Armstrong.[21] Others had been invited, among them Dr. DuBois, but his passport had been confiscated by the anti-communist State Department of John Foster Dulles. Although Roy Wilkins, head of the NAACP, had been invited, neither he nor any other member of the civil rights establishment attended. This was somewhat rectified by

1960 when Thurgood Marshall and other Afro-Americans, such as Professor Leo Hansberry of Howard University, attended the ceremonies on the occasion of Ghana becoming a Republic.[22]

Nkrumah's first visit to the United States as a new head of state occurred in late July of 1958. A typical newspaper headline describing his wildly enthusiastic reception by Black Americans said, "Harlem Hails Ghanaian Leader as Returning Hero." On July 27, his twenty-five-car motorcade was met by ten thousand cheering people on Seventh Avenue in Harlem and as the parade reached the Armory at 143rd St. and Fifth Avenue there were a reported 7,500 "cheering persons packed inside."[23] Once inside, Nkrumah emphasized that Africans and African Americans were held together by "bonds of blood and kinship" and appealed to "doctors and lawyers and engineers to come and help us build our country."[24]

The next day, Nkrumah met with a hundred of his fellow alumni of Lincoln University and talked with them about the importance of economic development. The Lincoln connection had been fruitful because Dr. Robert Lee and his wife, both dentists, had gone to Ghana to live and work; another alumnus, Robert Freeman, who had been president of the United Mutual Insurance Company in New York City, went to Ghana in 1955; another alumnus had set up the successful Ghana Insurance Company.[25] Speaking at a luncheon that evening, Nkrumah acknowledged the ties between Ghana and African Americans and confirmed his invitation, saying: "Back at home, we think of them still as brothers and we can assure them of a warm welcome whenever they choose to visit the land of their forefathers."[26]

The following evening Nkrumah was hosted at a dinner reception organized and presided over by several Black leaders, including Dr. Bunche, United Nations under secretary, and Nobel Prize winner; the NAACP's Roy Wilkins, and Lester Granger, executive secretary of the National Urban League. Wilkins made remarks which could be characterized as less strongly Pan African than those of Nkrumah. He affirmed both the African and American heritage of Blacks in the United States, saying that if Blacks renounced Africa, they would also be renouncing Concord, Valley Forge, Gettysburg, and Iwo Jima. But he did say that as other "loyal Americans looked upon their homeland with affection and pride . . . so we look upon Ghana and the emerging nations of Africa. Your struggles and your successes have aided us in our trials and tribulations here . . ."[27] Granger's comments were similar. "Between Little Rock, Arkansas and Accra, Ghana," he said, "8,000 miles of land and water stretch. But there is no more than the whisper of a bird's breath between the hopes and aspirations of the Black citizens of Arkansas in the Deep South and the triumph and expectations of the Black men and women of Ghana who walk the streets of Accra proud and tall in their status as free citizens of no mean state."[28] So there was on this occasion a polite but unmistakable validation of the ties that held Ghana and the African-American community in the United States together. At the same time, he struck a note of political support in suggesting that, while America had made some progress in dealing with the evils of racial segregation, "no stable world order could be built upon a foundation of political subjection, racial inequality, economic exploitation and wide-spread misery."[29]

Kwame Nkrumah then left New York City for a three-day visit to Chicago, where he was hosted by Mayor Richard Daley. The scenes repeated themselves as thousands of Blacks on the South Side lined his motorcade route, cheering and waving Ghanaian flags as an expression of their own Pan African commitment.[30] This was evidence that the independence of Ghana was an event of national significance that provided an opportunity for an outpouring of the Pan Africanism latent in the community.

Thus, the combination of the enthusiasm of African Americans over the independence of Ghana and their symbolic presence at the independence celebration, together with Nkrumah's direct appeal for them to come to Ghana and share the fruit of its independence, acted as magnets for African-American immigration to the country. All of this was underscored, however, by Nkrumah's personal philosophy of Pan Africanism. Nkrumah's vision that the independence of Ghana would be meaningless unless all of Africa was liberated was stated in his independence celebration speech, and in the view of many African-origin peoples everywhere, it was the correct vision for the unity of the continent and, eventually, the unity of all African peoples. In addition, the final declaration of the 1958 Conference of Independent African States and the Conference of All African Peoples, both held in Accra, contained sections devoted to the eradication of racism and racial prejudice, even though the strongest example cited was that of South Africa.[31] At the latter meeting, Nkrumah remarked that he was happy to see so many delegates from the African-American community present. In addition, the Ghanaian constitution adopted in 1960 contained a provision prohibiting racial, religious or sexual discrimination. Thus, beyond theoretical Pan Africanism, the antiracist nature of the Ghana regime, firmly established, would be of special interest to African Americans.

This strong antiracist posture would, of course, continue throughout the life of Nkrumah's regime not only because of altruism toward other Africans in the Diaspora, but also because of the association in Ghanaian minds between imperialism and racism as a "basic factor of instability in Africa." [32] This dynamic was a part of the analysis of Pan Africanists as a part of the process of colonialism and neocolonialism. In fact, Nkrumah's speech on the theme of unity to his parliament on the occasion of the creation of the Organization of African Unity expressed the following thought that it was within this context that one had to consider the problem of racism within the United States, saying further that after having been dragged into the country, the Afro-American had experienced the contradiction between living in an advanced technological country which touted the dignity of the individual, and suffering group racism. Despite this, he felt, the Afro-American had excelled in many fields of human endeavor, and as a consequence America had a moral duty to accept the essential humanity of Afro-Americans.[33]

Nkrumah's antiracist ideology, thus, was functional and consistent in providing a temporary basis of legitimacy—as it happened—for the African Americans living in Ghana and for those who passed through.

The Afro-American Response: Community

In the second manifestation of the political significance of the African independence movement, many Africans in the Diaspora began to drift "homeward." This group included African Americans who were attracted to Ghana out of many motives, but the most important stimulus was the fact that, because of Kwame Nkrumah's leadership, Ghana had become the hub of Pan African activity, and as such the country was a symbol of the aspirations of many peoples of African descent for the future viability of the continent. The country was regarded by many African peoples at that time as "the center of the Black World," being a sanctuary for African revolutionaries and the center of Pan African thought and practice. African Americans were also attracted because of the specificity of Nkrumah's vision—he had lived in the United States and he understood the role of Black Americans in the African freedom struggle. Many Black Americans who had already been alienated from America began to drift in from other corners of the world, especially from Europe.

No one knows for sure just how many African Americans went to Ghana during the early 1960s, for many reached there by both legal and illegal means. But of the thousands who came through, it is known that a relatively stable community of a few hundred expatriates from America settled there, together with a somewhat smaller number from the West Indies. The "stable" group was augmented occasionally by a considerable number of short-term transients, essentially visitors, tourists and businessmen. Here, I make a deliberate distinction between visitors and tourists, between those who may have come for any one of a number of politically serious reasons and those who were coming to an exotic place—much like their white counterparts—on holiday.

At the top of the expatriate structure there was a group of Black Americans who were very close to President Nkrumah, among them W. E. B. DuBois and Dr. Alphaeus Hunton and their wives, Shirley Graham DuBois and Dorothy Hunton. They had been invited by Nkrumah to produce the first *Encyclopedia Africana*, a project first envisioned by DuBois that would contain the history and the demography of all the African peoples of the continent. Nkrumah placed the project under the Ghana Academy of Sciences, headed by Dr. Ernest A. Boateng. The encyclopedia has since come to fruition, but its pages have scarcely honored this initial contribution.[34] Nkrumah revered DuBois, considering him the father of the Pan African movement and, as a result, DuBois was respected and cared for by the Ghanaians who called him "Father." The expatriates also included Drs. Robert and Sarah Lee, black dentists from Virginia who had known Nkrumah as students at Lincoln and who had come to Ghana to become citizens.

Other individuals came, like Maya Angelou Make, who had had a successful acting career and had spent two years in Cairo as a journalist; she hoped to place her son in the University of Ghana and move on to a job in Liberia.[35] She worked at the Institute of African Studies at the University of Ghana for Professor J. H. Nketia. Others were Alice Windom, from St. Louis, who had received a M.A. degree from the University of Chicago; Sylvia Boone, with a Masters degree in Sociology; artists Tom Feelings, Ted Pointiflet and Herman Kofi Bailey; Lesley Lacy, a former graduate student; Jim and Annette Lacy (no relation to Lesley), elementary school teachers; Frank Robinson and Carlos Allston, who had a plumbing company; Vicki Garvin, a former union organizer who had spent some time in Europe; and Pauli Murray, a law professor at the University of Ghana. Indeed, Lacy describes an amazing variety of individuals of assorted professional persuasions—artists, writers, architects, professors, actors, industrialists, small businessmen, physicians and so on who comprised this community of expatriates. Some stayed from 1958 until the overthrow of Nkrumah, others were members of this community for shorter periods.[36]

Then there were individuals who simply materialized without passports of any description; one such person, whose name was Otis, was nicknamed "dirty" by the American group. But there was also Dr. Preston King, whom the Georgia Draft Board had tried to induct into military service[37] and who joined the staff at the University of Ghana.

The acknowledged leader of this group (characterized by Lacy as "politicals," "non-politicians" and "opportunists"), however, was Julian Mayfield, an author and playwright. Mayfield had become involved in the armed self-defense movement in Monroe, N.C. with the militant Robert Williams in the late 1950s, and after a shootout with the authorities, both fled the country. He ended up in Ghana as a journalist and as assistant to Yaw Eduful, Nkrumah's press secretary. Mayfield's proximity to President Nkrumah and the fact that he was often called upon to solve problems within the African-American community lent credibility to his role as leader. However, Mayfield himself says that he had far less influence with Nkrumah than outsiders perceived.[38] Meetings of the community leaders were often held at Mayfield's house and, thus, a sense of social organization evolved. This, as well as a perception among Ghanaians, defined the group as a distinct community, and even though some of the more sophisticated Ghanaians were aware of the political differences existing among the expatriates, they still considered them to be a functional cultural entity within the Ghanaian context.[39]

Pan African Expectations

As is possible to see from the brief listing above, the motivations of those who came to Ghana are connected to their expectations of what they might experience there. Generally speaking, the phenomenon of "the return" was a search for original identity, a search for an authentic expression of the "African roots" from which Africans in America were taken. The specifics, however, varied according to the individuals and, so the motivations varied, some coming to Africa for the same reasons as Europeans, as Mayfield said, "to sack it!"

It was observed repeatedly that some travelers arrived in Ghana, getting off the plane and kissing the ground, expecting to be swept up into the arms of the first African they met and welcomed home after such a long sojourn in America. Angelou put it best: "Since we were descendants of African slavery torn from the land, we reasoned we wouldn't have to earn the right to return, yet we wouldn't be so arrogant as to take anything for granted. We would work and produce, then snuggle down into Africa as a baby nuzzles in a mother's arms."[40] She writes that the justification for this attitude was that "our people had always longed for home. For centuries we had sung about a place not built with hands, where the streets were paved with gold, and were washed with honey and milk."[41] The last reference was to the biblical expression for home, which signaled the symbolic desire of the African to be released from slavery. However, more explicit statements and activities of African emigrationists left little doubt that the object of their return to Africa was to go back to their home, since they did not consider themselves American either by law or custom. In the 1960s returnees were, however, fraught with ambiguities; because of their longer socialization to Euro-American culture, there was among them at least the development of a dual sense of commitment, which fostered the well-known concept described by DuBois as a "dual consciousness."

The racial edges of the Ghanaian were not as sharp as those of the Americans. A Jamaican settled in Ghana observed: "When an Afro-American is talking about colour and race he is using terms that are totally alien to Africa."[42] I might have suggested that this is true in many parts of Africa, but Francophone African intellectuals have traditionally been keen to point out the racial distinctions that exist between Africans and Europeans and even between sub-Saharan Africans and North Africans. As we have seen above, a major debate continues today over the juxtaposition of the philosophies of Négritude and socialism in the struggle for genuine African independence and development. Otherwise, the racial explanation for various societal problems generally has relatively less saliency in racially homogeneous societies, whether in Africa or the Caribbean.

Ghana represented the first tentative opportunity for many African Americans to experience Africa. Given this fact, they were seeking not only the affirmation of their own individual identity, but the experience of living in a valid cultural environment. In a sense, the Black presence in America has been unnatural, the unnaturalness of a people made a "minority" who came from a land where they had been in the majority. To live again in a place where majoritarian culture was Black meant getting used to seeing Black people in every conceivable role, in contrast to their prior experience with the limitations placed upon the horizons of Black people by the strictures of racism. Thus, it was in Ghana that many for the first time saw what William Gardner Smith called "the visible signs of Black sovereignty"—a Black president, Black members of parliament, Black High Court judges, pilots, bank managers, media producers and directors, and others in natural positions of power dictated by their people's independent status and majority position.[43]

These aspects of Ghanaian society—natural-given Ghanaian sovereignty and majority status—were unnatural to American Blacks raised in a social minority situation. Thus, the question of race came to have a different meaning for Ghanaians than for African Americans. Oppressed because of racism, African Americans had developed over time a "minority conscious- ness," which elevated race issues and racial solidarity.[44] Thus, they attempted to connect to Ghanaians initially on the basis of racial solidarity, of a physical Pan Africanism, of a shared knowl- edge of mutual pain and suffering from the process of imperial- ism. They often expected that Ghanaians would identify with them on the obvious basis of their shared African heritage. One visitor to Ghana said, "I would talk about Malcolm, about race, about Black brotherhood and black beauty, about the goddamn white man, and people would just sort of stare at me blankly like they didn't understand what I was saying. I couldn't make it, baby. I couldn't make the contact. I couldn't get across."[45] The Ghanaian psycho-social framework did not utilize generalized race identity as a basis for relationships, but rather utilized cul- turally specific references. The question was: "Are you Ga, or Ewe, or Ashanti, or Fanti?" To challenge them with any other basis for the establishment of immediate relationships was to violate a learning-curve that traversed centuries. What often acted as a rough substitute was the vague knowledge that here was someone who had come from America and whose people might have been taken away long ago—the Omawale syndrome or the "child returned home." Thus, African Americans often attempted to "relate" to Ghanaians on the basis of a generalized "African brotherhood" concept, because specific knowledge of the situation of African Americans in the United States was the province of only a handful of African intellectuals. For most Af- rican Americans, the search for social acceptance on the basis of cultural specificity was impossible. Their basis of cultural speci- ficity comprised their own community and extended family ties, their regional origin in the United States, their state of residence, or their biological history, little that was functional within the cultural context of Ghana.

In 1959, for example, an African-American jazz clarinetist,

Edmund Hall, decided to live and play his music in Ghana. At first, he later said, there were many questions about the technique and style of the music, but it soon became clear that Ghanaian musicians wanted only to play their highlife music; most eventually drifted away from his classes. Unable to make the adjustment his expatriate forefathers had made in 1914, Hall decided to return to America.[46]

Maya Angelou has discussed the ever-abiding consciousness of the differences in culture and the unavoidable comparisons made between each aspect of Black American and Ghanaian behavior and physical appearance. The frustration among Black Americans was often the strongest when the rejection came from Ghanaians, because it meant that one had at all times to affirm that which they had attempted to reject—their Americanness. Lesley Alexander Lacy says he arrived in Dakar shouting that as a brother he was glad to be home in Africa and that despite tales that Black Americans weren't wanted, he was happy to bring greetings from all of our people. The reply was not to welcome him as a brother, but to ask if he had any American dollars. Suddenly, he says, "It was as clear as the hot sky above."[47]

Maya Angelou also relates that the closest she ever came to feel that she was at home—finally—was when she was mistaken for a member of the Bambara tribe of Liberia. She went along with the pretense because "I didn't want to remember that I was an American. For the first time since my arrival, I was very nearly home. Not a Ghanaian but at least an African. The sensation was worth the lie."[48] Nonetheless, this sensation, however precious in the annals of Black identity it has surely been, was based ultimately upon a falsehood which she, much earlier in her narrative, readily admits.

I doubted if I, or any Black from the diaspora, could return to Africa. We wore skeletons of old despair like necklaces, heralding our arrival, and we were branded with cynicism. In America we danced, laughed, procreated; we became lawyers, judges, legislators, teachers, doctors, and preachers, but as always, under our glorious costumes we carried the badge of a barbarous history sewn to our dark skins.[49]

This character portrait drawn by Maya Angelou is accurate to the point that it begins to define the consciousness of African Americans. Despite the cultural difference with Ghanaians, this consciousness was not as bad as the sentiment of racism and so, those in the Afro-American community in Ghana felt that at least they might make a contribution in Ghana whereas in America making a contribution had been extremely difficult.

Another problem with race and color in the African context generally is that the "outsider" of the same color but not of the same culture poses a threat of subversion, both cultural and political. Important work has been done on the "stranger" that has anthropological significance and is also useful in explaining the suspicious reaction of Ghanaians and other Africans to African Americans. To begin with, many Ghanaians were hostile to the presence of Afro-Americans for many reasons, including the fact that the latter were considered aggressive, more Western, race-obsessed, different. That some Africans could come to the conclusion that there was a connection between African Americans and the U.S. intelligence service was natural, especially since it has also often been painfully accurate. William Sutherland, long-time adviser to African governments, affirmed the existence of a "feeling in parts of Africa that America is going to use its Afro-Americans as a possible 'fifth column'."[50]

For many Africans, the first Americans with whom they came into contact were associated with the American government through the many branches of its Foreign Service. In fact, Professor St. Claire Drake describes the presence of a considerable number of African Americans in Ghana connected with the U.S. government in various capacities, such as embassy officers David Bolen and Alan Dean, cultural affairs officer Lindsey White, and other assorted technicians and Peace Corps workers.[51] While the motives of many of these individuals connected with the American government may have been positive in some way, their fundamental role as information gathers and reporters for the U.S. foreign policy decision-making establishment obviated the possibility of any genuine trust between them and Africans. Africans, then, often have difficulty distinguishing "the good guys from the bad guys" in the general Afro-American community.

Ironically, in the African context some African Americans become super American patriots. Those in the American foreign service, for example, often were suspected as being subversive by their white superiors and so had to prove their loyalty to the government agency which sent them there. On the other hand, there were the culturally rejected who were unable to assimilate into Ghanaian society. Pauli Murray, a law professor at the University of Ghana, said that even though her experience in Ghana had clarified whatever negative elements remained in her African identity, "it also strengthened my conviction that I was of the New World, irrevocably bound to the destiny of my native America."[52] Both groups, vulnerable to the charge of spying, lend credence to a generalized charge to all African-American expatriates.

In this context, the news—not long after the Ghana coup in 1966—that the American Society for African Culture was discovered to have been infiltrated by the CIA was disastrous. This charge had also been made about the organization which was to be its successor, the American Negro Leadership Conference in Africa, a project of the "big six" civil rights organizations. An organization of both Ghanaians—or "Ghana patriots," as they would refer to themselves—and African-American nationalists in the United States voiced their opposition to the Leadership Conference in a publication launched in Ghana on the grounds that it represented "American colonialism, imperialism, and exploitation" and that it sought to "disorganize African labor" and consisted of "quislings" seeking diplomatic appointments.[53]

Leslie Lacy described another such case involving his friend, Dr. Wendell Jean Piere, a professor at the University of Legon in Ghana, who was deported by the government for spying.[54] In any case, while African Americans are busy fending off charges of being spies, the far more serious problem in most African countries is the extent to which *indigenous citizens* have been attracted by the U.S. and other intelligence services. In most countries, however, little subterfuge is necessary to penetrate the core of African state operations, since the combination of Africans who had been trained by European police and military agencies, lingering cultural deference to whites and functional technological dependence upon whites means that access to most information is easily obtained.

In many African countries, the problem of which African American is working for U.S. intelligence, however, has been taken too far and suspicions have been indiscriminately cast upon the entire group of expatriates. This has happened, no doubt, to the delight of the managers of the intelligence machine whose objective is precisely to sow such confusion, doubt and suspicion among Africans and African Americans so that no meaningful Pan Africanism is possible.

Roles: Nation Building

However, one must add to the "barbarous history" the ecological factor that Black Americans are the most urban African population in the world and that their ability to cope using modern technology is buttressed by their employment in the most advanced industrial and service-oriented society. This means that, as Mayfield observed, habits of work and thought are socialized into standards of efficiency and pace different from those in Africa.

Julian Mayfield related the story of Otu, a middle-aged Ghanaian raised in the tradition of the British colonial civil service, who worked as a typist beside an Englishwoman named Jean. They were preparing documents for the Ghana General Assembly when Mayfield noticed that Otu was typing half as fast as Jean; the deeper problem, however, was that when he raised this issue with Otu, the latter felt that Jean *should* be able to type faster because she was British. Mayfield said this attitude was typical among those he encountered coming out from under the political and psychological control of British colonialism. Mayfield saw this as a lethargy comprising a lack of confidence not unlike that which afflicted Black Americans who had been beaten down by the system of slavery and whose sense of self had to be redeemed if self-determination would be achieved.[55] The Otu's, Mayfield said, had lived so long "in the bosom of a power that appeared unbeatable that, at first, they could not even grasp the 'arrogant' thrust of people like Martin Luther

King, Jr. who was considered by many Blacks both in Africa and in America to be a trouble-maker."[56] Some Ghanaians pictured African Americans as immediate professional rivals and objected to their presence, often more strongly than they did to the presence of white American consultants, professionals or temporary workers.

Some Africans made very little distinction between what they considered to be the negative traits of white Americans and Blacks. This was demonstrated by Mayfield in a story about his immediate superior, Yaw Eduful. When President Kennedy was assassinated, Mayfield entered Flagstaff House, the government headquarters, only to be told by Eduful to "get out!, I don't want to see any American today. You're all so damn violent. Killers, all of you." And when Mayfield protested that his people were "different," Eduful replied: "I don't care what kind of American you are, get the hell out of here!"[57] Therefore, Blacks often had to work harder to prove that there was a distinction between them and whites in their political consciousness, including their attitude toward American activities around the world. To renounce American activities that were counter to the progressive values of Africa and other emerging countries without renouncing all that America stood for was the special and delicate balance the African-American expatriates had to keep in their relationship with Africans.

Without awarding to Nkrumah the gift of total prescience, it was likely that, since he understood political, historical and psychological situations both in America and in Ghana, he also sensed that "seeding" Ghana with militant, even antiwhite African Americans might help to break the psychology of colonialism; the development of national consciousness might be hastened by bringing in people who were already detribalized, and this movement might attract people who possessed many of the ready-made skills necessary to assist in administering the government. When Richard Wright visited Ghana after its independence, he cautioned Nkrumah that he would have to purge some Africans who had adopted the colonial mentality through their service in the British civil service. Nkrumah, however, could not have helped but be aware of this through his own struggles within the United Gold Coast Convention, his initial political party, but the fact was that Ghanaians had worked in close proximity with the English as well as South Africans, who had been sprinkled through the administrative, educational and economic system of the colony. In this sense, encouraging the return of race-conscious, loyal Black Americans was a pragmatic risk worth taking, even if the possibility existed that they would stir some modest resentment among indigenous Ghanaians.

Roles: "Légitime Défense"

If the cultural price of identity for African Americans was too high, the political price was much easier to bear. The African Americans fell back upon their own unique culture and upon that culture based a rudimentary social organization as a distinct community of immigrants among Ghanaians. As such, they had a political characterization since they were so strongly identified with President Kwame Nkrumah and supported his programs for Pan Africanism and African liberation. In fact, Leslie Lacy says of the "politicals" that, not only were they "religiously loyal to Nkrumah" and "to zealously following the ruling party's line," but that they were honest and, though lacking in "revolutionary sophistication," hard working and believing in Nkrumah's commitment to change.[58] This mindset was important because, as Lacy also reports, several African Americans "walked in the corridors of power."[59] They were, thus, frequently able to contribute directly to Nkrumah's Pan Africanism, but often could not successfully caution him against over-optimism. Smith, for example, reports an exchange with Nkrumah as the Accra Conference of Heads of African States approached; Smith raised the question as to whether Hastings Banda of Malawi or Houphouet-Boigny would support the idea of a central African government.[60] Clearly, one of the roles of the expatriate became that of defending the aims of the Nkrumah regime, in this case, the aim of building a socialist state.

One of the first individuals to have the role of defending Ghanaian independence to Africans in the Diaspora was George

Padmore. As previously suggested, his main task as a principal adviser to Nkrumah was to help prepare Nkrumah's Pan Africanist approach to continental liberation. However, Padmore also noted that there were sections of the British press that were opposed to Ghanaian independence from its inception and, when the Ghanaian government deported a Sierra Leonean journalist and two northern Nigerian businessmen in 1957, Padmore strongly defended this action.[61]

Somewhat later, Julian Mayfield, who in the minds of many became the leader of the Afro-American community, frequently wrote for Ghanaian newspapers. In an article on "The Afro-American and Kwame Nkrumah," Mayfield wrote that it was a "privilege to live and work in a socialist country that is surging forward."[62] He also defended Nkrumah from attacks by the Western media opposing Nkrumah's policy of "neutralism and non-alignment," saying that the "President of Ghana was a constant target of vicious elements of the Western press . . . because he will not involve his country in a cold war fight." He described Nkrumah as "the world's leading Pan Africanist," citing this as the reason why "the lackeys of capitalism and colonialism hate him." But, Mayfield argued, "22 million Afro-Americans have a guide: they say if the white man hates him, he must be up to something good." Then, he concluded with this thought: "I believe in scientific socialism, but I write here in racial terms, for I am first of all a Black man who knows that within the framework of capitalism and imperialism, racial doctrinairism has been the hammer used to destroy the Black man's personality."[63]

Again, while Nkrumah had defined the central aim of the independence of Ghana to be the building of a socialist state under the principles of "scientific socialism," Mayfield had to nod in that direction, but adhere to a racial analysis in his translation to Ghanaians of the intentions of the West toward Nkrumah. And, while this explanation in defense of Nkrumah might have worked for outsiders, it is likely that it was far less effective for most Ghanaians than Nkrumah's own explanation of the West as both capitalist and imperialist.

Loyalty to the regime by Afro-Americans was important because many expatriates fervently believed in the possibility of African socialism, but it was also useful in coping within the new environment where race was not a strong basis for legitimizing one's presence. Thus, the act of defending the regime and its direction might also function as a method of gathering the necessary social standing in which to legitimize the Afro-American group's presence. This activity was also evidence of the fact that it was possible to connect—or to enter into positive social relationships with Ghanaians—on the level of *political* relationships where *cultural* relationships were for the most part proscribed.

It is possible to say that the movement emerging in the United States among Blacks had not developed a firm ideology at the time of the independence of Ghana and that certainly the movement had adopted no firm position toward either capitalism or socialism, but a clear anti-racism was paramount. Indeed, the McCarthy period had just emerged, a period when many progressives were under the presumption of being communist, and so the social stigma of having been identified with socialists of whatever stripe was a healthy negative to say the least. The Council on African Affairs, harassed by the McCarthyites, closed its doors in 1955, four years after the six-month jailing of Dr. Alphaeus Hunton in New York City for refusing to turn over to the House Un-American Activities Committee the record of its financial supporters.[64]

I have referred to the fact that the American Society for African Culture, born about 1955, was eventually infiltrated by the CIA, and in this period two giants of our time, W. E. B. DuBois and Paul Robeson, were politically handcuffed by the Federal Bureau of Investigation, having had their passports taken and been virtually silenced by the Smith Act. The emigration to Africa took place within a highly volatile competition between the United States and the Soviet Union in a Cold War context, and the U.S. intelligence apparatus was undoubtedly quite active in attempting to shape the evolution of the Ghanaian state system toward the West. As a factor in this intrigue, the anti-racist ideology of African Americans would help to tilt the balance against rather than for the United States in this competition. In fact, Hoyt Fuller reported a conversation with an American official in Guinea who admitted: "Yes, we are keeping Black radicals away from the Africans, and we will succeed. There's a damned good chance that we'll have the French back in control here after a few years."[65]

So the fact that within the United States the Black movement emerged from the left, but without a strong left ideology, meant that those authorities who would keep the movement from developing such an ideology had to be on guard. Nkrumah's announcement that he wanted to create a "socialist" Ghana, then, must have given the old guard civil rights leaders considerable pause; just as important, Nkrumah's decision would begin to shape the ideology of those who would seek to return seriously to Ghana to participate in nation-building activities. To some extent, it was a challenge to choose Ghana; to American authorities, however, such a choice was probably interpreted as a choice between the Soviet Union and Americanism. Americanism, however, became more and more unpopular in Ghana, partly because the growth of the civil rights movement taught Africans more about what American Blacks were suffering internally, partly because of the deteriorating relations between the American and Ghanaian governments.

In December of 1962, Senator Thomas J. Dodd, Democrat of Connecticut, began a campaign focusing on Ghana as a "center for subversive communism in Africa."[66] In July of 1963 Dodd, vice chairman of the Senate Internal Security Committee, reiterated the charge, saying Ghana was "the first Soviet Satellite in Africa . . ."[67] This accusation was not only refuted by the State Department and the Ghana government, but also by St. Clair Drake, then head of African studies at Roosevelt University. Professor Drake pointed out that Americans who often objected to policies of "positive non-alignment," African socialism, the one-party state and militant Pan Africanism had a tendency to label all of these orientations as communist. Drake underlined that "Pan Africanism is not a communistic movement and not a menace to the United States."[68]

Although the call for socialism was not new and evoked no opposition among African Americans in Ghana, perhaps the most conflicting issue was Nkrumah's creation of a "one-party state," under the banner of the Convention Peoples Party. Nkrumah's last defense of the one-party form of government was in a speech before parliament in February 1966, the year in which he was deposed.[69] He argued that the one-party system is workable in the African context and where there are socialist states because of the relatively equalitarian nature of the society, whereas

in capitalist countries the two-party system is often a manifestation of class cleavages. Despite Nkrumah's justifications, the creation of a one-party state was an additional cause for alarm on
the part of the Western nations, and although G. Mennen Williams, head of the State Department's Africa Bureau,
appeared to take a relatively relaxed view of this development,
clearly there was opposition both within white and Black circles
in the United States.

For example, Professor Martin Kilson, an Afro-American lecturer at Harvard, who was at the University of Ghana before
Nkrumah was overthrown, wrote a critique of African socialism
for *African Forum*, the journal of the American Society of African
Culture, in which he took a relatively dim view of the phenomenon.[70] Kilson suggested that upon economic grounds bureaucratic interference with the market was demonstrated to have
been counter-productive in Ghana. Kilson used the stated views
of Arthur Lewis, a West Indian and Nobel Prize-winning economist whom Nkrumah had invited to Ghana to study the process
of its industrialization, who declared that "the single-party system is largely irrelevant to the current economic problems of
West Africa."[71] Then, John A. Davis, editor of *African Forum* and
president of AMSAC, wrote in an editorial that "American Negroes, do not favor rule by the military . . ." and that, while they
were saddened by the military takeover in Ghana, the "denial of
civil liberty" was also "a source of anxiety."[72] The same issue of
the journal contained an article by Lt. Gen. Joseph A. Ankbah,
leader of the Revolutionary Council that had deposed Kwame
Nkrumah. One wonders whether or not he would have been
permitted to publish in the pages of the journal *Freedomways*.
Indeed, Shirley Graham DuBois published an article in *Freedomways* explaining the rationale for the military coup from a progressive point of view.[73] So, there was some African-American
opposition to Nkrumah's concept. The "politicals," then, supported Nkrumah's call for socialism and found simultaneously
in Ghana a base from which to strike at American racism. One
opportunity to do this was provided by the August 28, 1963,
March on Washington; the "politicals" organized a sympathy
march to the American Embassy in Accra on the same day.
Another opportunity appeared with the visit of Malcolm X
in 1964.

Fighting Racism

The tradition of utilizing the base of Ghana to fight racism was a tradition developed by none other than Kwame Nkrumah himself shortly after the country's independence through an incident quite probably stimulated by the few political African Americans in Ghana at the time. It involved Jimmy Wilson, a fifty-five-year-old illiterate handyman in Alabama who was convicted of stealing $1.95 from an eighty-five-year-old woman in a nighttime burglary in July 1957 and was sentenced to die in the electric chair on October 24, 1958. An inquiry made by the Ghana government about the case to the American government initiated a series of protest demonstrations around the world. This resulted in pressure from Secretary of State John Foster Dulles on Governor James Folsom of Alabama to reconsider the grossly unfair sentence, and Governor Folsom eventually commuted this sentence to life imprisonment![74] This is the only known case where, almost as a direct result of external pressure from an African government and negative international public opinion, the sentence of a Black American was changed.

Somewhat later, when the African-American community matured and the civil rights movement in the United States became a truly national phenomenon, this tradition of fighting racism from the Ghanaian base also matured. Having largely subdued Marxism among Black Americans in the 1950s, U.S. policy makers and police authorities probably did not expect that an additional challenge to capitalism and to the mystique of American national unity in the fight against the Soviet Union would come by way of Black Nationalism. This development was made all the more probable since, despite the cordial welcome accorded Nkrumah by Black leaders on his visit to the United States in 1958, most were cautious about the new regime. Into this vacuum of neglect stepped Malcolm X, the most prominent Black American leader to go to Ghana since DuBois. Although upsetting to American diplomatic officials and super-patriotic Black Americans, his visit was undoubtedly more desired by the "politicals" than that of any other Black leader.

To begin with, Malcolm X was partly responsible, as we have suggested, for new militance among young people and for the

conclusion that new leadership was needed in the Black community. Not only Louis Lomax, but even earlier, Professor Frank
Lee noted that the emergence of the more militant tactics of Rev.
Martin Luther King, Jr. was made possible by the moderate approach to civil rights in the South.[75] Clear evidence exists that
there was antipathy between the younger, more politically conscious Black Americans in Ghana and Black leaders who, in
1962, had formed the American Negro Leadership Conference
on Africa. One of the sages of Harlem, Richard B. Moore, notes
that a January 1963 issue of *Voice of Africa* carried an article entitled, "Negro Stooges Bid for Africans Challenged," ostensibly
written by "Ghana Patriots."[76] Apparently, the Ghana patriots
charged that these Negro leaders attempted "to move ahead of
the African nationalist in America," branding the leaders "opportunists" and suggesting that the organization represented
"American colonialism, imperialism, and exploitation."[77]

Secondly, Malcolm was a kindred spirit, for he was the only
prominent Black leader forcefully to utilize a Pan Africanist analysis in his lectures and his approach to Black problems. By the
time of his famous "Message to the Grass Roots" speech in November of 1963, Malcolm had grown used to setting the problem
of Black people in America within an internationalist context.
For example, he referred to the fact that when the Bandung conference was held, Africans from various parts of the continent
had an opportunity to understand that, though they were from
different cultures and regions, the European was their common
oppressor.[78] He used this precedent to suggest to his audience
that they in America must also know their common enemy.

Nevertheless, it is surprising how successful Malcolm was in
making his Ghanaian audience understand his perspective,
given the Ghanians' low social acceptance of racially-based explanations for political problems, as we observed previously.
His tactic, however, was again to set the American racial problem within the context of Pan Africanism by drawing parallels
that his audiences would understand. The following response
to a question posed to him at a news conference in Ghana constitutes an example:

> I said that the 22 million Afro-Americans in the United States
> could become for Africa a great positive force—while, in turn, the

African nations could and should exert positive force at the diplomatic levels against America's racial discrimination. All of Africa unites in opposition to South Africa's apartheid, and to the
oppression in the Portuguese territories. But you waste your time
if you don't realize that Verwoerd and Salazar, and Britain and
France, never could last a day if it were not for United States support. So until you expose the man in Washington, D.C., you
haven't accomplished anything.[79]

This was a powerful rationale for challenging American relationships with imperialist nations, not from the base of a socialist or
communist ideological or political program, but from a Black
Nationalist and Pan Africanist direction. This strategy of exposing America was not based solely on its relations with other
Western colonialist nations, but also on its internal vulnerability,
its racist record on civil and human rights. Malcolm wanted to
expose this record before the world court of public opinion by
taking the issue to the United Nations, and for this he needed
the support of African states. Maya Angelou records him as saying that if this issue could be debated in the United Nations
"then we would be taken seriously," and that this should be possible since South African Blacks were able to petition that body
for redress of their situation.[80]

Malcolm, however, would underestimate the degree of control still exercised in the United Nations by the Western nations.
While they took some tentative steps to enact an arms embargo
against South Africa in 1963, they were totally unwilling to let
the searchlight examine their own internal racial policies. In addition, the African states faced severe limitations in pushing the
racial dilemma of Black Americans in the United Nations since it
was also that body which dispensed crucial economic development assistance and influenced other international financial
agencies—and since most of the funding would have to come
from Western states.

Malcolm was excited about visiting Ghana, to him "the very
fountainhead of Pan Africanism."[81] It would be here that he
would form a chapter of his Organization of African Unity
among the considerable African-American community resident
in Ghana at that time. As Malcolm would later note, this community, led by writer Julian Mayfield, formed a Malcolm X Com-

mittee to facilitate his visit and meetings with government officials, students, intellectuals and just plain folk. Among these,
he also met with figures conversant with the long struggle for
Pan Africanism, among them Ras Makonnan, financier of the
Manchester Pan African Conference, with whom Malcolm
talked about "the type of Pan-African unity that would also include the Afro-Americans." He met with Shirley Graham Du-
Bois, who took him to the DuBois home and talked with him
about her famous husband's activities in Ghana. He met with
President Nkrumah, a meeting he would describe as "my highest single honor." They discussed the unity among African
peoples, Malcolm later saying that he and Nkrumah "agreed
that Pan-Africanism was the key also to the problems of those of
African heritage." [82]

There was, of course, a feeling by the "politicals" that the
American authorities were vexed at the reception given to Malcolm X by Ghanaians and to his views describing American activities around the world and its treatment of African-American
citizens. Was it, then, a coincidence that G. Mennen Williams,
assistant secretary of state for African affairs, the government's
chief spokesman for Africa, was traveling in Africa at the same
time? Some in Malcolm's entourage also felt that the American
ambassador to Ghana was attempting to counter Malcolm's popularity with Ghanaians at the various events he attended where
Malcolm was the guest of honor. William Atwood, American
ambassador to Kenya, was explicit in relating that he attempted
to tell Kenyan leaders "who Malcolm X really was" and to alert
other American posts in Africa to his presence on the continent. [83]

Another political act by the "revolutionary returnees" consisted of a march in August 1963 in sympathy with the March on
Washington. Maya Angelou describes the derision provoked
when Julian Mayfield mentioned in a group meeting at his
home that Martin Luther King, Jr. was leading a march on Washington, D.C. "The ridicule fitted our consciousness. We were
brave revolutionaries, not pussyfooting, nonviolent cowards." [84]
This evidence of antinonviolent consciousness, preceding the
militant Black Power period beginning in 1966, is important in
mirroring the anti-nonviolent mood among militant, Black conscious activists in America. However, whereas in America activ-

ists had other outlets, the "politicals" in Ghana eventually decided to mount a march to the American Embassy or a "march against the Embassy" as a modest expression of their anti-racist politics.

Dr. Alphaeus Hunton led the more than 200 marchers. Their march at midnight August 27 took place in unity with the crowning moment of the civil rights movement, a kind of national legitimation of moderate politics; it took place amid sorrow over the death of Dr. DuBois that day in Ghana, a refugee from Afro-America but a Pan African patriot to Africans on the continent; it took place in Ghana where there should have been thousands of Ghanaians to join it, but where there was an incomplete understanding of what the march meant.

After an all-night vigil, the marchers set out with placards toward the American embassy. Once at the embassy, Hunton and a five-person delegation presented a declaration drafted by the "politicals" to Oliver Troxel, the acting chief of mission, and intended for delivery to President Kennedy. It read in part, "We remind you that 20 million Americans of African descent are products of more than 300 years of slavery and inferior status in a white supremacist society, which boasts to the world that it is the land of the free and the home of the brave. Such a boast is hollow as long as America's Black citizens are denied the fundamental liberties which white citizens take for granted." [85]

Conclusion

Perhaps one of the most fruitful ways to gain a more objective assessment of the Pan African experiment of African Americans and the Nkrumah government from 1957 to 1965 is to compare this black expatriate experience to that of whites in Africa. [86] To begin with, a distinction must be made between the expatriate community and settlers. The white community in several countries, notably in Southern Africa and Kenya and Tanganyika, could be divided into two classes: the expatriates who were businessmen, civil servants and other whites in the country on a temporary basis for specific purposes, and the settlers who were more or less permanently resident. In some countries the distinction was important, and in others the two white forces constituted parts of one community; perhaps the difference was in the relative size of the overall white community and the fact that its control over the economy supported a large expatriate class.

The African-American community in Ghana might be considered one that was not large enough to have an important distinction between expatriates and settlers. In fact, the strong expectations with which many came to Ghana initially resembled those of settlers rather than expatriates and only changed when it became clear that the circumstances would not support their expectations for permanent residence. Thus, it is easy to conclude that there were few permanent settlers among the Black Americans and, in addition to this difference, the Black and white communities in Africa resembled each other only in the fact that they were constituted as distinct communities.

It is interesting that they appeared to constitute distinct communities for the same reason, but this appearance breaks down under closer scrutiny. Most whites were not seeking to assimilate culturally with Africans, but the Black American community probably would not have been as strong as it was if its assimilation into the Ghanaian community had been easily accomplished. As suggested, because assimilation was difficult to impossible, Black Americans fell back upon their own distinctive culture. This culture had a certain attraction to Ghanaians because it was Western and because they had been colonized by a Western culture. In addition, Blacks had changed this culture in important ways to create interesting new syntheses and had achieved a professional base, however small. It was not the "Americanness" of the black expatriate that became most functional, but the "Blackness"—the synthesis of the African and American experiences. Those who posited their Americanness within the Ghanaian experience most often maintained some official relationship which made this necessary. The few who maintained a high profile for their Americanness and did not have an official reason were suspected of being spies and often were not easily able to function within the Ghanaian situation, especially as Ghana became more openly critical ideologically of Western foreign and domestic policy.

Franck further explained that because the white expatriate was not a permanent resident, "he has the further advantage of being a political in a highly political society. This makes him particularly useful in sensitive positions. Dr. Nkrumah, for example, finds it prudent to retain a British 'expatriate' supreme commander who can be trusted to steer clear of local internecine plots and intrigues."[87] That other expatriates were also utilized by Nkrumah quickly to bolster his cadre of politicals—individuals who were ideologically committed to his independence strategies and professionally competent—is supported by the fact that there was a white expatriate community in Ghana as well. Its members were largely concentrated in the university, business and civil service sectors. Shirley Graham DuBois recalled the disappointment she felt at her husband's reluctance when Nkrumah asked his advice about appointing Dr. Connor Cruise O'Brien, an Irishman who had fought to keep the Congo free of international exploitation, to the presidency of the University of Ghana.[88] No doubt, W. E. B. DuBois saw the potential danger in expanding the number of European expatriates in Ghana.

Nevertheless, it was important for Nkrumah quickly to secure his own base with loyal and competent individuals in view of the fact that even in the first year of Ghana's independence, the charges of "authoritarianism" to characterize Nkrumah's stewardship had begun to be used by former white colonials, Western journalists and academics and his political enemies among the Ghanaian elite.[89] Thus, while Nkrumah may not have had cynical motives in deliberately using African Americans as a foil against his political enemies and a resource against the residual colonial mentality among Africans and whites in Ghana, he did seek real and immediate results from Pan African theory.

A second very important difference between the white community and the African-American community in Africa was that the colonial process had left a residue of white control and, thus, effective power—the economic, technological and educational spheres bred a white-dominant/Black-subordinate distribution of power, even in newly so-called independent states. And whereas the white expatriates and settlers were desperately attempting to hold to their power, the Black American expatriates formed an important Western elite with economic, technological and educational resources that were under the control of the government. Complicating the ability of foreigners of any description to live close to the social scale of Ghanaians is the fact of extremes of poverty and wealth left by the process of colonialism. Part of the problem was the structure established that paid expatriate professionals of all kinds more than ordinary Ghanaians, often for the same work. Some African Americans benefitted from this and, thus, another barrier stood in their way to "live as an African." [90]

Thirdly, the racism that whites practiced in the settler colonies and in the independent states was largely missing among African Americans. To some extent, it was replaced by the air of arrogance and a suggestion of being closer to white culture and Western standards that some African Americans carried, but in general, the cultural expectations and strivings of African Americans bred an air of seeking acceptance and common ground in the quest for cultural legitimacy—something that could only be obtained from Africans. Few Africans were able, for example, to grasp the view often expressed by African Americans that the racism they experienced existed to the extent that the process of neocolonialism was managed essentially by white, racist European and American countries and that many of the reasons for the policies visited against them were related not only to their powerlessness, but to their color and the historical legacy of inferiority it invoked in the European consciousness.

Pan African Politics

The use of independent Ghana as a base for fighting racism was clearly secondary in the eyes of the "politicals" to their main task of supporting the political objectives of the Nkrumah government. In a crucial theoretical sense, it is important to suggest that these objectives were one and the same, that is to say, by being in Ghana and supporting the government, the "politicals" constituted a refutation of the racist view that Africans would not unify, that Pan Africanism itself was a rebuttal to Western arrogance. In practice, however, there were clear priorities; supporting the regime came first. Here, it should be recognized that "the government" is being used as a euphemism for the social, economic and political policies of the government, a term covering all the activities of African Americans in fields as diverse as plumbing and political science. Then, when there was an opportunity, other anti-racist activities might be mounted, even though there were seldom direct opportunities.

The role of the "politicals" in facilitating Malcolm X's visit, for example, struck a direct blow against racism at "home." For, just as Ghana has become a base for revolutionary groups seeking to overthrow their colonial masters on the African continent, it had also become a base for the "politicals" in their struggle to forge "liberated zones" of anti-racism within the United States political culture. Thus, to the extent that a powerful motive for those who supported the overthrow of Nkrumah was to rid the country of these bases and so an important source of anti-Western activity and propaganda, there simultaneously existed the motive to eliminate the African-American source of anti-Westernism.

Franck's realistic view of the "politicals" as existing in a highly political situation would appear itself to pose barriers to the objective some African Americans possessed of moving from a status as expatriates to that of settlers. In fact, the African political elite would move against any group which stood in the path of its acquisition of power, and as the political African Americans were supportive of the regime, they were vulnerable. The community, in fact, was vulnerable even if only part of it was openly supportive of the regime. In this sense, the vulnerabilities of Nkrumah were shared.

I have not provided a political analysis of the policies of the Nkrumah regime in this period, since this was outside the scope of my investigation. It is worth noting, however, that in a frank critique of the Nkrumah regime—among the many which have been written by various kinds of detractors—C. L. R. James, an admirer of Nkrumah and one of the great Pan Africanists, concludes that Nkrumah made some intractable errors. James felt that not only was Nkrumah's fall deserved but that this was so because Nkrumah himself made his fall inevitable by the policies he pursued. He believed that in the rush to modernize the economy, Nkrumah split the nation apart and in the process of keeping his enemies at bay, robbed the people of the basic fruit of independence, the creation of a democratic state.[91] Those who played various roles in support of the policies of Nkrumah's government, then, were also destined to be judged guilty.

There is in this, however, a double-edgedness. For, on the one hand, the quest for a functional Pan Africanism cannot in itself be assailed, but on the other, it carries an awesome responsibility. Many of the roles played by African Americans in Ghana were significant, from the initial role of George Padmore in the Pan African Bureau, to that of DuBois and Hunton in initiating the *Encyclopedia Africana* (and in giving Nkrumah general advice in other matters), to the role of Shirley Graham DuBois as director of Ghana Television, to the role of Julian Mayfield in administration and propaganda, to the professional expertise of so many others in medicine, economic development and education. These roles seldom were traceable to the shaping of specific policies or political strategies, but they did provide crucial support for the general administration of policy.

On the other hand, there is very little evidence of the struggles with Nkrumah over direction of the government. There is the possibility that the African-American community, Ghanaians and outside supporters—all were driven by two factors. First, they viewed Nkrumah's Pan African thrust toward the liberation of the continent as correct, since it was grounded in the history of the movement since 1900 and in the more recent nationalist movement for independence. Second, Ghana constituted the first Black African country in a wave of emerging states after the break-up of the colonial system and, as such, its leaders were new to the experiment of managing the state. African Americans certainly could not have advised Nkrumah, and his political opposition had only the politics of the developed powers and their models as guides. Under these conditions, to suggest that C. L. R. James' hint of inevitability of disaster was correct is a gross understatement. All were in uncharted waters;

Nkrumah, the captain of the ship, was moving with full throttle open. The African American experiment, then, was also headed toward a collision course.

One conclusion is inevitable: that the political role—or political specificity—is risky and may be antithetical to the long-term maintenance of community in this context and, thus, to the pursuit of the type of Pan Africanism that allows the African American to play a role in the development of an African country. In this sense, it is possible to make a distinction between types of Pan Africanism—political Pan Africanism and developmental Pan Africanism as the proper substance of Africans who are expatriates. This is not to oppose the historical role played by the "politicals" who, we clearly understand, did not comprise the entire African-American community, but by their vocality often represented it. In fact, it is well understood that because of the environment of the times, what with the symbolism of the independence of Ghana and the history and personality of Nkrumah, this role was probably unavoidable. But this conclusion is clearly something to consider for the future, if it is possible to move from expatriate to settler to citizen as the most viable form of Pan Africanism within the national context of an African state.

4
The Anglo-Saxon Diaspora: Britain and the United States

This chapter will focus primarily on the United States and Britain as places where the African population is similarly in the substantial minority, following the "ghetto" pattern of residence as a comparable frame of reference as discussed in chapter 1. I will address the Pan African politics of both communities in their interaction with the dominant white population in each country.

This examination will emphasize two elements which form an overall paradigm for understanding the discrete aspects of the political behavior of Africans in a Diaspora situation. The first is the comparative analysis of political events or activities that have no organic connection between key actors or institutions, but that have taken place in Britain and the United States during the same period of time for approximately the same reasons. The second approach is the Pan African approach, by which we mean to select situations which have found African-origin people in both Britain and in the United States engaged in the same events or activities through actual linkages among key actors and institutions.

First, however, it will be necessary to explore the environmental parameters for this study by examining the extent to which Britain and America do provide an empirical context for the analysis of the political dynamics of the African Diaspora, by suggesting that their "special relationship" led to a similar development of "race relations" policy and techniques as the response of these nations to racial problems. Subsequent chapters will address the problems of Pan Africanism and the comparative positions of Black communities.

In the words of A. S. Eisenstadt, a "special relationship" has existed between the United States and Britain that has hardly been regarded as "terra incognita," but rather has been the subject of considerable analysis by writers and scholars of the two countries.[1] More profound, however, is Eisenstadt's observation that this relationship has been one in which the two countries consider each other to be mutual "polities of reference."[2]

It is possible to illustrate that with respect to cultural, economic and political factors, the United States and Britain are so integrated as to constitute linked systems of transnational behavior. However, it should be noted that this also involves linkage, of course, among more than just these two countries, including the more formidable grouping of Western European countries as well. In this sense, there really is a "Western Europe" which has functional integrity at the level of broad cultural behavior, as has been affirmed by such students as Ronald Inglehart.[3]

I conclude this brief introductory statement with the thought that if the two systems are thus fundamentally linked, then it is not illogical to assume that they have followed similar approaches to the question of race. This means that there are empirical similarities which provide an appropriate setting for the study of African life in both societies. Next, I will examine the response to African communities in both Britain and America, describing broadly their approach to "problems" presented by the existence of such communities in their midst, beginning with their treatment of "race relations."

The Rise of "Race Relations"

Race relations, of course, become a social imperative from the time of the initial contacts between individuals representing diverse racial groups. But in societies such as Britain and the United States, "race relations" are only raised to the status of national prominence when sufficient numbers of racially different peoples emerge in a social situation (by whatever method) and pose, for those controlling the situation, a question concerning how they will associate with this group, as expressed in national social policy. We will examine only the most modern manifestation of this problem since the Second World War by describing the U.S. approach, since it matured earlier, and then the British approach.

Two of the historically most consistent features of the relations between the African community and whites in America has been the control by whites of the conditions of Black entry into and maintenance in society and the consequent pattern of racial stratification that has resulted in Blacks being at the bottom of the social system and whites at the top. This control, initially an effort to make the most efficient use of Black labor, institutionalized patterns of social behavior and thought that have long outlived the particular institution of slavery and are active today.

In the post-slavery period, this control, which cannot be separated from the various cruel forms of oppression that made it possible, was regulated by the power of national governmental institutions as well as by social ideology. In the first half of the twentieth century, for example, legal discrimination existed in almost every sphere of life in American society, and an especially virulent form of Anglo-Saxon Nativism made the physical mutilation and elimination of Blacks a common practice. As these practices ended in the post–World War II period, race relations were still marked by race prejudice which led to discrimination and forms of rank exclusion and segregation. Indeed, some writers have suggested that historically Blacks have been given only two choices—to conform or to be excluded. As one observer wrote, "The prevailing attitudes of the dominant group toward Blacks and Indians have been remarkably similar in regard to the issue of cultural assimilation, in spite of the vastly different histories of the two groups. In both cases, rigid adherence to white cultural standards has been the only alternative offered to exclusion."[4] However, earlier nineteenth-century theories of race, developed essentially by prejudiced social scientists, held that Blacks were basically unassimilable.[5] This led Swedish social scientist Gunnar Myrdal, in his comprehensive study of the African-American community published in 1944, *An American Dilemma*, to develop the concept that the so-called Negro was a "problem" in American life, albeit of the creation of whites.[6]

It should be noted, however, that the "Anglo-Conformity Doctrine" was directed as much toward the European immigrant community as it was toward Blacks. This doctrine and its institutionalization thereby became the principal agent for the socialization of dissimilar ethnic groups into a fundamentally English society.

> They [immigrants to America] must cast off the European skin, never to resume it. They must look forward to their posterity rather than backward to their ancestors; they must be sure that whatever their own feelings may be, those of their children will cling to the prejudices of this country.[7]

The above extract from a letter, written by the then Secretary of State, John Quincy Adams, in 1818, has been a useful guide to the immigration policy of the United States. The effect of that policy has been to so amalgamate, acculturate and assimilate white European immigrants into the dominant cultural nexus that there can truly be said to be a "white" consensus in America with regard to most racial questions. And if the Anglo-Conformity Doctrine was insistent concerning the conduct of the immigrants, how much more so would that doctrine be intolerant of a Black community which exhibited any behavior other than unquestioning service and loyalty to whites, whatever the treatment?

With such a history of race relations, Blacks could not automatically look forward to the establishment of national mores and policies that benefitted them, without themselves persistently and determinedly raising the question of social justice for their community.

One of the potent side-effects of Black American participation in the Second World War as part of the armed services, as well as in the homefront war industries, was the fact that it increased the material resources of Blacks and gave them an advanced domestic and international awareness of social progress and how this related to their own status. Race relations were beginning to change according to the increasing ability and willingness of Blacks seriously to struggle for resources with whites, utilizing all of the political instrumentalities available to them—the courts, protest action, the vote and institutions such as labor unions.

What appears to have happened after the war is that Blacks across the country, with the assistance of organizations such as the National Association for the Advancement of Colored People, launched a challenge to various forms of majority control. The response to this at the national level was the promulgation of executive orders such as President Truman's ban on discrimination in the armed forces (Executive Order 9981 of 1948) and the establishment of the President's Committee on Civil Rights. At the same time, various states were abolishing legal segregation by enacting laws to protect the civil rights of Blacks in such areas as employment, public accommodation, transportation, voting, and education. In the area of education, the legal battle spearheaded by the NAACP reached a dramatic climax when the Supreme Court decided to hear five similar cases testing the principle that separate educational facilities, maintained in many areas by race, were inherently unequal and that such inequality was a denial of "equal protection of the laws" afforded all citizens of the United States by the fourteenth amendment and by the "due process" clause of the Constitution.[8]

The decision in this case was hailed as a major advance for the principle of racial integration which black organizations had established as a goal to combat segregation, and the confirmation of this objective by the highest court in the land had an immediate impact upon other areas of civil rights activity. In fact, it led directly to the testing of Southern-style segregation in transportation by the establishment of a movement in 1957 known as the Montgomery (Alabama) Bus Boycott and to the rise of Rev. Martin Luther King, Jr. to presidency of the Montgomery Improvement Association and, eventually, to found and lead the Southern Christian Leadership Council.[9] For all practical purposes, the movement of 1957 launched the modern era of civil rights protest which was to last through the 1960s and which was key to shaping the national consensus that led to the passage of civil rights legislation by the federal government.

In the wake of the enlivening protest movement on the part of Blacks, the first of a series of civil rights acts was passed in 1957, establishing the federal Commission on Civil Rights. The duty of the commission was to make investigations, carry out studies, hold hearings on various aspects of the denial of civil rights, such as voting or other activities where equal protection of the law is guaranteed by the Constitution. It was also concerned with protecting those threatened or otherwise intimidated in the act of exercising their right to vote.

In 1960, another civil rights law was passed by the national government that further extended the activities of the commission and established access to federal voting referees by those who could legally establish that they had been denied the right to register. However, the first landmark law of the period was the Civil Rights Act of 1964. This far-reaching piece of legislation was focused primarily on the access of Blacks to public accommodations (Title II) and Equal Employment Opportunity (Title VII). Title II outlawed discrimination (on the basis of race, color, religion or national origin) to places such as hotels and motels, restaurants, lunch counters, movie houses, gasoline stations, theaters and stadiums, and other such establishments licensed by the state as a facility serving the public.

Equally important, Title VII established the Equal Employment Opportunity Commission with a mandate to enforce nondiscrimination among employers and unions of 100 workers or more (later changed to 25 or more). The commission could hear complaints but could only conciliate (negotiate and seek agreement between complainant and employer) except where states had established fair employment laws. This step, as well as Title VI, which established the principle that every federal agency providing financial assistance through grants, loans or contracts had to adopt nondiscriminatory policies, has been singularly responsible for the advancement of thousands of Blacks, other racial minorities and women (to whom the act was later extended). Passage of the act also culminated the long drive by Blacks begun during the war to establish a national Fair Employment Practices Commission (FEPC).

Another piece of legislation of equal significance with the 1964 act was the Voting Rights Act of 1965. For many years, the true electoral power of the Black community could not be expressed because of the generalized prohibitions on voting, ranging from literacy examinations as requirements to register to physical threats and actual killings. The intimidators were aware of the fact that with the Black population in the South concentrated at levels of well over fifty percent to just under fifty percent since the war, Blacks could politically control many cities and counties and strongly influence the political complexion of the states and the region. The result of the passage of the 1965 act was that, whereas in 1965 fewer than 100 blacks held elective office, the expression of black voting power made possible remarkable increases: 1966—159; 1968—248; 1969—388; 1970—711; 1972—873; 1973—1,144.[10] By 1979, there were 985 Black elected officials in the South, constituting fully 60 percent of the total number of such officials in the United States.[11]

This law, covering any state which maintained a test or device for voting as of November 1, 1964, included the deep South states of Georgia, Louisiana, Alabama, Mississippi, South Carolina and Virginia, plus Alaska and 26 counties of North Carolina. It outlawed such devices as tests and special taxes, enforced the system of federal voting examiners, and stated that the U.S. Attorney General had to review and approve any changes in election law in covered jurisdictions that might affect the right to vote or the equal effect of the vote.[12] (Even today, many city and county councils are filled by "at large" elections, rather than through smaller districts corresponding to racial or ethnic populations. Such "at large" elections destroy the equal effect of the black vote by preventing it from ever electing a representative.) This law was amended in 1975 to include Spanish language districts and thus protect the Hispanic population.

The only other significant piece of legislation in this civil rights series was the 1968 Fair Housing Act, Title VIII of which made discrimination in the sale or rental of housing in the United States unlawful. The law forbade discrimination in financing and in the provision of brokerage services, and also made it unlawful to threaten or intimidate individuals seeking access to housing.

In the decade of the 1970s, civil rights legislation was virtually nonexistent, with the important exceptions of the renewal of the Voting Rights Act in 1975 (for an additional seven years) and amendments giving the Equal Employment Opportunity Commission power to sue for damages directly. This lull, as indicated in the public opinion polls, meant that white Americans had largely withdrawn their support for further civil rights laws. On the one hand, thy felt that enough had been done and that the pace of change was about right. On the other hand, they were seized with the new problems of high inflation, high unemployment, a generally worsening economy, and the impact of these factors upon their living environment.

Britain

In 1969 a report, *Colour and Citizenship: A Report on British Race Relations,* was published by the Institute of Race Relations in Britain. This report was a landmark study in the social dimensions of race relations in the United Kingdom, but it also marked an earlier debt to the Myrdal study in explicit references. Indeed, it was this model which convinced the Nuffield Foundation to fund such a comprehensive study of race in Britain, but rather than taking as its conceptual basis Myrdal's standard of the "American Creed," the authors focused the study on the technical problems of citizenship.[13] Despite the attempt by the authors to "deprecate" the U.S. experience in British race relations, their admission of its relevance leads us to delve further into the question by assessing the similarities and differences between the two societies.

To begin with, there is the question of the extent to which British society is "racist" or prejudiced in its attitudes toward colored peoples. After the Second World War, one study (1948) of British attitudes suggested that the population fell into three broad groups of roughly equal sizes: one-third tolerant of colored people, one-third mildly prejudiced, and one-third extremely prejudiced.[14] The results were similar to those of a U.S. study showing that only 35 percent of whites approved of residential integration.[15] By 1963, in the United States, this figure grew appreciably to 64 percent, but by 1978 there was some indication that very little additional increase had been observed.[16] In the 1969 British study conducted by Rose and Associates, however, there appears to be some confirmation of the 1948 thesis; their survey found that 27 percent of the English population was either "prejudiced or prejudiced-inclined," 35 percent were "tolerant," and 38 percent were "tolerant-inclined."[17]

Secondly, there appears to be a similar pattern of control in the two countries. Both Britain and the United States are industrial societies, and although Blacks form a much larger proportion of the population in the United States, the transition from rural to urban residence and the attendant problems of coping with a metropolitan environment took place relatively recently, occurring largely in this century. Similarly, the transition by Black immigrants to Britain from the colonial situation to the metropole was much like the transition by American Blacks from a rural to a metropolitan environment, but because of the more stark differences in residence, culture and technology, it has been argued that the adaptation of the African peoples in Britain has been more difficult. This may make the agents of control and oppression of the immigrants more harsh in the modern urban context, and, in fact, the Black immigrants to Britain have been given the same options as Black Americans—to assimilate, separate or tolerate—with one additional option—to repatriate. Otherwise, the form of oppression is also very similar, arising as it does out of the colonial framework and the system of "indirect rule" exercised by the British.[18] (Very early Professor E. Franklin Frazier suggested that this "indirect rule" was a feature of American race relations.) Amid the wealth of similarities, perhaps the main difference is that, while the Black American has acquired a functional socialization and yet a somewhat different culture from mainstream whites, Caribbean African people have a more distinctly defined culture and, therefore, experience more cultural distance from the normative Englishman, even though much of Caribbean culture is also English derived. As we have suggested, this factor intensifies racism and makes problems of adaptation more difficult, producing a syndrome of white resistance and black alienation.

Britain's colored immigration began in earnest after the Second World War, and here, too, the United States played a role through the McCarran-Walter Act, which controlled the flow of immigration from the Caribbean to the United States so severely that most of it was forced to Britain. Coupled with this "push" factor, the most important "pull" factor was the British economy itself. Britain had had a restrictive immigration policy since before the First World War, but its economy, fueled in part by massive Marshall Plan economic assistance from the United States after 1947, suffered from a chronic labor shortage which caused a reconsideration of these restrictions. "It is the existence of these pockets of labor shortage which the local inhabitants have been reluctant to overcome which has led in some measure to the tapping of new sources of immigrant labor in the tropical Commonwealth."[19] Thus, it appears that Britain, with the help of the United States, substantially created the conditions for Commonwealth immigration, and through an "extensive recruitment campaign" turned first to the white immigrants who were displaced persons of wartime Europe and then to the "colored" commonwealth territories.[20]

These "colored" peoples were mainly in Africa, the Caribbean and Asia, where the political process of independence was taking place simultaneously with economic recovery of the metropoles that controlled them. India and Pakistan, which became independent in 1947, applied for membership in the British Commonwealth in 1948. This was a stimulus for the British Nationality Act of 1948 whereby these Asian Commonwealth countries fit their citizenship provisions into the overall framework of British citizenship. On the other hand, the independence process in the Caribbean paralleled that of most African states, occurring for the most part in the 1960s, but the lack of independence was no barrier to labor migration, and the Caribbean peoples, as British subjects, fell under similar citizenship provisions. Thus, when the immigrants came, there was a built-in contradiction between their perception of having access to full citizenship rights and the perception of white Britishers that the immigrants were essentially guests at best and, at worst, unwelcomed wards of the state.

The pace of immigration from African origin territories between 1951 and 1966 can be seen in Table 1. The figures in Table 1 should be appreciated as much as 15 percent because of the

Table 1. Black Immigration to Britain (thousands)

	Caribbean	Africa
1951	15.3	5
1961	171.8	19.8
1966	267.9	36.0

Source: Census of Population and Home Office Returns, cited in E. J. B. Rose and Associates, *Colour and Citizenship: A Report on British Race Relations* (London: Oxford University Press, 1969), appendix, table III, IV, "Adjustment of Census by Reference to Net Arrivals."

considerable undercount of the Black population. Nevertheless, as Table 1 indicates, a potent movement of people were absorbed into the workforce, mainly into the factories, the transport system and hospitals. The figures in Table 2, for example, show the distribution of Jamaican labor.

The official policy response, at first, was to do nothing about the flow of immigration, largely because the ambiguity referred to earlier was also present among those in government from both the Labor and Conservative parties. Nevertheless, the ensuing debate which surfaced solutions ranging from control to stoppage of immigration was settled in 1961 with the passage of an immigration control bill, the Commonwealth Immigrants Bill. Because of intensive lobbying on both sides of this legislation—among the lobbyists were government representatives from the Caribbean areas effected—the widespread assumption was created that immigration would be cut off, and this, in turn, created among the immigrants a new flood to "beat the ban." The Commonwealth Immigrants Bill essentially established a system which required the prospective immigrants to apply for and receive work vouchers in various classifications of skills (with entrance priority given to the most highly skilled) in order to enter the country. However, as will be shown, this has not had the effect of severely limiting immigration on any grounds. What we see in the figures presented in Table 3 is what the British regard as their dilemma. While immigration as a la-

Table 2. Industrial Classification of Jamaican Immigrants (%)

	Males	Females
Agriculture and mining	4	1
Chemicals, metals, engin.	38	18
Textiles, clothing, leather	4	22
Food Manufacturing	9	11
Wood, paper, rubber, etc.	6	7
Building	11	—
Gas, electricity, water	3	—
Transport, distribution	16	14
Admin., hospitals, misc. services	9	27
Total	100	100

Source: R. B. Davison, Black British: Immigrant to England (London: Oxford University Press, 1966), 76, table 37. (Sample: 98 persons)

Table 3. Types of Commonwealth Entrant (selected years)

	Total	Holder of Labor Voucher	Dependent	Student
1962	72,549	51,121	8,832	12,596
1965	66,974	12,880	41,214	12,880
1966	61,318	5,661	42,026	13,831
1972	66,958	1,803	45,494	19,671
1976	91,701	1,364	61,139	29,198

Source: Butler and Sloman, British Political Facts, 1900–1979, 5th ed. (London: Macmillan, 1980), p. 300.

bor category has been curtailed, the immigrants have "adjusted" their applications accordingly, placing more emphasis on their status as either dependents or students. Both of the latter categories also indicate the growing maturation of the African community in seeking to stabilize its community structure through immigration of family members and add to its competitive skills through study.

By 1964, immigration had become a serious subject of British politics, and as the transition was made that year from a Tory to a Labor Government, Labor responsibility for action culminated in a White Paper of 1965. This executive statement proposed to make police registration a condition for entry if the immigration officer doubted the reasons for immigration; it gave the Home Secretary power to deport a citizen of the Commonwealth; it established a limit of 8,500 work vouchers per year, and it reduced the permissible age for dependent children from 18 to 16.[21]

In 1968, Asian immigration touched off an emotional political issue, prompting Tory shadow government leaders to call for increased controls to stop the "invasion" by Pakistanis and by the Asians forced to leave Kenya; the latter numbered potentially 95,000 British passport-holders, but eventually less than half that number went to Britain. The response of the Labor government was the Immigration Bill of 1968, which restricted entry to British passport-holders having "substantial" connections with the United Kingdom (the place of the applicant's father or grandfather); further reduced the work vouchers to 1,500 per year, and further restricted the ages of dependent children and parents wishing to join the immigrants.[22] This bill was considered by those affected and by liberal Britishers to have devalued the British passport by denying the right of citizens to enter the country of their citizenship. National policy had successfully aligned itself with policies originally proposed by the racist National Front Organization.

A further onslaught against colored immigration to Britain gathered steam when the conservative elements in British society, such as the National Front, found a spokesman in the Conservative M. P. Enoch Powell.[23] Powell preached that the streets of London would be flowing with "rivers of blood" and he incited racial passions on both sides as he called for the complete stoppage of colored immigration and the repatriation of those who had already come to Britain. He thus created both an embarrassment for the Tory government and a pressure to act; to this the Tories responded with a new immigration bill in March 1971. This new measure reflected Powell's views, making it necessary for those who were admitted for a short time to register with the police; it established the standard that those applying for five years or more of residence must possess "good character" and a sufficient knowledge of English, and it provided new powers for the government to finance the repatriation of immigrants. The act divided individuals seeking entry into Britain into two classes: "patrials" and "non-patrials." Patrials were defined as British passport-holders who were born in Britain or whose parents were born in Britain; they had the "right of abode" under the law. This provision would grant virtually unlimited right of entry to white Commonwealth immigrants. Non-patrials, however, were defined as having no right to settle in or bring dependents to Britain and had to apply for specific work permits for specific jobs for a given period of time. Like the alien, the non-patrial needed permission to change jobs and had to register with the Department of Employment rather than the police while retaining the right to vote.[24] Regarding the effect of this act, one observer was led to say:

> With the enforcement of the 1971 Act (in January 1973), all primary immigration virtually ceased. The only immigrants who were allowed in beyond the specific needs of the British economy were the dependents of those already settled here and such special categories as U.K. passport-holders from East Africa (mainly Asians) and 'male fiances.'[25]

What the British government had attempted to do with controls it obviously felt it had to accomplish with regard to race relations. The incident which triggered government action on the immigration question was a race riot that occurred on August 23, 1958, in Nottingham and Notting Hill, where three thousand and two thousand Blacks lived respectively. Up to that time, one observer says, "the official policy of the British government was that the best way to deal with the problems that were arising was to leave them alone in the belief that the problems would solve themselves in time."[26] The racial venom that surfaced publicly gave evidence of far deeper problems that the government attempted to address by creating a Commonwealth Immigrants Advisory Council as a part of the 1962 bill. At the same time, on the initiative of the Labor Party, proposals were drafted for an integration policy and published in the pamphlet, *Integrating the Immigrant*. This policy, however, was not distilled until the 1965 White Paper and the Race Relations Act.

The Race Relations Act dealt with restrictive clauses in leases and sales agreements for homes and apartments, discrimination in public places, and incitement to riot. In order to deal with open racism, it banned public incitement to racial hatred by voice or pen. But it also set up a Race Relations Board with local conciliation committees, and gave labor access to voluntary conciliation of complaints. If this approach was reminiscent of that contained in the U.S. Commission on Civil Rights and the approach of the U.S. Equal Employment Opportunity Commission set up in 1964, it was because a delegation from the British government had visited these agencies and adopted what it considered to be some of the more salient features of the American legislation to Britain's situation. It is necessary to understand the judgments of observers that in fighting racism and discrimination the legislation was ineffective in both situations. In the British situation, this led to the Race Relations Bill of 1968, also under a Labor party government.

This bill was also debated under the shadow of Enoch Powell's tirades against the continued immigration of colored peoples to Britain, raising the question to national proportions and paralyzing the attempt by the Labor government then in power to adopt anything resembling a strong piece of anti-discrimination legislation. Generally, the bill permitted employers to operate undefined racial quotas and permitted shipping companies to have segregated cabins. But it also contained a new general definition of discrimination, minor concessions in relation to housing, and minor changes in the machinery used to investigate complaints of discrimination. One evaluation of the Bill stated: "An initiative which was intended to provide a sound basis in law and practice for a constructive programme of community action has misfired."[27] This judgment illustrated the government's failure to devise effective race relations policy and therefore did not address the speeches of Enoch Powell or the growing assertiveness of the National Front and other fascist groups. Thus, the increasing polarization in British society itself was the most fundamental dividend of the lack of clear or forceful action in this arena.[28]

Next, I will examine the Race Relations Bill of 1976, a bill that became obviously necessary as a result of the twin realities of the failure of the community relations effort enshrined in previous law and the awesome legacy of the American riots. As early as 1971, some observers had suggested after serious consideration that the government-sponsored effort in community relations had been a failure because it was "weak in financial resources, low status, and lacking in executive power," that its (local) committees "usually fail," that the community relations officers (CROs) "would consider their general councils to be ineffective, a loose, uncoordinated assortment of people meeting annually . . . ," that "representation on the committees . . . is overwhelmingly middle class," and that the funding level of £127 million over a three-year period was inadequate by the standard set by the American War on Poverty.[29]

On the other hand, nearly every speech in Parliament on the bill stressed that the new race law was needed to prevent the kind of civil disorders seen in the United States, especially the Detroit rebellion of 1967, which seemed plausible in the wake of the rapidly maturing Black Power movement in Britain. Indeed, earlier the White Paper of 1975 had also declared that the "frustration of legitimate expectations" carried the risk of conflict and left those suffering discrimination with "no option but to find their own redress," closing with the thought: "It is no longer necessary to incite the immense damage, material as well as moral, which ensues when a minority loses faith in the capacity of social institutions to be impartial and fair."[30] These forces made it possible for the Labor government of 1976, augmented by the considerable race relations lobby which had grown up, to create a substitute for the acts of 1965 and 1968, breaking new ground in several aspects. One of those aspects was in the definition of discrimination, which, while it retained the first form of "direct" discrimination where people are treated less favorably than others due to their color, race, and so on, also held that "indirect discrimination" (similar to the concept of "institutional racism" used in the United States) existed where "everyone is treated the same, but there are conditions or requirements which put members of a particular racial group at a disadvantage compared with others and which cannot be justified on non-racial grounds."[31]

Other new features provided that victims of discrimination could take their cases to an industrial tribunal when employment was the issue and to a County or Sheriff Court in all other cases, and made possible individual remedies for alleged discriminatory victimization. The new act also replaced the Race Relations Board with a Commission for Racial Equality (CRE) with much greater investigative powers and enforcement and absorbed the Community Relations Commission as well. The CRE, for example, could issue nondiscrimination notices advising those guilty of discriminatory actions to cease and desist and require that necessary changes in behavior and practices be made. These powers, it will be remembered, closely follow those also won by the EEOC in the United States, though the British laws were somewhat stronger.

Nevertheless, the effect of such new powers in the race relations area was cancelled out by the contradictory policies of the government in the area of immigration. The problem here was that while the government appeared to be affirming the access of the immigrant to certain rights and protections of citizenship, including the right to domicile and to be treated decently, it also appeared to be saying by its immigration policies that the immigrants were in the country on sufferance and that their presence was increasingly troublesome and provocative of attempts to force them to leave. Just as odious and confusing, the race relations laws assumed that the denial of justice could threaten the public peace and order, while implicit in the immigration law was the notion that immigrants were in fact a threat by their mere presence. Such contradictions made the effects of the 1971 statute severely tenuous in implementation and consequently nearly meaningless in its amelioration of the problem of race and citizenship.

Finally, the clearest evidence that the policy actions of the preceding decade did not resolve the problem of immigration and race relations are found in the British Nationality Bill adopted in 1981 and amended in 1988. Briefly, this bill established three classes of citizenship: British Citizens, Citizens of the British De-

pendent Territories, and British Overseas Citizens. British Citizens are those born in the United Kingdom to a British Citizen
or to a parent who is "settled" in Britain; citizens of the British
Dependent Territories are people born in the dependent territories, and all other citizens of the United Kingdom and colonies
(under the former law) are British Overseas Citizens. The key
here is that there are strict controls over who among those not
born in the country can become British citizens through a process of naturalization. Then, where there are ambiguities such
as that which suggest that the Home Secretary would exercise
wide discretion in granting or withholding such rights. The
Government White Paper, published in 1980 only five months
before the bill was drafted, made clear that the controls would
include such subjective features as deciding to naturalize only
those of "good character," negating those of "dubious reputation" or those who have been "known to be working against the
interests of the country or who have no sense of loyalty to it, and
to have a 'sufficient knowledge' of English or Welsh." This Bill
was the subject of intense interest, debate and consternation in
the colored and Black communities because it set up various categories of second-class citizenship and introduced a more intensive police surveillance upon the Black communities with regard
to the legal status of persons in the country.[32]

In summary, the American legal experience in race relations
covering especially civil rights has constituted a legacy from
which the British have sought to mold their own solutions to a
very similar problem. In America, the state of these race relations—and one must assert that the definition changes with the
nature of contemporary problems—in the new stage is marked
by the struggle for empowerment through the acquisition of resources by the African community. In Britain, however, the constitutional issue that will provide the framework for the solution
of the problem of civil rights is very much at the center of the
race relations conflict, as the reaction to the Nationality Bill illustrate. This is compounded by the fact that there are current signs
that the second stage struggle over resources has begun. Nevertheless, there is one important difference between the approaches of the British and United States governments to the
issue of immigration. The British government appears caught
between the need to "do something" about race relations be-

cause of the reality that there is a substantial Black and colored population in Britain, while at the same time entertaining the illusion that the race aspects of its immigration policy might make possible the elimination of these people and, therefore, its racial problems. In this section, we have attempted to describe this "staging" process from the perspective of benchmark policy activities of the British and the American governments. Next, we examine this process in terms of the political response of the African communities themselves, following the approach of our original hypothesis.

5
Comparative Linkages in the African Diaspora: Britain and the United States

The political culture which comprises the relations between Black and white communities in both Britain and the United States is heavily conflicted, primarily as a result of the presence and condition of the Black population in these countries, the response of white people and the governments to the Black presence, and the consequent reactions of the Black populations. This type of problem has been common in the American experience and, likewise, forms the basis of the idea that the definition of what is "political" must be extended to most activities where race relations are involved. The minority size of the "African" communities in no way mitigates either their lower status or visibility, making them most vulnerable for attack by individuals, institutions and government. The quest for cultural continuity, for survival and development, therefore, becomes an incessant struggle against the dominant white group and the effects of its civilization.

John Rex attempts to provide a definition of types of conflict which arise in such situations, where "a minority group is seeking to enter a stratification system from below," where "two or more groups are in competition for limited resources," where "punitive policies are pursued by one group against another," where "one group seeks systematically to exploit the labour of another," and where "there is a situation of virtual civil war."[1]

The implication which Rex leaves by his subsequent discussion of these typologies is that there are rather distinctive minority-majority group situations to fit each. Nevertheless, it would not be difficult for the average member of a Black minority group in either America or Britain to recognize that all five of the categories presented above are but various aspects of the same fundamental conflict process in which they are engaged. In any case, the categories are not analytically discrete, even though an aspect of minority group experience is not included in our study.

Other writers, however, have attempted to overcome this fragmented approach to the analysis of race conflict in society by reference to such holistic theories as racism or internal colonialism. The theory of classic colonialism as well as that of internal colonialism encompass both class and race theory. However, both theories contain a variety of measures, the most potently negative of which have been the pervasive racial discrimination and subjugation and the unstable and battering effects of the system of capitalist economy upon the material well-being of Black communities. Needless to say, no consensus concerning which may be the "correct" analysis is forthcoming immediately, and indeed correctness may lie in some sort of synthesis of these theories—and others. Throughout all of these analyses, the only constant factor is the victimization of the African community and its need to organize various of its resources to defend and promote its very presence and its objectives. This "political activity" is the subject of this analysis.

For example, the two greatest working-class resources in Britain or America are housing and employment, and in obtaining these the conflict experienced by African-origin immigrants (both West Indian and African) has been profound. In 1958, immediately after the London riots, a study commissioned by the Institute of Race Relations in England contained a report of complaints processed by a Committee for the Welfare of Colored People in Nottingham that included representatives from the West Indian, Indian and Pakistani communities. Most such com-

Table 4. Complaints of the Colored Population, 1957

Issue	Number of complaints
Employment	96
Family and Personal	42
Housing	35
Travel	16
Education	11
Miscellaneous	22

Source: James Wickenden, *Colour in Britain* (London: Institute of Race Relations, 1958), p. 10.

plaints of racial discrimination came from West Indians, who outnumbered the other two communities, and revealed an important litany of issues with which they were concerned. Table 4 profiles cases dealt with in 1957.

Again in 1966, the Institute facilitated the publication of a study based on 1961 census data which found considerable dissatisfaction with housing and employment, while among 215 cases only five specifically mentioned racial discrimination in employment.[2] Then, in 1969, the Institute, in its extensive study *Colour and Citizenship,* reported the results of an earlier study carried out in 1966 which confirmed incidents of discrimination by whites against Blacks in housing and employment.[3] While one is aware that difficulties obtaining such resources as housing and employment may be related to factors other than race discrimination, still immigrants are often unaware of or afraid to report incidents of racial discrimination in these areas as a consequence of their precarious status in society.

These key resources are important because they are the means by which a community establishes a beachhead, reflecting that it is able to pay for ancillary services and necessities, thus supporting a wider network of family members, and for social institutions. The areas of Black settlement in London today are the Notting Hill and Brixton areas where the battle rages to stabilize and destabilize the Black community. Low-income working-class Black areas have been established such as Broadwater Farms in the Nottinghill area, which is reminiscent of the Barry Farms housing projects in the poorest and Blackest sections of Washington, D.C. From these areas and others, the Black community in England attempts to expand as its socioeconomic resources make it possible to acquire and hold housing units in various areas of central cities.

The establishment of such an African community in Britain, including West Indians and Africans from the continent, invited heightened prejudice and physical attacks by many of the native white residents and attempts to drive them from some neighborhoods. A practice of "Paki-bashing," or attacks on Pakistani immigrants, engaged in by young white toughs known as skin heads, often spilled over into the Black neighborhoods. At the same time, there was an attempt by the police to enforce a harsh pattern of public social control, and although the issues of housing and employment in the 1970s undoubtedly grew more difficult because of the worsening economy, these volatile issues were exacerbated by the expanded use of police power against the African community.

In the establishment of the community, political strategies were devoted to those structures which are responsible for the maintenance of protection and development, and in the case of both Britain and America we may describe this roughly as "welfare politics," though not in the institutional welfare sense. In the United States, for example, the Community Action Program (CAPs) created by President Johnson's "War on Poverty," brought a substantial number of Blacks into participation in a variety of community programs and decision-making roles.[4]

These programs were being established in the mid-1960s simultaneously with the rise of a militant Black ideology known as "Black Power," which was grounded in precepts of Black self-determination and which logically meant that Blacks should struggle to control these programs in their areas and to use them as instruments of Black community development. Such an attempt to make governmental programs coincide with Black community political strategy was the source of a tremendous conflict which destroyed many of these programs, yet in the operation of these poverty programs many Blacks gained political skills and a knowledge of the functioning of an urban environment.

Many of these skills, as well as the transfer of resources (contacts, organizations, funding strategies, and so on) from the poverty program to individuals and organizations, made possible the rise of a new Black middle class in the 1970s, thus successfully challenging the notion of inherent Black inferiority.[5] Although these programs made possible the diversification of the Black middle class occupational base and new political strategies such as electoral politics through the rise of Black elected officials, they did not provide the basis for the long-term strategy of Black economic or political empowerment, since they were governmental in nature and the priorities of government changed with the coming of the Nixon Administration in 1969. But what could also be said of the poverty politics era is that it augmented the role of moderate Black political groups, such as those which had so strongly advocated and agitated for civil rights, binding them even closer and focusing their attention even more narrowly to the role of the Democratic Party and the federal government in implementing their strategies for social change.[6]

Similarly, the Community Relations Commission, part of the Race Relations Board of the British government, was set up in the 1960s as a response to racial problems. For many Blacks who became employed on the various local and national boards and committees, a veritable "race industry" emerged that performed the function of providing occupational mobility, somewhat akin to the Equal Employment Opportunity jobs in the United States which grace most of the agencies of the federal government and many private corporations. At best, the race establishment was paternalistic in both instances. It was monitored in the United States by a Congress which took a wary and highly selective approach to race equality, positing a goal of "access" to "equal opportunity" rather than equal treatment in fact. In Britain, the paternalism of the race industry was guaranteed as well by the fact that Blacks were seldom in key roles of decision-making at the local or national levels, and so their status was merely "advisory" to those who made policies. This paternalism was also challenged by the Black Power movement in Britain in the 1960s, but its main effect was to integrate a larger number of Blacks into the formal race relations system.

The second effect, which appeared deliberate, was to pose the "race industry" as an alternative to the surging Black Power movement, and so to "buy off" militant leadership. Thus, what happened in Britain and in the United States was that a significant number of those who had led aspects of a challenge to authority from the basis of community and national organizations were absorbed into "race industry" jobs or into roles funded by race industry related agencies. In the United States, many of the "poverty politicians" of the 1960s, who had benefitted directly from the various political movements we will later discuss, became elected politicians, consultants, Equal Opportunity officers, Community Relations officers or heads of programs funded by governmental grants. In both countries, this "strategy" was deemed desirable, even at the expense of the continuation of the various political movements. One Black British observer, however, put the race industry into illuminating perspective. He suggested that the Community Relations Commission and the Race Relations Board created channels for the administration of immigrant affairs under white control, a fact appreciated by British politicians who were believers in "proper channels." This was necessary because as British political parties were established based upon *class* conflict in society, *race* was perceived as being outside this arrangement, and so the racial dilemma was "subcontracted" to the bureaucracy. However, this solution was ineffective because Blacks and even the ideological and activist Right wanted to make the racial problem one of the central concerns of British society.[7] Under such circumstances, then, both in the United States and Britain, the concept which holds that such agencies may be responsible for anything resembling "community development" may be merely an illusion because of the sophisticated insight of those whose fortunes would be guided by what they view as oppressive and inadequate bureaucracies.

Yet the political strategies in both cases have yielded to substantial participation with the political party perceived to favor the race relations industry, the Labor party in England and the Democratic party in the United States. Indeed, both parties have been more favorable to welfare and race bureaucracy approaches than have the Tory and Republican parties, and in both cases the Black population has given them allegiance overwhelmingly throughout the past two decades.

In the United States, there has been a rather explicit coalition of forces inside the Democratic party, including Blacks, women, labor, Jews and other minorities, which has held together the race approaches mentioned above, the coalition only beginning to erode badly only in the 1970s.[8] In Britain, however, one of the more significant differences from the American situation arises from the fact that the Labor party is not only a force in Parliament, but also has direct effect upon working-class politics and economics through its ability to wage class warfare in the factories and among the various unionized occupations. Although the Black population is in the working-class sector of the British economy and is heavily unionized, it is not more so than the other colored minorities, which in industrial cities such as Birmingham and Manchester are well represented in the factories and have supported the class politics of the Labor party.[9]

Today, the main vehicle for the mobilization of the Black community in England is not strictly through the working-class base, but through the community organization base and the Black ethnic neighborhood institutions that encompass all classes of Blacks. Indeed, the fact of racism has caused the inevitable clash of interest and priorities between Blacks and the leadership of the Labor party, and the response of community leaders has been to raise the question of "Black Sections" within the Labor party. As one observer put it in a forum on the Black Sections issue by *Race Today*, ". . . by itself the Labor party is not the way forward. Its past betrayal of Black people demands that a certain distance be maintained."[10] More important: "A mixture of white racism and black nationalism has created amongst black people a discernibly high level of black collective consciousness. It's almost as if black people constitute a sub-nation within Britain."[11]

One of the issues revolved around the question of who would benefit by the organization of Black Sections. Darcus Howe, Editor of *Race Today* and a Marxist intellectual, was an early supporter of this movement, but he cautioned that it was a movement of an upwardly mobile Black middle class as distinct from the struggles of the Black working class.[12] He saw the emergence of the Black Sections question within the context of a move on the part of some black middle class activists toward obtaining seats in Parliament, a companion movement that would not bear fruit until 1987. In fact, some Black Sections existed at the local level, as in Paddington, where Diane Abbott worked to recruit Black people into the Labor party; she was subsequently elected to the House of Commons. Nevertheless, Howe objected to the claim of the Black Sectionists "to represent the 'black masses' when in fact all they can do is to represent themselves and their aspirations."[13]

Initially, some Black activists and leaders opposed the Black Sections issue on the grounds that it contradicted the essential unity of the working classes, but such opposition has waned to the point that the prevailing position is that "the right to independent self-organization is . . . absolutely crucial to our existence and progress in this country," that it is "the only way forward."[14] However, even the more ideological of the leaders came to believe that the opposition to Black Sections from whites has taken the predictable forms of assessment that Blacks were creating a "ghetto" for themselves, or that Black Sections would destroy the movement of the party toward integration, and the like. Some Black party activists, however, such as Bernard Grant, former leader of the Haringey Council in London, felt that Blacks were "being used" by the Labor party because Blacks were voting for the party without being rewarded with concomitant rewards.[15]

Proof of this assertion by Grant was found in the Vauxhall by-election, caused by the resignation of a Labor MP, in May of 1989. The Vauxhall district contains Brixton, a largely Black area which makes the entire district approximately one-third Black. Local Labor activists constructed a short list of candidates which included a popular Black woman, a Nigerian feminist universalist, Martha Osamor, but the party's national executive committee chose a white woman, Kate Hoey, as candidate for the seat against the Tory opponent.[16] The local Black community and progressive whites widely perceived this selection as an "imposition" upon their district.

The issue was first debated in the Labor party Congress of 1984 and as the leadership rejected it, it was voted down badly by 92 percent of the delegates, or delegates representing about 500,000 votes as opposed to delegates representing 6 million. In 1985, the outcome of the vote was essentially the same, and in 1987 though the opposition began to lessen, delegates were still overwhelmingly opposed, and it did not pass the 1989 Labor party Congress.[17] The proposal is for a single socialist society existing within the local and regional branches of the Labor party.[18]

In preparation for a continued offensive, the leaders of the Black Sections movement prepared a policy document, "The Black Agenda," in response to criticism of some Black activists that the movement lacked a program. The document covered such issues as racism, problems of the inner cities, police, immigration, education, employment, youth, and international issues such as those of South Africa, Israel and the Arabs and Northern Ireland. The content of these issues, which are predictably left-of-center, covered the interests of Blacks and Asians and were specific as to the definition of the problems and their emphasis on policy solutions.[19]

There was a striking resemblance between "The Black Agenda" and the Peoples Platform, constructed by the National Black Leadership Roundtable in the United States, chaired by Congressman Walter Fauntroy. It, too, was a policy document directed toward influencing the positions of the Democratic party in the election of 1984. For example, "The Black Agenda" called for a "full employment economy as the main priority of a future Labor government," while "The Peoples Platform" supported the Humphrey-Hawkins (Full Employment and Economic Growth) Act "as a means of achieving balanced economic planning and growth and full employment . . ."[20] The British document suggested that "one powerful tool [for achieving equity for Black people in private industry] is through 'contracts compliance,'" while the American document suggested that proposed regulations which might curtail affirmative action in the Office of Federal Contract Compliance should be rescinded.[21] The urban policy sections were very similar, and in the international section similar issues like South Africa and the Middle East were included. There were many, many other similarities and in some cases identical wording of problem formation or proposed policy solutions in the two documents.

In this case, there were also substantial differences in the Black British and American cases. In the United States, for example, in the Democratic party Blacks form at least 10 percent of each of the national committees, including the governing Democratic National Committee itself, and since the Carter Administration Blacks served in top leadership positions in the party, with Ron Brown being elected chair in 1987. At the same time, there were 7.3 thousand Black elected officials in 1990, with more than half being municipal officials, and with over three hundred of these being Black mayors. Blacks serve as mayors of some of America's largest cities such as Los Angeles, New York, Atlanta, Cleveland, Washington, and Kansas City, with many serving as mayors of cities having over 100,000 population. Blacks have also made substantial increases in the national government, with twenty-three serving as members of the House of Representatives, and hundreds of senior appointees may be found to have served in key roles in the executive branch in past administrations. Finally, in 1989 Douglas Wilder was elected Governor of Virginia. This picture is a marked change from a time at the beginning of the civil rights movement when Blacks were relegated to the community level of politics.[22]

Black Britishers have, in the recent past, had virtually no meaningful representation in significant decision-making roles of the government at the national level. This state of affairs is a direct result of the instability fostered by, on the one hand, the Black Britisher himself who, in the past, regarded residence in Britain as a temporary phenomenon and did not bother with formal political participation or aspire to integration into political institutions. But on the other hand, this instability was fostered by Britons who were hostile to Black immigrants, regarding them as "guests" and, therefore, were unlikely to consider them as fit candidates for election to key political roles in the parties, local councils or national government.[23] Such a view was put vividly before the white population by racist and fascist organizations such as the National Front, which has in the past decade begun vigorously to contest local seats in Parliament as a means of putting forth its racially biased viewpoints and blocking Black advancement.

This situation is beginning to change. In 1987, four Blacks and one Asian were elected to the House of Commons. Bernie

Grant, born in Guyana and a resident of Britain since 1963 was elected in the Tottenham district. Diane Abbott, born in Jamaica and a graduate of Cambridge, was elected from the Hackney North and Stoke Newington district. And Keith Vaz, born of Indian parents and educated at Cambridge, represents Leicester and became the youngest member of Parliament. Paul Boateng, of Ghanian and English parents, elected from Brent South, is a solicitor educated at Cambridge and a rising star in the Labor party. The longest serving Black Parliamentarian is Lord David Pitt of Hampstead who was granted a life peerage in 1975. Lord Pitt has had a distinguished career in medical, political and race relations leadership, continuing to champion issues related to the poor and inner city communities.

Again, assessing the speeches on the floor of the House of Commons by the new Black members, one finds that their concerns are very similar to those of their counterparts in the Congressional Black Caucus. For example, in his intervention on the Local Government bill, Bernie Grant pointed to the situation of his constituents: "Black people are four times as likely to be unemployed as their white counterparts, and those who are employed are in the most low-paid and menial jobs. They suffer the worst housing, education and health care, and they have the worst chances in life of any group in society."[24] Grant, whose speech could easily describe the African-origin community any place in the Diaspora, went on to oppose the government's tampering with contract compliance or labor clauses in local construction contracts. In a wide-ranging debate on Southern Africa in December 1987, he took the floor to describe in some detail the reason why the British government must oppose Apartheid in South Africa, why the existing government's position was put to "shame," why he considered that government to "collaborate with the dictators in Pretoria" and why its view of the African National Congress was indefensible. He continued lucidly to point out flaws in the government's approach to the Namibia situation and to support economic assistance for the Southern African Development Coordinating Conference.[25]

On March 10, 1987, in her speech on the floor, Diane Abbott attacked the Inner Cities legislation put forth by the Conservative government, saying that the government's answer to the poor and homeless of the inner city was "to build prefabricated housing on the outskirts of London" and amounted to a policy of "bringing yuppies in and shipping the poor and homeless out"; she suggested that this was a "disgraceful and squalid episode."[26] Paul Boateng, also a passionate supporter of housing for the poor, pointed out in debate in May 1987 that the government had cut housing spending from 6.7 billion to 2.7 billion pounds in action that mirrored the housing cuts of the Reagan Administration. The government, he said, should listen to Mother Teresa about the housing needs of the poor—"The odor of sanctity clung as it never did to the Prime Minister."[27] Boateng also chose the occasion of the debate to denounce the government's "Action for Cities" policy as "a shameless deceit" because, with unemployment in his district having risen 273 percent since 1979, the government's approach amounted to high gloss. The government's plan, he said, was to spend only 22.2 million pounds on housing repairs, while the need was for 146 million pounds.[28] Similarly, immigration is a sensitive concern to Black residents, and accordingly, Boateng and Abbott attacked the government's attempt to add administrative powers to regulate those who overstayed their leave in the country as being unnecessary, given the low incidence of such cases.

Party politics, however, are most effective when those involved have a substantial relationship both to the key roles in the party institution itself and to the governmental bodies where the party attempts to implement its notions of public policy. The treatment of community issues at the policy level makes it possible for us to see how the national interest of the Black community competes with other interests within national political institutions.

In Britain, therefore, the Black community has served and is serving as the incubator of strategies whereby the community secures its place in society.[29] It would appear that these communities must be stabilized before launching national political strategies or being able to function effectively in roles outside of the community base. As we have previously suggested, resistance has been necessary because of physical attacks upon members of the Black community by groups of whites, but especially, the threat to the community safety has come from the police itself. Howe, however, is correct in that there has been the inevitable rise of a Black middle class, but rather than decrying this fact, it should be embraced because it makes possible the pursuit of a wider range of political strategies.

The international image of the difference between American and British societies is that the latter is more civil, less prone to violence, while the former plays out an unrestrained saga of the "wild wild west." The decade of the 1960s in America was a particularly violent one; crime, including incidents of murder with handguns, generally shot up; there was more police corruption; there were sensational political assassinations; there were mass murders—and in the middle of this, a gigantic struggle between the police and a youthful protest generation.[30] A generation of white youths was protesting American involvement in the Vietnam War, while Black youths were protesting the denial of civil and human rights. Temporarily diminished were the distinctions between class and race as the battles between the police and protesters illuminated the role of the police as the first line of defense for the established policies and resources of the dominant group. Even in a very favorable assessment of police behavior, an author says that "abrasive police-Negro relations" was only a symptom of a much greater dilemma. This was typically illustrated by occasions when city officials sent the police, visible representatives of their power, into Black communities to contain political protest, for example, against the lack of employment. When conflict occurred, the suggestion by city officials that "a police review board was needed" was logically referred to by the author as "shallow thinking."[31] Indeed, it is shallow thinking for anyone to suggest that the police are more than agents of social control; in this era the "higher authorities" attempted to aid them by the passage of the Omnibus Crime Control and Safe Streets Act of 1968, an act which put additional resources into police training, community relations and the purchase of sophisticated weapons and defensive armaments for urban police to quell riots. The act also set up new agencies such as the Law Enforcement Assistance Administration to fund a massive data gathering effort.

Still, there is the fact that police reacting to protest often carry their duty to maintain public order too far, and certainly in the 1960s police action followed the pattern of racism in society, brutally injuring most severely and most repeatedly Black citizens.[32] For example, after the Detroit rebellion of 1967, surveys revealed

that while 36 percent of respondents felt the rebellion had occurred because of racial discrimination, 38 percent felt the police
had a role in triggering the precipitating incidents.[33] And more
than half of those interviewed believed that police brutality was
practiced regularly on blacks.[34] The U.S. Riot Commission Report confirmed these data and others which indicated that the
tension between youths, especially Black youths, and the police
was extremely high. The report explained that young people
were often the most aggressive and visible elements in the community on the streets of urban neighborhoods and that the police had made natural targets of youths because of their substantial and growing role in the commission of crimes. Thus, police
harassment was considered in some cases by police and community residents alike as a natural part of crime prevention.
Such policing tactics as "stop-and-frisk," aggressive interroga-
tion or "move-on" orders were known collectively as "aggressive preventive patrol."[35] Such contact of police with community
residents often led to death, usually the death of a resident at
the hands of the police, and the incidence of such deaths of minority residents is still disproportionately high.

One organization which monitors the criminal justice system
in America defined police brutality as "the psychological, verbal
and physical misuse of authority." In addition, they suggested
that the court system supported this misuse of authority: "In
every major American city the long list of 'Justifiable Homicide'
returned (as a verdict) in the wake of eye-witness testimony to
the contrary has caused many blacks to live in fear of police and
creates a mistrust of the court as a place where justice is done."[36]
The report went on to say that of 3,860 persons executed by various methods in America since 1930, 54 percent were Black, and
of the 405 men executed for rape (generally of a white woman)
90 percent were Black. The report also pointed out that while the
Black population of the United States was officially 12 percent of
the overall total, nearly 40 percent of the prisoners in American
jails were black.[37]

What is seldom adequately covered in surveys of police attitudes among Blacks, or in reports of the external symbolic value
of police as a social target for alienated peoples, is the role police
assumed in surveillance and disruption of Black organizations
through informants, police raids, electronic eavesdropping and

by other methods. So pervasive was this surveillance in the 1960s for example, which increased as the rise of Black militant groups produced added tensions, that special operations mounted by the Federal Bureau of Investigation, the Central Intelligence Agency, the Internal Revenue Service and other agencies focused on the most moderate groups such as the NAACP and the Southern Christian Leadership Conference.[38] In addition, the psychological burden that finds Black people constantly under suspicion for wrongdoing was reinforced by the passage of laws strikingly like the "sus" law enacted in Britain and actually in force in America at the turn of the century, laws that permit the police to stop, interrogate and detain individuals suspected of crimes.

In the early stages of substantial contact between the colored community and the police in Britain, the government considered that the function of police was solely one of maintaining public order in places of immigrant settlement; and the Home Secretary praised the police for its handling of the Notting Hill and Dudley disturbances in 1958 and 1960 respectively. However, even in this period, the Campaign Against Racial Discrimination (CARD) and the West Indian Standing Conference began to level a barrage of complaints against police conduct in their areas, complaints that quickly outnumbered those of whites three to two.[39] As Professor Michael Banton observed it was becoming clear that "it is necessary to see his [the policeman's] activities as being governed more by popular morality than by the letter of the law" and that "public morality" was a basic factor in the attitude of the police toward colored immigrants.[40] Still, there was an increase in the appointment of "liaison officers" by Scotland Yard as both the Yard and the higher authorities believed, naively it appears, that the police might play a role in mediating and regulating the civil aspects of race relations beyond the "criminal" policing function.

Crime in Britain, as in the United States, continued to rise in the 1960s, and as British racial homogeneity lessened and police control tactics intensified, the image of Britain as more tolerant and civil than the States began to disappear. The problem was that with the establishment of a community zone (or ghetto, if you will), what is defined by law enforcement officials as mere "crime" may be a reflection of the poverty or cultural difference of neighborhood residents or an expression of their alienation toward white authority or acts which manifest a strategy of survival and are, as such, part of the political socialization of the newcomers. In this situation, the British police exercised a dual function, maintaining civil order, but also as an arm of the immigration apparatus, carrying out an aggressive mandate to capture "illegal aliens."[41]

This dual function, together with the implementation of white community norms and values, led the police to employ a variety of tactics against the Black population which Clifford Lynch, of the West Indian Standing Conference, described as "the systematic brutalization of black people and police blackmail, planting drugs, trumped up charges and physical assaults."[42] To add to this, the British also found themselves in the midst of a Black social movement in the 1960s and responded by a "Law and Order" campaign similar to that introduced by President Nixon in the United States. It also entailed the use of Special Squads and new laws, such as the Industrial Relations Act and the Prevention of Terrorism Act.[43]

A 1981 report indicated that numerous isolated events occurred, among them the "battle of Atlantic Road" in which a Nigerian diplomat who was visiting Brixton was arrested just as he was about to drive off in his own car, a white Mercedes, and was charged with stealing the vehicle; even after the diplomat presented proof of ownership, the arresting officer said, "I don't bloody care. I want you to say you stole this car."[44] This report went on to detail six attacks upon Black people in the Lambeth (Brixton) area by the Special Patrol Group (SPG) between 1975 and 1979. "Over 1,000 people were stopped on the streets," the report said, "and 430 people arrested; 40 percent of those arrested were black, more than double the estimated black proportion of the local community. The SPG operation was concentrated around four housing estates, all with high black populations."[45]

Another report confirmed this view of the activities of the SPG, a section of the Metropolitan Police, suggesting that its activities in Brixton were not isolated and that similar incidents occurred in other areas, such as Peckham, Lewisham, Tooting, Stoke Newington, Kentish Town, Hackney and Notting Hill, all areas with high Black populations. In addition, the report said,

"The SPG has changed from its original function as a police support anti-crime unit to a police commando unit conducting indiscriminate stop-and-search activities in these 'high crime' areas and for use against demonstrations and pickets." [46] The report inferred the political use of the police against those expressing forms of dissent against public policies related to race or acts of police or government misconduct; the extremely flexible tool of "sus" law was thus exploited. Section four of the 1824 Vagrancy Act requires the evidence of two police officers that the accused "acted suspiciously on two separate occasions" (which could be minutes apart), while under the Immigration Act of 1971 the police have the power to arrest without a warrant anyone "suspected" of being an illegal entrant. The combination of these two laws gives wide discretion to police, and as a result the Black community's evaluation of the police has grown more strongly negative since 1958.

The Black community protested, through its own organizations, newspapers, and other means at its disposal, police brutality which they suffered on the streets, in shopping centers, and other common areas of life, where the police often set upon individuals, attacking them and making arbitrary arrests. These arrests, the author says, were often the first step in a policing process which "appears to have become a means to a very different end, that of controlling a whole community." [47]

It is important to establish that the attacks upon the Black community, although they rose in volume, did not prevent the establishment of a community as the base of Black politics in Britain. In fact, one can see in the attacks evidence of the growth of community institutions and political strategies of protest mobilization, education and the articulation of group interests. For example, the Black population has been associated with the act of "mugging," a crime closely related with material deprivation. [48] But just as in America with the growth of the Black Panther party from the "lumpen-proletariat" elements of the Black community, the hustler has also often provided forms of community leadership in Britain, as George Jackson and Eldridge Cleaver had done. [49]

In 1970, the Mangrove Restaurant in Notting Hill, a gathering place for West Indians, was raided three times by the police in search of drugs—which they never found. But the attacks provided the occasion for a demonstration to defend the Mangrove, and although this event touched off a full-scale riot with about 500 policemen battling demonstrators mainly armed with placards, the "Mangrove 9 Struggle" became institutionalized as a highlight of West Indian culture, politics and history.[50] The "New Cross Massacre" occurred on January 18, 1981, when a petrol bomb was thrown into a house where a birthday party was being held. As a result, thirteen black youths died and twenty-seven more suffered serious injuries. Although this attack took its place in a line of growing racist murders and fire bombings, the black community leadership chose this event to make a dramatic response, and the resulting demonstration on March 2 saw nearly ten thousand people, mostly Blacks, march through central London in an important display of solidarity in opposition to such racist violence.[51]

Then, there is Carnival, which began in Notting Hill in 1975 as a festival of Caribbean culture, including music by steel bands, revelers in the parades in colorful costumes, and dancing like that in the traditional festival held in Trinidad each year. In 1976, white residents of the area made a serious attempt to ban Carnival from the streets, thus provoking a struggle by Blacks for the right to hold it. After a pre-Carnival incident involving young Blacks, the police masked the concern of white residents about strange music and noise and the sheer audacity of the Blacks in sponsoring such a public event by arguing that Carnival was a "threat to the public" and an "occasion of hate and violence."[52] So, as Carnival grew, the police presence grew from sixty in 1975 to nearly twelve hundred in 1976, making a clash inevitable in the view of some participants and subverting the fact that the demeanor of the nearly quarter of a million revelers in the past was generally peaceful.

One observer felt that this conflict over Carnival was symptomatic of that which faced the Black community over the trials involving other conflicts, such as the Notting Hill defendants, and that government officials were aware from the previous conflicts of Peckham Fair in 1972, Brockwell Park in 1974, the Cricketwood Club in 1974, Leeds Bonfire in 1975, and others that they had the potential to involve Blacks in the criminal justice system.[53] As the act of countering the court system would often entail strong organizational efforts within the Black community, it was inevitable that some activists came to see the battles over Carnival as productive of a "revolutionary" ethos.[54]

Given the events in the establishment of Carnival and the battles with the police during Carnival, these activities become part of the general interpretation of race conflict so prevalent in Britain today. The act of organizing Carnival organizes the Black community and becomes a platform for community politics of another variety.

Now, the importance of dealing briefly with manifestations of the police/Black community conflict is to show that there is indeed a conflict of serious proportions growing with the police/Black community aspect of the conflict being merely symbolic. It has been one thing for the authorities and their representatives at the community level—CRC, RRB, the police and so on—to deal with new immigrants ambiguous about their permanent status in Britain, either because of their own objectives or their perception that British society was hostile to them. But it is quite another thing for a new generation of Black youths, most of them born in Britain, to declare that they are, indeed, permanently in residence and that they will fight for the rights extended to all British citizens on the basis of racial equality.[55]

Such determination means that the response of symbols of oppression like the police or other agents of social control are likely to be qualitatively different in the future and that the range of political strategies is likely to diversify. More immediately, however, it means that the rebellions which broke out in Britain in June and July of 1981 are but a manifestation of that sentiment to establish, through their own violent struggle, the right to a place in society, the right to be treated without discrimination and the right to experience access to the acquisition of individual and community resources the society has to offer—also on terms of racial equality. The rebellions, then, become part of the arsenal of community protest strategies by which the Black community has broken through its containment and secured the undeniable attention of the national authorities with a powerful presentation of its grievances.[56]

Again, some clues to this phenomenon can be found in the Black experience in the United States. In the period 1964 to 1971, an estimate of the magnitude of the rebellions indicates that there were approximately 1,300 incidents with 65,000 people arrested; 7,000 people injured and 250 people killed—the great majority of all of these being Black. Estimates of the monetary damages have reached \$1–2 billion or more.[57] Generally, the incident which precipitated violence was some contact between the Black community and the police, and the participants can be said to have represented the entire spectrum of the Black community, as one observer suggests:[58] "If the survey research, arrest data, and impressionistic accounts are indicative, the rioters were a small but significant minority of the Negro population, fairly representative of the ghetto residents, and especially of the young adult males, and tacticly supported by at least a large minority of the black community."[59] What happened is not in dispute, but the *meaning* of why it happened is not clear from the numerous analyses which were performed, usually by white social scientists,[60] immediately after the events had occurred. The above statement continues: ". . . the 1960 riots were a manifestation of race and racism in the United States, a reflection of the social problems of modern black ghettoes, a protest against the essential conditions of life there, and an indicator of the necessity for fundamental changes in American society."[61] The explanation contained in the above statement is that the rebellions were protests designed to bring about "fundamental changes" in American society in its treatment of Blacks. But this general notion has been construed to mean, in the words of some Black Power leaders, that the actions constituted "revolutionary" activity, while others characterized them as "revolts" or "rebellions" to relieve deprivation.[62] But while social scientists found in many cases that analyses of the standard "relative deprivation" rationales did not fit the socio-economic pattern of many "riot cities," they failed to comeasure in any serious detail the more potentially explosive ingredient of alienation among Blacks of all classes arising from unjust treatment of themselves or others like them in the wider national Black community. This factor would be consistent with other findings which hold that Blacks are the most cohesive national ethnic grouping in some patterns of political behavior such as voting.[63]

In this sense, the homogeneous communities in which Blacks have either been forced to reside or have chosen to reside constitute their basis of social cohesion and, therefore, the fostering of community-based political strategies such as this strong protest method of expressing community interests (grievances and goals). Some analysts, on the other hand, have found that, rather than the pluralist notion of harmonious ethnic relations existing on the basis of equally shared values, social movements represent "social deviance" and that the real social situation is one of competition for resources, with protest movements being an effective weapon in the various struggles.[64] If this situation exists for the larger society, then how much more so for Blacks?[65]

Americans, however, have no monopoly on the misunderstanding of social protest and its forms among the most severely dispossessed in society, as indicated by the attempts of British social scientists to connect protest potential to the various social classes. For example, utilizing data from a survey conducted in 1973 and 1974, one author sets out to prove, apparently, that "simplistic theories that relate protest to crude measures of class, income or ideology simply do not survive even superficial confrontation with good quality data."[66] In the end, he finds that "colored immigrants" are least likely (by a factor of two) than "student protestors" or "revolutionary groups" to utilize protest tactics.[67] This finding, determined from the respondents' answers to surveys, severely misrepresents the history of Black resistance to oppression, and rendered the author and other scientists totally unable to foretell the rebellions and massive peace protest demonstrations which occurred in the first half of 1981.

We have mentioned the "Day of Action" March in the spring of 1981 in retaliation for the New Cross Massacre. Just as in many ways this massive march of nearly 10,000 people was the culmination of many such marches in London, the Midlands and other areas, the rebellions occurring in April and July of 1981 also represented the culmination of other such protest actions. Implicit in these activities was a strategy of retaliation for both the material deprivation of the Black population and the psychological effects of racist harassment, intimidation, rejection, and elimination of the Black population by the white population or their agents—the government, the police, the race industry bureaucracy, and other institutions such as the schools.

The 1981 outbreak of rebellion started traditionally with contact between the Black youths in the community and the police, and while confused, reports suggested that on the night of April

11 in Brixton, an incident began after an altercation between a Black youth and a policeman that quickly escalated the throwing of stones and petrol bombs by 700 or 800 youths as extra police units were coming in to quell the disturbance.[68] Fortunately, it was not lost in the British accounts of the violence that in the Brixton area approximately 40 percent of the Blacks and 20 percent of the white youths had "no jobs and no chance of jobs, no money and nothing legitimate to do all day or night."[69] But more importantly, there were also reports that this incident took place during "Operation Swamp," a program of stepped-up "stop-and-search" actions targeting the Brixton area for its "high crime" profile, which itself was a prelude to the London-wide "Operation Star."

For days before the rebellion, the police launched a team of plainclothes officers to implement Operation Swamp in Brixton, and during that period four thousand people were stopped and questioned. Young Blacks interpreted this as a show of force by the police and their retaliation was a serious response to the misjudgment that the Black community would take this harassment—as they previously had done—without any opposite show of force.[70] Other reports indicated that out of 1,000 people in Brixton stopped by police only 150 were arrested. "That meant 850 people stopped without justification. The mixture was ready to explode."[71] The rebellion left nine buildings demolished, six additional structures damaged and over 150 looted; in the areas where revolt occurred, 42 percent of those arrested were youthful whites.

As the area calmed down and the authorities sought to assess the situation, on July 3 violence erupted in heavily Asian Southall and spread into other industrial centers, bringing out both Black and white as well as Asian working-class youths, many of whose jobs were threatened or had been eliminated as a result of a worsening economic situation. The fact that working-class white youths were involved appeared to have induced a rational tone to the debate over what policies the government should follow in making what then Prime Minister Thatcher called "reconciliation."[72] Most notable of the reported comments among politicians on the issue were those of the shadow home minister in the Labor party who suggested that a massive infusion of funds would be necessary and perhaps the establishment of occupational quotas, both in the style of the American response to the crisis of racial inclusion.[73]

The British government responded to the riots as a police matter, but it might pay more attention to the reoccurrence of this problem created by the lack of a sustained national social policy. Whereas the rebellions in the United States contributed to a backlash, producing the highly flawed thesis that the poverty programs of the 1960s were wasteful and bankrupt, rarely is it acknowledged that these programs, together with a growing economy, were responsible for a 15 percent increase in the nominal Black middle class in 1970.[74] Also, every indication shows that the Equal Employment Opportunity effort both within and outside of government has been beneficial to Black occupational advancement.[75] At the same time, trend data show that Black male participation in the labor force has declined since 1970.[76]

Just as important, the result of these policy approaches appeared essentially to have heightened class divisions within the Black community, and because the majority of Blacks are worse off, the relative position of all Blacks to whites in society worsened. What was being attempted in both the American and British responses to race was mild facilitation policies without making it possible for Blacks to own enough institutional resources to make possible the elevation and maintenance of their social development. This is what is meant by "fundamental change"— ceding enough of these public and private resources to Blacks and other dispossessed minorities would require changes that those who manage the national resources have, thus far, been unwilling to make but which circumstances may force them to consider. After all, even in America, the strategy of rebellious retaliation as a political strategy continues to be the last desperate course of Black communities, frustrated by the lack of material and social justice. Witness the incidents in 1980 in Chattanooga, and the 1989 incidents in Miami, and Bridgeport, Connecticut.[77]

Thus far, I have been discussing the comparative aspects of the African Diaspora by analyzing ways in which aspects of the political socialization and political strategies of Black communities in America and in Britain may be successfully compared as similar responses to the attempt to control these communities and make them conform to the pattern of social adjustment (assimilation, separation, repatriation, and so on) prescribed by the dominant white group. In conducting this discussion, I have omitted important aspects of Black American and Black British politics in an effort to enter another type of analysis that illustrates the extent to which Pan African relations are operative in the Diaspora. In the following chapter, I entertain a brief discussion of some salient examples of Pan African relations in the British-American African Diaspora.

6
Pan African Linkages in Britain and the United States

I have posited that the second way of analyzing relations among African peoples in the Diaspora is through the "Pan African" approach. In addition, I originally suggested that the case studies of relations among Africans studied by Shepperson and others constitute an empirical approach rooted in the discipline of historical studies.[1] In chapter 1, however, I suggested that St. Clair Drake's criterion of unity among Africans in Diaspora constitutes an appropriate objective and approach because of its potential for illuminating the interactive aspects of social relationships between African-origin communities.

Thus, the modern Pan African movement was anchored by leaders like Malcolm X who reaffirmed the basic value of this approach.

Unity between Africans of the West and the Africans of the Fatherland will change the course of history. Just as the American Jew is in harmony politically, economically and culturally with world Jewry, it is time for all African-Americans to become an integral part of the world's Pan-Africanists, and even though we might remain in America physically while fighting for the benefits that the Constitution guarantees us, we must return to Africa philosophically and culturally, and develop a working unity in the framework of Pan-Africanism.[2]

What is clearly stated by Malcolm is that the second meaning of Pan Africanism implicitly posits the unity of African peoples in a specific kind of revolutionary process that is an "integral part of the world's Pan Africanists reality," "physically fighting" in America, but having a dual responsibility to develop a functional unity with other African peoples *in a modern and evolving sense*.

The distinction is that, unlike traditional historical analyses that were concerned to focus the impact upon Africa, these cases consider both events on the continent and those outside Africa in the developed industrial Diaspora of the West.

Below, we will attempt to present several aspects of this case study to illustrate Malcolm X's approach to the African Diaspora, using the special environment of the U.S. and British African communities. Those aspects will include the Campaign Against Racial Discrimination, the Black Power movement and its effect on the Black Panther party and the Racial Action Adjustment Society, and the formal Pan African movement itself.

CARD

It is widely known in the United States that one of the results of the Montgomery Bus Boycott (1955–1957), through which Blacks in that Alabama town won the right to integrated bus transportation, was the emergence of Dr. Martin Luther King, Jr. and the Southern Christian Leadership Conference. Little known, however, was the fact that a few years later this boycott would provide a model for the political strategy of Blacks in Bristol, England. In April 1963, a Bristol bus driver said to a Black West Indian attempting to board the bus, "Sorry, no colored." This was to become the catalyst for a movement against a common injustice. Fortunately, Paul Stephenson, a young Black West Indian, born in Bristol, had just returned there from a three-month stay in the United States where he had observed the tactics of the civil rights movement, then in full swing. As an official of the West Indian Development Council, he called for a boycott of the buses to force the transport company to adopt a policy of integrated service; as a result of subsequent demonstrations, the management capitulated on August 28, ironically the day of the March on Washington. In addition, while Black Americans were marching in Washington, Black Britons were marching in sympathy and solidarity with them from Notting Hill to the American Embassy in London.[3]

This identification with the American civil rights movement set the stage for the recognition given Dr. King by the Black leadership in Britain in December 1964, when he was en route to Oslo, to accept the 1964 Nobel Prize for Peace. On December 7, at a reception given in his honor in London, he suggested that one way for the Blacks in Britain to fight injustice and discrimination was to launch a civil rights movement, but that to do so would require an organization.[4] This seemed a useful suggestion and was accepted enthusiastically, particularly since the recent successful passage of the 1964 U.S. Civil Rights Act demonstrated that this strategy could work. In addition, this had been a time in Britain of escalating physical violence against colored immigrants and especially of intimidating behavior by groups such as the North London branch of the Ku Klux Klan, which had physically attacked Blacks, burned crosses and sent hate mail.[5]

In response, the Black leadership in London organized the Campaign Against Racial Discrimination at a public meeting in February 1965; its first conference was held a few months later in July. The Campaign was to be a multiracial organization that would encompass the main colored groups, such as the West Indian Standing Conference (WISC), the Indian Workers Association-Great Britain (IWA-GB), and the National Federation of Pakistani Associations (NFPA), all of which had previously been involved in various aspects of race relations work.

The work of the organization was carried out by a national council which met quarterly and was elected by the annual delegate convention, an executive committee which met monthly, and special committees on various subjects. At the outset, the organization called for effective antidiscrimination laws in housing, insurance and credit as well as public accommodations; fair immigration laws and repeal of the Commonwealth Immigration Act of 1962 and the 1965 White Paper, and equal education for children of immigrants, including special language services.[6] Under the chairmanship of Dr. David Pitt, a prominent civil rights leader and physician, CARD set objectives to fight prejudice and racial discrimination against colored people and all minority groups, to achieve effective legislative solutions to the problem of racial integration, to coordinate the work of organizations already in the race field and to maintain liaison with other organizations having similar goals.[7] CARD's literature suggested that it would accomplish these tasks through the tactics of publicity, boycott, protest action and industrial action.

Accordingly, CARD set up projects dealing with employment testing for discrimination (sending whites to apply, then Blacks); it fulfilled requests for speakers on race discrimination all over Britain, established a complaint bureau concerning discrimination in public accommodations, employment, or personal abuse, established a voter registration program. There was also established a legal committee to work on immigration cases and legislation and to conduct investigative work with local race relations boards on police and other community matters.[8]

Perhaps the most significant aspect of the work of CARD was its legislative lobbying during 1965 for the repeal of the Commonwealth Immigration Bill of 1962 and of the White Paper of 1965 which had set the stage for the Race Relations Bill of that same year. In November, the organization sponsored a lobbying session; nearly 800 people attended meetings and then went to the House of Commons to lobby against the government's ineffectual approach. Government proposals included providing "voluntary liaison committees" to monitor racial problems and "immigrant advisory councils," all of which would provide a new source of jobs and, therefore, obscure the demands of Black leaders without seriously addressing the central issues.[9] CARD's lobbying activity did not influence the government, which went straight to the promulgation of the Race Relations Act with many of the assumptions contained in the White Paper. CARD's

objective was to replace proposed criminal penalties for race of-
fenses (which many did not believe would be allowed as bona-
fide charges against whites by the various courts) with an administrative agency to handle the large volume of complaints
and to adjudicate them. This would be a special agency, modeled after the U.S. Civil Rights Commission, a body which had
already established that it was not easy to bring suit for civil
rights violations.

CARD was instrumental in initiating what came to be the
Race Relations Board, although that board, too, had little power
except the highly unsatisfactory right to urge voluntary conciliation.[10]

A second project conducted in the summer of 1966 aimed at
both voter registration and stimulating discrimination complaints. The model for this was developed by a CARD official
who had been in the United States observing the 1964 summer
project sponsored by the Council of Federated Organizations
and civil rights groups (such as the NAACP, SCLC, SNCC,
CORE).[11] That project for Amnesty International invited hundreds of interracial volunteers into the deep South for that summer to conduct voter registration campaigns, teach in freedom
schools, participate in sit-in demonstrations, and carry out other
acts related to the civil rights struggle. The CARD project included the conduct of a survey, begun in 1965, of more than
5,000 individuals in an effort to determine the extent to which
colored people were experiencing discrimination. The survey
concluded that "over 95 percent of the people visited had suffered from Racial Discrimination in one form or another."[12] So
effective had CARD's debut in race affairs been that Martin En-
als, general secretary of the National Council of Civil Liberties,
voiced the widely held view that up to the end of 1966, "CARD
has done an enormous job in shaping public opinion into a position where it accepts the facts of discrimination."[13]

In 1967, the organization's main legislative aim was to secure
the amendment and extension of the 1965 Race Relations Act.
The proposals, contained in a private member's bill drafted by
the CARD Legal Committee, cumulatively would extend the
scope of the act to prohibit racial discrimination in all places of
public resort, employment, housing; it would also provide in-

surance and credit services.[14] This act would be closely modeled after the 1964 Civil Rights Bill in the United States which prohibited racial discrimination in public accommodations, Title VII prohibiting discrimination in employment, and the Equal Employment Opportunity Commission.

That CARD was somewhat effective in testing for discrimination was evidenced by the growing complaints from whites that its tactics were "deceptive."[15] Actually, many of these tactics, such as testing and picketing, were growing and involving the rank and file of the member organizations.[16] Tactics also included other familiar ploys used by black civil rights leaders in the United States, some of which had been the subject of presentations given by Bayard Rustin, a former strategist for King, on his visit to Britain in February 1967. Urging the members of CARD to militant action, Rustin said he knew that perhaps the "time is not ripe for mass action" in Britain on the race question, and that while there were parallels with the American situation, he knew there were important differences. But he emphasized that the problem would only be solved through the dedication of those who made up their mind to stay in Britain and become mobilized into action, saying: "In the United States until Negroes took to the streets in sit-downs and pickets and many other kinds of direct action, the essential character of the American people was that 'they like it—there is nothing to be done'; 'what are you other people getting excited about, when they are not excited?' "

Also, Rustin, a student of labor union organizing, said that the trade union movements in both Britain the United States won the right to organize not because of the largess of their parliamentary bodies, but because the workers created "social dislocations" that were "disruptive for the nation." Then, he continued: "We are going to have to find the early methods of creating—if not physical dislocation—that moral and spiritual dislocation that comes from the dedicated action of the few."[17]

To adopt these militant tactics, as suggested, would expose internal contradictions of both class and race for the organization, since there was a serious question as to CARD's capacity for militant action beyond those endeavors which had been attempted up to that time.

With respect to the racial contradiction, the formation of CARD was taking place at the very time when the Black Power movement in Britain was launching an entire series of organizations grounded in the grass-roots working-class Black communities all over the country. Tensions began seriously to surface when in 1967 Obi Egbuna, leader of the Universal Colored Peoples Association (by then a Black Power organization), drafted a manifesto addressed to the more than 40 organizations by then affiliated with CARD, urging not only a Black, but a radical program of action, a call he reinforced in a series of speeches.[18] The effect of this was to break open the festering opposition of many Black organizations to the fact that the white liberals and radicals had largely taken over the CARD leadership. These events came to the critical point at the third annual conference of CARD when the white and moderate Black leadership was ousted and Blacks took over in a bitter, confused atmosphere.

In the center of the militant movement within CARD was Johnny James, West Indian assistant secretary of the organization and its international secretary. A proposal to change the constitution to reflect the radical changes failed the two-thirds test, but the vote carried more than half of the delegates. James had supported the proposal, and his attitude can be seen in the following statement taken from a November news conference. In a highly emotional answer to the question "Why are we angry?", he pointed to the constant attacks against Black people in Britain, the generally disappointing state of the race legislation effort, and the attempts of the communists and assorted leftists to undermine the Black movement within CARD. Then he said:

> The colored majority of CARD members and supporters is at the stage of red-hot explosion when we turn our attention to the suffering of our brothers and sisters in our own homelands, Asia, the Caribbean, and Africa. When we think generally of Rhodesia, South Africa, Anguilla Aden, the Middle East generally, the Afro-American struggle, Viet Nam, Hong Kong, etc. And when white liberals and a few Uncle Toms tell us "IT IS NOT OUR BUSINESS, THAT WHAT IS HAPPENING THERE AT HOME TO OUR BROTHERS AND SISTERS, PARENTS, RELATIVES AND FRIENDS, IS NOT OUR BUSINESS,

WE MUST NOT BROADEN CARD ETC., ETC. THEN THE BLOODY LIMIT
HAS BEEN REACHED AND PASSED![19]

The main effect of this sentiment and the movement within the
organization reflecting this attitude was to drive the remaining
white moderates into the National Committee for Commonwealth Immigrants (NCCI), a quasi-governmental race-relations
agency set up in 1964 to advise the government on its approach
to immigration reform legislation. Precipitously, whites and
some Black bodies, such as the West Indian Standing Conference, had left CARD as an organization and joined NCCI in an
advisory capacity. They, thus, became absorbed into NCCI employment and voluntary advisory structure. By 1968, there existed two large competing organizations, one largely Black and
growing more alienated from government solutions, and the
other largely white and growing more official in status. Indeed,
the 1966 Race Relations bill would replace NCCI with an official
Community Relations Commission. CARD, caught between
these trends and the surging Black movement, could not survive
the year, its death reflecting the tension in the divergent streams
of race politics.[20]

Although the comparison was made between CARD and the
National Association for the Advancement of Colored People in
the United States, it is more appropriate to compare CARD to
the Leadership Conference on Civil Rights, an interracial civil
rights coalition of more than a hundred organizations. It was
understood from the beginning, however, that the lead organization in the leadership conference would be the NAACP and,
perhaps, had this been explicitly understood in Britain, CARD
would have been spared a painful lesson. The other lesson
which the case study of CARD illustrates was also experienced
earlier by COFO: when the coalition partners have individual
objectives that supercede those of the collective coalition, the organization itself becomes dysfunctional. The implication here is
that these coalitions probably were doomed to have race problems for various reasons, but their equal vulnerability to class
problems should be recognized in James' unsuccessful attempt
to "broaden" CARD. Perhaps the survival of the Leadership
Conference on Civil Rights, could be attributed in part to the fact

that it made little pretext of "broadening" the organization to include grass roots groups at all.

The Black Power Movement

Spokespersons for the new militant Black movement in Britain, like their counterpart in the United States, felt that concerns of assimilation and integration should be replaced with gaining group power. They knew that power emanated from the difficult and often "unrewarding" tasks of organizing people into a unified ability to express common demands for progress. Thus, they also knew that possessing real power did not entail having a large number of passive supporters, a militant-sounding newsletter, contacts with high officials, or political patronage. Real power, they felt, could only be gained by mobilizing the entire community: "This is the one lesson a Black British Movement must learn from the Black American Experience."[21] In these words, Chris Mullard, a Black Briton, was obviously concerned with the theme of power and, in this, he was reflecting something powerful which had come upon the scene after 1967. But it will be necessary to assert that part of the reason why the Black population in Britain was prepared to accept this new doctrine lay in the dynamism of Malcolm X. Malcolm X preceded the movement which he sparked, and although it is ironic that Mullard's references to the Black American movement mythologizes it (though not beyond recognition), it is clear that the Black movement acted as a model with Malcolm X as its progenitor as much outside the United States as within it.

Malcolm X's contribution to Pan Africanism is fundamental, as was evidenced by his reception among heads of African states, in the Organization of African States and in Britain, testimony to his impact in a modern context less than one year after the death of W.E.B. DuBois in Ghana. Immediately before the famous march for voting rights, he had spoken in Selma, Alabama, then he left to visit Britain and France. Arriving in Britain for his second visit in February 1965, he spent three days meeting with local Black leaders and with the Council of African Organizations in London.[22] Then, after his attempt to enter France had been refused by the French government, he returned to Britain for a debate at the London School of Economics, afterward making a trip to Smethwick near Birmingham for a BBC Radio interview.[23] After observing that the treatment of Black people in Smethwick could be compared to the treatment of Jews in Nazi Germany, Malcolm made the controversial statement that he "would not wait for the fascist element in Smethwick to erect gas ovens," thus angering the local government representatives.[24] Malcolm stayed in London for a week, reportedly enjoying his notoriety and the debates with the press and others to whom he was exposed. Then, upon returning to the United States, he evaluated the state of Black people as having been divided in England, France and other places in the Diaspora, by the lack of pride in common cultural roots. But as Black pride in the African independence movement became a reality, the common bonds were discovered and Black people began to want to come together. What was needed, he suggested, was "someone to start the ball rolling."[25]

Someone did get the ball rolling in Britain, but it was not until 1967 that Stokely Charmichael, then head of the Student Non-Violent Coordinating Committee (SNCC), would popularize the slogan "Black Power." Just as importantly, Carmichael was invited to a conference on "The Dialectics of Liberation" at Round House in London, and his visit in July can directly be dated as the birth of the Black Power movement in Britain.

On July 18, 1967, Carmichael gave his speech, "The Dialectics of Liberation," making four essential points. First, he distinguished between acts of individual racism and what he called a "more subtle" variant that had come to be known as institutional racism, marking it as even more deadly than the first because it effected potentially more people in more fundamental ways.[26] Secondly, he talked about "cultural integrity" as a necessary goal and process by which an entire range of behaviors, information and self-images were evaluated in an effort to see the world through one's own perspective, one's own history and culture.[27]

Then, most important, his ideology married the fight to eliminate capitalism with the opposition to imperialism around the world. Positing that the Black masses were in key positions in the urban Western industrial centers, he said that "a capitalist system automatically includes racism, whether by design or not," that "the struggles to free these internal colonies related to the struggles of imperialism around the world."[28] However, the most controversial element of this position was that the struggle against racism is most fundamental; British Marxists up to that time had posed the struggle against capitalism as most fundamental.

Carmichael was careful to point out that the struggle could not be only against racism, because this led to the philosophy of integration as the solution, which was unacceptable. "Because of the integration movement's middle-class orientation, because of its subconscious racism, and because of its nonviolent approach," he said, "it has never been able to involve the black proletariat."[29] The implication here was also a "class-struggle" dimension.

Finally, he suggested that the struggle against racism was an international struggle, allied with the struggles of other progressive peoples such as the African liberation movements, the Vietnamese, and the guerillas of Latin America. He added that while the West was concerned with the "violence" of armed struggles, the United States Black liberation movement had not moved to that stage; it was a political struggle, and "the White West will make the decision on how they want the political war to be fought" (that is, with or without violence).[30] Still, even though "Black Power . . . means that black people see themselves as part of a new force, sometimes called the Third World, we see our struggles as closely related to liberation struggles around the world."[31] At the same time, he held to the view that "it is necessary to understand that our analysis of this country [The United States] and international capitalism begins in race. Color and culture were, and are, key in our oppression; therefore our analysis of history and our economic analysis are rooted in these concepts."[32] Carmichael's speech was well received, and this address as well as his talks at Speakers Corner in Hyde Park were of historic proportions for the movement in Britain.[33] For, even though these concepts were put forth at a time when some prominent Black spokespersons in Britain and in the United

States were denouncing Black Power, his effect was overpower-
ing. Obi Egbuna was to say, "It was one of the best speeches [at
Hyde Park] I have ever heard Stokely make, and his impact on
the audience, both Black and White, was electric. By the time he
finished speaking, it had become evident that, if he was lucky
enough to get away from Britain without being arrested, he was
destined to be banned from coming back. A new phase of Black
history had begun."[34]

The effect of Black Power in Britain was similar to its impact
in the United States in that it legitimized a body of Black political
theory developed in earlier Pan African movements, the concepts of Marcus Garvey on racial integrity, and those more recent concepts of Malcolm X. But it also spawned a series of organizations and converted others to the new Black religion of
social change.

Obi Egbuna, an accomplished Nigerian novelist and playwright, had seen first hand the effect of the new Black movements in the United States on a previous trip. He was editor of
the newsletter, *United Africa,* then the organ of the Council of
African Organizations, the organization before which Malcolm
X had spoken on his trip to Britain. So, because of his previous
identification with Black Power, Egbuna became involved in the
conversion of the Universal Colored Peoples Association, a
Garveyite organization, to Black Power, and at the meeting
where this occurred he was elected its chair. Shortly thereafter,
the organization became mired in bitter wrangling over direction and competing claims of legitimacy on the part of other factions claiming they were the "real" UCPA. In April of 1968, Egbuna resigned as chairman and member of UCPA and formed a
chapter of the Black Panther party in Britain. His experiences
had taught him that he should have an organization whose core
of individuals shared the same political ideology and a similar
level of commitment to organizing.[35]

In July 1968, not long after the formation of the Panthers,
however, Obi Egbuna was jailed for writing a document threat-
ening the life of a policeman in Hyde Park and that of Enoch
Powell, an arch racist Member of Parliament. During his six-
month incarceration, the Panther organization wrote a poignant
letter to the police authorities that rejected the charges against

Egbuna and two compatriots and contrasted the right of free speech enjoyed by Enoch Powell with the restrictions placed on Black militants. Then, warning that the patience of Blacks had grown thin, the organization issued a warning that "Detroit and Newark will inevitably become part of the British scene and the Thames may foam with blood sooner than Enoch Powell envisaged!"[36] Despite the considerable support for Egbuna in the Black community, he was found guilty and drew a one-year suspended sentence. After his release, he found that the problems which had beset the UCPA had now engulfed the Panthers, and he receded into the background of the leadership.

Meanwhile, the Panther Party continued to follow essentially the Marxist ideology of the American organization, but in substantial respects it believed in Black Power. This problem was highlighted on a visit to Britain in February 1970 by Connie Matthews, representative of the international office of the Black Panthers in Algiers, which was headed by Eldridge Cleaver. In her talks in the Handsworth district of Birmingham and in Clapham and Earls Court in London, she drew about 1,000 people altogether. She emphasized such points as the Marxist nature of American Panther ideology which incorporated a cooperative role with whites—even though the latter could not be members of the Panther party. Sensing the small party cadre in Britain, Matthews also urged higher levels of political organization and education among the masses. Perhaps she had also seen newspaper reports quoting British Special Branch, American CIA and South African Intelligence Service estimates to the effect that the overall party cadre strength numbered less than 100 in all of Britain.[37]

For example, later on that year in demonstrations aimed at protesting the incarceration of Bobby Seale, the American chairman of the Black Panther party (West Coast), hundreds of Blacks in Britain and some whites marched; at one such event on March 2, in a clash with police, 16 people were arrested. The trial served to again highlight police provocation as the testimony included the eyewitness account of a white American film editor accidentally on the scene.[38] In this period, the ideological force of the movement remained the Black Power thrust. There had been riots in Leeds (1969) with officials inevitably placing the blame on such extraneous factors as the desire on the part of

Blacks for "beer" and suggesting as always that the provocation had come from "outsiders."[39]

Effectively after 1971, the Panther organization pased from the British scene, never gaining as much strength of publicity as it had in the United States. But the year of action was 1970, a year during which numerous demonstrations for Black Power had been held and a weltering variety of Black organizations had come on the scene, such as the Black Racial Action Adjustment Society (RAAS), the Black Peoples' Liberation party, the Black Workers League, the Black Unity and Freedom party, and the Black Power party. Especially important in this regard were the various magazines, newsletters and other publications of these organizations, among them the important *Black Voice* newspaper of the Black Unity and Freedom party, *Race Today* of the Race Today Collective, *Race* which became *Race and Class* after a takeover by progressives of the Institute of Race Relations in 1972, *Bradford Black,* an affiliate of the Race Today Collective in Bradford, and somewhat later in the 1970s, *Grass Roots Newspaper,* operating from a bookstore in Brixton's black community.

An important difference between the Black Power movement in Britain and the United States at this point was that while in the States the movement was relegated (even in the case of the Panthers) to those of African descent, in Britain immigrant struggles incorporated so-called "colored peoples" so that Black Power had the potential to mobilize other colored groups. Indeed, Pakistanis and East Indians also marched in many communities under the banner of "Black Power." Sometimes they protested alone, as when 600 angry Pakistanis marched on Downing Street in May of 1970 protesting attacks by "skinheads," often with West Indians and Africans.[40] Such a phenomenon has not occurred in the United States, perhaps because of the special variety of racism in America reserved for peoples of African descent and distinguishing between them and all other "colored immigrants." On the other hand, because of the size of the U.S. African community relative to other colored immigrant communities and the growth of its leadership class (both community and bureaucratic), there would be a strong resistance to the inclusion of other foreign groups in African-origin protest organizations. Then, too, many foreign immigrants pick up racist cues from the social structure and learn quickly that their social progress depends upon the *disassociation* of their lives from the lives of Blacks. Thus, colored immigration often adds another layer of racism to the existing system of stratification.

One of the main groups that mobilized during this period marking the high point of Black Power was the Racial Action Adjustment Society (RAAS), headed by Michael X (also known as Michael Abdul-Malik and Michael Defrietas), who counted himself a disciple of Malcolm X, whom he had met on Malcolm's trip to London. Michael X had come to Britain about 1951 and worked in the Cardiff dock area of Tiger Bay where historically there had been a Black community.[41] He was a self-taught intellectual, former rent collector, minister, and leader of the Black Muslims in London. The news media depicted him as an apostle of violence and as head of the Black Power movement in Britain because he had briefly been jailed in 1967 for fomenting violence in his Black Power speeches and because of his association with the Black Muslims, other Black Power groups and Stokely Carmichael.[42]

And yet, in a speech at Oxford University in November 1969, he abruptly quit the Black Power movement, resigning all of his posts and signing over all buildings registered in his name. He was reported to have felt that Britain no longer needed a Black Power movement and to have said: "Those people whose interest is the avoidance of the polarization of the races and its inevitable consequences—bloodshed, I will continue to serve."[43]

The reason for this startling turnabout became clear when Michael X revealed in 1970 that he would be opening Black House, a complex of buildings at one site which would house a resident population of 1,000, a cultural center, supermarket, meeting hall, boutique, museum and restaurant.[44] In 1969 a minor furor had been created when Nigel Samuel, son and heir of the fortune of Howard Samuel, a real estate magnate, announced the transfer of £250 thousand of his assets to Parsimony, a company that had Michael X as one of its directors. This company would finance the Black House complex which Michael X said would cater to Black and white alike. Benefits were held to raise funds, and Muhammad Ali, John Lennon, Mick Jagger, Sammy Davis, Jr., and others participated and gave funds and other valuables.[45] Actually, Black House had been in existence since 1969 and already contained a small resident population of Blacks living under a set of rules forbidding fornication, white women, card-playing or gambling, drugs or alcohol. The emphasis was on self-help, Islam, Black education, Africa and African languages and a radical view (quasi-Marxist) of British society.[46]

RAAS had 27 chapters across Britain, but even in its reformulated state after 1969, it could not escape its identification with the Black Power movement. For example, in January 1970 a fire, possibly set by an arsonist, destroyed the cultural center and damaged the prospective site of the supermarket, planned as the main income-producing arm of Black House.[47] All the vendors demanded full cash payment in advance for all services or materials delivered to Black House. Police harassment was constant for members of Black House and those in the immediate neighborhood.

One of the more notable incidents happened in July of 1970 when a Black youth was arrested by police. In response, Michael X called a meeting of Black militant organizations which decided to take the radical action of going to the police station to retrieve the youth forcibly (as Malcolm X had done in 1960 in Harlem).[48] The Black House group, the Black Panthers, and the Black Eagles, altogether numbering about a hundred, tried to enter the police station, causing injury to six police officers. After the confrontation, Michael X also used the well-known tactic of bluster and conciliation, angrily declaring that Blacks were going to "take matters into their own hands," charging that they could take anyone out of the police station because "under the uniform of the policeman is a man," ending with the thought that, although "all it would take is matches and petrol," he would much rather "find ways of working to establish harmony between peoples."[49]

The incident which led to the undoing of Michael X, ironically, was precipitated by two Black Americans. The police and courts charged Michael X with robbing a man of five pounds "and demanding three with menaces."[50] The Black House version of this incident, published in a news release, held that Leroy House, a 23-year-old actor stranded in London, had gone to work for Mervin Brown, a job placement operator who allegedly extracted £3 illegally from House's wages. A friend of House, Ray Draper, took him and his problem to Black House, whereupon Michael X decided to confront Brown and demand the return of the money. Eventually, Brown did so (because Michael and his compatriots had taken some of Brown's papers as surety), but when his papers were returned Brown promptly swore out a warrant upon the Black House leaders.[51] Michael X was tried in absentia, having fled to his native Trinidad and expressing the view from there that he could never receive a fair trial in Britain.[52] Michael X remained in Trinidad and was subsequently tried and executed for murder. Black House faded away with no part of the proposed structure having been made operational.[53]

The Pan African Movement

Another Pan Africanist aspect of the linkage among black communities in the Diaspora may be found in the formal activities of the Pan African movement itself, as it related to the liberation struggles on the continent of Africa. The massive sweep of the Black Power movement had touched virtually the whole of the progressive movement in the Americas and Canada, including the Caribbean, Europe, even Africa and as far away as Australia.[54]

The main instrument of the propagation of a Pan Africanist ideology was Stokely Carmichael, along with other members of the Student Non-violent Coordinating Committee. One of the reasons their role was possible was that by the time Black Power had developed, SNCC had within its leadership cadre politically sophisticated and internationally minded individuals, such as Charles Cobb, Jr., Courtland Cox and James Forman, and their international activities extended initially to such projects as visits to North Vietnam to shore up their progressive posture and support the developing opposition to U.S. involvement in the war.

In 1968, the theme of African unity became an explicit part of Carmichael's rhetoric. In one speech, he said, "We are coming together. We are an African people with an African ideology, and we are wandering the United States. We are going to build a peoplehood in this country or there will be no country."[55] Later that year, he evinced a maturing concept of Pan Africanism when he said on one occasion that Pan Africanism should be based on a concrete understanding of African economic and political systems.[56] By 1969, Carmichael was studying at the feet of Kwame Nkrumah, one of the fathers of modern Pan Africanism, who had been overthrown as Ghana's president in a 1966 coup and was living under the protection of President Sékou Touré in Guinea. Addressing the opening of the Malcolm X Liberation University in Greensboro, North Carolina in October 1969 from Guinea, Carmichael said, "Now we must recognize that black people, whether we are in Durham, San Francisco, Jamaica, Trinidad, Brazil, Europe or in the mother continent, are all an African people. We are Africans, there can be no question about that."[57] In this same speech, Carmichael also cited the explicit references of Malcolm X to the term and the meaning of Pan Africanism. By the time he returned to the United States in 1970, he had concluded that Black Power "logically leads" to Pan Africanism and that "the highest political expression of Black Power is Pan Africanism."[58] It is from this understanding that Carmichael concluded that, since the political expression of Pan Africanism is the African revolution, and since revolution is defined by the struggle over land and the Black man's land base is in Africa, then the most concrete form of Pan Africanism involves a return to Africa to participate in the progressive transformation of society ensuring the use of African land and resources for the benefit of the masses rather than the elite.

This doctrine guided the birth of the Pan African movement in the United States under the leadership of such individuals as Maulana (Ron) Karenga, Owusu Sadaukai, Imamu Amiri Baraka, Jimmy Garrett and Irving Davis. The meeting of the Congress of African People in Atlanta in 1970 helped to stimulate the observance of African Liberation Day on a modest scale in 1971 in places such as Washington, D.C. But the most impressive demonstration, involving more than fifty thousand Blacks, was organized by the African Liberation Support Committee, under the leadership of Owusu Sadaukai, in 1972.[59]

In Britain, the observance of African Liberation Day began on May 25, 1973, under the influence of the movement coming from America and the visits of Carmichael, Baraka, Sadaukai, and others, as well as the fact that ALD had been observed the previous year in Toronto, Dominica, Antigua and Grenada, all sources of West Indian migration to Britain. The African Liberation Committee sponsored a public meeting on that day, held at Brixton Town Hall, and a cultural presentation in Holloway at Keskidee Center.[60] Through the poems by Andrew Saulkey and the messages of the African Liberation movement representatives, it was clear, as one account indicated, that this event was an expression of the "same struggle," albeit in working-class terms.

> The system under which we as black people—belonging to the working class—live in Britain is the same system that exists from the U.S.A. to Japan, with the exception of a few countries trying to build socialism. The struggles of Black people living here, fighting for basic democratic aims are linked with the struggles of oppressed and exploited people the world over, because the system we're fighting is the same system—capitalism/imperialism, which has many faces. Whether it is the Black people of the U.S.A. fighting for basic democratic rights (with total liberation as the long term aim), or the peoples of the West Indies and African or Asian states fighting against their lackey ruling class subservient to Western Imperialism, or against the white settler rulers, the fight is the same—it is an international one.[61]

What is somewhat ironic about this Pan African sentiment is that despite the larger number of Black people directly from the African continent in Britain, there did not develop a Pan African movement with the strength it possessed in the United States. Perhaps this may be accounted for by the great factionalism within the Black community in Britain with regard to such issues as native country and culture. For example, there was a substantial Nkrumahist movement in Britain in the mid-1970s, but the membership conformed greatly to those from that region of English-speaking West Africans.

Another important point of contact which helped to institutionalize African Liberation Day was the Sixth Pan African Conference, held in Dar es Salaam in July of 1974. This meeting, held in the tradition of the previous Pan African Conferences begun in 1900 and continuing through 1945, attracted delegations representing African communities from around the world, including a delegation from Britain and with the largest from the United States, numbering over two hundred. Although the British delegation by comparison was extremely small, numbering fewer than 25, its position paper at the meeting reflected a mature grasp of the concept of Pan Africanism and a thorough understanding of the statistical dimensions of the Black community in Britain and how this translated into a conflict of values and other aspects of life with the dominant group.[62] But it was also here that the British delegation heard the practice of observing ALD reinforced most pointedly in the speech of Owusu Sadauki.[63] With this reinforcement, national observance of ALD in Britain was held in Nottingham in 1975, moved to Liverpool in 1976 and to Birmingham in 1977.[64]

In 1978, under heavy police surveillance, a march was held from Brixton to Clapham Common and, although the speakers included Horace Campbell and Ron Phillips, they also included representatives from the Institute for Positive Education in Chicago, headed by Haki Madhubuti (Don Lee), a well-known poet.[65] Then, in 1979 the venue was moved to the West Indian Center in Manchester, and by 1980, it was held in four cities, Nottingham, Manchester, Birmingham, and London, thus substantially decentralizing ALD into most of the centers of heavy Black population.[66] Moreover, since the formation of the African Liberation Committee by the Croydon Collective and the Black Unity and Freedom Party in 1973, the aims of the Pan African movement appeared to have been consistent. As expressed at that time, the movement sought to establish links with the liberation movements on the continent of Africa, to provide material support to those movements, and to create a platform to educate peoples about those struggles. These objectives were largely followed thereafter, even though the original leadership was no longer in control.[67]

Parliamentary Politics

Finally, there was also a parallel development. After a long period of community struggle with generalized and systemic racism and classism, there emerged a Black middle class in Britain that was able to mount a political offensive in the policy arena by winning elections to Parliament. Just as in the United States, the form of racism moved from the overt physical prohibitions of mobility by nonwhites, where the obvious signs "no blacks, dogs or Asians" were displayed, to more subtle forms. Here also, it was the product of institutions, as much as the conduct of agents of the white majority such as the police, that was at issue. And here also, the chief manifestation of the problem was not only racial discrimination directed against nonwhites, but also, because of England's more rigid class system, the distribution of benefit according to class.[68]

As mentioned previously, in 1987 three Blacks and one Asian were elected to new seats in the House of Commons. This development was important internationally, because they were the first to have won direct elections to a parliamentary body in all of the countries of Europe. In the heat of the campaign of 1987, these candidates agreed that if elected, they would work together because they recognized that their ability and, indeed, their responsibility to attempt to affect some change extented beyond their individual constituencies to the whole of Britain. What is important for our discussion is that the formal initiation of the Parliamentary Black Caucus (PBC) took place by an act of Pan African interaction.

Once elected, and having served nearly a full term in Parliament, the members of the Parliamentary Black Caucus decided to invite the Congressional Black Caucus of the United States (CBC) to share in the formal inauguration of the organization.[69] Accordingly, in the spring of 1969, a delegation led by members of CBC traveled to London. The CBC delegation comprised four members (Ronald V. Dellums, Chairman; Charles Rangel, George Crockett and John Conyers), together with the heads of various organization of Black politicians, such as Black mayors, county officials, legislative officials and lawyers, as well as board members of the Congressional Black Caucus Foundation.

To PBC, its supporters and detractors, this was a sign that in spite of its relatively small membership, it was able to command the support of a much larger body of fraternal legislators in a show of concrete camaraderie. In fact, the U.S. delegation was greeted by Bernie Grant, PBC chair, as "our kith and kin from across the water."[70] Lord Pitt said this moment was "pregnant with meaning." In fact, a common theme in the dinners, seminars, news conferences, and the speeches at the gala ball with 1,000 in attendance, was unity among Black and oppressed peoples in the world. An Asian newspaper, for example, commented that "the single thread of the common oppression which faces the visible minority communities—whether of African or Asian descent—in the United States or in Britain . . ." was the essence of that unity.[71] A Black community newspaper *The Voice* wrote that despite the fundamental differences between British and American cultures, the unity must reach a functional level, adding: "For far too long we have put Black America on a pedestal—a role model always out of reach and out of touch both culturally and economically. But now it is time to stand up and link up with our American cousins. It is time to forge a lasting dialogue between the two Black communities that will benefit both of us in the future."[72] The writer went on to praise the experience of Rev. Jesse Jackson's Rainbow Coalition and its attempt to be victorious within Democratic party politics.

A Black Member of Parliament, Bernie Grant, left no doubt about the meaning of the joint inaugural affair when he said at the CBC-sponsored black-tie gala dinner at the Royal Lancaster Hotel that "the reason we are here tonight is political, and we are not making any apologies whatsoever."[73] Dismissing any possible unhappiness on the part of Neil Kinnock, leader of the Labor party, at this obvious strengthening of the idea of Black political organization within the party, he went on to say that "there are many rooms in Mr. Kinnock's house and we occupy just one of them."[74] Kinnock, as suggested in the previous chapter, had been cool to the idea of Black Sections within the party, along with his ally Paul Boateng, the one newly elected Black MP who had refused to join the Black Caucus. Despite Boateng's rejection of the caucus, all of the PBC members responded to his absence at the dinner with conciliatory statements. With these minor distractions, the event was pronounced a success by press and participants alike, an illustration that African unity was being utilized as a weapon in the fight for an institutional share in the Labor party.

There are basic reasons for the obviously similar love-hate attitude of Black people in Britain toward the Labor party and the Black American attitude toward the Democratic party. This attitude exists because the two parties are liberal enough to embrace some of the social agenda necessary to give the Black community a promise of viability, but occasionally give strong signals to Blacks that they are also as capitalist and as racist as the Republican and Tory parties, so that their support for the Black agenda is undependable. Given this undependability, Black political strategies in this arena are unstable, bending to the currents of support from their major coalition partner at times and standing alone at other times, unable to follow the lead of the more conservative political direction of the Tory and Republican parties. Thus, activists are often driven to a politics of independence as a way of bring maximum leverage and discipline to the process, and the rewards are often minimal. And while Jesse Jackson's presidential bid is a variation of this strategy in the United States, it is interesting that at this writing the seeds of the strategy are beginning to appear in England as well.[75]

A 1987 Runneymede Trust Report on Black politics in Britain concluded that with their growing political participation Blacks are simultaneously concerned "that no party should take their votes for granted and to demand equality in the political as well as in the economic sphere."[76] This theme was also sounded by Bernie Grant shortly after he was elected to Parliament.[77] This concern reaches the uppermost part of the Black leadership; in 1987, Bernie Grant admitted that the Labor party had little knowledge of or respect for the aspirations of Black people.[78] In America this concern in part accounted for the startling drop in Black turnout in the 1988 election.

As a result of the Vauxhall by-election issue, explored in the previous chapter, Bernie Grant threatened to withhold the votes of Blacks from the Labor party as a sanction against the party for its choice of candidate, a choice which went against the wishes of local party activists. Grant was aware, then, of the necessity to use the unity of PBC within Labor party circles; when the Vauxhall incident occurred, he wrote "as Chair of the Parliamentary Black Caucus" to convey the feelings of Black constituents on the matter.[79] Grant and PBC have proceeded to construct a modest but substantive program urging the sponsorship of a policy institute (such as the Joint Center for Political Studies), the unification of Europe as a single market by 1992, and Black business development.[80]

Conclusion

This closing discussion will briefly address the main theoretical findings of the case study and comments upon the substantive question of political strategy among Blacks in Britain.

With regard to the theoretical aspect, I will discuss the initial assumptions in chapter 1 that there were at least two approaches that might be used in the analysis of political dynamics in the African Diaspora, the comparative method and the Pan African method.

Given the high degree of similarity between British and American experiences in the overall relations of the Black communities and their leadership structures to the host white community and its authority structures, I believe the comparative method to have been very useful. The conclusions of social system similarity which follow assume also that there exists an underlying empirical relationship among them. Thus, the analysis found:

1. structural similarity of social, political and economic systems between Britain and the United States promoting similar policy approaches to race relations;

2. cultural similarity with regard to racial attitudes of whites in Britain and the United States;

3. similar political and social reactions by whites, to the presence of Blacks—given the maturing state of the British Black community;

4. similar political reaction by the respective Black communities to the reception by the white host societies;

5. similar violent racial conflict patterns in each society.

Regardless of the admittedly important differences between the British and American societies, I believe that there exists a relationship among such factors as the overarching system of authority, the cultural attitudes of citizens with respect to race, the racial policy of officials, the political reaction of Blacks to discrimination and subordination, and the consequent level of social conflict in society.

This study was centered less formally on the question of stratification as the normal focus of "race relations" studies, but rather more explicitly on race and social conflict and on the use of political power, both legitimate and illegitimate, by the Black communities. In this, we were cognizant of a pre-existing study by Ira Katznelson which emphasized the same major variable: "The relative power of racial groups to make and carry out decisions and nondecisions—institutionally expressed and organized—is the most significant independent variable for the student of race politics."[81] In his study, Katznelson uses the methodology of comparative politics to examine the political participation of Blacks for the relative periods 1900–1930 in the United States and 1948–1968 in Britain in an attempt to measure similar institutional outcomes given the best empirical situation.

This study has assumed that it is possible to measure both societies within the period of the past three decades, roughly 1960–1990, but this need not obviate the simultaneous understanding that Black British society is in transition, engaged in an effort to solidify the basis of the community by attempting to acquire the resources of adequate social services, employment, stability in immigration policy, favorable administration of race laws, and decent treatment of individuals and groups within the community by the established authorities. At the same time, the violent rebellions illustrated that there is a permanent Black British presence that is expressing itself and, thus, exhibiting the demand for permanent community status with dignity, providing the basis for a fair comparison with a similar African-origin community in the United States.

In any case, I formed the judgment after a short period of field work in Britain, as early as 1972, that the differences illustrated that the two communities were about one decade apart in the pace and style of similar race dynamics, and this schedule appears to have held firm. However, it is an open question, given the Black experience in the States, whether and to what degree the relationship between *community political strategies* materially changes the distribution of *power* in favor of Blacks as the rapidly maturing Black community in Britain gains stability.

Nevertheless, I have utilized a comparative approach to examining community relations, party politics, police-community relations and the rebellions as a way of establishing the comparative baseline of race conflict; it has been shown that the approaches between societies by both Blacks and whites, even to the adoption of striking similar institutions and strategies in the competition, have been amazingly close. In this, I confirm Katznelson's findings[82] and have attempted to show in addition that whereas the main causal variable for the institutional production of policy outcomes and resource distribution is state action (power), an analysis of the effect of this use of power upon the Black communities shows the autonomous organizational and cultural base of the community itself to be a key dependent variable as it responds politically to the initiatives of the dominant group.

The study referred to above makes a convenient departure for a discussion of the Pan African method because it replicates the approach of many political scientists in comparing the political dynamics which emerge from the vertical relations between the Black community and the polity. We have asserted that the Pan African method involves an analysis of functional interaction, and in this sense, it is concerned with the *horizontal* relations of transnational African communities as a resource for each other's competition (struggles) with the dominant systems of each society. In addition, while the comparative method artificially restricts the comparison of variables to the selected units of analysis (i.e., Britain and the United States), the Pan African method also recognizes and utilizes horizontal linkages which emerge from other influences exerted by other African communities. In this sense, the Pan African method of study is based on a assumption similar to that of Black studies in that it recognizes the dominant influence of the racial variable within the context of the analysis of domestic relations, while the Pan African method recognizes the dominant influence of African identity, history and culture in the transnational relations of Black peoples in the African Diaspora.

Given this, it is necessary to reject the bald assumption contained in the following statement in the study *Colour and Citizenship* that, "None of these (Martin Luther King, Jr., Malcolm X, Bayard Rustin or Stokeley Charmichael) visits (except perhaps King's) deserved to be recorded for their direct consequences in the United Kingdom." These visits illustrate the importance of the interaction by Black American leaders with their counterparts in Britain, by showing their impact upon the development of organizations and movements, and thereby support the claim of the credibility of Pan Africanism as concept and reality. Ironically, the author goes on to suggest that these visits are irrelevant because the ideas the visitors espoused were not limited to America, but had relevance to Britain, a relevance intensified by the "attention paid to the American race relations by the British press."[83] This statement belies a gross level of awareness of and appreciation for the empirical relationships reconstructed, even in this casual examination of the interaction between Blacks in Britain and the United States. I have attempted to show that, indeed, the visits of the individuals named and others, while some may have considered that they did not have obvious consequences for British society and government directly, did influence the course and character of the Black response to the control agents of British society by stimulating the use of political tactics to oppose racism.

In this sense, I have pointed out the extent to which Black American activists were involved in the founding of organizations such as the Campaign Against Racial Discrimination and even such competing groups as the Black Panther party and the Black Muslims, and through the Black Power movement itself spawned a whole host of other organizations. More importantly, this movement developed an ideology of resistance to British racism and a conception of the Black community as a source of power potential through which strategies could be operationalized to confront police, white liberal race experts, local government councils, social service programs, landlords and so on. In fact, based on an historical note unearthed by Dr. David Pitt, chairman of CARD, which found that in response to Black rebellions taking place in the United States in 1919 there were similar rebellions by Blacks in Liverpool, London, Cardiff, Hull and other British cities in 1920, and together with what we know of the influence of Marcus Garvey, I would also suggest that the Pan African syndrome may have influenced British society much longer than anyone has dared to imagine.[84]

7
The Environment for Race Politics in the United States and South Africa

I have attempted to demonstrate that a theory of Pan Africanism has analytical implications—that its explanatory power can be used to examine aspects of Black life in the African Diaspora. In this case, I will show that the African continent also provides fertile models for comparative and Pan African analysis. Here our examination of the Black communities in the United States and South Africa will not be groundbreaking, for other scholars interested in "race relations" have long pointed to the similarities between U.S. and South African racial development. One of the most important of these has been George Frederickson in his book, *White Supremacy*.[1] Also, Bernard Magubane, Gail Gerhart and others have alluded to the involvement of African Americans in the political and cultural life of Black South Africans.[2]

I will discuss, first, the environment for race relations in both the United States and South Africa, then, in subsequent chapters the comparative aspects of political life in the two communities and the Pan African relations between the South African and American Black communities.

198

The Evolution of South African–United States Race Environment: A Brief Historical Introduction

The first and most prominent distinguishing feature of the South African–U.S. environment for race relations was the monopoly of political power by the European-origin racial group in both societies. In the United States this fact may be viewed as more natural in one sense because the dominant group in the population is by far numerically larger. On the other hand, as Gunnar Myrdal noted in his work, the American "dilemma" exists because the practices of cultural, political and economic superiority by the white majority conflict with the equalitarian principles that are supposed to govern the entire political order and to result in the equitable distribution of social benefits.

The result of this "dilemma" is a racially stratified society that resembles the South African system in terms of its objective possession of power.[3] In both systems, Blacks are at the bottom of society. In the South African case, however, there is a system of racial separation and dominance by the European minority enforced by law, politics and the police power. South Africa acknowledges no such moral dilemma since its practices are consistent with its legal concepts. Its dilemma arises from the equally objective fact that it is a minority—a white minority—in a Black population which is launching a challenge to its continued domination. This is a political dilemma for the South African whites somewhat different in nature from that political dilemma which exists in America.

In this context, the monopoly of power in South Africa made possible a more oppressive racism which, although it was founded upon the back of Black people, was applied to Asians as well. Thus, the definition of Apartheid—the segregation of Blacks and whites—would be meaningless without the fact that it was also the segregation of whites with superior material status and political rights from Blacks who have inferior material status and political rights. In any case, the syntax changed historically to reflect the policies of a given government, for example, from "separate development" to "multinational development."

This kind of inequality marked the classic definition of the term "herrenvolk," a kind of social system that emerged as a by-product of European civilization. That America was a part of this process is confirmed by an early psychologist, who said: "A child brought up in the Southern states of America's Union learns first to think of man in general; but later he learns to discriminate between white men and 'niggers,' and their differences become so accentuated and their similarities so neglected that, but for his command of the word man, he would be in danger of forgetting that black and white men are varieties of one species of Man."[4] America shared the patrimony of the European system of social (racial) perspectives, the same system that was operative within South Africa. This made possible a certain intercourse of Americans with other whites in South Africa during this period. For instance, Americans supported the British in the Anglo-Boer War partly on the assumption that a victory by the British would liberalize race relations in South Africa and that this would be good for the developing commerce in gold and diamonds. In fact, an American publication, *Review of Reviews*, was able to say in 1903: "The authorities of British South Africa are observing with interest the progress of Negroes in America, and are expecting advice and help from them in promoting the advancement of the Negro Tribes that now come under their [British] Jurisdiction."[5]

This sentiment helped to foster Black American ties with Black South Africans, because of the parallel desire of American white industrialists to exploit passive, trained Black labor as well. Thus, the American Black leader, Booker T. Washington, who developed the Tuskegee educational institution, sought— with the encouragement of American and South African white business owners—to expand to South Africa his "model" of making Blacks suitable for industrial labor. From an early period in the history of these two states, then, it is demonstrable that in both situations the role of Blacks in the labor force was a paramount concern. Such has been the case in the modern period as well.

For instance, it is a modern feature of the workings of the American and South African capitalist economies that Africans suffer high levels of unemployment, with the unemployment rate in both instances running at about 15 percent. Also, in both cases the official rate probably grossly understates the real situation. In South Africa in 1980, the official Black unemployment rate was listed at 9 percent, but if the "economically active" Black population included all Blacks potentially in the labor force, the rate would probably double.[6] In the United States, the undercount of the Black population and the much higher rate of short-term unemployment for Blacks mean that the real rate could also be as high as 30 percent of the potential Black work force.

At the same time, in both countries, Blacks make up the largest proportion of the unskilled work force, and the economic projections for such labor are not bright because employers are adding technologically sophisticated capital equipment and trained employees. This development has been responsible for the downward trend in Black male labor force participation rates in the United States during the past three decades. In South Africa, the only factor which makes possible the growth of the Black labor participation rate is the easing of the job reservation system, making possible the hiring of semi-skilled Blacks in jobs formerly reserved for whites. Nevertheless, South African economists admit that the economy is currently unable to generate the requisite jobs needed to keep pace with the expanding African population.[7]

Neither American nor other foreign investment was able to contribute to the generation of jobs for Black South Africans at a pace that would promote full employment. The initial impetus for American investment was the belief that South Africa constituted a "stable" social system under white control where vast profits might be made. In this regard, one finds expressions such as those by the President of Jeffrey Company of Ohio, who said in 1965, at the opening of a factory in South Africa: "We have complete faith in the soundness of the South African economy, full confidence in the stability of the country . . ."[8] In that same year, a companion attitude was expressed by the chairman of the Norton Company of Massachusetts at the opening of a new factory: "I think South Africa is going to remain a strong country, led by white people."[9] These plant openings were stimulated by the fact that after 1950, profits grew in South Africa at average rates of 15–20 percent, but wages for Blacks increased, for example, by only 22 cents between 1950 and 1975.[10] This situation inevitably led to an explosive period of opposition to South African Apartheid in both its racist and capitalist dimensions. With the rising effectiveness of the opposition both in South Africa and in the United States, many American companies have withdrawn from South Africa.

Yet the American situation itself is dangerously skewed. In the 1970s there arrived a substantial Black middle class, now amounting to about one-quarter of the entire Black population, and highly visible Blacks were placed on corporate boards, in foundation and government administrations, and the like. The appearance projected was that the overall status of Blacks as a group was sufficiently high. However, one trend has been the rise of class cleavages among the black middle class, where many with vested interests in moderate, often individualistic solutions and programs have neglected internal Black community development. These individuals and groups often constitute a potential buffer to more aggressive Black strategies to achieve socio-political resources. The white minority regime in South Africa has observed this process and appears to be on the same tenuous course; South African industrialists are suggesting that progressively Blacks should form a middle class which has enough of a stake in the existing order that they would not threaten its existence or continuance.

The Reagan Administration, however, helped to expose the fragility of this strategy in the United States because its fiscal and monetary approaches to economic development transfered government resources from the Black and poor sectors to the already wealthy and white middle-class sectors of the society. The withdrawal of funds from a government-dependent community such as the Black community was a shock in itself. And it was done with an attendant edge of racist public policy so that it elevated both the material and psychological advantages of white Americans. It is, then, small wonder that a president whom the leadership of the moderate Black organization, the NAACP, could call "racist," could support a policy of "constructive engagement" with South Africa. This policy of closer cooperative relations with South Africa was justified on strategic and economic terms.[11]

The third major factor was the resulting failure of pluralism. In both the United States and South Africa, the basic effect of political and economic inequality was to widen the disparity between racial groups. Despite the rise of a black middle class of some significance in the United States, as suggested above, the overall status of the black population as compared to the overall white group worsened in terms of income, position in the labor force and poverty rates. At the same time, there is strong attitudinal evidence that even though there has been economic and social cleavage within the Black population, there appears to have remained a dominant consensus among Blacks generally on racial issues.

The South African situation was far more explosive because the idea of a "Herrenvolk Democracy" both in law and practice has remained a reality. It was the objective of the Herrenvolk (master race) to extend the benefits of a democratic system only to those having membership within the white group, a group which exercises the monopoly of political, economic and social power. But the freedom of the Black majority would be sacrificed to this principle and severely controlled.[12] The explosiveness of this situation resided in the fact that in the time since the promulgation of the original doctrine, a sizeable Black urban population had grown up in South Africa numbering probably three times the entire white population. This group signaled that it would not remain passive while the white South African government carried out the ultimate Herrenvolk doctrine and partitioned the country into separate "homelands" or even "independent" nations based on a false and sham ethnic nationality.

At the same time, the white attempt to impose the cultural manifestations of the nineteenth-century Herrenvolk doctrine upon the young was directed at an urban population. These young people, aware of their oppression within the context of an Afrikaner-dominated society on the one hand, and understanding the clear possibility of social advancement under a different system on the other, challenged the further institutionalization of Apartheid. The inevitable result was an increase in aggressive behavior of all varieties, from labor strikes to urban insurrections to educational strikes. There was even a sense in which the release of pent-up anxieties, the result of a new vision of society with the release of Nelson Mandela and the virtual legalization of the ANC, set off violence even within the Black community as well.

Perhaps it is with regard to the limitations placed upon Black Americans by their minority status that we may make a distinction between their response to whites and that of the Black South Africans. In America, Blacks have not yet rejected the national framework of constitutional democracy which has given them a continual vision of the possibilities inherent in a free and open participation in American society. In South Africa, however, the vision of a Herrenvolk Democracy which acts to subordinate Blacks as a structural fact of South African life in all its facets was resoundingly rejected by the Blacks but maintained by the majority of the whites. This led a segment of the Black South African population to believe that the only way such a system could be removed was through a violent revolution which rearranged the distribution of power and the purposes of the state. This concept, illustrated by the Black liberation movements now active in South Africa, forms the major difference between the two societies in the failure of true pluralism.

Next, it should be mentioned that, just as the African Diaspora forms one of the elements in the environment for the analysis of comparative and Pan African race relations, we follow the earlier concept in suggesting a conflict between the African and the European Diaspora as it exists within South Africa. Of course the Boers, who comprise 60 percent of the white population, are descendants of French Hugenots, Germans and Dutch, while the much smaller English community stems from Great Britain. There are also today Jews (mainly from Eastern Europe), Germans and other Europeans, forming smaller groups within the white population.

Given this unity within diversity of cultural origin, there was not, in terms of political attitudes, what one might regard as a monolith of views among all of these ethnic actors. There is a liberal-to-radical community which believes in the possibility of a multiracial society in South Africa and, as such, opposes Apartheid. Yet, the largest element of the white community in South Africa (which includes non-Boers) is united in the preservation of white status and is opposed to the voluntary relinquishment of its power and privilege.

The hardliner in South African terms is called the Verkrampte in the Afrikaner community, the individual who has put the preservation of the white privileges and the survival of the Afrikaner way of life above all, which means that he or she must follow the traditional attitudes and practices of approving policies which result in the effective subjugation of Blacks at all cost. This is also close to the position of those who are not Afrikaners but who are, nonetheless, members of one of the white ethnic groups and who feel that their lot must be cast with those who direct the power of the government to the maintenance of the status of whites. The challenge for the De Klerk government in particular is, therefore, how to yield to the Black challenge to Apartheid by creating a new political situation which does not destroy the framework of superiority that the whites have created.

In America, there is an analogous grouping which has no real sectional genesis, but which has been more openly found among whites in the Southern part of the country. Despite much talk recently of there being a "new South," the main difference is that they have been socialized to the ways of Northerners such that they do not express racial feelings as publicly as was previously acceptable. Otherwise, the main changes in Southern racial thought and behavior is marked by a decrease in the physical abuse of Blacks, but there has been a marked intransigence in terms of sharing meaningful political or economic power in ways which would define a genuinely "new" situation.

There is also a liberal community in South Africa (verligte) on racial matters, a grouping of whites basically committed to seeing the ideals of a fair and democratic society prevail and the nightmare of Apartheid abolished.[13] But this group is caught on the horns of a dilemma—how to achieve equity for Blacks and not give up any of its status when some sacrifice is required. The result has been the same as that in the United States, that is, the liberal has vacillated between poles of strong support for the rights of Blacks—essentially civil rights—and opposition to the provision of human rights that would be costly in terms of social resources. This choice was not problematic as long as the liberal could guide and direct the demands of the Black freedom struggle, but when this effort was directed by Blacks, then whites had to confront the issue of choosing. This was strikingly illustrated by the opposition of Helen Sussman, a leading liberal white South African politician, to the imposition of economic sanctions against South African Blacks. The result, both in the United States and South Africa, has been that in many instances the role of the white liberal in the Black freedom movements has been substantially reduced.

Next, there are those whites who are committed to the Black freedom struggle to the point that they have joined it and become a functional part of the movement. These people generally constitute a very small segment of the population in both countries, but apparently they have understood the dilemma of the liberal and sought to overcome it by placing their services at the disposal of the Black movements and respecting their leadership.[14] Black consciousness groups in both countries have taken the position that a functional relationship with white revolutionaries is possible, though generally not within Black organizations but by whites playing their role in the white community where the essence of the problem of oppression exists, or as leaders in multi-racial organizations, where resources essentially are obtained from the white community.

Finally, there are the moderates. In South Africa, there are few moderates because racial polarization is so pervasive that, as indicated, most whites measure their ultimate fate in terms of white racial unity. One Afrikaner said to journalist David Halberstam that the racial politics of South Africa was not "fun" like it was in America, like it was during the McGovern convention, which liberalized Democratic party politics in 1972. He felt that in South Africa there could not be a McGovern convention, that in fact, they could not afford to take any chances with racial liberalization. He continued to say: "Here we have the politics of survival. That's all that bloody matters. Here you make a mistake and it's your ass."[15] This comment tells much about what is on the mind of Afrikaner conservatives; their perception of how to survive as a white minority carries with it the survival of their privilege, and so liberal strategies are rejected because they do not have the potential of guaranteeing the survival of a total way of life.

In America, the situation is somewhat different. First, the whites are in the vast majority, constituting 80 percent of the population. And although the racial dynamic had been the most consistent factor of internal conflict in the history of the country, it is cyclical in that it tends to become a crisis occupying the attention of the great majority, then fading from public view, only to recur again. Most white Americans confront racial problems only occasionally, and then not as a question related to their survival. If they choose to do so, most are able to escape a fundamental engagement with Blacks or their problems. The result is an attitude of indifference at worst and at best a large population that may be favorably disposed toward Blacks—so long as the latter stay within the boundaries of the traditional dominant-subordinate system of relationships.

Comparatively, therefore, there are many more moderates in America than in South Africa, and it is even possible to suggest that they are the controlling factor of American racial dynamics, constituting the great grey battleground where committed protagonists, seeking either liberal or conservative outcomes, must contend for their attention and their approval for changes in the body politic that would rectify problems of racial oppression.

The abominable reputation of South Africa has made it difficult for governments such as the United States government to have "normal" relations spanning the full range of exchanges without internal political friction. This has been true despite the fact that there is a strong element of "kith and kin" sentiment in the feeling between the white populations of the two countries. Take the example of Hodding Carter, former editor/publisher of the Greenville, Mississippi, *Delta Democrat Times*. Carter, a "liberal" in the context of Mississippi politics in the United States (and father of the progressive Hodding Carter, Jr., former Carter administration official), had two uncles who were mining engineers in South Africa, one of whom fought on the side of the Boers in the war against the English. The two uncles collectively account for his six cousins born in South Africa. Small wonder, then, that Carter opposed the proposed policy of "One Man One Vote" for all the people of South Africa as disastrous.[16]

There is probably more than a little of the kind of relationship referred to above than supposed. However, historians have provided scant documentation concerning the culture of the slave masters and their international linkages. For example, from the period of the rise of slavery in the United States in the late seventeenth century to the development of the need for labor in the Natal of the 1850s spanned nearly 200 years of American experience with slavery. In addition, the British colonial period in

America spanned about 130 years of the period when the British controlled the Cape Province. Where are the studies which indicate the sharing of customs and practices, the similar concerns and solutions which must have been a part of the legacy of the British colonial heritage in both societies? For example, in 1910 the Union of South Africa was accomplished, and early in that same year, one observer hinted at the linkages which existed among British colonies in their parallel use of slave labor in the growth of cotton. "In self-governing Natal, though still existing, it [forced labor] was officially condemned, and elsewhere it was minimized. But in our [British] parliamentary debates of 1910 it was admitted that it had been made use of in several of our African protectorates at the first starting of the experimental growth of cotton."[17] So, by this time, although slavery had also ended in the Americas "officially," varieties of it could be found in South Africa in the practice of forced labor to produce a similar commodity. Meanwhile, vengeful and defeated white Southerners had at this time unleashed a reign of terror and oppression against blacks, reinstituting many of the older slave patterns in the utilization of labor.

Studies of American public opinion on South Africa had consistently shown that whites have been far less willing than Blacks to sanction punitive measures against South Africa.[18] And, while expressing opposition to Apartheid, white Americans were not willing to support measures which have the effect of severely weakening South Africa or causing a revolution in the social system if that results in Black rule. Such opinions had been held, perhaps, for a number of reasons having to do with the perceived importance of South Africa to the United States as a source of minerals, as a bulwark against communism or as a white Christian nation which has been historically identified with the history of the West.

As a result of the positive supports for American relations with South Africa, until 1986 there existed unrestricted social intercourse between the two nations with immigration, business and tourist travel unimpeded. And while overt military alliances were avoided and an arms embargo imposed by the United States, vital economic relations grew unimpeded until 1986. For example, in 1980, trade, investment and financing proceeded unobstructed until the U.S.–South Africa trade volume (imports and exports) reached $6 billion a year, amounting to about 20 percent of total continental African trade volume; U.S. investment amounted to $2.6 billion in 1980, and outstanding loans from private U.S. banks amounted to $2 billion or about 25 percent of the total South African exposure.[19] There were at that time about 350 American firms doing business in South Africa, including automotive, electrical, heavy industrial equipment, chemical and other enterprises represented in the Fortune 500.[20]

The attraction of South Africa to the U.S. government was strong because of its supply of strategic minerals, many of them important to the maintenance of a high U.S. standard of living; they included uranium, chromium, ferrochromium, vanadium, tungsten and manganese. What appeared to be missing in calculations of the importance of the supply of such minerals was their availability at an affordable price. The low price of many such minerals is maintained by the slave wages paid to Black South African miners who endanger their lives to bring the ores up from deep shafts. Thus, the maintenance of economic Apartheid is in the interest of those customers who consume the products of the mines. No doubt, if the Black South African miner was paid a wage equivalent to those paid to the American miner or the white South African miner, the profits of mine operators and owner would not be as substantial.

Finally, the mutual interests of the United States and South Africa in anti-Communism as an operative political ideology gave the two countries a basis for foreign policy interdependence. While a full discussion of this factor in its impact in international politics is outside the scope of this work, it should be recognized that both countries paid considerable attention to the activities of groups inside their countries that were regarded as Communist. These groups, in the case of the United States, were subjected to surveillance, disrupted and in many instances harrassed to the point where they had to cease operations. At the same time, many non-Communist groups fighting for social change were labeled as Communist-oriented and subjected to the same treatment. When one assesses the results of the McCarthy period of anti-Communism paranoia in the United States, and the government's long period of absorption in its internal effects, it must be understood that Communism was not the central threat to American domestic tranquility. In fact, the 1960s showed clearly that racism and economic inequality held this status and still do so today.

Shortly after the victory of the Nationalist Party in South Africa in 1948, the Boers promulgated a number of repressive laws, among them the Suppression of Communism Act of 1950. This law outlawed the South African Communist Party; in 1951 the government made the act retroactive in an effort to silence extraparliamentary opposition, harrassing groups that had protested unjust pass laws and other aspects of the Apartheid system as "Communist" or their activities as "Communist-inspired."[21]

This concern with Communism gave the United States and South Africa a basis for empathy in both their internal policies and their wider foreign policy approaches to the region, as South African activities in opposition to the liberation movements in Zimbabwe, Mozambique, Angola and Namibia demonstrated. The internal concern with Communism in South Africa resulted in added measures of social control, directed against some white individuals who were the most militant allies of the black community and against some members of the Black community itself.

In summary, there is, then, up to 1986 a substantial basis provided for the analysis of comparative and Pan African political dynamics which suggests that, even though the United States and South African political systems provide a similar historical approach to the problem of race relations, the late twentieth century saw them taking different paths. The United States accepted full legal status for Blacks and afforded a modest amount of racial integration and economic, political and social mobility. However, while there has been some absolute change in the status of Blacks, the dominant material conditions and the pattern of social stratification between them and whites has remained largely unchanged. The South Africans, on the other hand, attempted to maintain the idea of Herrenvolk Democracy and in the face of challenges by the Black majority developed modern schemes that would have institutionalized the geographical, economic, political, social, technological and other disparities in status. In any case, in South Africa, the pattern of racial stratification was maintained, and there was no discernible improvement in the legal status of Blacks, except at the margin. It is the continuing fact of this pattern of racial stratification which mirrors the distribution of power and status in society, and the economic and political ties which exist between the United States and South Africa which provide the strongest aspects of the environment for our analysis.

Therefore, it is possible to conclude specifically the following:

1. The establishment of settlements in America and South Africa by whites followed a similar pattern of expansion into the interior, and the conquest, extermination, and subjugation of the indigenous peoples. The two subjugated groups, however, were the African and the American Indian whose comparative condition strikingly resemble each other in terms of the relegation to reservations of the surviving groups, often by treaty, on what was thought to be unproductive lands, while the victor took possession of the dominant land areas of the country. In this sense, the African enters American history at a different place, though he comes to serve the same purpose and is relegated to even a lower status. What made it unfeasible to exterminate the African was his value as human capital, and so he was allowed to survive to serve economic, social, and political functions.

2. Both in South Africa and America, there were sectional disputes over the status of the African, but while the Boers resolved this problem by the formation of separate republics, the attempt to do so in the American South met resistance and defeat. The price of this resolution in the Americas was the partial elimination of the contract of economic bondage and the partial inclusion of the African in the social contract which governed the nation. The Boer, on the other hand, did nothing to alter Herrenvolk Democracy which, by definition, excluded the African from the social franchise, and only a half-hearted attempt to institute British paternalism was made in the English colonial provinces.

3. In any case, by 1910 with the Act of Union, the whites in South Africa established the basis for consolidating the separate and lowly status of the African which they proceeded to enshrine by a series of laws. In America, however, this dangerous period of the ascendancy of vengeful whites in the South experienced a ruthless reinstitution of white subjugation of the African through terror and extermination. What saved some Blacks was migration out of the South and a renewed value of Blacks as industrial laborers in the North and some areas of the South.

4. In the first half of the twentieth century, the social pro-

cesses of two World Wars, industrialization and urbanization to some extent gave the African in America and South Africa greater social and economic mobility, and in both places, politicized classes were produced which began to agitate for further reforms to provide greater social, economic and political participation. In South Africa, despite the fact that the African was a part of the dynamic processes mentioned, the reactionary power of Afrikaner nationalism succeeded in institutionalizing a segregated state based on the doctrine of Apartheid. Then, because the African was in the majority, the white minority refined the legal and technological basis for the control of black movement, residence and social activity throughout the country.

In America, in many places the segregated status of the African was just as firmly maintained; however, greater mobility was achieved by Blacks principally because: (1) the "scab" potential of Black labor provided the leverage factor which made it possible for Black workers to be absorbed into the white labor union movement; (2) the continuing liberal promise of an inclusionary democracy was capitalized upon by various movements led by Blacks, and (3) the combination of Black agitation and national social policy enabled various institutions of government to include Blacks in the economic recovery of the 1930s, the war industries of the 1940s and to attack serious aspects of race discrimination directly in the 1950 and 1960s.

5. Relative to South Africa, the United States appears to be a more liberal state on the racial question because its strength in material resources and the size of its white population provide room for the absorption of a significant Black middle class which obscures the survivalistic nature of its management of the racial question. Whereas in South Africa the degree of racial antagonism is driven by the unwillingness of the ruling white minority to include the Black middle class or other Blacks in either the social or economic sectors.

Nevertheless, in both societies the essential disparity of the resources and social status of blacks and whites continues to fuel a high degree of Black alienation and white resistance which is the basis of race politics.

8
Comparative Black Politics in the United States and South Africa

We have learned from the above conclusions that the most salient basis for comparative analysis of Black politics in both South Africa and America resides in the extent to which there is in each society an enduring pattern of race stratification based on the white dominance–Black subordinate model and that this pattern owes its maintainance to such factors as the persistence of institutionalized race prejudice and capitalism. These phenomena provide the parameters within which we will make a comparative assessment of such political strategies as community organization and the defense of community objectives by such tactics as demonstrations and rebellion. In addressing this problem, we will make very little attempt to describe the rural situation in South Africa or to describe the liberation movement activities because we assume that although there exist some parallel activities associated with African Americans, the dominant comparative frame of reference is the urban context and the political activities that flow from it.

Community Organization

As previously suggested, African Americans are the most urbanized African population in the world with about 70 percent residing in cities and, therefore, having to respond to the pervasive utilization of urban technology in the daily tasks of living. Again, this is the result of migration of Blacks out of the South into industrial areas in an effort to better their situation. The resulting pattern of residence was most often a core community located in the center of the city (if an industrial city) or near an industrial activity and on the fringe of the town if it was not a heavily industrialized city. These areas came to be the base of the "Black Community," and it was from them and within them that Blacks became socialized into the habits of urban living. The "Community" made up of many formal and informal institutions regulated the social lives of Blacks and was invaluable as a resource for the survival of individuals and their families and, hence, the whole group.[1]

Professor E. Franklin Frazier, an eminent Black sociologist, once argued that "the spatial pattern of the community is the basis of a moral order."[2] Reflective of this fact is the racially segregated nature of most core Black communities from most white communities. Second, there is a low level in the extention of the services and technology of the city (those things which make it function), such as the transportation service, sanitation service, and information services to the Black community. Third, the low economic level of members of the Black community relative to the white community defines its relative material status as well. For example, the average yearly income of the Black family in 1988 was 58 percent of the average white family; 33 percent of the Black community (nationally) was classified as poor compared to 9 percent for white families; unemployment was 14 percent for Blacks and only 5 percent for whites. While there were an estimated 250,000 Black businesses, total assets of Black businesses would constitute only $10 billion, or the equivalent of the assets of the twentieth enterprise in the listing of the top fifty American corporations' earnings.[3]

Politically, Blacks hold only two percent of all elected positions, and in fact it has made slight difference that Blacks have held political power in some cities when in those same cities effective economic decision-making still remains in the hands of whites.[4] On the whole, even in places where Blacks are in the leadership, the Black community still retains a dependent relationship to those who make effective decisions governing the distribution of resources. The nature of this relationship, combined with the subservience of the Black community to the police power of the white community, has often been the basis of defining the relationship as *colonial* in nature, as we have seen in the comparative analysis of Britain.

The dependent status of Black communities in America is vividly reflected in the decisions of those who direct the development of urban areas, influencing the very location of the Black community by controlling the access, availability and price of housing in certain neighborhoods. For example, the effect of federal housing policies through Urban Renewal, Model Cities, Section 8 and other programs has often hidden policies designed to concentrate Blacks in certain sections of cities or disperse them according to the prevailing political mood or the demands of local economic interests.[5] Ironically, however, the pattern of an urban, identifiably Black core persists as the dominant locus of the Black community, and even where some dispersion has been accomplished the existence of racism has often resulted in resegregation of Blacks in suburban areas.

The last point for comparative analysis concerns the existence of a Black middle class. In the 1960s, several forces, including a 40 percent growth in the GNP (1960–1970), the rise in the average income of the Black family by 30 percent, the initiation of a federal "War on Poverty," a rise in the number of Blacks attending college by more than 500 percent between 1968 and 1972, and the implementation of affirmative action job laws, all resulted in an increase in the number of materially affluent Blacks. In 1964, nine percent of Blacks had income of $15,000 or more; this figure increased to nineteen percent by 1974 and 27 percent by 1990.

Together with the increase of this group within the Black community, there began to be indications of "class cleavage," as a popular manifestation of the difference in the observed behavior of the traditional Black "lower classes" and that of a newer middle class in terms of residence, comportment, consumption and other areas.[6] Attendant to this phenomenon is an emerging debate over whether or not this new class represents a "buffer" between the Black "underclass" and the white power structure to the extent that the true conditions and demands of the more disadvantaged group are distorted and not clearly visible as the reflection of the dominant portion of the Black community.

As for the class structure of the Black community in South Africa, the observation of Professor Frazier, quoted previously, was never more insightful in that the spatial situation of the Black population is highly reflective of the morality of Apartheid. In this sense, it may be somewhat absurd to think that a legitimate "Black community" exists. Nevertheless, Black people there have preserved aspects of their indigenous culture and institutions, and in urban areas have forged new community institutions for their survival despite the despotic conditions they face.

There are currently (1990) twenty-nine million people in South Africa. Of them, five million are whites, twenty million Blacks, three million coloreds and one million Asians. Of this number the urban population has been growing rapidly. By 1974, official South African estimates indicated that 8.5 million Blacks, 700 thousand Asians and 2.3 million coloreds, or about 52 percent of the nonwhite population, lived in areas alloted to whites. These areas included the mines, ports and industrial cities and the prime agricultural lands.[7] The largest urban concentration is in the Johannesburg-Pretoria area where one-third of all whites live, and there whites accounted for only 36 percent of the total population.[8] Cape Town's "legal" African population is listed at 100,000, but the actual Black population is estimated at double this size. The African population in urban areas is projected to grow; official estimates expect that in the year 2000 the total African population will stand at 30.5 million and that 22.8 million of them will be living in the urban areas.[9]

There are basically two types of urban residence. The first is composed of the "white cities," though they are not entirely white; some Africans have permission to reside in them to serve white homes and industries. However, the Apartheid laws were based squarely on an understanding described in a 1922 statement of the Transvaal Local Government Commission, saying: "If the native is to be regarded as a permanent element in municipal areas there can be no justification for basing his exclusion from the franchise on grounds of colour. The native should be allowed to enter the urban areas when he is willing to minister to the needs of the white man, and should depart therefrom when he ceases to minister."[10] This mind set led in 1923 to the Natives (Urban Areas) Act which required local white authorities to set up segregated areas and to establish the administrative machinery to regulate the residence of Africans. Special attention was given to the "superfluous" African population— wives and children of male workers and unemployed Africans. In 1959 the Promotion of Bantu Self-Government Act was promulgated mandating the establishment of Bantustans largely as places to which "surplus" or "undesirable" Africans from the urban areas could be exported. However, the basic act governing residence in the urban areas was spelled out in Section 10 of the Natives (Urban Areas) Consolidation Act of 1945. In summarized form, it states that no African may remain in an urban area or area designated for white residence more than seventy-two hours unless he or she has resided there continuously since birth, has worked for only one employer for more than ten years, is the wife, unmarried daughter, or son under the age of eighteen of a resident African, or has been granted permission to reside in the area.[11] From this law and others the infamous "passes" developed, documents Africans had to carry at all times and containing information related to the above noted laws. By inspecting these passes South African police officials could determine whether or not to arrest individuals for violations. In the 1960s and 1970s, arrests for pass law violations averaged an estimated 2,000 per day in an average year, and massive numbers of Africans were kept on a treadmill from the urban areas to jail, to labor camps, to the Bantustans or "Homelands," back to the urban areas to begin the cycle again. In the process, one could easily see the challenge to the concept of community presented by such forced mobility which disorganized the family and regularly subtracted resources from the entire community.

The second and most frequent form of residence for urban Africans is a township near the "white city." These sprawling Black towns were initiated in the early 1960s in order to stem the flow of Africans to the white areas and to build up convenient nearby reserves of African labor to serve the white cities. One description of Soweto (*South West Township*), a well-known township about thirty miles from Johannesburg covering an area of about twenty-one square miles and holding more than five million people, called this largest African city "less a city than a dormitory," with no industry or normal city-styled amenities and where the largest building are the police station and a few others that are government controlled. Fundamentally, the author describes it as a sprawling ghetto of long rows of three- and four-room one-story houses stretching endlessly over the landscape, except for the few double-story houses of the small Black professional class.[12] This stark picture of Soweto holds true for literally all of the African townships in South Africa.

The townships are populated by a mixture of Africans from the 10 major ethnic groups (Tswana, North Sotho, Ndebele, Shangaan, Tsonga, Venda, Swazi, South Sotho, Zulu, Xhosa), depending upon the area of the country where they are found. It has been official South African government policy to divide the nonwhite population on the basis of racial and ethnic characteristics, making the population politically easier to deal with. For example, the term "black" in the context of South African society includes Africans, Asians, and so-called coloreds, while the African population is separately known as African. There are colored but no Asian townships, and both groups have permission to reside in some white urban areas (cities) in segregated "divisions" or districts. The "Homeland" policy envisioned each of the African ethnic groups having citizenship in a separate "independent nation" forming a "constellation of states" led by South Africa. The government, therefore, made a great deal of the separate identities of the various African ethnic groups, but this concept ran counter to the dynamic force of urbanization which tended to harmonize the differences among Black ethnic groups to the point that urbanized Africans cared less and less about ultimate ethnic identity and more about the common oppression exercised upon them because they are Black.

The Blacks do not control the townships; rather, they are administered by provincial boards in cooperation with the South African central government. No Blacks or Africans serve on these boards; instead, local township advisory councils have been created with Black mayors who have little authority over any of the normal functions of law and order or over government-owned housing. African authority is only tolerated as traditional tribe authority in the homelands under the watchful eye of the South African government, and there are attempts by the traditional homelands leaders to extend their authority into the townships.

A good example of this is Inkatha, the political organization of Chief Gatsha Buthelezi, head of the Zulu Homeland, who often visits the largely male Zulu-populated hostels in Soweto during social events as a symbol of Zulu ethnic leadership. Such a role, as noted by the urban African, especially the youths, plays into the hands of the South African government in its "divide-and-conquer" strategy.[13]

As may be assumed, the standard of living of the urban populations is patently low by comparison with that of urban whites. For example, one observer says that in 1973, the white 17 percent of the work force held 68.2 percent of all salary and wage payments; the coloureds making up 9 percent of the labor force received 7.9 percent of the jobs, the Asians composing 3 percent held 2.8 percent of the jobs, and the 71 percent who are Black received 21.1 percent. "Simple deduction from these figures suggests that the average overall white/Black income differential is slightly over 13½ to 1, though of course the differentials from the ownership of wealth, as opposed to income, would be astronomically higher."[14] This disparity should be further seen in 1980 figures which suggest that for a family of six to live in the Johannesburg area a minimum income of $156 (R135) would be required, while the average Johannesburg worker's take-home pay was an estimated $60 (R52).[15] Therefore, despite the fact that they live near the country's prime urban area and in somewhat better conditions than others, the Soweto Africans should be regarded as generally poor and in severely overcrowded conditions.

Finally, those who do not reside in the urban areas on a rather permanent basis are viewed as migrants, usually getting only a few weeks at home before renewing their yearly contract. So, many Africans form "squatters" camps near principal white cities. One such area was known as Crossroads, a town of some 20,000 people, which in 1979 was scheduled for destruction. On August 11, 1981, as had happened in so many other cases, the white authorities moved into Crossroads and began to burn and tear down the flimsy wooden lean-to and corrugated metal huts that had housed many of these families. They scattered the inhabitants, placing many in jail for violations of the pass laws and the Section 10 residence law.

At the same time, a visiting American congressional delegation asked to see Crossroads people, who were still clinging to the settlement even though their only protection from the elements were plastic garbage bags within which they huddled. The South African authorities prevented the delegation from going to Crossroads, and Black Congresswoman Shirley Chisolm wept at the news of what was occurring. Black Congressman Gus Savage angrily broke off from the delegation and went to Kenya.[16]

In both America and South Africa, it is obvious that there are still massive disparities in status between the African and white communities. Nevertheless, there had existed in both countries a framework of Black "community" based on the construction and maintainance of social institutions. In America, because the reign of physical terror eased after the turbulent decades of the early twentieth century, social institutions (including economic organizations) grew strongly behind a wall of legally enforced segregation. More recently, while physical racism has made the transition into institutional racism, and a measure of social integrated mobility had led to the emergence of an affluent Black elite, it may be observed that some of the strongest Black institutions have suffered from lack of Black support and the "community" reality has diminished accordingly. These institutions—the church, the school, the social centers, the eating establishments—all shift according to the wind that blows from the dominant community's attitudes and activities.

The same is true in South Africa, except more profoundly so because of the more tightly controlled circumstances within which Black people live. The white South Africans have made a point of deliberately withholding the material fruits of the South African political economy in an effort to ensure their own survival and privilege. The Black African has developed the rudimentary institutions of social living out of this material deprivation and has also utilized the resilient resource of indigenous African culture to maintain these same institutions.

In both countries, then, whatever its form or strength, *community* is a vital resource not only for living, but for the daring attempt to recreate an African future under conditions of wrenching oppression for the masses of the Black population. It is the basis out of which political strategies are designed to resist this oppression and to posit the Black community's own collective and individual humanity.

Next, I will compare some of the political strategies which have been used in both societies by African peoples in an effort to change their national status. In this, we will examine three themes—accommodation, resistance and revolt—in order to focus on the challenges inherent in the more radically oppressive situation faced by the Black population in South Africa.

Accommodation

The tradition of accommodation is strong among any oppressed people as an acknowledgement of the power of the oppressor. In America, this tradition most certainly did not begin with Booker T. Washington, or else slavery would never have had so rich and illustrious a history. Yet it was with Washington that accommodation was rationalized into an ideology of race advancement and raised to the level of national strategy of race relations. We find Washington at the Cotton States' Exposition in Atlanta, in September of 1895 uttering the speech which was to become his model of race relations, suggesting that Blacks should glorify common labor, that they should "cast down your buckets where you are," that "the wisest among my race understand that the agitation of questions of social equality is the extremest folly, and that progress in the enjoyment of all the privilege that will come to us must be the result of severe and constant struggle rather than of artificial forcing."[17] This was not the only statement that could have been made, but Washington knew it was the only prescription that would have a tremendously positive reception among a Southern white power structure and among Northern industrialists.

One of those who followed the alternative prescription of resistance was W.E.B. DuBois, who was one of the founders in 1909 of what came to be known as the National Association for the Advancement of Colored People and who felt at the time of Washington's famous Atlanta speech that "Mr. Washington represents the old attitude of submission."[18] While DuBois was undoubtedly correct from a Northern perspective, it is highly unlikely that, given the temper of the times, if he had attempted to have founded the NAACP in any of the states of the Confederacy, the attempt would have been successful.

A distinguished professor of Black history, Carter G. Woodson, located the tendency toward accommodation in the flawed education of the "Negro," suggesting this as the reason why Blacks have often chosen "the line of least resistance rather than battle the odds for what real history has shown to be the right course." He continued: "A mind that remains in the present atmosphere never undergoes sufficient development to experience what is commonly known as thinking. No Negro thus submerged in the ghetto, then, will have a clear conception of the present status of the race or sufficient foresight to plan for the future; and he drifts so far toward compromise that he loses moral courage."[19] This Woodson called "moral surrender" that often led "Negroes" to "exultingly champion the cause of the oppressor."[20] The only course for Woodson, then, would be for Blacks to resist attempts of others to prescribe their education in order to socialize them politically to the acceptance of their status and by so doing, control their attitudes and behavior.

E. Franklin Frazier attempted to describe the basis of this tendency by suggesting that it constituted an important feature of the "Black Bourgeoise," resulting from their dependency and their drive for an elusive equal status with whites. He writes:

In his role as leader, the Negro politician attempts to accommodate the demands of the Negro masses to his personal interests which are tied up with the political machines. He may secure the appointment of a few middleclass Negroes to positions in the municipal government. But when it comes to the fundamental interests of the Negro masses as regards employment, housing, and health, his position is determined by the political machine which represents the propertied classes of the white community.[21]

This structural relationship, Frazier suggests, is the reason why Black leadership has not acted independently in many cases, but accommodated ultimately to the dictates of those who basically controlled the resources through which these Black leaders fulfilled status desires and which allowed them to "escape from their feelings of inferiority in the delusion of power." [22]

The accommodationist tradition, to be sure, arises because of the existence of men who compromise the goal of race advancement for their private ends, and also because good men feel that political objectives may be achieved through cooperation and coalition with those who control the instruments of policy. For example, the 1964 Civil Rights Act was signed into law on July 2, but the price may well have been Black support for the presidential candidacy of Lyndon Johnson at the Democratic National Convention that same month. James Forman has poignantly described a pivotal meeting at the convention during which leading figures, Black and white, attempted to persuade a Black delegation from Mississippi, the Freedom Democratic Party (MFDP), not to embarrass the party and the president by openly challenging the right of the racist white Mississippi delegation (which excluded Blacks) to represent the entire state. Some of those attending the meeting were Rev. Martin Luther King, Jr., Bayard Rustin, Jack Pratt of the National Council of Churches, Senator Wayne Morse of Oregon, Joseph Rauh, James Farmer of CORE, Bob Moses, Stokely Carmichael, and Courtland Cox of SNCC, and Fannie Lou Hamer and other members of the Freedom Democratic Party.

The issue at the meeting was whether or not the Freedom Democratic Party would accept a ruling of the credentials committee that sought to resolve the dispute by seating the all-white delegation from Mississippi, awarding the MFDP two at-large seats and even naming the two delegates! Perhaps it would be enlightening to the reader to have a brief illustration of the tone of the meeting as indicated by Forman's paraphrasing of the speeches of two key participants. The first was Bayard Rustin, who counseled the MFDP delegation that institutional politics required its participants "to give up protest" and "be willing to compromise." [23] Then, Martin Luther King said that the Democratic party, despite its segregationist elements, was the best that Blacks could hope for, and transmitted promises made to them by Lyndon Johnson's vice president, Hubert Humphrey.[24] Predictably, the SNCC delegation spoke against the compromise offered by the credentials committee, and finally, the compromise was rejected by the Freedom Democratic Party leader, Fannie Lou Hamer, who said, "We didn't come all this way for no two seats!"[25] The MFDP challenge to the party threatened the explicit consummation of the marriage between the Black civil rights leadership and Northern white political power within the Democratic party. This relationship had been implicit since 1932, but would become the basis of a new electoral coalition, the result of which for Blacks would be the fulfillment of the civil rights agenda. This explicit coalition functioned well for about a decade, but now that it has ceased to function, the habit of accommodationist politics—even in the early 1990s—remains a reflexive response.

In South Africa, as previously stated, the government evolved a vision of its final solution for the problem of "sharing power" with the Black majority. We suggested that the evolution of this policy began in 1913 when, as Sol Plaatje, a turn-of-the-century Black Nationalist said, he awoke to discover that he was "a pariah in the land of his birth."[26] He was responding to the fact that the Native Land Act, just adopted, legitimized the theft of 87 percent of the land by the white minority. The movement continued when in 1959 the government adopted the Promotion of Bantu Self-Government Act establishing the so-called Bantustands or "Homelands" as the only places where Africans could have elections, territorial assemblies and extremely moderate amounts of self-government. It continued in 1970 with the Citizenship Act which made the Homelands the source of ultimate African citizenship, allowing for a while a fiction countenancing dual citizenship of Blacks electing to choose both South Africa and a Homeland. It moved, in 1977, to the point where the Homelands were declared "independent states" one by one and, as each becomes independent, the ethnic group supposedly represented by the Homeland lost its citizenship in the Republic of South Africa![27]

The response to this usurpation of the land and birth rights of Africans by the government surfaced the predictable array of political tendencies, among them the accommodationist tendency. The similarity to the U.S. situation arose in the fact that some of these accommodationists, too, were motivated by their desire to hold on to a certain status, were cowed by the power of the white establishment, and had ultimately come to feel that collaboration was the compromise that would protect both their interest and those of the people they purport to represent. But illustrative of a widespread African attitude toward them is the observation that Black leaders such as Chief Gatsha Buthelezi, leader of the Zulu, Chief Kaiser Matanzima, head of the Homeland Transkei, and Lucas Mangope, leader of the Bophuthatswana, are regarded to be "stooges" of the South African government. Buthelezi has walked the line between opposition to the Homeland policy of the white minority regime and acceptance of the authority of the South African government and has been an outspoken opponent of the more revolutionary approach to social change. Similarly, Mangope and Matanzima accepted the designation of their territories initially as "Homelands"—actually wastelands for dumping the surplus Black population—and later, separate "states" within the framework of the "separate development" policy of the regime. One pertinent observation was that while such leaders considered themselves "political realists" or "pragmatists" using the "art of the possible . . . using the available legal platforms," there was little hope of them ever gaining the allegiance of oppressed people.[28] The striking similarity between this line of reasoning and that of American Black accommodationists will be immediately evident. In line with their heavy emphasis on cultural difference between themselves and the Africans as the basis for their political approach, the white minority carefully preserved tribal authority as the basis for African leadership in the Homelands while at the same time attempting to extinguish revolutionary, progressive or legitimate urban leadership among the detribalized Africans. Thus, the chiefs could also be regarded as an appendage of the regulatory mechanism of the South African government, since their authority was vested in the Native Administrative Acts of 1927 and the Bantu Authorities Act of 1951. Section 8 of the latter says, "He [the Chief] must carry out all the lawful orders which he receives from or through the Native Affairs Commissioner or another government official properly authorized thereto in writing by the Secretary, the Chief Native Commissioner or the Native Commissioner."[29]

Mantanzima, who is mentioned above, was tribal Chief of the Transkei, and in the first campaign for election of the Transkei Territorial Government in 1963, he said: "As the future Chief Minister of the Transkei, I wish the people to know that: 1. I stand for the policy of separate development which is the cornerstone of Transkei Constitution Act which had granted self-government to the Transkei."[30] Mantanzima thus unabashedly aligned himself with the policy of the white minority regime and went on to institutionalize it in the leadership of the Transkei government. As we see, separate development was the "cornerstone" of the Transkei Constitution, and Mantanzima's Transkei National Independence Party formulated a loyalty oath for members requiring them to swear allegiance to the principles and program of the party which also uphold the separate development approach. The rationale was clearly illustrated in a party manifesto aimed at the 1968 election, which said:

> I/We believe in the policy of separate development, since it has proved that it is the only policy that can successfully be applied in South Africa. Since it is the hereditary right of the people of the Transkei to govern themselves in their own country and according to their own wishes, we honour and observe the Transkei constitution and will act in accordance with the principles laid down in it.[31]

By the early 1970s, however, it had become clear to the tribal leaders that the so-called "independence" model offered by the South African government left something to be desired.

Mantanzima gave the opening address at a congress of his Party in March 1973, and his initial remarks showed his allegiance not only to the ruling white minority government, but to his chiefly colleagues as well.[32] Nevertheless, he voiced some concern about the promise of separate development in ultimate practice. "I stand for separate development," he said, "provided it is carried out to its logical conclusion. If it fails, as it seems to be failing, the alternative is an integrated South Africa with full equality amongst all races."[33] Mantanzima then asked, "What is meant by 'logical conclusion'?" And he suggested that the promise of true nationhood as the basis of the policy of separate development should carry with it control over the government administrative system, as well as control over police, budget and army. But in the shaping of the 1977 Independence Constitution for the Transkei, it was clear that the South African concept of "independence" for Africans within a "constellation of states" was not the internationally recognized concept of independence, and accordingly no state recognized the three so-called independent states. This struggle with the definition of the rights of Africans under "separate development" helps to illuminate the objectives of whites under any new political arrangement and provides a framework for assessing the objectives of moderate and conservative Blacks at the same time.

For example, Chief Mangsoutho Gatsha Buthelezi, head minister of the KwaZulu, was also a traditional chief in the paid service of the South African government, accepting the infamous doctrine of separate development. Although Buthelezi is a moderate and considered an accommodationist by the more militant young Africans, he has managed to appear militant enough to achieve considerable popularity among ordinary Africans. For, while accepting the separate development concept, he rejected its ultimate step of the loss of South African citizenship via an "independent" status which has not achieved international legitimacy.

Buthelezi, for example, was a consistent critic of Apartheid. He explained that he supported separate development because it was imposed upon his people by fiat of the South African government and that he was exploiting it "for what it is worth." The government tolerated his criticism, it was thought, largely because of his popularity and because he was able to unify the two million Zulus within the framework of the Homelands policy. At the same time, he exercised some influence on the approximately two million Zulus living outside the Homelands in the urban areas.

For example, he supported strikes by Zulu workers at the aluminum smelter at Richards Bay. It is worth noting that Richards Bay, an industrial area with a port, has been excised out of the Zulus' Homeland.[34] Perhaps this is the key illustration of why Buthelezi's past objections were based on the lack of economic viability of the Homelands and the relationship between this fact and their questionable independence. In 1974, he suggested that he did not believe that breaking up the "integrated economy" should be part of the further establishment of separate development, because that economy was the "life blood of all the people of South Africa."[35]

Yet it was clear that he functioned as a part of the system for controlling Africans that the South African whites had created. In January 1975, there was a conference between then Prime Minister Vorster and some "Black leaders." And in a dialogue whose tone could have been used by the same "Black leaders" in a meeting with the president of the United States, Buthelezi told Vorster:

> I reminded him that by co-operating with his government in implementing this policy [separate development], we had been slated as "collaborators with the oppressors" by certain elements within South Africa, and others outside South Africa. I reminded him that there were amongst us who do not believe in Apartheid as a philosophy but who have cooperated merely because there were no other alternatives to finding a peaceful settlement.[36]

It was equally clear that on other issues, Buthelezi attempted to distinguish himself from the others of his colleagues in supporting various aspects of separate development. At the same time, he objected to the criticism of some Blacks that he and his colleagues were not qualified to present to Vorster the case of urban Africans.

Buthelezi also postured as a national legitimate political leader through his revival of Inkatha, an ancient Zulu cultural organization that he has embued with fractures of the Black Consciousness movement ideology and style. This enabled him to have a vehicle through which he could mobilize ethnic opinion and activities across rural-urban lines and stave off, to some extent, the encroachment of the Black Consciousness movement into his own strongholds. Inkatha's manifestations in songs, colors, and so on were also strikingly patterned after the ANC liberation movement and Inkatha's stated aims are to promote "National Cultural Liberation" and achieve the incorporation of Blacks into political decision-making (majority rule).[37]

This ambitious program for Inkatha was a contradiction to Buthelezi's fence-straddling act and did not keep him from being evaluated basically like any other functionary of the separate development program of the government. In 1976, for example, one month before the Soweto rebellion, students at the University of Zululand demonstrated against the award of an honorary doctorate degree to Chief Buthelezi and stoned his automobile.[38] Also, in 1978, Robert Sobukwe, the revered leader of the PAC, died; Buthelezi appeared at his funeral and was stoned by some members of the Black Consciousness movement.[39] Then, in 1990, as the De Klerk government appeared to be preparing for negotiations with the ANC concerning a new future for South Africa, fighting between Zulu Inkatha and ANC supporters broke out in some townships. Speculation about the role of Buthelezi centered on his refusal to meet with Nelson Mandela and his apparent sanctioning of "self-defense" for his Zulu warriors and raised the possibility that he was signaling to the government that his faction had to be included in any negotiations.

Resistance

In setting forth a rationale for the discussion of this subject in comparative terms, one should note at the outset that there are two forms of popular resistance—violent and nonviolent. Both of these strategies, however, may be addressed to the same objectives—drawing the authorities' attention to a grievance, demanding immediate redress of the grievance—and while violent strategies may accomplish this more dramatically, often nonviolent strategies are just as effective. In this discussion I will consider first the nonviolent strategies utilized by the African communities in South Africa and in the United States, categorizing them as either institutional or extra-institutional in nature. Institutional nonviolent strategies involve the use of institutions to oppose acts of law, public policy or regulations that contribute to the oppression of Blacks and that often emerge in the judicial, legislative or executive branches of government. Extra-institutional nonviolent strategies, however, involve nonviolent protest demonstrations of various kinds—marches, rallies, boycotts, and so on. Secondly, we will consider violent resistance as occurring in the form of urban Black rebellions and associated tendencies toward urban guerilla warfare.

With regard to *institutional nonviolent strategies,* long before the abolition of slavery in America, Blacks petitioned both local and national governments for redress of grievances and therefore the movement for civil rights has had an early and expansive career. Nor did the NAACP, an early protest organization, begin the quest for civil rights in the 1950s or 1960s. Indeed, the Niagra Movement, forerunner of the NAACP, in 1907 created the first "Department of Civil Rights" to be established by a Black organization. Also, in the 1911 meeting that, for all practical purposes, founded the NAACP, there was an explicit demand "of Congress and the executive: 1. That the Constitution be strictly enforced and the civil rights guaranteed under the Fourteenth Amendment be secured impartially to all."[40] Having taken this "radical" step for the times, as is well known, the NAACP went on to become the leading organization in working through the dominant governmental institutions to secure civil rights for Blacks, although other such organizations were also active.

For example, in 1948, on a challenge by the NAACP, the Supreme Court struck down the "white primaries" that had prohibited Blacks from exercising their voting power in the primaries of the Democratic party. Then, in 1954, again on a challenge by the NAACP, the Supreme Court, in the case of Brown v. Board of Education, found segregated education unconstitutional, setting the stage for the implementation of a policy of integration in American public schools. This was followed by pressure upon the executive branch to implement the Civil Rights Acts of 1957, 1960, 1964, 1965, and 1968, by helping to initiate the Leadership Conference on Civil Rights, a group of 125 interracial civil rights-oriented organizations, led by lobbying expert and its director, Clarence Mitchell.[41]

Then, in the 1970s a second source of institutional focus was created with the large number of Black elected and appointed officials coming into the dominant institutions and into the legal profession and its institutions. And so there began to be substantial resistance waged inside American governmental institutions. For example, the Congressional Black Caucus opposed the attempt to roll back civil rights gains by voting against punitive measures such as federal budget cuts, offering its own national budget, attempting to transfer funds from the military to the social side of the national budget, and by many other actions.

At the same time, in the Carter Administration, two Black attorneys, Drew Days, head of the Justice Department's Civil Rights Division, and Eleanor Holmes Norton, head of the Equal Employment Opportunity Commission, developed favorable regulations concerning access to jobs by Blacks. Andrew Young, as U.S. ambassador to the United Nations, was able to establish a more favorable climate of relations between Africa and America, reversing the low priority Africa has been given by American diplomacy in the past. Also, Justice Thurgood Marshall, Black associate justice on the Supreme Court, undoubtedly had an impact in opposing the Bakke suit, a challenge brought by a white male who claimed that affirmative action programs had kept him out of a University of California medical school. And there were other effective acts of outright opposition and resistance by Black officials.[42] However, the problem with this official approach has been its lack of overall effectiveness, its inconsistency, its reliance upon bureaucratic rules of procedure, and its incremental outcomes.

In South Africa, because the whites went to such great lengths to keep Blacks from effective political participation, Blacks as yet cannot vote for representation in the White House of the South African Parliament. And since they do not hold positions in the Executive Branch, Blacks have little formal access to legitimate channels of institutional nonviolent action to redress their grievances. As we have seen, the South African government utilized the tribal chiefs and their "parliaments" in the Homelands as instruments through which to obtain advice from African rural leaders. Also, the government fashioned the Bantu Advisory Board (1923) and Urban Bantu Councils (1961), both of which included elected and appointed members. In 1977, Community Councils were created and "mayors" were permitted in the various townships.

These institutional bodies did not offer Africans either an adequate administrative apparatus or a valid platform for resistance to the oppressive acts of the South African government, because they had no effective relation to or sanction upon the power of the government either in political or legal terms. The official status of the Blacks within them was, then, meaningless. Alternative bodies, such as the Soweto "Committee of Ten," were created in Soweto. But the most important antecedent to the committee was the rise of the Black Consciousness movement in the period 1967–1970.

Extra-Institutional nonviolent resistance finds it base of initiation within the Black community and its institutions, where resources exist for the formation and maintenance of resistance strategies as one function of community organizations. Above, we used the NAACP as a model of an organization which pioneered in working through formal governmental institutions to establish a baseline of resistance as its main strategy. It should be noted that this organization also engaged in protest demonstrations of various sorts. However, its history and experience with institutions intersected with the growth of protest organizations, such as the Southern Christian Leadership Conference, led by Martin Luther King, Jr., the Student Non-Violent Coordinating Committee, and the Congress of Racial Equality in the early 1960s, to form a powerful dynamic through which actions in the field were linked to action within institutions. One observer said of this movement: "With the techniques of nonviolent action it was possible to picket and boycott and sit-in, with consequences which, though they might involve manhandling or imprisonment for some, were far short of bloody conflict. . . . he had found that such tactics bore fruit."[43] The SCLC and SNCC came into the movement as a result of the upsurge created by young people protesting the lack of access to public accommodation because of segregation and racial prejudice, and launched a broader movement. The broader movement attacked such injustices as the lack of the right to vote, the lack of jobs, the inferior status of housing available to Blacks and its segregated access. In building this surge, they did so under the prevailing ideology of nonviolent protest. This could be attempted because the right to protest peaceably for the redress of grievances had been upheld by the First Amendment guarantee of the right to free speech and assembly. American history has seen other ethnic groups and special interest groups utilizing this method to accomplish their social objectives. These groups, however, did not have to use the philosophy of nonviolence because they were not at the same time confronted with racism which detracted from their right to the tradition of protest without additional moral sanction.

Thus, the civil rights movement was initiated by the reaction to white racists challenging the right of Black youths to go to integrated schools after the 1954 Supreme Court decision. The news coverage of these youths walking to school under the protection of the National Guard in Little Rock appeared to spark a mood of popular resistance. Sit-in tactics were begun in 1958, and there were also pray-ins, wade-ins, freedom (bus) rides and other evidence of popular resistance tactics initiated by individuals and unheard-of groups.

But the dominant features of the movement were the news-making events, such as the bus boycott of the Montgomery Improvement Association in 1957 leading to the desegregation of bus service; the 1963 March on Washington bringing 250,000 demonstrators to Washington; the Birmingham demonstration in 1963 which led to the Civil Rights Bill of 1964, and the Selma demonstration of 1965 which set the climate for the Voting Rights Act in 1965.[44]

In 1966, when Stokely Carmichael began to use the term "Black Power," a new set of strategies was introduced into the movement. One strategy was related to the acquisition of civil and human rights, but proposed Black Nationalist tactics to achieve them. The other two identifiable strains led toward Pan Africanism and "Black Liberation"—or the possibility of a total transformation of America through a violent revolution. The antecedents of this movement were clearly evident as early as 1961 when Malcolm X stepped upon the scene; between then and 1964, when he was assassinated, Malcolm provided an important counterpoise to the civil rights ideology, strategy and tactics.

Although the civil rights movement was a resistance movement, Malcolm could not accept the nonviolent resistance strategy as one that would either be successful or endow Blacks with the dignity of human integrity as men and women. His philosophy of self-determination was clearly spelled out by May of 1964 at the founding meeting of the Organization of Afro-American Unity, a "human rights" organization he built to operationalize his strategies. Reading from the Charter of the OAAU, he said,

"We assert that in those areas where the government is either unable or unwilling to protect the lives and property of our people, that our people are within our rights to protect themselves by whatever means necessary."[45] But in one of the most stringent rejections of the philosophy of nonviolent resistance, he said, again reading from the OAAU Charter:

> If you have a rifle, I must have a rifle. If you have a club, I must have a club. This is equality. If the United States Government doesn't want you and me to get rifles, then take the rifles away from the racists. If they don't want you and me to get violent, then stop the racists from being violent. Don't teach us nonviolence while those crackers are violent. Those days are over."[46]

On this same occasion, however, Malcolm expressed the desire not to be "too hard" on Black leaders inasmuch as many of them had expressed support for the aims of the OAAU. Nevertheless, in the second meeting of the new organization, he expressed an opinion on the newly enacted 1964 Civil Rights Act and pointed out that the OAAU's objectives would also be related to the achievement of humane public policy and adequate social resources. Noting that in the "hullabaloo" over the Civil Rights Bill a little Black boy was lynched in Georgia and "no-knock" and "stop-and-frisk" police laws went into effect, Malcolm criticized the bill as not having been designed to prevent job, housing or educational discrimination or the police from exercising violence against Blacks.[47] This and other themes of the Black Power period were anticipated by Malcolm X, and by 1966, there was a substantial cadre of individuals, unorganized but understanding the critique of nonviolent strategy, who began to organize extra-institutional groups to express opposition to racism without regard to the philosophy of nonviolence.

One of the individuals who reflected Malcolm's thinking in the early 1960s was LeRoi Jones. As early as 1963, in an article entitled "What Does Nonviolence Mean?" he expressed the feelings of a formidable, largely youthful Black force growing more and more opposed to the use of such tactics, and he characterized the Black leadership class in the following terms: "The NAACP, SCLC, CORE, and any other group who advocated moral suasion as their weapon of change (reform) have been members of the Negro middle class, or at least bound by that class's social sentiments. These organizations, and others like them, are controlled by the Negro middle class and sponsored by white liberal monies."[48] These ideas were certainly instructive because LeRoi Jones was to become Imamu Amiri Baraka and a leading activist in the Black Nationalist and Pan African movements after the death of Malcolm. In a later essay in 1965, Jones explicitly detailed the legacy of Malcolm X as a call to Black Consciousness and through it to an understanding that Black people constituted a nation and that the destiny of nationalists was to struggle for control over their land space.[49]

What we have established to this point was that there existed in the 1960s a strong tradition of resistance to oppression which was founded upon two dominant approaches—nonviolent active resistance and Black Power—and which, while it did not preach violence as a strategy, was secure in its belief in the right to self defense and to oppose violence with violence. I will now explore the notion and activities of resistance in South Africa before moving to the final discussion of rebellion.

Just as in the case of the American Black community, the resistance struggle in South Africa for Blacks has had a long history. The modern phase of that movement, however, strikingly has some of the same origins. For example, Steve Biko was a student, as were Stokely Carmichael and his companions in SNCC who launched the militant phase of the resistance movement. Likewise, Biko felt that it was time to examine the value of Black organizations, rather than integrationist organizations, as the basis of the resistance movement. He held this view not because he was inherently embued with Black consciousness, but because he had come to feel that integrationist organizations had bred a politics which stagnated the authentic expression of Black objectives and tactics. And "If allowed to persist over many years as a pattern in black-white political relations," he said, "this accommodation, in SASO's [South African Student Organization] view, was bound to lead eventually to an acceptance by blacks of the entire framework of 'separate development.'"[50] Biko based this statement on the belief that the accommodationists had moved toward "comfortable politics"—"comfortable politics in the sense that we must move at a pace that doesn't rock the boat"—and that the style of politics adopted by the older leaders was "shaped in the sense of working out an approach that won't lead them into any confrontation with the system."[51] Here, we have the essence of the new resistance movement Biko and his companions were to initiate in founding the South African Student Organization in the period 1970–1971.

Although I will later discuss the relevance of the Black Consciousness movement within a Pan African framework, here we are concerned with the fact that *Extra-institutional nonviolent* methods were also being attempted which assumed community political mobilization to confront the fear bred by government violence. For instance, it had become clear to SASO that there would be severe limitations to the movement if it did not have a strong adult counterpart and if it was not comprehensive in scope. And so in mid-1972, SASO helped to launch the Black People's Convention. The latter contained a combination of labor, religious and community service leaders, and its ideology strongly echoed the Black Consciousness ideology.[52] We see this influence boldly emerging in the principles and aims of the convention's Constitution. They resolved, for example, to utilize the philosophy of Black Consciousness to unify Black people, as a tool of liberating them from oppression. In accomplishing this, they would adopt an educational policy for Blacks, and a fair economic system, and construct the framework of an egalitarian society through the philosophy of "Black communalism"—sharing resources equally, while also making religion more relevant to the needs and aspirations of Black people.[53] At the same time, BPC began to take stands on issues that were extremely sensitive to the South African government; it passed a resolution rejecting foreign investors and their investments and called "upon foreign investors to disengage themselves from this white-controlled exploitative system."[54] Apparently, BPC struck a responsive cord in the Black community nationally; by late 1973 there were in existence forty-one branches of the organization.

Steve Biko himself, testifying in 1976 at the trial of the SASO Nine, characterized BPC as a political organization whose aim was to confront Apartheid by first confronting the fear resident in Black people that kept them believing that white people should rule, that their opposition was futile, and that they were less than human beings and, worst of all, ashamed of their

Blackness. Biko said, for example, that "BPC more than any-thing else was seen as giving a hope to the people."[55] But be-yond hope, the impact of BPC was infectious. One observer says that the SASO/BPC connection was responsible for stimulating community organizing efforts relating to Black self-help pro-grams, legal aid, medical aid, self-education and other commu-nity programs. These efforts gave birth to a new rash of organi-zations, including the Black Arts Theatre, the Black Press Project, the Black Workers Project of the Black Allied Workers Union and the Black Theology Project. Altogether, some 20 or-ganizations were affiliated with BPC by 1975.[56]

One of these new organizations was Black Community Pro-grams (BCP), begun in 1972 and sponsored jointly by the South African Council of Churches and the Christian Institute of Southern Africa. This was an organization very much like BPC in that it believed in Black Consciousness and sought to support the cause through a variety of programs such as leadership training, economic self-sufficiency activities, welfare work, and establishment of small businesses. Its publications office issued a Handbook of Black Organizations; BCP itself was divided into Youth, Church, Educational, Health and Workers depart-ments.[57]

Steve Biko himself went to work in 1972 for Black Community Programs as an organizer when he was expelled from medical school, and worked in Durban and even in King William's Town, the place to which he had been directed after having been banned in 1973. It was clear from his testimony that by working with BCP, Biko kept open a line of communication with BPC; these two organizations worked together on some programs. One example of their cooperation was the Black Workers Project mounted in the area around Johannesburg; a facility was set up to provide advice to workers and, although it was supposed to have been taken over by a Black trade union, BPC, BCP and SASO all found themselves working together in the facility.[58]

The Black community leaders were in a position in the early 1970s to organize a number of mass demonstrations. One such event in 1974 commemorated the victory of FRELIMO in Mo-zambique over the Portuguese; that victory had a profound im-pact upon the black movement in South Africa. The rally was set for September 25 at Curries Fountain in Durban, but it was vehemently opposed by whites who were apprehensive about the rally's possible results and also frightened by the example of FRELIMO. As the crowd gathered, police blocked entry to the Curries Fountain stadium and then set upon the crowd, scattering people in all directions. This event could perhaps have been similar in impact to the demonstration in Selma where the police also set upon the Black protesters with dogs and clubs. But there was no sympathetic press at Curries Fountain, no TV coverage, no sympathetic legislature, nor indeed the necessary sympathetic public opinion.[59]

In addition to this event, between 1974 and 1976 a wave of strikes occurred in the mines and auto plants, giving evidence that the message of Black Consciousness had permeated through the institutions of the community to the people who were the victims of the system of Apartheid. The reaction by the plant managers was swift, entailing firings, jailings, and bannings; among those banned was Drake Koka, who was the head not only of the Black Allied Workers Union, but also of the Black People's Convention. After the rebellion of 1976, which touched all over South Africa, a frightened government banned the entire range of individuals and organizations responsible for various aspects of the movement. It was no accident, then, that Steve Biko was brutally beaten to death in October 1977 by the police, which no doubt deemed him just as dangerous to the maintainance of white power as Martin Luther King, Jr. or Malcolm X were to J. Edgar Hoover, FBI director, during the 1960s.

Violent Resistance

It is, of course, extremely artificial to draw a line of demarcation between the Black Consciousness movement and the events which sparked the Soweto revolt in 1976 or between the Black Nationalist movement in America and the urban rebellions which began in 1964. I do so only to mark the difference in the quality of political strategies. I mean to suggest that the events were, indeed, part of a cohesive dynamic of op-

position to oppression. Certainly, the link between consciousness and action was evident in the above noted series of events.
Even though violent resistance to oppression is, in one sense,
more obvious than nonviolent protest, it is also more difficult to
assess empirically because the participants often do not leave
neat piles of evidence. Still, we conceive of rebellious activity as
a strategy of violent revolt against oppression carried out for the
same objectives as described at the outset of this analysis.

In the previous discussion of the situation in Britain, I noted
that much of the tension that sparked the rebellions in America
was precipitated by community attitudes toward the police.
However, some observers believe that the police were merely
representatives of the larger white community and its power
structure, suggesting that the rebellions grew out of an increasingly violent social struggle between two societies.

The pattern of events began in 1963 and 1964 with outbreaks
of nascent violence. The Report of the National Commission on
the Causes of the Disorders states that in 1963 racial disorders
broke out in Birmingham, Savannah, Cambridge, Maryland,
Chicago, and Philadelphia and that the fighting between Blacks
and whites was often more intense than battles between Blacks
and the police.[60] In addition, in 1964, in Jacksonville the arrest of
a civil rights demonstrator provoked violence; a Black woman
was killed by a sniper in a passing car and for the first time Black
high school youths used Molotov cocktails to set fires. Two
weeks later, violence erupted between Blacks and police in
Cleveland, and in July youths demonstrated for several days
after an off-duty white policeman shot and killed a 15-year-old
Black. By 1964, then, the pattern of violent retaliation was established, and in 1965 a major eruption of violence occurred in the
Watts section of Los Angeles, leaving 34 dead and millions of
dollars of property destroyed.

This was not a purely sectional Northern phenomenon in origin. It is also important to note that the national Black community was stunned into anger in 1963 by the bombing deaths of
four small Black girls in a Birmingham church and by the televised images showing police power being unleashed upon unarmed Blacks. It is possible to draw the conclusion that the ideology of Black Power was at least three years behind a militancy
in the Black community, a militancy that had climaxed in acts of

physical retaliation prompted by the growing violence and counter-violence of the civil rights movement. For even though the movement ostensibly utilized nonviolent strategies, its demonstrations, ironically, precipitated violence, a violence that actually was useful to the cause of civil rights because it gave moral weight to those who did not engage in violence and would not retaliate when violence was used against them.

However, to those who did retaliate both in the South and the North, the battle began to evolve, with the police becoming more and more the target of angry demonstrators and the combatant for the white community. Jesse Gray, a Black activist, symbolizing this mood, called for "one hundred skilled Black revolutionaries who are ready to die to correct the police brutality situation in Harlem," this in a speech to about 500 people described as Black Nationalists on July 19, 1964.[61]

The distance between the leadership style of Jesse Gray and Martin Luther King, Jr. may be summed up by what occurred when King was called to travel to Watts on August 15, 1965, to help mediate an end to the violence. David L. Lewis says that a delegation from SCLC containing Martin King, Bayard Rustin and Andrew Young walked through the rubble of the rebellion. Besides the fact that the youth were hostile to them and seemed not to know who King was, they astonished him with their attitude. "A group of young Blacks boasted 'We won.' 'How can you say you won' Martin asked, 'when thirty-four Negroes are dead, your community is destroyed and whites are using the riots as an excuse for inaction?' 'We won because *we made them pay attention* to us,' they told him" (my emphasis).[62] This distance defines the character of the mood and helps one to understand the complex of factors operating in the urban North and West that gave a certain legitimacy to the strategy of rebellion and prolonged its use for nearly a decade.

Ironically, and tragically, Martin Luther King, Jr. himself was killed by a sniper in early April 1968, and the response was an orgy of retaliatory violence and outrage by Blacks all across America. The response of the white power structure was to bring as many "responsible" Blacks and headline Black entertainers into various cities to denounce violence and call for calm, dignity and a cessation of the rebellions. Such was the case on April 6 when Roy Wilkins, executive secretary of the NAACP,

Dr. Wyatt T. Walker, minister of the Canaan Baptist Church of Christ in Harlem, and entertainer Sammy Davis, Jr., appeared before the cameras of ABC News television. Wilkins said, "It seems to me that what's taking place now, over the country, is largely subteenagers—children eleven, twelve, thirteen, fourteen and fifteen years old—desecrating the man's memory with a sort of spree, a picnic-like attitude, with dangerous and frightening overtones of thievery."[63] This theme was quickly picked up by Davis who said: "I somehow want to disown those people. Those people, who were laughing less than forty-eight hours after our leader died, and stealing . . . those are not really brothers. Those cannot be the people who are striving for the dignity that we should have at this point."[64] These remarks by Wilkins and Davis called for solemnity as the only mode of expressing a sense of loss and anger over King's murder and, again, established a great distance between themselves and the youth described as "thieves" making a "carnival." Another explanation, however, was that propounded by Frantz Fanon, who, in *The Wretched of the Earth*, said that expressive violence was a "cleansing" social act. This thought was echoed by Professor Charles Hamilton, coauthor of the book *Black Power*, who said:

> . . . there is something very important about violence as a means of cleansing people, and you cannot build a movement on non-cleansed people. You must begin from a base of consciousness— of ability to act. You must build a movement on a base of people who believe in themselves, and the cumulative effect of centuries of black-white relations in this country has left acts of expressive violence, unfortunately as the only means for the black man to create such a belief in himself.[65]

Obviously, this statement explains the distance between some Black leaders and the young rioters by clarifying the behavior of the youths, linking expressive violence to the preparation for participation in a more civil political movement.

In the case of the Black community in South Africa, it is similarly difficult to draw definite linkages between the new self-assertiveness that came with the ideology of Black Consciousness and the rebellions touched off in Soweto in 1976, but a relationship is highly likely. This leads to the suggestion that the Soweto rebellion also grew out of a process of social struggle, in this instance beginning with an aspect of Apartheid, the educational system, then the police. In making this analysis, it should be recognized that there is a theoretical difference in police tactics in the United States and South Africa. It is rather explicitly understood that the police in South Africa have the duty to protect the interests and property of the white community. Therefore, it is difficult for Africans, knowing that they do not stand under the equal protection of the laws as a concept of government, to charge the police with "harassment" or brutality." The police in South Africa are the first line defense force for the white areas, and since in America they are also perceived by Blacks as defenses of white interests their function is therefore symbolic of the larger conflict that exists in both societies. Indeed, in the United States where there is the theory of equal protection of the laws, more Blacks were incarcerated than in South Africa by 1991.

Still, we cannot deny the fact that, as Professor Leo Kuper says, "Characteristically, race riots in South Africa involve the police and Africans, since the police are the main agents of racial aggression to which the African reaction is likely to be the destruction of the government and municipal property in the locations . . ."[66] I will then examine some of the more fundamental reasons for rebellious activity during the events in Soweto in 1976.

A number of factors account for the June 16, 1976, uprising in Soweto. In the aggregate, I have illustrated that developments in the African community were responsible for producing a heightened sense of political consciousness among organizations and individuals, and especially among the youth. The combustible materials, therefore, were already set and what was needed was the match, eventually provided by Dr. Andries Treurnicht.

Treurnicht was a hard-line Afrikaner ideologue from the Transvaal who was so politically popular in this conservative region and among Afrikaners in general that he was said to have threatened the political popularity of Prime Minister Vorster himself. Vorster, therefore, brought him into government service in January of 1976 in a cabinet shuffle and made him deputy

minister of Bantu education. The department had had some difficulty enforcing a new ruling that 50 percent of the instruction
in Black schools would be conducted in Afrikaans, the language
of the ruling Afrikaner white minority.

Treurnicht was determined to enforce this policy. When asked
in Parliament for an example of the opposition among the African headmasters to the policy, he replied, "I do not deem the
requested information of such importance to instruct my department to undertake the time-consuming task" (of counting the
number opposing this policy).[67] He appeared to make the enforcement of this policy an indication of his continued maintenance of conservative Afrikaner political ideology.

The Bantu Education Act, enacted in 1953, put the territorial
schools under the direct authority of the central government
rather than the territorial assemblies. It was thought that this
would be a better way of directing the educational strategy to fit
into the overall Apartheid scheme; the imposition of Afrikaans
was considered necessary to reinforce necessary subservience
by allowing the dominant class to communicate its power to the
subordinate Black class directly in its own language.

Africans by and large hated the system of Bantu education
and regarded it as training their children to become "hewers of
wood and drawers of water," because Bantu schools were under
orders to teach in the so-called languages of their ethnic "nations." This new step, they felt, was demeaning because Afrikaans was the language of their oppressor, and to learn it would
effectively cut them off from English civilization, the symbol of
modern society and progressive ideas. This step, therefore, was
the last straw, and the students decided to resist it.

The atmosphere was ripe for resistance. In March of 1976,
25,000 Blacks in the township of KwaThema initiated a bus boycott to protest fare hikes; on March 18 Black Consciousness
members launched a demonstration protesting the trial of seven
members of the National Youth Organization (youths clubs that
had grown out of the BCM); thousands of Blacks rallied on
March 21 to commemorate the Sharpeville Massacre of March
21, 1960; in May the dramatic testimony of Steve Biko in the trial
of the "SASO Nine," charged under the Terrorism Act, swept
the Black community, adding backbone to the new political consciousness. Then, on May 17, students at Soweto's Orlando

West Junior Secondary School, numbering about 1,600 between the ages of 12 and 14, launched a strike protesting the imposition of Afrikaans and when police intervened, stoned and burned police cars.[68] The students, led by Tsietsi Mashinini, president of one of the chapters of SASM in Soweto high schools, decided to strengthen the strike by holding a demonstration on June 16. Tactics for the demonstration included having different groups of students move out from the various high schools at different times so that they could not all be controlled by the police and that some of them could reach Orlando Stadium.

On the morning of June 16, they moved out singing the anthem of the liberation struggle, "Nkosi Sikeleli Afrika" (God Bless Africa), shouting "Amandla" (Power!) with raised clenched fist, bearing placards which read, "Afrikaans is Oppressors' Language."[69] Through all of the strategizing, the SASM students hoped that they could have a peaceful demonstration. As one later said, "The demonstration we planned was to be peaceful because as students we were, of course, unarmed. But we knew that the police would be violent against the students. So we said no, immediately there is violence from the police, we would have to defend ourselves and, if possible, hit back."[70] Predictably, the police moved in with revolvers and machine guns and immediately the happy mood was broken as panic developed and bodies fell, as accounts by eye witnesses reported.[71] The government brought in its paramilitary anti-terrorism unit for the first time.[72]

Although by June 19, the official toll of deaths had risen to 109 (the unofficial toll counted nearly 700) and the government was pronouncing that "it would not be intimidated," the rebellion spread into other urban areas, townships and even into the Homelands, where students at the University of Zululand burned down the administration building, and students at Bophthatswana ignored the entreaties of Chief Mangope not to protest.

In July the government officially reversed its policy on the imposition of the Afrikaans language and offered other concessions, such as allowing Blacks in Soweto to have 30-year leases on their houses, but this could not stop the uprising. Also in July, the SASM Action Committee, which had played a part in

initiating the movement, became the Soweto Student Representative Council under the leadership of Mashinini, who
promptly went underground to direct the resistance campaign.

By August, SSRC had been successful in organizing the Black
Parents Association, an umbrella organization of prominent figures from the BCM to the YWCA, to support the struggle. Also,
solidarity strikes broke out in the Cape; 2,000 "Coloured" students began a class boycott that led to street fighting with the
police, and by September 8, the number of casualties in Cape
Town had reached seventy-three.[73]

As the resistance campaign grew, it became more political.
First, there were the inevitable attempts by the government to
use paid tribal agents to stop the violence; and Chiefs Lucas
Mangope, Gatsha Buthelezi, and others cooperated because the
uprising posed a serious threat to their authority. But this only
made them and other government collaborators stand out and
sharpened the internal resistance movement, making possible,
for example, a challenge to the Urban Bantu Council in Soweto
and the establishment of the unofficial "Committee of Ten"
Black leaders as the legitimate grassroots body representing the
Black people of Soweto.

Second, the ANC was quick to attempt to capitalize upon the
uprising by distributing leaflets urging "Amandla Soweto!"
(Power Soweto) and a popular uprising against the white minority regime. Since the formation of SASM in 1971, there had been
discussions among high school students, initiated by the ANC,
about their commitment to revolutionary struggle; as a result,
some of these students were recruited for training as armed
guerilla combatants outside of the country.[74] As the rebellions
wore on, the ANC was active in stimulating their spread by attempting to guide the tactics of resistance employed.

The effect of the movement's spread had an influence on the
political culture of the black community. For example, SSRC was
able, as indicated, to spur the formation of additional organizations committed to the resistance in the Black communities.
Also, the rebellions had an impact upon the nature of the identity of the participants; "Blackness" took on a political coloration
that affected the attitude of the Coloreds and Indians, already
re-examining the divide-and-rule tactics of the government.

Finally, other kinds of strategies of resistance were launched in this atmosphere, among them the labor strikes in September that saw an estimated five million Black workers striking in the Johannesburg area in the biggest stay-home action South Africa had ever known. This set off a series of one-day strikes across Cape Town and in other areas. By the end of the year, SSRC leaders such as Mashinini were forced to flee the country, 4,200 persons had been arrested, and 697 persons had been detained for security reasons.[75]

Conclusion

Despite the dissimilarities of culture, history, demography, legal structure and other important elements of state between the United States and South Africa, there does exist a basis for the comparative analysis of Black politics in the two countries. It rests upon the similar characteristics of the internal political dynamics examined previously between the white and Black community in each society. This has created a similar framework of race relations where the causitive factors of racial politics also rest upon similar bases.

The similar patterns of race stratification, where most power is held by the white community and its leaders, has produced a broad framework of power inequality in both societies and has produced similar patterns of Black adaptation. The pattern of accommodation is clear, in that some Blacks have assimilated the institutional and cultural values of the powerful and have become their instruments for accomplishing objectives in the Black community. To some Blacks in both societies, accommodation is useful as a personal ideology and practice for achieving individual status goals and as a rationalization for a passive political strategy. Still, there has also been a similar pattern of mild resistance, though such resistance takes place in nonviolent institutional and extra-institutional ways; this mode essentially characterized the civil rights, community organization approach in both countries. Finally, there are those in both societies who have developed a violent extra-institutional mode of expressing resistance to oppression and who have a program of serious op-position to the state that challenges its actions, structure and le-gitimacy. For example, teenage youths in both societies devel-oped a pattern of expressive violence, but in South Africa, the emphasis became much more intense, sustained, organized and purposeful because of the more severe nature of the oppression.

The framework for the comparative analysis has demon-strated a similar pattern of Black community objectives and po-litical strategies as well. Generally, in neither society has there been any dimunition of the drive (or the will) among Blacks to establish community—a valid conception of social relations that places value on the individual and institutional resource aspects of building a community. Beyond merely reacting to the general framework of race relations, the goal of the Black community has required the establishment of specific objectives, such as the elimination of racism, especially institutional racism; an end to unemployment; an end to limitations in job mobility caused by racism; the right to unionize openly and effectively; the right to receive a fair return on their labor on equal terms with white workers; the right to decent and adequate urban facilities and access to residence in the urban areas; the provision of housing, and rights to ownership in and control over their neighbor-hoods.

Finally, one of the most striking differences between the two societies is ideological. The ideology of political inclusion inher-ent in the constitutional form of American democracy gave Blacks the tools with which to forge a political struggle to change their condition. In South Africa, however, the idea of "Herren-volk Democracy" that legally excluded Blacks from social, polit-ical, and most economic participation, set severe limitations upon Black achievement and on the consequent social status of the Black community. Still, in both cases, the relative power of the Black community to the white community finds the former still at the bottom and subject to similar treatment such as that by the police, and while a relatively larger Black middle class emerged in America than in South Africa, effective economic power in both cases is largely absent. So, although the function of these two ideologies has made the absolute trend toward so-cial advancement by Blacks far more rapid in the United States than in South Africa, in relative terms, their progress is about the same. In addition, with the prospect that the Apartheid system may be eliminated and a system constructed where Blacks would achieve the kind of political participation that should result in areas of control of the state, the means may be at hand to enhance Black community development within South Africa more rapidly than in the United States in the future. The comparative ideologies of democratic inclusion and Herrenvolk, therefore, have produced a distinction without much of a difference in the relative social status of the two Black communities.

9
Pan African Politics of Black Communities in the United States and South Africa

The modern post-war period witnessed the rise of the African National Congress, an organization dedicated to the acquisition of Black civil rights within a multiracial South Africa. To achieve this goal, there was continuous agitation. For example, in 1946, strikes called by the African miners union brought out more than 70,000 miners. In 1949, a mass protest in Johannesburg ended with the killing of 18 Black Africans by the police, and in 1952 the ANC Defiance Campaign saw 8,500 Africans voluntarily go to jail to protest repressive laws. By 1957, African women protested the hated pass laws by burning their pass books; 200 were arrested in the violence that followed. However, these protests kept up sporadically in 1958 and 1959 and in the latter year, 330 were arrested protesting the Bantu Authorities Act and the cattle culling program in Natal and Sekukuniland. And in 1960, a PAC (Pan African Congress) anti-pass law campaign led to demonstrations and to the killing of 69 Africans and wounding of others in the infamous massacre at Sharpeville. After this period, the ANC and the PAC were forced to go underground and a program of sabotage and guerilla activities was launched by a new ANC organization "Um Khonto We Sizewe," The Spear of the Nation which had "Poqo" or small paramilitary units.[1]

After Sharpeville, the ANC was closely allied with the Communist party of South Africa, and the heavy influence of white liberals and Communists kept the objectives of the organization rooted in multiracialism. Such leaders as Dr. A. B. Xuma and Chief Albert Luthli, the Nobel Peace Prize winner, were moderate in outlook and method, and they were respected in the sense that Martin Luther King, Jr. was both feared and respected by whites in America. But this was not always the case. Beginning about 1944, there arose a Black consciousness movement in the form of the ANC Youth League to challenge the multiracialism of the older leaders. Robert Sobukwe, Walter Sisulu, Nelson Mandela, Oliver Tambo and Peter Roboroko were the core group that began this movement of rejecting all forms of white domination and demanding "Africa for the Africans"—the early slogan of Marcus Garvey. These impatient young breakaway militants formed the Pan Africanist Congress in April of 1959. The charismatic Anton Lembede, however, was considered the originator of the Africanist ideology of the PAC.[2] Lembede, a lawyer, died at the age of 33 in 1947, but his legacy lived on in that the PAC came to be influenced by the ideas of W.E.B. DuBois and George Padmore, whose book *Pan Africanism or Communism?* made them suspicious of the motives of Communists and distrustful of Communist influence in the ANC.

In the ensuing years the Black population reacted to the growing knowledge that the white minority would not readily share power and that only a forceful movement could change power relationships. When this became clear the objectives of the whites were no longer simply the maintainance of the status quo and the objectives of the Blacks were no longer the simple elimination of the racially discriminatory aspects of Apartheid.

Internally the South African situation moved quickly in the direction of polarization and growing violence on both sides of the equation. By the early 1980s Professor Gwendolen Carter could write that her visit to South Africa in 1964 was the last permitted by the South African government until 1979 and that one striking impression she shared, actually sharpened by the hiatus, was that the pace of the government program of separate development had increased to a pronounced degree. She relates witnessing on her 1979 visit much more of the institutionalized separation of the races than was present in 1964.[3] She also had the vivid impression that young Blacks were more militant and less tolerant of the pace of change than their brothers in the 1960s.

Into this volatile situation in the 1970s stepped an important group of Black American civil rights leaders and others. For example, in early 1972, an alert group of artists in New York, later to form an organization known as the Committee of Concerned Blacks, discovered that a number of prominent Black artists had made plans to tour South Africa.[4] As a result, the tours of these entertainers were all eventually canceled. At about the same time, Roy Wilkins, NAACP executive director, accepted an invitation to visit South Africa, and thus came under pressure from the committee. In a letter to Wilkins, Louise Merriweather attempted to explain the essential rationale for the adoption of a policy of boycotting South Africa altogether by the committee: "The purpose of our committee is to disseminate the facts and figures contained in our paper to the black community and to publicize our position that any accommodation with South Africa strengthens that racist government, is an act of treason against the Africans in rebellion underground and those fighting wars of liberation in Mozambique, Rhodesia and Guinea-Bissau." Elsewhere in this letter, Merriweather said that Wilkins' presence would be used to full advantage by the South African government and would illustrate the fact that while the United States, Britain and France had "no difficulty sticking together" in support of the South African white minority regime, Blacks in the Diaspora were not united in support of fellow Africans. This she said, "would be detrimental to Black unity throughout the world."[5]

About two weeks later, Wilkins replied, saying, "I am sorry, but if I am given a visa to visit South Africa I shall go." He added that his invitation came from the Association for the Educational and Cultural Advancement of the African People of South Africa (ASSECA) and that there was a distinction between his visit as a consultant and that of an entertainer. His letter continues: "Moves from the outside which are calculated to aid the plight of black Africans should, of course, continue. But it is the

NAACP position that its director cannot refuse a plea for aid from inside the country, made by the very people whose situation we wish to improve."[6] By March 27, however, Wilkins had arrived in South Africa and on that day visited a Black township outside Johannesburg where he announced that he "was not impressed." A news report, however, quoted Wilkins as strongly defending U.S. business involvement in South Africa, saying, "How many black jobs would be lost if General Motors went back to Detroit, if John Deere and Chase Manhattan pulled out? If these American corporations were not here and South Africa corporations had those manufacturing units, would they not have the same or a worse pattern?"[7] This view, the story in the *New York Times* continued, represented an attitude developing among prominent Black leaders, suggesting that the theme of "jobs before rights" was one that found acceptance among Black State Department officials, Black business executives and others.[8] Merriweather and Dr. Mburumba Kerina, a Namibian leader in exile and an official spokesperson for the committee, went on the offensive to counter Wilkins' remarks, suggesting that "supporting . . . revolutionary acts should be the role of American blacks rather than defending American companies. Is Roy Wilkins speaking for the NAACP membership or for the American corporate structure?"[9] They further pointed out that the organization sponsoring the trip, ASSECA, had recently been the recipient of a $10,000 grant from the Polaroid Corporation. Polaroid, however, was experiencing considerable harrassment from the Black-led Polaroid Revolutionary movement in Boston that opposed Polaroid's presence and activities in South Africa. Black employees of Polaroid discovered that they were involved in manufacturing the cards for the South African identification system mandated by the infamous pass law. After months of mobilizing against this involvement, the Polaroid Corporation donated $10,000 to Boston's Black United Front; while this was apparently designed to split the anti-Apartheid effort of the Black community, the Front contributed $5,000 to the Polaroid Revolutionary Movement and $5,000 to other community organizations.[10]

ASSECA was founded in 1968 by a group of individuals who were alarmed over the 1967 matriculation results for Black children and who resolved to point out the problems of "Bantu education" and attempt to resolve them within the framework of the Apartheid system as a non-political organization.[11] It is well to remember that by 1968 the ANC and the PAC, liberation movements devoted to armed struggle, had been in existence and operating for eight years and that the ASSECA stood in relation to these organizations where the NAACP stood to the Black Panthers or the Revolutionary Action Movement in the United States.

Nonetheless, in early 1971 when leaders of the South African Student Organization (SASO) sought to establish an umbrella organization for the strengthening of the Black Consciousness movement, it invited ASSECA and five other organizations to meet and form this institution. From this meeting, M. T. Moerane, editor of a Black South African newspaper, *The World*, and president of ASSECA, emerged as chairman of the group, but much to SASO's consternation, it developed that Moerane, who had been an original member of Lembede's ANC Youth League, had mellowed over the years and resisted militant politics in favor of a very moderate course. In the end he did not join what came in July 1972 to be the Black Peoples Convention. Despite characterizations of ASSECA as more moderate and accommodationist then even Chief Buthelezi of Zululand, however, the white minority government banned ASSECA in 1977.[12]

Another civil rights leader who went to South Africa in this period was Rev. Jesse Jackson, national president of Operation PUSH, who visited in late July of 1979. His interest in South Africa had been expressed earlier in the year when he waged a successful campaign to prevent white South African boxer Kallie Koetze from coming to the States to box. This campaign signaled that Jackson had a wider interest in opposing the policies of the racist government. It was small wonder, then, that his application for a visa was not received cordially by the South African government, but an intercession on his behalf by Secretary of State Cyrus Vance made his trip possible.

Reports reaching the United States showed that Jackson had an emotional impact upon Blacks in South Africa. For example, at Crossroads, a "squatters" camp of 20,000 people who were there "illegally," according to South African residence laws, people responded to the familiar refrain "I am somebody!" and to the chant that "this land is changing hands!" It was reported that "women in the audience repeatedly broke into hymns, and some wept. Afterwards, as Mr. Jackson made his way among the tin shanties clustered on the sandflats he was mobbed, with people of all ages reaching out for his touch. Not since Senator Robert F. Kennedy visited South Africa in 1966 has a visiting American caused such a stir among Blacks and whites as Mr. Jackson."[13]

Rev. Jackson's visit lasted ten days and he met and talked before varying groups, including university students and faculty, business leaders (especially American business leaders) and government officials as well as Black leaders. Although he had promised not to prescribe American policy on the question of disinvestment by U.S. businesses in South Africa, by the end of his visit he was leading four thousand Black South Africans in Black power chants urging President Carter to oppose U.S. investment in South Africa.[14]

And so we have seen visits by a moderate and a militant Black civil rights leader to South Africa. The question posed by their visits is, what was the impact of their direct contacts with peoples of African descent whom they considered as "brothers and sisters." The major impact appears to have been at the level of identification with the prevailing moods in South Africa. Clearly, there is in South Africa a group which reacts to the presence of Blacks as they did in a meeting with Black American tennis star, Arthur Ashe there in 1974. This group said: "If we isolate them, they're forced to change. . . . Cut off South Africa, boycott it. Don't you see: we blacks wouldn't suffer any more than we already do. We are used to suffering. Only the whites would suffer more. Power! Power!"[15] A contrasting point of view was expressed as follows: "Somebody like you comes, it shows us an inspiration, not just to excel at something, but not to be intimidated by the bully. Enough of you come and show us, then pretty soon, we don't have no bully no more."[16] Now the optimism of the latter attitude paled beside the realism of the former, for it was highly unlikely that the South African government would permit Blacks there to begin to "be like you [Black Americans], free." The first attitude derives from the many situations where Blacks have had the opportunity to test the reactions of the whites to their exercise of freedom, in the mining sector, in labor strikes, at Sharpeville, in the Soweto rebellions and at other times in the history of that relationship.

More fundamentally for this study, the actual and potential repression exercised by South Africans was the reason direct contacts by both moderate and militant Black leaders had little impact upon that situation in an *institutional* sense. No new movements were fostered, no new organizations sprang into existence, and no events were reported as a direct consequence of these visits.

The history of this issue since that time suggests that it was not necessary for Blacks to have gone to South Africa to have had an impact, that where these Black leaders and their messages were largely unsuccessful in stimulating mass movement, the Black Power movement *in America* succeeded. Perhaps the correlation of its power arose from the fact that this movement was not at all directed toward obtaining an American civil rights type of freedom; rather, it was aimed at doing something the white South Africans could not control—it affirmed the worth and dignity of Africans as individuals and emphasized that Black survival in South Africa depended not on obtaining more freedom within white domination, but of applying the power of their Blackness toward the goal of eventually governing the land.

It is possible that the visits by Black leaders did far more in the United States in that the controversy helped to legitimize the boycott policy in the South African struggle as a part of the American Black agenda and it identified Jesse Jackson with the issue in a manner which would contribute to his subsequent role in projecting a progressive view of American foreign policy toward South Africa in the context of his 1984 and 1988 presidential campaigns.

Thus, at this point, I will assess the direct connection of the idea of Black Consciousness as it emanated from the Black Power movement in the United States, and the philosophical development of the concept of Black Consciousness into a full blown ideology of Black community mobilization in South Africa. The organization that espoused this ideology was the South African Students Organization, led by Steve Biko. Of course, its own antecedents were important in the development of this ideology, since the "Africanist" ideology of Anton Lembede of the African Youth League of the ANC as suggested was briefly popular in the 1940s and was adopted by Pan Africanist Congress militants in the 1960s as the basis of their organizational beliefs.

When the SNCC leader Stokely Carmichael uttered the words Black Power during a demonstration in July 1966, this sentiment found fertile root in the Black masses and launched a new movement for "Black Liberation," setting it apart from the civil rights projection of the immediate past period. The power of this movement, like the Garvey movement before it, raced into the far corners of the Black world, and South Africa would be no exception. We may illustrate this with regard to the definition of Black Power itself. For example, in their work *Black Power*, Carmichael and Hamilton write: "The concept of Black Power rests on a fundamental premise: Before a group can enter the open society, it must first close ranks. By this we mean that group solidarity is necessary before a group can operate effectively from a bargaining position of strength in a pluralistic society." [17] At the same time, the SASO policy manifesto adopted in July 1971 also defined the movement. SASO defined Black Consciousness as an attitude of mind, a way of life that rejects values that make Blacks foreigners in their own land; that promotes self definition rather than definition by others; that considers group unity the key to wielding power, politically and economically; and that attempts to reach the entire community with the message of Black Consciousness. Then, in a section identical to that cited above in the book *Black Power*, the manifesto said:

> SASO accepts the premise that before the black people should join the open society, they should first close their ranks, to form themselves into a solid group to oppose the definite racism that is meted out by the white society, to work out their direction clearly and bargain from a position of strength. SASO believes that a truly open society can only be achieved by blacks. [18]

There is some evidence that this statement, expressing obvious connection with the terms of reference of Black Power in its emphasis on adopting a Black "value system," on "closing ranks," on "group solidarity," and on "bargaining from a position of

strength," was being operationalized even earlier in the formation of SASO, as indicated by statements from a training session
conducted by the organization in September of the previous
year. SASO executives who attended the training seminar were
split up into various groups, and one group was instructed to
study the importance of the statement "before entering the open
society, we must first close ranks" that appeared in the Carmichael and Hamilton book.[19] We see, then, that the discussion in
September of 1970 crystallized into the SASO policy statement
of 1971 as an official part of the organization's ideological understanding.

It is also important to note that while utilizing the concepts
outlined in the American Black Power movement, the SASO
leadership was careful to make the distinction between the
American situation and that which they faced in South Africa.
They understood, for example, that when Black Americans indicated a desire to "close ranks," they wanted to do so as a tacti-
cal ploy to create, out of their minority status, the organizational
resources to acquire the power necessary to alter their status
within society. But SASO also understood that the goals of
Blacks in South African society perforce were different. SASO
recognized that the entire power relationship between the Black
majority and whites had to be changed to reflect the situation
there. In this sense, the meaning of an "open society" with its
many possibilities changed substantially as one moved from the
United States to South Africa.

We are taking one slice out of the cultural and political communications of Black America to illustrate the connection with
the South Africa Black movement. But we should be aware that
a much broader band of currents also crossed the waters—the
speeches of Martin Luther King, Malcolm X and others and the
writings of James Baldwin, Julius Lester, Nikki Giovanni and
many others. And so there was an impact of the Black American
1960s atmosphere in a time of political movement that tran-
scended the impact of any one organization or personality. Barney Pityane, a founder of SASO, evidenced his awareness of the
"discontent seething" within Black Americans; of the history of
mass mobilizations like the Selma to Montgomery march and
the rhetoric of Martin Luther King, Jr. and Malcolm X, which
"reverberated across the oceans, to break the hot, still air of the

black ghettoes in South Africa." He continued, suggesting that what shook the "complacency in the hearts and minds of the black students sitting in a tribal 'bush' college in South Africa," even more than the call for Black liberation in America was the formidable essence of the racist system of Apartheid itself.[20]

Pityane also pointed out that the South African government established a commission, known as the Schlebusch Commission, to investigate Black organizations. The commission, in Pityane's words, concluded that "Black Consciousness" was nothing but an importation of Black Power ideas from America, as if that was wrong in itself," that it was inspired not by local conditions but by imported problems, and that it was meant to inspire racial polarization.[21] While noting this charge, Pityane goes on to identify some of the various influences and powerfully similar descriptions of life constructed by Black American and South African Black writers and ideologists. At the same time, he suggests that there are also certain negative influences on Black Consciousness that arise from "Afro-Americanism," such as that which glorifies capitalism, exhibited by images depicted in the pages of *Ebony* magazine emphasizing Blacks involved in conspicuous displays of affluence. But in the final analysis, he points out that as a concept which fosters a certain way of life, Black Consciousness emanated from and, thus, identifies with many similar life experience of Black Americans.

> It is obviously true that both black Americans and black South Africans were victims of capitalist-imperialist economic system. The excesses in wealth and deprivation are to be seen cheek by jowl in the same locality. People are imbued by the system with the notion that they have only themselves to blame for being without the necessary means of livelihood. There is lack of housing for blacks, discrimination in employment and thus poverty.[22]

This catalogue of similar conditions in South Africa and America, he strongly infers, explains why the ideology of Black Power was so welcome among the Black South African masses and assisted them in organizing institutions to reflect the vitality of the new ideology. For, although it has been previously mentioned that the student movement attempted to form an umbrella organization devoted to Black education, we should be aware that this tremendous surge in the expression of Black self-determination fostered the development of a new series of organizations in the Black South African community. For instance, the Black Peoples Convention, the adult manifestation of the movement, was born in July of 1972; in August 1972 the Black Allied Worker's Union was formed; a Black cultural movement was started, and the Black clergy was also infected with the new ideology.

I should say a special word about the clergy inasmuch as it is possible that their influence was among the first to bring the doctrine of Black Consciousness to life by way of the "Black Theology movement," itself an outgrowth of the Black Power movement in the United States. In July 1966, shortly after the cry Black Power! unleashed a tremendous force, a group called the National Committee of Negro Churchmen met in New York City to affirm the principle of Black Power and issued a statement which was published in full in the *New York Times*. It said:

> From the point of view of the Christian faith, there is nothing necessarily wrong with concern for power. . . . At issue in the relations between whites and Negroes in America is the problem of inequality of power. Out of this imbalance grows the disrespect of white men for the Negro personality and community, and the disrespect of Negroes for themselves. This is the fundamental root of human injustice in America.[23]

And so, early in the Black Power period, Black churchmen struck the theme of the ill-usage of power on the Black personality and the consequent damage to the Black psyche. As they saw it, Black Power would become the corrective force that restored the Black man's sense of himself and his perspective amid the oppression raging around him.

From this, the manifesto went on to do as Carmichael and Hamilton had done and condemn the notion of integration fostered by the Black and white civil rights movement as a perversion because it was founded not upon an equal distribution of power that would make the participation of Blacks effective, but upon a paternalism in which whites held power over so-called "integrated" institutions and political coalitions.

As Professor Gayraud Wilmore points out in a masterful analysis of the relationship between this movement and religion, between 1966 and 1970 the Black Power movement was moving toward an institutionalized place among Black churchmen.[24] Spurred on by a searching and inspirational article by Dr. Vincent Harding, "Black Power and the American Christ," published in 1967, the National Committee of Negro Churchmen (later called Black Churchmen) authorized a further examination into this phenomenon that became the "Black Theology project." But then, almost as a response to this call, in 1968 Rev. Albert Cleage's *The Black Messiah* was published, presenting an *historical* rather than an eschatological challenge to the "blackness" of American religion by positing the blackness of Jesus Christ. In 1969 the appearance of Rev. James Cone's *Black Theology and Black Power* took center stage in establishing a theological basis for the ideology of Black Power.[25]

By 1969, the challenge of Black Power to the American church had reverberated to the World Council of Churches in the form of the demand for reparations, resulting in the formation of the Interreligious Foundation for Community Organization (IFCO), a largely Black-led agency of the American Council of Churches. IFCO proceeded to fund a Black economic development conference, headed by James Forman, former SNCC executive director, held in Detroit in April 1969. The manifesto that emerged from this conference was used within days by Forman as the basis for the demand for reparations; he boldly walked into Riverside Church in New York City and demanded $500 million in reparations for the role of the church (all Western churches) in the oppression of Blacks.

Just as important for our purpose, Wilmore recalls that this incident initiated a series of church "liberations" and an associated series of events both in this country and overseas. For example, on May 23, the World Council of Churches, meeting in London, adopted a "Declaration of Revolution" setting up the allocation of funds to South African political prisoners and African liberation movements, and leading to the Council's Program to Combat Racism, an agency that has since provided critical support to the world-wide anti-Apartheid movement.[26]

By 1967, in South Africa, two liberal white clerics, Basil Moore, a Methodist, and Colin Collins, a Catholic priest, had established the University Christian Movement (UCM), a multiracial organization containing a substantial number of Black students. It was, perhaps, the fact that UCM showed a strong interest in Black Theology that ironically made Black students susceptible to the overtures of Steve Biko in August of 1968 to form an all-Black student organization that eventually became SASO.[27]

Sabelo Nwasa became the first director of UCM's Black Theology Project in 1971 and was instrumental in initiating a series of conferences on Black Theology across South Africa in that year. However, he was placed under house arrest in 1972 and his writings were banned. Mokgethi Mothabi became director of the project after he refused to return to Catholic seminary training at Hammanskraal in the Transvaal following a student strike. He, too, was banned, and it was left to Basil Moore to bring out the volume of papers from the previous conferences in 1972; the book was promptly banned in 1973 by the censors.[28] UCM no longer exists, and Basil Moore was banned under the Suppression of Communism Act and fled to London in 1972.

But in this remarkable volume of essays on Black Theology in South Africa, Moore included an essay by Rev. James Cone, leader of the American Black Theology movement, entitled, "Black Theology and Black Liberation." In the essay, Cone defines the relevance of the concept, writing: "The significance of Black Theology lies in the conviction that the content of the Christian gospel is liberation, so that any talk about God that fails to take seriously the righteousness of God as revealed in the liberation of the weak and downtrodden is not Christian language."[29] In another place he says, ". . . we conclude in America that Christian Theology must be black. In a society where men are defined on the basis of colour for the purpose of humiliation, Christian Theology takes on the colour of the victims, proclaiming that the condition of the poor is incongruous to him who has come to liberate us."[30] It was the consensus of the other writers in the collection that Black Theology should have special relevance to South African Blacks since the dehumanization suffered by Black people is the beginning place of the humanity and privilege of its white population. In their own article, Ntwasa and Moore support the contention by the Black American clerics that because of the depth of their suffering, Black people have a special perspective upon Christian theology, suggesting that

Black South Africans also know, "better than any other man," the experience of dehumanization, where the basic decisions over the lives of Black people are made by whites.[31] They find that even Western theological authoritarianism has been used to support the status quo and challenge this "twisted application of God's authority" by encouraging Blacks to reject all that flows from it as "nonsense."[32]

These bold assertions of the humanity of Black people through the Christian religion and the writers' identification with the striving for Black liberation as a natural consequence of belief in God and Jesus as liberators found support in the Black student movement. In this same volume, Barney Pityane, as I have noted, wrote that "Black Theology . . . is an extension of Black Consciousness," that "both Black Theology and Black Consciousness are instruments of construction," and that "the Relationship between Black Theology and Black Consciousness is that one is a genus of the other." But he best defines the relationship as that described by James Cone, who said: "Black Theology seeks to commit black people to the risks of affirming the dignity of black personhood. We do this as men and as black Christians." Cone continues: "In a nutshell, then, Black Theology concerns itself with liberation, and liberation presupposes a search for humanity and for existence as a God-created being."[33] This affinity between the two doctrines is the reason why, as Pityane noted, a resolution was passed at the SASO Conference in July 1971 affirming the belief that Black Theology "is an authentic and positive articulation of the black Christians' reflection on God in the light of their experience."[34]

Another important aspect of the Pan African dimension of relations between Black Americans and Black South Africans has been the extent to which a rather important group of political exiles from South Africa have been resident in the United States and have, to a large extent, functioned within the parameters of the Black community. Here, one may mention as representative writers Bloke Modisane, Willie Kereopsitsili and Ezekiel Mphalele, labor leaders such as Drake Koka, entertainers such as Miriam Makeba, journalists such as Jordan Ngubane and Percy Quoboza, professors such as Bernard Magubane, Dennis Brutus and Chris Ntete, activists refugees such as Dumisani Matabani, Dumisani Kumalo and other representatives of the various movements, including most notably Johnny Makatini of ANC and David Sibeko of PAC.

There have also been frequent visitors representating various tendencies inside South Africa, such as Bishop Desmond Tutu, general secretary of the South African Council of Churches; Rev. Alan Boesak, former head of the Dutch Reformed Church of South Africa; Chief Gatsha Buthelezi, head of the Zulu Homeland and of Inkatha, a Zulu political organization; Nyati Pokela, president of the Pan Africanist Congress of Azania, and Oliver Tambo, president of the African National Congress of South Africa. In the process, an extraordinary Pan African relationship has been formed between the members of some of these organizations such as the ANC and especially with representatives of the United Democratic Front (UDF), an umbrella organization formed after the 1976 rebellion to represent a coalition of Black organizations involved in the freedom struggle with the Black American lobby organization TransAfrica. I will very briefly examine the activities of TransAfrica somewhat later in this chapter.

These individuals have been an invaluable source of inspiration and education to the American Black community on the life of Black South Africans and the oppression they face through the policies of Apartheid. But perhaps one of the most important of these individuals was David Sibeko, PAC representative to the UN. Sibeko, a big jovial man with a booming voice and an unavoidable presence, was also seriously political. He was a constant force in the American Black community from the time he began to come to the United States regularly in the late 1960s. He knew well many of the key activists in the Black community and never turned down an opportunity to speak before Black groups on the nature of Apartheid. His presence in the Black community was truly inspiring and unique at a time when many Africans residing in the United States were basing their main activities in the white communities with individuals and families who often were their political and financial sponsors and patrons. His presence came precisely at the time when a strong Pan African movement developed in the United States, and with his considerable world-wide contacts he was an important source of guidance and information on the entire liberation struggle in Southern Africa. Articulate and powerful as a

speaker, he represented the less well endowed of the two liberation movements—PAC's support came mainly from the
People's Republic of China—and the less approved-of group because its ideology was inclined to be more Black Nationalistic
than that of ANC. Yet, to many in America and around the
world, he was the authentic voice of the Black South African
freedom struggle. When David Sibeko was assassinated in an
internal conflict within the PAC in June 1979, he had become
PAC's director of foreign affairs and a member of its executive
committee.

In this same period of the surge of Black Power and the resurgence of the Pan Africanism movement, perhaps no one did as
much as Miriam Makeba to popularize the situation of the Black
people in South Africa through her rendition of South African
folk songs expressing Black resistance to Apartheid. In this
sense, Makeba was a political figure, but her role diminished as
she became more identified with American radical movements
through her marriage to Stokely Carmichael in the early 1970s
and as her concerts became more explicitly political.

More recently, the void left by Sibeko was filled by other
forceful representatives, in particular, Johnny Makatini, ANC
representative to the United Nations from the mid-1970s to the
mid-1980s, who died in 1987, understood the American political
process perhaps better than any of the other expatriate South
Africans and frequently availed himself of the Black leadership
in America to push the cause of the South African struggle into
the corridors of United States foreign policy. He was one of the
most tireless lobbyists for this cause within the UN political
framework, in Africa and in the United States as well.

So effective were these individuals who alerted Black Americans to the South African plight that as early as 1970 groups involved in the Black Nationalist/Pan African movement, such as
the Republic of New Africa, could easily identify: "To begin with
it is important to understand that we in the Republic of New
Africa look upon ourselves in the same way that the brothers of
Azania [South Africa] look upon themselves vis-a-vis the white
South African. The Azanians are fighting to free their land from
a white oppressor; we New Africans are doing precisely the
same thing."[35] Few American Black groups would admit to such
a close identification with the goals of Azanian freedom fighters

because ANC has been legitimized by a substantial portion of the international community as the most effective group in mounting a serious challenge to the South African white minority regime. The animosity between ANC and PAC has split some segments of the Black American community into two ideological camps. The Black Nationalist and strongly African-oriented organizations tended to favor PAC, while the Marxist organizations supported ANC. In the middle, most of the American Black community support the ANC leadership because of its visibility.

The fact that African Americans identify with the South African issue through the ANC prism was illustrated by the tremendous reception given to Nelson Mandela on the occasion of his visit to the United States after his dramatic release from prison in February 1990. At the moment of his release, Rev. Jesse Jackson, who had traveled to South Africa for the occasion, was the first American to greet him, and Jackson and his family were received by the Mandelas very warmly. Jackson had come to South Africa from Britain where he had met with Prime Minister Margaret Thatcher to urge the British government to support Mandela's release and to continue to apply the modest economic sanctions it had in force. Jackson had tried without success in his 1984 presidential campaign to make South Africa an issue among the other Democratic candidates but he succeeded in doing so in his 1988 presidential campaign.[36]

The lead organization in hosting Mandela and the ANC delegation was the Free South Africa Movement (FSAM), a formation sponsored by TransAfrica, originally to broaden the opposition to Apartheid by demonstrations conducted in 1985, a campaign that succeeded in influencing the passage of the anti-Apartheid Act of 1986. That FSAM was given this role was testimony to the close relationship between ANC and this American formation. By 1989, an ANC office had been opened in Washington, and its director, Lindiwe Mabuza, a Black South African, helped to solidify these relationships.

At a meeting in London in January of 1990, sponsored by the ANC leadership, Mandela reception committees were established in each of the countries the ANC leader was visiting as a part of the tour. In the United States, committees were established in New York City and in Washington, with Randall Robinson having substantial responsibility through the TransAfrica/ FSAM leadership.[37] The planning for the American venue in June included visits by Mandela to cities where he could be well taken care of, and some of these cities had African-American mayors.[38] And even those who opposed the Black community on issues such as affirmative action were bound to admit this truth, as neoconservative Harvard Professor Nathan Glazer acknowledged, that the political power of the Black community was central to the form of the reception in several cities, including New York.[39]

When Nelson Mandela arrived in New York City, he was hosted by Mayor David Dinkins and the Black business and professional community. This scenario was repeated in Detroit, Oakland, Birmingham, Baltimore and Los Angeles. In Washington, the city officials greeted the Mandela party while its Black mayor, Marion Barry, a strong supporter of the anti-Apartheid movement, was standing trial for alleged involvement with drugs. In Miami, another major city visited by Mandela, the mayor refused officially to greet his party because Mandela had voiced continuing support for Fidel Castro.

Nevertheless, the essential story of the Mandela visit, substantiated by public opinion polls and the turnout of African-origin peoples, was one of a massive outpouring of love and support for Nelson Mandela, the Black South African leader who had spent 27 years in prisons for his anti-Apartheid activities. Seldom in the history of Black America had there been such a public witness for another Black leader. White Americans were said to be experiencing "Nelson Mandela burnout" from what they felt was too much media attention to the Black leader, but this attitude certainly did not extend to African Americans. A survey showed that 58 percent of America's Blacks followed his visit in the United States via the media as opposed to just 20 percent of whites.[40]

Howard Dodson, director of the Schomberg Library in Harlem, was to set the tone for the awed perspective of most African Americans in suggesting that the visit was an "extraordinary and unique moment in history."[41] Most often, Blacks marveled at Mandela's integrity and his consistency in the pursuit of his principles for 27 years. As a result, he was able to raise $10 million on his tour in the United States, and he achieved a heroic status among Black leaders of the world. A careful understanding of Mandela's speeches explaining his commitment reveal that there were several keys to understanding his heroic qualities. First, when he spoke, he often used the collective term "we" to indicate that the positions which he was espousing emerged from a collective process arrived at through an organizational effort. Second, it was clear from the first moment that he had subjected himself to the discipline of ANC, not appearing to be more important than the organization and the goals for which it had struggled. Third, he often referred to historical events and, thus, grounded himself in a continuum of concepts such as the Freedom Charter, the 1985 constitution containing ANC's principles for the construction of a nonracial South Africa. His use of such concepts validated them for the succeeding generations now in the movement. Finally, his integrity was a personal quality visible in his historical commitment and his refusal to be swayed from a militant course or induced to disavow ANC's revolutionary tradition. The kind of leadership forged in a situation of intense struggle is bound to be somewhat different than bureaucratic or administrative leadership.

On his U.S. visit Mandela was subjected to considerable pressures to bend, as when he was asked by President Bush at one point to disavow violence. Instead of succumbing to a powerful president's request, he said the president was misinformed on this question, asserting that because of the violence of the white minority regime the Africans had no alternative and that as long as peaceful channels were open, there would be no need for violence.[42] A few days earlier on the Ted Koppel TV program "Nightline," while he appeared to intimidate the usually unflappable Koppel, he had also refused to disavow Yasser Arafat, head of the Palestine Liberation Organization (PLO), saying that Arafat had helped the ANC when it had few international friends and that it would not befit any leader with integrity to turn his back on comrades. He maintained this position throughout his visit.

As a result of the personal values and characteristics Nelson Mandela exhibited, he engendered no little speculation on the quality of current African-American leadership by comparison. The tendency of the African-American leadership to compromise to the detriment of the masses, to eschew the accountability that comes from adhering to organizational discipline, to speak in a manner devoid of African or African-American historical precedents and personages, and to manifest little personal integrity are all traits which affect not a few in the Black leadership class today. As a result, some have voiced the concern that there is now no one of the stature of a Nelson Mandela in the United States. It should also be understood that heroic circumstances also contribute to the emergence of heroic leadership and, to that extent, the ascendency of electoral politics as a moderate methodology of social change and the lack of an intensely emotional crucible of change in the United States in this era have perhaps deprived African-origin peoples of the opportunity to have such leadership as well.

Conclusion

I will comment first upon the comparative aspects of the methodology used in this set of chapters dealing with the South African case, then conclude with some observations on the Pan African method.

To begin with, the South African white minority regime ran a political system that represented a caricature of the United States in its tight control of the Black population, based upon an elaborate legal code of Apartheid, and backed up by the brutal use of police power. Thus, while South African whites made little pretense of employing a legal regime of equality such as the "equal protection of the laws" contained in the United States Constitution, there have been frequent occasions in the United States where the Black population was treated just as brutally and where the theory of law was no comfort. As suggested, this is more obvious in the use of police power than in any other area, even though in some cities the mayors are Black and the police forces are both integrated and led by Blacks. This significant degree of racial integration in many American cities has prevented neither disproportionate police use of deadly force against Blacks nor a national rate of incarceration of Blacks that is greater than South Africa's, as previously observed.

The comparative assessment of both countries, nevertheless, yielded an interesting understanding that the course of political modernization—as determined by the progress of the incorporation of Blacks into society—has not been linear in either society. However, in the United States, the regime of law was helpful in creating a framework of justice for the achievement of a moderate amount of fairness and progress by the Black community in political participation, employment, education and public accommodation. To this extent, there is no equivalent in South Africa to the record of contributions by Black Americans in various areas of American life such as entertainment, sport, or government at present.

"At present" is important, because Black South Africans stand on the threshold of a new political regime as a result of both their internal and external challenges to Apartheid. Combined with the positive assistance of the rest of the world, this broad challenge to Apartheid has created the pressure for unimagined changes, such as the release of Walter Sisulu, Nelson Mandela, and other political prisoners and the scrapping of most of the legal infrastructure of Apartheid. These changes, implemented by F. W. De Klerk since he was elected president in August of 1989, may lead to constructive negotiations for power-sharing with the whites and may eventually build the foundation for economic and social progress of a substantial nature. For example, Black South Africans are already traveling to the United States to inquire about such issues as governmental participation and business ownership, but they are also interested in measures which have broad affect on the labor force, such as affirmative action.

At the same time, in the United States there is the general feeling that because of the growth of a virulent conservative political culture since the 1980s, social progress for Blacks is actually deteriorating as gains in civil rights are steadily being attacked, undermined and eroded. Consequently, the political institutions created by South Africans in the future may be even more comparable to those in the United States and, thus, make the analysis of comparative political phenomena of Black communities even more valid.

Considering the entirety of this case study, I will look at the basic criteria of the Pan African method—the quality of the historical dimension and the nature of unity achieved in strategy and objectives. But to comment first on the question of history, in our consideration of the early stages of the contact between Black South African and African-American intellectuals, what impresses is the extent to which the series of events marked by the meetings at international conferences (including the Pan African conferences) and the borrowing of "progress" strategies represents the history of a class in both societies. It represents the history of Black leadership of a subordinated people attempting to find ways of making race progress in their respective situations within the established framework of institutional procedures.

Both classes, however, appear to have been overtaken by events after World War II, when a new group of leaders came upon the scene more militant in style and in substance. In South Africa, civil rights and educational solutions of change gave way to the quickening call of "Amandla" and to liberate "Azania," and in the United States, the civil rights movement was replaced with the movement for "Black Power" and "Pan Africanism." The difference in the nature of the demands in the latter stages of each movement meant that the militant phases of history diverged at this point from the more moderate solutions. This phase was apparently not sustainable in the context of a situation where African-origin peoples held a minority status as in the United States, with fewer competitive resources, and where the goals were either inclusion or some form of group self determination. However, the militancy of the movement could be sustained where the group was in the majority as it was in South Africa, where the internal power deficiency was supplemented by overwhelming international legitimacy and support, and where the goal was the more expansive one of achieving state power.

It is clear that in many ways these struggles contain substantial differences as illustrated above by the constitutional nature of the states in which they reside, the kinds of control to which they have been subjected, the comprehensive vision of the place of Black people in society, and the terms of their ultimate objectives. However, it is also clear that the struggles of Black peoples in South Africa and in the United States have the capacity to remain connected because of the irony that in the pursuit and administration of the various elements of state power, African

Americans have more experience than any other group of Black peoples in the world. They, thus, constitute a resource which might be utilized in the future by African people in South Africa; and in a reciprocal way, this kind of empowerment can assist in liberating African Americans as well by providing them viable options for economic and cultural progress.

10
Pan Africanism in Brazil: Comparative Aspects of Color, Race, and Power

       The African presence in Brazil has followed a course in world history similar to that of other peoples in the Americas, but with some profound differences. One major difference is that because of the great number of Africans captured and imported into that country, Brazil contains the largest population of African-origin people outside of the African continent. This number is variously estimated to amount to from 50 to 60 percent of the total population, double the number of African peoples in the United States and more than the total in the United States, the rest of Latin America and the Caribbean combined. This fact puts into context the potential for the expression of an "African personality" different from that in Africa itself, but nonetheless significant in world affairs.

       The imagination is stirred with wonder as to the possible impact of Black Brazilians upon the character of that nation and its future social, political, and cultural development. Clearly, the impact of this number of Black people upon the future relations between peoples and nations in the Americas will be extremely significant. Finally, if these dynamics materialize, the African population in Brazil cannot help but affect the relations of that country and the relations of Black peoples in the Americas with Africa and the rest of the world.

The elements that would provide the basis for a developing influence by African peoples in Brazil are changing. Brazil has been independent since 1822; since that time its political system has evolved from a "patronage" form of authoritarian system based on large land-holders and plantation owners, so prevalent in premodern Spain, to a system of military dictatorships for the years between 1964 and 1990. These political systems stifled open discussion about race and the effectiveness of the few Black political organizations that did arise for most of this period.

In December of 1989, multiparty elections for president were held. The advent of a civilian government may signal a new climate within which the social fabric of Brazil may be examined in a more tolerant light. Certainly, there has been a rise in the number both of organizations exhibiting a "Black" political consciousness and of bodies espousing deliberate forms of political action. This new "movement" or "proto-movement" which has been germinating for several years gives evidence of the emergence of a new stage in the political development of Black people in Brazil.

Brazil, therefore, is a fascinating and potentially explosive element in the Pan African world and worth considerable attention by Pan Africanist scholars and activists. In keeping with the format of consideration of other topics in this work, I will address first the Pan African linkages between Afro-Americans and Afro-Brazilians and then discuss the most fertile emphasis in this case study, the comparative political and cultural features of both Black communities.

Abdias do Nascimento

From Brazil, there have been a series of visits by Black scholars and politicians to the United States in the period since 1960. By far the most important, in my estimation, has been Abdias do Nascimento, Black artist, activist and scholar. In 1944, he founded the Experimental Black Theater (TEN) of Rio de Janerio and from that base began to examine the nature of Brazilian racism. This led to the founding of the Museum of Black Art in Rio in 1968. He became such a vociferous and unapologetic critic of racism that after the military coup of 1964, he left the country. In the early 1970s, he joined the faculty of the State University of New York at Buffalo, becoming director of its Puerto Rican studies and research center, and began to interact with Black scholars engaged in the formation of the discipline of Black studies. They learned about the situation in Brazil, and Nascimento deepened their appreciation of the philosophy of Pan Africanism. He eventually founded the journal *Afrodiaspora* and moved to the University of Ife in Nigeria, where he published *Racial Democracy in Brazil*, an analysis of the condition of Black people in that country. Ultimately, his passport was confiscated by the Nigerian military government and he was considered persona non grata.

Abdias do Nascimento's influence was felt not only as a teacher and writer in universities; he became the *unofficial* representative of the Brazilian Black population at several international conferences, including the Sixth Pan African Conference in Dar es Salaam in 1974 and the Second World Festival of Black and African Art and Culture (FESTAC) in Lagos, in 1977. In Lagos, he was initially denied the opportunity to make his presentation on the floor of the colloquium because the official Brazilian delegation was in attendance and Nigeria had important trade ties with Brazil. But after protests to the chairman of the colloquium by the U.S. delegation and others, he was allowed to speak.

Shortly after FESTAC, the First Congress of Black Culture in the Americas was held in Cali, Colombia, in August of 1977. He was elected president of the working group on ethnicity and miscegenation. Nascimento made a proposal for a single language to be spoken by all people of African descent, echoing the proposal put forth by Wole Soyinka and reconfirmed at FESTAC.[1] Just as important, he was instrumental in promoting the concept of the "Afro-American" identity to extend beyond

American Blacks to include all African-origin peoples in the Americas. In the early 1980s, his citizenship rights were restored and he became politically active in the Democratic Labor party (PDT), being designated as a deputy to the Brazilian Congress.

He has continued to examine race relations from the base of an organization he founded, the Institute of Afro-Brazilian Studies and Research. The institute has played a major role in promoting additional congresses of Black culture in the Americas, and in 1985 sponsored an important conference on Namibia.[2]

Abdias do Nascimento is important because his work in Brazil and his residence in many parts of the world clearly shows that as a militant Pan Africanist, he has illuminated to many African-origin scholars and activists the workings of racism in Brazil and the struggle of Black Brazilians to overcome racism. He has also played a direct role in organizing a process for the analysis of Afro-Brazilian culture and in relating this activity to politics—in Brazil, in the Americas, and in the African Diaspora.

In many ways, the climax of his theoretical contribution to the Black Brazilian movement is the concept of "Quilombismo," an adaptation of the Pan African concept to the particular circumstances and cultural perspective of Brazil. For Abdias, the historical antecedents of the Black politico-cultural groups that have emerged in the past three decades is the paradigm of the "quilombo" and the revolts against Portuguese colonialism that established them.[3] Paralleling the Maroon societies in other parts of Latin America and the Caribbean, they were communities formed by runaway slaves in Brazil and represented the liberation space for the autonomous pursuit of African civilization.

In this study of the politics of Pan Africanism, we have taken for granted the phenomenon that is central to political organization—cultural identity. Here, we have an opportunity to examine the complex situation of culture and politics as it exists in Brazil in an effort to summarize an important relationship in the overall theory of Pan Africanism. In doing so, we make a comparison of the role of culture in politics in Brazil and in the United States, with the emphasis clearly on Brazil, taking up such topics as cultural identity, religion, culture and politics, and political organization.

Cultural Identity and the
Racial Democracy Myth

In the European colonial experience, most of the major countries involved—among them, the United States, England, France, Italy—confronted Africans and individuals with African blood as part of a collective African population. The "one-drop" theory, as it developed and was perfected by the British, became the norm. In Spanish and Portuguese cultures, however, the admixture of African blood to the blood of whites or Indians was categorized into different social groupings, producing—as it did in South Africa—a complex set of social identities with consequent cultural behavior manifestations and degrees of access to privilege.

The reasons for this difference, in the first instance, might appear to be based on the different attitudes of these colonial cultures toward miscegenation. In fact, it can be explained by the frantic attempt of the colonialists to maintain a system of white supremacy in countries where they were grossly outnumbered by Blacks and Indians and where they were forced to cohabit with them because of the shortage of white females. The few white women who came to the colonies or were born during the colonial era were often sent to nunneries so that they could retain their "sexual purity" until they were old enough to marry their own kind and produce white children. Brazil was the largest consumer of slaves from the fifteenth to the eighteenth centuries, accounting for 38 percent of all imports into the Western Hemisphere; by contrast, in the same period, only 4 percent were imported into the United States.[4] Imports of slaves into the Americas have been placed at 400,000 for the period 1701 to 1870 in North America, 1,184,600 in Spanish America, and 3,036,800 in Brazil.[5] The strong urban complexion of Brazilian slavery, the relative paucity of Europeans until the mid-nineteenth century, the presence of Indians, these were the ingredients of a strong "mestizo" or mixed race foundation in the population, though of strongly African origin.

Next, for a period beginning near the end of the nineteenth century up to the Second World War, the Portuguese-origin Brazilians dominating the country encouraged massive European immigration as a way of reducing the predominance of the Black population. While an explanation of this complex process is outside the scope of this work, it can be noted an outgrowth of this historical fact was the gradual emergence of a social (or sexual) method of maintaining racial hegemony—the absorption of various groups by skin color preference, or the pernicious doctrine of "blanqueamiento." This Portuguese word literally means whitening the population by means of each group marrying the lighter strains within the group until the Black population disappeared altogether![6]

A corollary to this doctrine has been the practice of an individual denying that he or she is "Black," denying an essentially African identity, even though the individual may be physically Black in appearance. It is as though there was a stench of Blackness from which everyone sought to flee. In fact, this stench was manufactured by those who gave the world the doctrines of the racial inferiority of African peoples as a way to rationalize the heinous crime of slavery and the continued subordination of Blacks.

African-origin peoples in Brazil suffered from this world-wide phenomenon as much—or more, considering their numbers— than Africans in other parts of the world. For example, Count de Gobineau, an infamous racist and author of "Essay on the Inequality of the Races" (1853), which clearly argued the theory of the inferiority of the non-European peoples, spent thirteen months in Brazil as representative of the French government.[7] One of those to be directly influenced by de Gobineau was Oliveira Viana, a mestizo who once championed the idea of a mestizo republic, but whose belief that the doctrine of natural selection had produced an Aryan racial supremacy included the thought that the Aryans had simply lost interest in Brazil.[8] Still, this doctrine buttressed the desire of successive Brazilian governments to import Europeans in a process that Viana would describe in 1922 as the "progressive Aryanization" of the country.[9]

There is, then, in Brazil, as in other Latin cultures, the concept of multiplicity of identities, typically based not on the an individual's racial origin, but on his or her appearance. The categories of appearance might include preto (black), moreno (brunette), louro (blond), mulatto (claro: light; escuro: dark), branco (white), crioulo (creole), pardo (brown), mestico (mixed blood), and so on. The most prevalent types, according to one author, are preto and mulatto, suggesting that most people in Brazil have some African blood.[10] Indeed, the Brazilian census of 1990 asked people how they would describe their color; and this exercise produced 137 different descriptive terms.[11] Yet the continued attempt of the Brazilian government to suppress racial identity may be found in the official data on the population which shows that only 6–8 percent of the country is "Black," while 30–40 percent is mulatto. In reality, in areas such as Bahia the African-origin population is dominant, while in the southernmost states, in Rio Grande de Sul it is as low as 17 percent. In this, the presence of a "middle race," such as the Indians from the Amazon region, has served the process of de-Africanizing the Brazilian population, for it is possible for an individual to claim that the particular form of miscegenation which resulted in him or her makes him or her a mestizo, rather than an African admixture.

This confusion of racial categories by the evaluation of individuals on the basis of appearance has dominated the ruling classes and led to the camouflage of the essence of the racial problem in Brazil. It has influenced even some of the working-class Blacks to adopt the belief that "there is no racism in Brazil," that there is a class problem of poverty and subordination that affects people because of their lower status and that the lower classes themselves are to blame for their status. This inverted perspective on the real nature of cultural subordination is best summed up by Abdias do Nascimento himself. To him, this is:

> A very special type of racism, an exclusive Luso-Brazilian creation, subtle, diffuse, evasive, asymmetrical, but so persistent and so implacable that it is liquidating completely what is left of the Black race in Brazil. This type of racism has managed to deceive the world by masking itself in an ideology of racial utopia called "racial democracy" whose entrenchment has the power of confusing the Brazilian people, doping them, numbing them inside, frustrating them or barring almost indefinitely any possibility of their self-affirmation, integrity or identity.[12]

There is, of course, a concept of "embranqueamiento" in the United States within the Black American community (and within every African-origin community in existence). Ever since slavery the advice has been given to sons and daughters, either subtle or overt, that they should "marry up," meaning to marry someone lighter than themselves; and, of course, there have been within-group prejudices and even some discrimination based upon color. Some Black organizations, including schools, churches, and social clubs, pretending to upper-class status within the community, were exclusionary on the basis of lightness of color. This practice operated on a subtle level because of the generally inclusionary principle of racial membership. At the same time, the "one-drop" theory of African race membership was often enshrined in the legal system of states, among them Louisiana.[13] So, even though both in Brazil and the United States informal color distinctions existed within the Black group, the official attitude toward race reinforced group solidarity in the United States, while in Brazil color distinctions have been legitimized through the doctrine and practice of "racial democracy."

The second factor that enforced a concept of group identity in the United States was the existence of rigid racial segregation that controlled the place of residence, work, recreation, burial, in short, all facets of existence. This enforced racial segregation was a pernicious aspect of racial discrimination and prejudice, but it also made possible the enforced participation of Blacks in the same institutions and, therefore, fostered a kind of socialization that made possible the evolution of a mass social consciousness that contained similar attitudes toward the world, including the white world. These attitudes made possible the predominance of racial solidarity in the pursuit of attaining social, cultural and political goals. In such a situation there could be a direct connection between racial identity and the definition of racial problems and strategies for racial progress. This is not to say that the question of class within the Black community did not often become the basis for the conceptualization of problems and the shape of remedies. However, it is remarkable, considering class differences within the Black community, that the major ideological divergences of moderate and radical tendencies have had adherents from all social classes. This fact has made possible a group orientation toward most racial questions in America.

Finally, then, the history of race relations in the United States was written essentially as a conflict between Blacks and whites, since the native Americans were all but wiped out and the remainder kept on isolated reservations away from the general population. There being a lesser middle race, miscegenation was clearly a net loss for the white population and a gain for Blacks and, thus, stimulated the intensity of separation and attacks on the Black male. Still, the native American did thrive and relate to the African such that even in America, the dominant "Black" racial type might be said to be a mixture of African, white, and Indian, just as it is in many parts of Latin America and the Caribbean.

More recently, there is a "middle race" phenomenon occurring; the American population is becoming more heterogenously composed of Third World or non-European peoples, such as Hispanics, Africans and Asians; thus, the stuff of racial conflict and miscegenation begins to involve more than the old paradigm of Blacks and whites in many communities. In an interesting way, this could develop a Brazilian type of identity confusion with the capacity to inhibit racial responses culturally and politically. The stimulus from this development could come from the necessity for "minority" groups to band together in order to confront the majority and become the new majority in certain situations. In this case, the basis of their political identity may change to become something other than Black, while maintaining the Black identity for cultural purposes.

The Socio-Economic Problem

The manifestations of Brazilian racism, as earlier suggested, are hidden in the definition of class conflict, but appear systematically in individual decisions with regard to intimate issues such as marriage and residence and in official decisions in such areas as the distribution of state resources.[14] For example, until 1950 racial selection in employment was legal, but in that year the Brazilian government passed Afonso Arino's law outlawing racial discrimination. However, Nascimento suggests that in practice the law has been almost totally ineffectual; it has never been enforced and no one has ever been prosecuted under it. Further, he says, employers have devised artful ways to evade its very broad prohibition; before the law, employment advertisements might have specified that no Blacks need apply, but afterward, the ads might say that only persons with "good appearance" need apply.[15] It should be mentioned that Afonso's law was enacted because Katherine Dunham, a noted Black American entertainer, embarrassed the Brazilian government when she was barred from a Sao Paulo hotel.

The social position of Blacks in Brazil is little different than that in any other non-African or non-Caribbean environment, where they are afforded upward mobility mainly in sectors of the society—art, music, theatre, and sports—that are "quite remote from the decision-making areas of the Brazilian socioeconomic and political structures."[16] Also, the Brazilian scholar Florestan Fernandez found Blacks resentful of the fact that whites managed the process of inferiorization by denying them access to opportunities other than in narrow sectors of Brazilian life—for example, cooking, football, boxing, the police, and the Army—and that whites, therefore, "made the Negro a specialist in these areas."[17]

Brazilians would probably agree with Professor Dzidzenyo's intervention, but many would not agree as to the causes. Even in 1990, the author heard the Black mayor of Porto Alegre state that the problem of Blacks in Brazil was one of "class not race!"[18] Most Brazilians would not believe, as Abdias do Nascimento has said, that "black cultural heritage exists in a permanent confrontation with a system designed to negate African culture."[19] This concept may be taken as a universal statement of the Black condition.

Indeed, the racial problem in Brazil is set within a disturbing economic picture. Brazil has one of the highest rates of inequality in income distribution between rich and poor in the world.[20] Such inequality is a product of the unequal opportunities in the labor force and in the distribution of property, especially in terms of the concentration of land and industry. For example, in a 1984 listing of 77,185 industrial firms, 5 percent were responsible for 49 percent of total sales and 47 percent of capital.[21]

Data from the 1980 census shows that a Black in Brazil has a

30 percent greater chance of dying before the age of 5 than a white and that life expectancy for Blacks is 50 years while it is 63 years for whites.[22] In addition, surveys in Sao Paulo and Recife carried out by the Brazilian Institute of Geography and Statistics (IGBE) in 1988 found the following pattern of inequality:

—the earnings of a Black physician are 22 percent less than those of a white;
—a Black engineer earns 19 percent less than a white;
—Black professors earn 18 percent less than whites;
—white chauffeurs earn 19 percent more than Blacks;
—a Black lathe operator earns 12 percent less than a white;
—a Black bricklayer earns 11 percent less than a white.[23]

In her work, *The Place of the Black in the Workforce*, sociologist Tereza Cristina Araujo found data in the 1980 census revealing that the Black person (those called Blacks and mulatto—who constitute sixty million persons or 44 percent of the country) exists in stark poverty. For example, of every ten Brazilians, four are Black, and of every ten poor people, six are Black. Education helps some, but as indicated above, does not eliminate the social disparities. Disparity in wages is great in the northeast of the country, where the work of a Black is generally worth only 50 percent as that of a white. However, in Sao Paulo, the disparity is greater, for the average difference in what is paid to whites and Blacks in eleven professions, according to IGBE, is 96 percent.[24]

Although data on the economic performance of various racial or "color-identity" groups are sparse, it is known that the northeast region, containing the largest number of African-origin people, has the lowest levels of income and the highest degree of inequality.[25] In 1980, approximately 54 percent of the poor families in the country were located in the Northeast, a larger share than in 1970, in an area with both urban and rural poverty.[26] A personal inspection of the areas known as "favelas" on the outskirts of Rio or virtually any of the larger cities would summarize for the reader the condition of Black people. While similar areas can be found in the inner cities of the United States and other major Western countries, in Brazil they develop outside the city, signifying the emphasis on urban development in the construction boom in the past four decades. The favelas also demonstrate that some of the relatively new cities, as in other countries, have been a magnet for the rural population; they have tended to settle on the edge of the city, and there an estimated 40 million people have become marginalized and largely ignored.[27] Many who drift into the favelas had been rendered homeless in rural areas because of development, and most of them are Black. Poverty, ignorance, and disease abound in these areas. They represent a national failure of social welfare to care for the dispossessed class. Sixty-five out of every thousand Brazilian children die in the first year of life; 35 million people are illiterate.[28] But the favelas, like the inner cities of the West, are sprinkled with elements of the Black middle class who also do not have access to housing in other areas of the city.

The state of the economy as a linkage to social mobility has been demonstrated in the North American context. It is an unassailable fact that in the 1960s the Black political movement created the pressure that forced the political system to distribute public policy resources in the direction of the oppressed Black community. It should be remembered that the situation in the United States had moved considerably beyond civil responses by Blacks and involved substantial violence in the streets, with the burning of buildings and a variety of military political actions. Yet the growth in the economy was also a factor in the rapidity with which the Black middle class was created. Educational enrollment in college achieved a 100 percent increase in the decade between the mid-1960s and the mid-1970s, employment rose, and average family income rose from 51 percent of that of white families in 1959 to 61 percent in 1969.[29] Whereas the number of Black families earning the national median income was 5 percent in 1960, the number rose to 25 percent by 1974. This was an illustration not only of the improving ratio of income distribution, but the distribution of mobility across a broader spectrum of employment occupations as well.

To conclude this brief survey of the socio-economic status of Blacks in Brazil, it should be noted that although there is a considerable mixture of colors within families and among neighborhoods that gives a facade to the integration of the Brazilian population on the basis of color, petty discrimination exists as a co-product of the larger framework of racial prejudice as illustrated by the comparative figures above. Brazilian Blacks, as is well documented, suffer the usual social slights and insults that accompany racial prejudice and discrimination all over the world in areas of interpersonal relations and public accommodation. This is an indication, however, of the fact that racial integration in Brazil has the same facile texture that characterizes integration within the United States, where different races may share the same physical space, yet possess very different value systems that consequently affect their status evaluations and social behavior. In a criticism of sociologist Waldir Oliveira's defense of the "racial democracy" thesis for Brazil, Abdias do Nascimento says ". . . the Black and the white in Brazil have been 'living together side by side' for four hundred years. Never have they 'integrated themselves' except for the insidious program of acculturation, assimilation, miscegenation and syncretism of Black peoples and their cultures *into* the dominant population and culture, processes that inherently involve their partial or complete destruction."[30]

This kind of "integration" assumes a sacrifice of values on the part of the African-origin person and does not value both cultures with equal integrity as a basis for integration. Thus, this form of "integration" does little to mitigate the more vicious aspects of white supremacy that are at the heart of the "blanqueamiento" philosophy in both societies.

The Political Response

The record of the resistance of African people in Brazil to their enslavement is to be found in the tangible fact of the "cimmarones," "palenques," and "quilombos"—the communities of escaped Africans established in liberated zones of the colonial countryside for four centuries. The modern age of political struggle against Brazilian oppression of African-origin peoples appears to coincide with that which occurred in other parts of the African Diaspora. For just as the "New Negro movement" was born in the United States, leading to the world-wide

emergence of the Marcus Garvey phenomenon, and the "Négritude" movement was born in France, so the Brazilian Negro
Front (Frente Negro) was born on September 16, 1931, in Sao
Paulo. Its first organ, *A Voz de Raca* (The Voice of the Race), was
launched in 1933, but soon vanished and another newspaper, *O
Clarim da Alvorada*, appeared in January 1924.[31] This paper's editor, Jose Correia Leite, was keenly interested in the Garvey
movement and also published articles on Frederick Douglass
and other Black activists. The attempt to transform the Frente
into a Black political party, however, did not succeed and it, too,
vanished in the 1930s. The Frente program was Black Nationalist ("only we can solve our problem") and separatist ("we separate in order to unite"), and yet, at the same time, it was determined to utilize this unity in order to achieve "total integration
of the Negro in all of Brazilian life."[32] Fernandez was to say that
"it remained in the political annals as a kind of historical landmark of the first demonstration of rebellion and force by the Negro people."[33]

A succession of organizations followed the Frente, among
them the Afro-Brazilian Democratic Committee (1945–1946), the
National Convention and Congresses of Black Brazilians (1938–
1950), the Black Cultural Association (1950–1955), and the Unified Black Movement, founded in 1978.[34]

The paramount political consideration of these organizations
was the achievement of justice for Black people in a way which
defined their own unique "Brazilianness," according to Fernandez.[35] He suggests that the "social rights movement" broadened
the cultural outlook of Blacks and bred in them a break with the
colonial past of dependency by fostering a new spirit of autonomy and self-confidence, teaching Blacks to develop their own
resources.[36] The end product of this effort, he says, was to eliminate substantially the stigma of inferiority.

Perhaps the most definitive statement of the Black movement
in Brazil, however, comes from Lelia Gonzalez, whose presentation at the United Nations symposium on the Namibian cause
in Latin America contained the following thought:

> When we talk about the Black Movement, we are referring to a
> complex of organizations and institutions which heirs of a long
> historical process of pan-Africanist resistance, fight for liberation

of the Afro-Brazilian community. Subject to extreme conditions of economic exploitation and racial oppression, and due to the fact that they fight against racism and its practices, they take to the ultimate consequences the process of unmasking the logic of capitalist domination. For this reason, the Black Movement has a much richer revolutionary potential than that of other similar movements that also propose to fight for a just egalitarian society.[37]

Gonzalez went on to suggest that the Black movement was undergoing the kind of transition that would make it possible to handle such considerable issues as the Namibian cause more effectively.[38]

One of the more recent organizations to emerge and express the sense of transition from a specifically cultural posture to a far more political position is the Unified Black Movement Against Racism and Racial Discrimination. In 1978, two Black workers were killed by the Death Squads which roam the favelas carrying out informal sentencing against the weak in a racist manner. In response, on July 7, two thousand people denounced racial violence in a demonstration in Sao Paulo; the coalition of groups that sponsored the demonstration went on to form this umbrella organization, setting up local cells called "centers of struggle."[39] The program of action adopted by the Unified Black Movement called for an amnesty for political prisoners, the abolition of racial violence (Blacks form the majority of the victims and the disproportionate subjects of police brutality), support for African studies, and promotion of Black Brazilian culture. The program also called for institution of Black Consciousness Day on November 20 in commemoration of the death of the nineteenth-century hero Zumbi as an alternative to the government-sponsored May 13 anniversary of the abolition of slavery.[40] UBM is the closest thing in Brazil to a national Black organization; it has chapters in various cities such as Rio de Janerio, Porto Alegre, Campinas, Sao Paulo, Belo Horizonte, Salvador, Brasilia, Juazeiro, and Recife.

With the relatively recent upsurge in Black political consciousness in Brazil, a number of new organizations have been formed. This is an important stage, for the strictures placed on race organizing by the military government had inhibited the development of Black political organizations, and so "cultural" organizations were formed. These were cultural in the sense that they their main agenda was to promote Afro-Brazilian art and cultural practices, including music, dance, and even religious practices. However, it is also obvious that in Brazil, as elsewhere, objectively cultural organizations laid the basis for the evolution of political action. For example, the Black Experimental Theater participated in the sponsorship of political forums such as the National Convention of Brazilian Blacks in 1946, and the convention manifesto was sent to all of the then existing political parties.[41] In fact, it was probably the political agitation of TEN that led to Afonso Arina's law following the incident in which prominent Black American artists such as Katherine Dunham and Marian Anderson were refused entrance into the Hotel Esplanada in Sao Paulo in 1950.[42]

This tradition may still be seen in organizations such as the Institute for Research on Black Culture (IPCN), the Odudua Imcorpomption Black Arts World and others based in Rio. ICPN in particular is an organization engaged in artistic culture preservation and promotion, complete with archives, but it also has become an interpreter of the ways in which Brazilian racism impacts upon the society. In addition, the institute plays a role in helping to galvanize community activists from other organizations on common issues.[43] In Porto Alegre and other localities, there are also cultural organizations such as the Black Cultural Association, the Solano Trindade Institute, and the Quilombista Movement, as well as political organizations such as PNB (Partido do Negro Braziliero), the Peoples Anti-Racist Movement, and many others.[44] Black women have manifested a rising political consciousness both as Blacks and as women with a special role in political struggles. This development has spawned such organizations as the women's section of the Unified Black Movement, the Nzinga Collective of Black Women in Rio, the Iya Dudu Black Womens Collective in Porto Alegre. Leila Gonzalez has noted that the well-known stereotype, "a white woman to marry, a mulatto to fornicate, and a Black woman to work," points to a second level at which the myth of "embranqueamento" works.[45] This level degrades Black and brown women. Women serving as laborers on farms and in domestic work have no standing in labor legislation protecting men, as was noted by the resolutions of the 1983 Namibia Conference. Thus, Black women believe: "We, too, seek to organize ourselves in the fight for our liberation and this necessarily implies struggling against all forms of racial, sexual and class exploitation."[46]

Political Work

An important task for many of the organizations involves the propagation of political values within the Black community that would create a Black political consciousness. For example, in 1988, the Brazilian Ministry of Culture sponsored an official commemoration of the ending of slavery, but it was boycotted by the more Black-conscious cultural and political organizations. President Jose Sarney attempted to appease them by designating a national park at the site of the seventeenth century slave rebellion that founded the Palmares Nation, an independent Black republic in Alagoas (1630–1697). He also established the Palmares Foundation as a national organization to sponsor Black cultural programs and named Carlos Moura, Black labor attorney and his adviser for Afro-Brazilian affairs, as its head. Private independent Black organizations, however, have maintained some distance from the Foundation, especially since it suffered financially under the radical budgetary constraints imposed upon government by President Collares in 1990, while Moura himself was appointed as ambassador to Cape Verde.[47]

Second, actions have been taken on a local and national level to further the political education of ruling whites with respect to the condition of the poor and Black communities. For example, in the spring of 1990, the Senate Chamber in Brasilia was taken over by hundreds of the country's estimated 24 million homeless children (most of whom are Black) in a demonstration designed to draw attention to their condition. Averaging age 12, they formed the Brazilian National Movement for Street Boys and Girls and demanded health care, education, and protection from violence.[48] Some of these children, who in news photos can be seen to be black and brown, were roughed up and arrested by the police.[49] This and other such demonstrations indicate that the government's social service budget is grossly inadequate. Private organizations are attempting to fill the gaps. In Belo Horizonte and other cities there are community organizations developing, such as Casa Dandara, which offer education and cultural programs for youth and women.[50] Given the fact that the community has shown confidence in such organizations, they are providing the base from which political influence may ultimately emerge.

Then, too, there are direct challenges to white oppressive acts carried out by the agents of government such as the police and other official bodies and by private organizations, including the press. What emerges from a review of news clippings in the early months of 1990 in various cities is that Black people are shown in conflict with the police authorities—being murdered by the death squads, handcuffed, arrested and taken away to jail, or in jail.[51] A number of organizations, including Coordenadoria das Promotorias Criminais, Movimento Negro Brasileiro, and Justica e Direitos Humanos, have protested against the death squads, which are suspected to be a combination of former military right-wing elements and the police. And a conference to consider strategies against discrimination and police violence in Brazil was held at the neutral site of the Municipal Center of Montevideo, Uruguay, under the sponsorship of the organization known as Mundo Afro (Black World), in April of 1990.[52]

Another direction of political action has been to seek involvement in the official political system through elections, a move that has produced a number of Black elected officials. For example, there are 12 "Black" members of the National Assembly, but only four who function as Black members. Of this group, Benedito da Silva, a black woman who rose from the favelas of Rio, and Carlos Alberto (Cao) Aliviera of the Democratic Workers party (PDT) are probably the strongest personalities with the most respect from their peers. The national program of this group of Black Deputados is little different from those of the Congressional Black Caucus in the United States or Britain's Parliamentary Black Caucus. Some Blacks have served as city mayors, among them Evaldo Brito of Salvador in the state of Bahia and Alecu Collares of Porto Alegre. Ironically, Collares, who interprets the problem of Blacks in Brazil as a matter of class, was not expected to win election because of the strong race prejudice in the conservative rural areas of the state.[53] Although there is no roster of Black elected officials as there is in the United States, one has the distinct impression that running for office and holding elected office is growing in popularity among Blacks, partly because office involves considerable life-time financial benefits. Holding office is also attractive because of the opportunities to attack the ills of the Black and disadvantaged communities through public policy. But the racial consciousness of both candidates and electorate is so distorted that the problems of Blacks and browns are not given the attention in the political process that they deserve, as a distinctly racial issue. The electorate does not vote on a racial basis; in fact, Black candidates are often shunned in favor of white candidates on the presumption that they are not as effective as whites. On occasion, there have been so many Black candidates that they have split the vote, and, thus, no Black was elected to office.

Political parties have invited Black leaders to join who possessed little hint of a Black program of action. One exception was the invitation of Abdias do Nascimento to become a PDT party official, later, he was designated a federal deputy and served in the National Assembly for two years. In that position, he attempted to put forth a program of Black cultural expression. Inasmuch as each political party acts as a patron, dictating who can and cannot stand for election, it would appear that the parties are complicit in the political disunity fostered within the Black community.

Moreover, there is an investment of many young progressive Blacks in party activism, and from the base of the party institution these young Blacks have attempted to organize the community to address its problems. The parties, however, have not been strong institutions for promoting racial consciousness, and so there is little that is equivalent to the "Black Sections" within the Labor Party in Britain or the Black Democratic Caucus within the Democratic party in the United States. More attractive is class-oriented party politics, some of it, of course, related to labor unions. This explains the tremendous attraction of Luis Inacio "Lula" da Silva, a common worker who founded the Metal Workers Union in Sao Paulo in 1978 and the Workers Party (PT) in 1980, among all sections of the poorer classes in the presidential elections of December 1989. During the 1989 campaign, Lula, who has been compared to Jesse Jackson, said: "I remember that at one time I feared I would not be able to hold my own in televised debates with great political scientists or economists. And I understand now why some workers imagine that to be a candidate for president one must have a college diploma. It is because the ruling class spreads that idea."[54] Lula came in second to Fernando Collor de Mello, candidate of the conservative Democratic Movement party (PMDB). Ironically, Lula may have been hurt by a racial incident in the last days before the election when the Collor forces surfaced a Black woman, mother of Lula's illegitimate 15-year-old child. The woman, who reportedly was paid $10,000 for her performance, charged Lula with racism and neglect of his child.[55] Lula did not emerge from the election as the leader of the progressive political forces, and that explains the continuing attraction of PDT, regarded as the most progressive of the parties. In any case, class politics is important in any country that has a tremendous concentration of wealth. The author Carl Degler has said that political participation in Brazil has been traditionally the preserve of the upper and middle classes, secure in their legal position from social and economic competition on the part of the lower classes. The upper class, he continued, used this security to solidify control over society while permitting a few individual Blacks to rise above their class since these few could pose no serious threat to their own position.[56] So, even though voting is mandatory in Brazil, the power of the Black and brown coalition has weakened because the political participation of Blacks has been controlled by upper-class whites through the manipulation of what Degler calls the "mulatto escape hatch," pitting the Blacks against the browns.

An investment of organizing work in political parties dominated by whites is questionable. Blacks might be better advised to focus on the development of autonomous centers of Black politics within the parties or outside the party system altogether. These centers would not only free Blacks from ideological or racial control, but also foster the development of a distinctly Black political agenda and the use of Black resources in the implementation of that agenda. Even this has not been successfully completed either in the United States or in Britain.

Prelude to Political Pan Africanism

The individual contacts between Afro-Americans and Afro-Brazilians in the twentieth century have formed the native substance of what might be considered a growing range of Pan African linkages in the American hemisphere. From America there has been a steady diet of visits by scholars, among them Dorothy Porter, former curator of the Moorland-Spingarn collection at Howard University, who developed one of the most substantive collection of Afro-Braziliana outside of Brazil. Also, two distinguished Howard professors, Rayford Logan and E. Franklin Frazier, traveled to Brazil in the 1960s and were captivated by the rich cultural legacy of Afro-Brazilians.[57] Logan, in particular, in 1942 made contact with the National Union of Men of Color in Sao Paulo and brought back to the United States a message seeking "closer cultural community with our North American brothers."[58] The two professors considered Brazil a veritable laboratory for the study of race relations. In the 1970s and 1980s, some Afro-American scholars were afforded the opportunity of spending extended periods in Brazil as a result of foundation work or scholarly research.

As has been illustrated, the dynamic of the Pan African movement in the United States entailed people moving out from the base of the American community to explore and experience Africa and the broader diaspora; these efforts often involved visits by delegations including hundreds of individual African Americans. An important series of festivals that entailed travel by such delegations was initiated in 1978 by Dr. Richard Long, a professor at Emory University and former professor at Atlanta University, editor of the journal *Phylon*, and expert in Africana culture. Long had been a college student in Paris and had been intimately familiar with the key figures in the Négritude movement, as well as with leading Black writers and artists in the United States. His goal for the festivals was summed up thus: "Black people being conscious of the totality of the African experience in a way that would enhance their understanding of their condition and their capacity to deal with it."[59] The initial African Diaspora Festival in Brazil, attracting nearly 200 African Americans, was facilitated by an interesting individual known as Jimmy Lee, of Miami, who had gained contacts and notoriety as a basketball player in Brazil in the mid-1970s. He became intensely interested in exposing African Americans to Brazilian culture and played a role as consultant to various travel and tourist agencies, both private and governmental, in facilitating such travel.

Another resource for the first festival was the cultural arm of the American government which, through the United States Information Agency, had made funds available for the travel of cultural groups to Brazil. On the Brazilian side, the Inter-American Foundation, a State Department-sponsored organization that ran an institute for Black studies, put up $50,000 for the festival. The Brazilian government, then under the control of a military junta and somewhat suspicious of the motives of this cultural program, eventually banned the IAF, but sanctioned the festival and approved minimal support by its own tourist agency. In Bahia, the Bureau of Cultural Affairs supported the event, but the government's opposition was inferred by the fact that Rosita Salgado, cultural affairs director of the city for many years, was dismissed and that the Rio sponsor, the Museum of Modern Art, burned to the ground a few weeks before the arrival of the delegation.[60] After much diplomatic maneuvering, the festival took place during August and involved the presentation of art works, music, dance, and literary expressions by African Americans and reciprocal presentations by Black Brazilians, focusing upon Salvador da Bahia and Rio de Janerio. The American delegation, which involved such leading Black cultural activists as Maya Angelou, Hoyt Fuller, John Henrik Clarke, Eugenia Collier, Margaret Burroughs, Eleanor Traylor, and Dr. Fletcher Robinson, appeared to have arrived at a time when the influence of the Black movement in the United States was being felt in Brazil, especially among Black activists in Rio and other large cities.[61] The Americans discovered, for example, that the "Black Rio" movement was underway, a term which was not translated into Portuguese but tellingly stated in English. In Sao Paulo, the newly formed Committee Against Racism read its manifesto on the steps of City Hall before a crowd of thousands.[62] The events illustrated was a new freedom of experimentation in Black music, and among some Black Brazilian activists there was a disparagement of the Samba which was popularized in the first half of the twentieth century, as being a "colonial dance."

There was also some considerable nervousness about the state of race relations in Brazil. Given the reactions of the average Black Brazilians to color, many were understandably puzzled by the "invasion" of such a large number of Black Americans, but after some reticence, Brazilians eventually came to interact with their "Black brothers and sisters" more easily.

After festivals in Haiti and Surinam, Dr. Long, with the assistance of Jimmy Lee, sponsored another festival in Brazil in 1988, again visiting Salvador da Bahia on the occasion of the celebration the hundredth anniversary of the formal abolition of slavery. Meanwhile, the National Conference of Artists, a delegation of 267 Black Americans, also visited Salvador that year and arranged a joint conference with about 300 Black Brazilian artists. Although the meeting was also facilitated by Jimmy Lee, it was led by Willard Taylor, a person with a long history of activism in the cause of Black advancement in America. The meeting focused on artistic presentations and workshops, and there were the inevitable political dynamics, such as the protest by the Black Brazilian workers who were being paid only 20 cents per hour to unpack and hang the art works. Similarly, the Black Brazilian artists, always conscious of the interplay of art and politics, took advantage of the cameras focused on this meeting to demonstrate their dissatisfaction with racism.[63]

As a result of the festivals organized by Long, other individuals and groups began traveling to Brazil on a more frequent basis. For example, at this writing, the African-American Cultural and Arts network was planning its third annual visit to Brazil, and other delegations were planning return visits for 1991 and beyond. Such visitations, apparently promoted by tourism and cultural/artistic interests, represent seeds being planted that may bear more substantial fruit in the 1990s and beyond.

Black organizations have the daunting task of bringing Brazilian racism to the surface as a national issue in order then to begin working for ameliorative measures. This was only accomplished in the United States and Britain through violent and nonviolent physical confrontation with the injustices involved in the national pattern of race prejudice and discrimination. The targets of racism in Brazil, at this writing, are obvious, but there is still a pervasive pattern of denial that race is the major driving dynamic behind the oppression of Blacks. It is not surprising that there is no protective legal shield against the racial discrimination that troubles a variety of areas of social, economic, and political life; the legal framework of racism is difficult to attack where no laws are erected to promote segregation as they were in the United States.[64]

Again, these specific legal protections did not arise in the States out of the largesse of American political institutions, but were won at considerable sacrifice of life and psychological and material comfort. This, I believe, is the challenge ahead for the Black political movement in Brazil. But in order to accomplish the task of broadening and deepening the movement, such cultural issues as the power of Black identity as a unifying force and the definition of the problem as a racial *and* economic problem must be generalized among the masses and important segments of the Black political elite.

11
Afro-Caribbean
Pan Africanism

An African Identity?

 The very title of this chapter exhibits the kind of problem that anyone who addresses the subject of Pan Africanism in the Caribbean must address—that of the possibility of Pan Africanism among nonwhite peoples who have become racially mixed in a substantial way over a long period of time. Still, because the process of European colonialism produced a culturally heterogeneous Caribbean, the problems and solutions indigeneous to this area of the Americas are not conceived in terms of an African identity. In fact, one of the oddities of the cultural question in the Caribbean, considering that the strength of African survivals identified by Melville Herskovits and others is so much greater than in the United States, is the fact that there is such ambiguity toward adopting a much stronger African cultural identity.[1]

It would appear that the question of personal and collective African identity in the Caribbean is problematic not only because of the multiracial nature of the area, but also for another reason identified by the distinguished West Indian writer, George Lamming.

> His [The West Indian's] relation to Africa is more problematic because he has not, like the American, been introduced to it through history. His education did not provide him with any reading to rummage through as a guide to the lost kingdoms of names and places which give geography a human significance. He knows it through rumor and myth which is made sinister by a foreign tutelage, and he becomes, through the gradual condition of his education, identified with fear: fear of that Continent as a world beyond human intervention. Part product of that world, and living still under the shadow of its past disfigurement, he appears reluctant to acknowledge his share of the legacy which is part of his heritage.[2]

Although Lamming makes a contention about the manner in which Black Americans retained their ties to Africa (a point that I will briefly examine below), he leaves us with a significant reason to ponder for the weakness of the African legacy in the Caribbean—and with a question. The absence of Africa in the educational system of the Caribbean leads to the conclusion that the vaunted system of "indirect rule" referred more to the political nature of colonialism than it did to the imposition of colonial culture upon subject peoples. Here, one remembers the statement by Dr. Carter Woodson that if the cultural apparatus works efficiently to socialize people to certain views of themselves, there is less need for direct political control.

In national terms, people in the Caribbean, of course, identify as citizens of their nation state, but they are very much part of a region, and so the people are culturally "West Indian." Just as the concept of Pan Africanism was created through the phenomenon of "externality," by people outside of the African continent, George Lamming says that "no Barbadian, no Trinidadian, no St. Lucian, no islander from the West Indies sees himself as a West Indian until he encounters another islander in a foreign territory . . . The category West Indian, formerly understood as a geographical term, now assumes cultural significance."[3]

And yet it also clear that the overwhelmingly African nature of the Caribbean has lent an irrefutable legitimacy to the fact that some of the most powerful contributions to the concept and the movement of Pan Africanism have come from a people who are a dynamic part of the historical experience of the African collective. Given what we have said about cultural ambiguity toward Africanity in the Caribbean, it is ironic that a Marcus Garvey emerges from the Caribbean to nurture Black and African consciousness to global heights through his United Negro Improvement Association (UNIA), having a monumental impact upon both African Americans and African-origin peoples all over the world. How does one account for the emergence of a Marcus Garvey if what we are saying about the acculturative process of colonialism is correct? Part of the key may lie in the fact that Garvey's Black and Pan Africanist ideology was rooted also in his physical blackness and in the physical blackness of most of his adherents, while, at least in America, most of those Blacks who opposed him were not only of the bourgeois class but often of another color as well. Is it possible that this phenomenon is at work in the Caribbean, that as one moves closer to the physically Black base of the community, one also moves closer to the African survivals? Obviously, throughout the African Diaspora, some lighter skinned Black people have manifested a more "Black" consciousness than their darker brothers and sisters, and some dark-skinned Blacks have a strong European consciousness. But the question is, are there strong correlations of class and color perceived among the broad sectors of the Black population? Probably. At least one close observer suggests that the Caribbean has managed to sustain an effective "elite skinocracy" where Europeans or those with European physical features are the beneficiaries of social status and power.[4]

This is important because the question of identity within the Caribbean has often shaped the substantive limits of Pan Africanism. For example, the official policy of racial identity established by the government of Jamaica has been "multiracialism." However, this policy is grounded in the reality that Jamaica is at once a Black majority country stratified according to a class system where the "brown man" or mulatto class is effectively the political, economic and social leadership and the Blacks are in the lower class. It has been estimated that 80 percent of the people are of "pure African descent," 8 percent of pure European descent, 1.7 percent of Afro-East Indian, 0.6 percent of Chinese extraction, 1.0 percent of Syrian origin, 14.6 percent are

Afro-European, 0.6 percent are Afro-Chinese, and 3.1 percent are the result of other mixtures.[5] In many ways, this sets up the same contradiction noted in other places such as Brazil that, whereas the majority of the population is of African-origin, the consciousness of the people tends toward the dominance of a Euro-centered or at the most a "neutralized" identity in which the African component is subordinated. And as in other situations, this is so because the minority who may be of European or Asian extraction or mixtures tend to be more dominantly represented in a ruling class, and so the national identity is reflected in the identity of the powerful rather than in the identity of the largest racial group. To this extent, then, the assertion of a strong Black or African identity would be regarded as antithetical to the notion of national consciousness, at least by the power that was fundamentally involved in the decision-making strata of national affairs.

Multiracialism or Black Nationalism?

One culturally powerful sector of the West Indian population that has exhibited a strong African consciousness and has, thus, been the carrier of a kind of Pan Africanism is the Rastafarian. Professor Nettleford states, for example, that the coming of Jamaican independence in 1962 also brought with it a Rastafarianism that, having emerged from the ranks of the Black lower classes some thirty years earlier, was so strongly African-conscious that it threatened the unity of society with a doctrine embodying the notion of separatism and eventually repatriation to Africa.[6] The Rastafarian perspective forcefully raised the view that even though Blacks formed the majority, they reaped little of the benefits of society through their long labor and that even with independence the "Brown man's government" have only managed bankrupt institutions that provided little better.[7] Meanwhile, lower-class Blacks held fast to the concept of "African redemption," championed earlier by Marcus Garvey, and promoted the study of African history and culture. This is seen as natural; for their own history merged with that of the Maroons whose revolutionary character was based on an anti-European perspective and a positive view of the African past. Professor Horace Campbell has suggested: "The convergence of the heritage of the Maroon, the religious movement—called Ethiopianism—and the emergent Pan-African movement which culminated in the U.N.I.A. were some of the forces which merged into the formation called Rastafari."[8] Thus, the Rastafarians played a role in liberating the question of African identity from the natural ambiguities of Caribbean cultural and political history.

Ethiopianism was a variety of Black Nationalist philosophy that became prevalent at the turn of the twentieth century. It was based upon the spiritual teachings in the Psalms that "princes come out of Egypt, Ethiopia stretches forth her hands unto God." This thought, repeated by Bishop Henry McNeal Turner, who traveled to South Africa and established the African Methodist Episcopal Mission in 1897, was the basis for Turner's Black Nationalist approach to the participation of Black Americans in African missions; it became the basis for the African rejection of white religious hegemony in many parts of the continent. And although the first Ethiopianist church was established in South Africa around 1900, the movement quickly became popular in other areas of Southern and Western Africa as well.[9] Yet the philosophy of "Ethiopianism" had wide currency within the African world of the first half of the twentieth century as a synonym for African nationalism and Pan Africanism.[10]

Embedded within the Rasta theology is the notion that Haile Selassie was the Rasta king and, therefore, the coming of the emperor to Jamaica in 1966 was, for thousands of Rastas and non-Rastas alike, an opportunity to identify with one of the most potent African symbols of the day. The reception given to Selassie by the Rastafarians in particular was another indication to the Jamaican elite that their variety of African consciousness threatened the fragile bonds of Jamaican nationalism then in formation. Still, groups such as the Rastafari Repatriation Association encouraged members to hold fast to the notion of repatriation while "building Africa in Jamaica," even while arguing that because of the nature of its population "Jamaica is Africa."[11] It was the emphasis of Rastas on the truth about the racial identity of Jamaica and others of the islands that made it possible for them to identify with the doctrine of "Black Power" emerging from the United States in the 1960s, just as they had identified with the Black Nationalism of Marcus Garvey at an earlier period in history.

There was in the adoption of the Black Power motif in the Caribbean a union of the cultural resistance of the Rastas with others who were posing political, economic and class questions and who urged political change within Caribbean societies such as Jamaica. Nettleford suggested that Black Power, by its very nature, ". . . possesses a relevance which accounts for its persistence, and explains in part the fear it arouses. Its young adherents, educated, alienated, share ideals with their counterparts elsewhere in the world in their demand . . . [for] not only a redistribution of the wealth and political rights . . . but a transformation of the morals, values and behavior patterns of the society."[12] Black Power sympathizers had become critical of the institutions of government set up for the satisfaction of the peoples' needs because they observed the social contradictions which correlated blackness of skin with the severest of poverty in a predominantly Black country. Yet, by identifying the contradiction of Black inequality among various groups in the multiracial social system, they did not believe that the adoption of Black Power carried an implicitly revolutionary threat to the existing government. Indeed, they took pains to say, at the First Black Power Conference in Montego Bay, held in September 1969, that Black Power instead was oriented toward Black dignity and pride.[13] Nonetheless, the political objections to the doctrine of Black Power were not only that it had penetrated the shield of "multiracialism," but that it had also penetrated the shield of corruption and government inattention to the needs of the disproportionately Black poor and inevitably would become revolutionary in its demand for structural and cultural change.

The Black Power ideology was disseminated from the United States through the various organic channels of human relationships that virtually cement Caribbean and African-American history in many fundamental ways. Still, its power potential ironically was greatly diminished by Stokely Carmichael himself. Carmichael's view was based on the narrow proposition of an African land base as the only concrete manifestation of Pan Africanism. This concept was fundamentally flawed because it negated the reality of cultural change within the Caribbean—a new base for Africa—and challenged the notion of Black self-determination within Black-controlled states outside the African continent. As such, his concept would have most assuredly been challenged by the very activists who came to lead the Black Power movement in the Caribbean. [14]

The Pan African Movement

In Montreal, in 1964 a small group of activists from the Caribbean, led by Tim Hector and others, founded the Caribbean Conference Committee. The committee began sponsoring a series of annual meetings bringing in key Black political thinkers and activists such as Stokely Carmichael and C.L.R. James. It was this committee which in 1968 sponsored the Black Writers Conference that attracted Amiri Baraka and Walter Rodney. At the meeting's end Rodney was barred from returning to Jamaica. This group, poised in white dominant Canada, established linkages with the U.S. Black Power and Pan African movements and played a basic role in internationalizing political support for the liberation movements in Africa. In fact, the Canadian group was the international wing of the African Liberation Support Committee founded, as indicated earlier, by African-American activists. [15] And so the seeds were planted that would internationalize the Black Power/Pan African concept, and it was no accident that the Black student movement in Montreal would seek to utilize these concepts in its struggle against racism at Sir George Williams University.

Clearly, much serious work on the dissemination of the Black Power and Pan African concepts had been accomplished by Caribbean activists by 1970, when the "Black Power virus . . . reached epidemic proportions in Jamaica and caught on . . . in Trinidad." [16] The writer Ivar Oxaal had predicted that the "virus" would cause a "mild infection" in his mythical analysis of the situation, but Oxaal's book, *Race and Revolutionary Consciousness*, indicates that it almost caused a revolution. The protest mobilization began in 1969 and was promoted by three major events: a Black Power leader in the United States, Stokely Carmichael, had been barred from entering Trinidad; in Montreal, Afro-Caribbean students attending Sir George Williams University held a sit-in, taking over the university's computer center, and bus drivers in Port-of-Spain organized a major strike.

The student action at Williams was important, for several of those involved had ties to American Black Power leaders such as Rosevelt Douglas and Ann Cools. The sit-in was calculated to expose the depths of racism within the institution and, as such, was part of the American struggle for Black studies and Black student self-determination. But it was also directed at Canadian racism perpetrated against Afro-Caribbean peoples in that society, and, therefore, struck a responsive note among the Black immigrant population. Ultimately, the students were arrested and deported, with the Trinidad and Tobago government paying their fines; that act became a source of anger in Trinidad, with activists charging cooperation between the Trinidad and Canadian governments in the oppression of the students. But when some of the students returned to Trinidad, it became evident that they had absorbed part of the radicalized Afro-American student culture. "Certainly the American styles and rhetoric of protest had already caught on among black youth in Trinidad along with soul music, Afro haircuts, and admiration for the flair and daring of the Black Panthers."[17]

In response, a radical organization of the unemployed, students, and alienated intellectuals in Trinidad was formed called the National Joint Action Committee (NJAC). In addition, in 1970, students and professors at the University of the West Indies became more radicalized, and Dr. James Millette, a history professor, formed a political party, the United National Independence Party. Other organizations were formed, among them a Black Panthers party chapter, the National African Cultural Organisation, the Afro Turf Limers, African Unity Brothers, Southern Liberation Movement, National Freedom Organisation, and Tapia House.[18] This development was an illustration of the force with which the movement had arrived. For, as previously indicated, one of the surest analytical signs that a movement is underway is a sudden upsurge in the formation of organizations carrying its banner.

In 1970, students at the University of the West Indies led a series of protest demonstrations in Port-of-Spain against such targets as the Canadian High Commission and the Canadian Royal Bank in support of the student protest at the Sir George Williams. In February, five of these students were arrested. The month of March was important to the mobilization; two massive marches were held. The first involved 10,000 people in Port-of-Spain and was led by Geddes Granger and Dave Darbeau of NJAC. The organization sponsored a "peoples parliament" which erected a shanty town in the main square and conducted a continuous speakout against government policies. Some key organizers and speakers were Granger, Aldwin Primus, head of the Black Panthers, and Russel Andalcio, a UWI student, as well as Abdul Malik, who it will be remembered was also a key figure in the Black Power movement in Britain before returning to Trinidad. The second march was directed at creating unity between African-origin and East Indian peoples, a unity that would allow them to attack working-class economic oppression; to make their point, they marched 28 miles into the heart of the sugar plantations.[19] The "peoples parliament" was still in session by late March. It grew more militant in its demands against the government, and ultimately some of the supporting organizations issued a call for a general strike. Subsequently, a major labor strike led by George Weeks of the oilworkers union got underway. With the demonstrations, fire-bombing and looting growing more intense, the government of Dr. Eric Williams began to show signs of panic; the police began to use tear gas against the demonstrators and marchers; government deputies began to resign, and ultimately a state of emergency was declared and 15 Black Power leaders were arrested and detained. This set off more intensive reactions, including a mutiny among the Trinidad Defense Force. As some of the mutinous soldiers were heading from their barracks in the Chaguaramas peninsula to the governmental center of Port-of-Spain, they were intercepted by the Trinidad Coast Guard and arrested. Had this not worked, Dr. Williams most certainly would have called for help from the American naval force stationed just off the coast.

The Williams government understood that this massive up-heaval was directed toward eliminating the racial division and inferiority dynamic contained in the social structure by de-Europeanizing the culture and toward democratizing the impact of capitalism upon the working class. Thus, Williams felt he had to do more than repress the movement. He began by acquiring government control of and regulating some key industries, a step that had broad social impact. He also empaneled the Wood-ing Commission with the assigned the task of attempting to de-mocratize the government through constitutional reform reduc-ing the powers of the executive.[20] The result was the declaration of Trinidad as a republic in 1976, with the powers of the chief executive somewhat reduced. However, the economic reforms never achieved the impact upon the people that the movement had hoped for.

Walter Rodney and Caribbean Pan Africanism

The impact of the Black Power movement upon Caribbean governments would explain the reaction of the Jamaican government, in particular, to the activities of a young proponent, Dr. Walter Rodney, in 1968. Walter Rodney, an activ-ist/scholar, was assassinated in his native Guyana in 1980, but his memory is revered among progressive West Indians. His very life as well as his intellectual productivity was a testiment to the power of Pan Africanism in the Caribbean and elsewhere in the world.

After completing his doctorate in 1966 at the School of Orien-tal and African Studies in London, Rodney taught history at the University of Dar es Salaam in 1966–1967, and in 1968 he taught at the Mona Campus of the University of the West Indies in Ja-maica. During his stay at Mona, he became an adherent of the Black Power philosophy that had become such a powerful force in the Black world. This led him to become a popular off-campus lecturer, teaching African history to middle-class groups as well as those in the "gullies" (back streets) of Kingston.[21] In a scathing attack on the Jamaican government's leadership, Rodney charged that the same government, then led by Hugh Shearer, which prevented Stokely Carmichael and other members of the Student Non-Violent Coordinating Committee from coming to Jamaica had committed other sins against the Jamaican people. In particular, he said, the government had used the police power of the state against the working classes. Because this class was also predominantly Black, the color question had also come "out in the open," facilitated by the Rastafarian brethren who had "been joined on this question by large numbers of other Black people—many of them influenced by the struggle and example of Black brothers in the U.S.A."[22] Rodney went on to explain how "white power" had been responsible globally for the definition of Black people as inferior and had managed the process of imperialism to the detriment of both Black and Third World peoples, especially those in Africa. While "Black Power" as a slogan was new, he said, it was really an ideology and a movement of "historical depth." And he linked this phenomenon to Marcus Garvey, Malcolm X and SNCC, examining this strain of Black Nationalist ideology which is the basis of Pan Africanism, to assess its relevance to the West Indies.[23]

For these transgressions, when Rodney attempted to return from the Black Writers Conference in Montreal, in October 1968, he was refused entry by the Jamaican government and his writings were banned. He, therefore, went back to the University of Dar es Salaam and remained there until 1974. During this time, he traveled among the Regions of East Africa, the Caribbean, the United States, and other parts of the world. In the United States, he was associated with the Institute of the Black World, a Pan Africanist institute in Atlanta founded in 1969 by a number of Black thinkers and activists who were at home with Black Nationalism, Marxism, and other varieties of progressive thought.[24] The institute was the major base for conceptualizing and organizing the Black studies movement in the United States; this eclectic group became a leading intellectual center for the propagation of Black thought until its demise in 1978. Rodney also spoke at a number of universities and, acting as teacher and comrade, moved among community activists in several cities who were part of the Pan Africanist movement in the United States.

In 1974, planning for the Sixth Pan African Congress in Dar es Salaam was underway and Rodney wrote an assessment of its prospects.[25] In this work, Rodney revisited the terrain of the class struggle in Africa between the masses and the emergent petty bourgeoisie that had taken over many of the functions of the former colonial powers in a number of countries. In his view, this class had appropriated the concept of Pan Africanism and Négritude in an effort to sanctify the existing structure of the state system in order to solidify its control over the masses in support of the neo-colonial imperialists, rather than align Africa with the masses and external revolutionary forces then contending for independence.

In his masterful analysis of Rodney's view of Pan Africanism, Robert Hill suggested that the view just presented actually has three components. To begin with, he argued that Pan African-ism for Rodney was "a critical tool for analyzing revolutionary new forms of genuine African liberation" which had the poten-tial to recapture the popular initiative against imperialism, thus preventing the usurpation of state power by the petite bourgeoi-sie. And, therefore, Rodney began his rigorous analysis of the Pan African dimension by examining the state structure in Af-rica and the Caribbean and the question of who controlled them. Second, Hill said, Rodney insisted that one must analyze the "class nature" of state power, or the way in which the petite bourgeoisie utilized it, which raises the perennial question, "in whose interest is power weilded?" Third, Hill said, Rodney used the mass criteria—or the perspective "from below"—in assess-ing the potential for struggle to be waged that would have the effect of intervening in the lives of the masses and improving their condition.

Thus, the criterion for Pan Africanism in this case was the de-gree to which it linked the peoples into common struggles: "We must begin to conceptualize the problems of Pan-Africanism as problems of forging links with social groups. The problem is to develop solidarity between the Caribbean peoples and the Afri-can peoples."[26] On the practical level, Hill suggested, Rodney labored hard to liberate the practice of Pan Africanism from "the simple process of mutuality" based on a "mystical racial union" and turn it into a Pan Africanism based on an examination of the specific forms of Black oppression and formulation of programs to combat oppression.[27] In Rodney's view, this required a non-romantic approach to organizing.

Thus, Rodney pointedly referred to some of the same questions that had been raised by Owusu Sadaukai about the Sixth PAC, such as what is the nature of state involvement and would progressive groups be represented from Africa and the Caribbean? "At the very least," he said, "the conference should be expected to record the firmest statement of support for the liberation movements."[28] Not only did the Congress eventually adopt this position, but in almost every other respect, Rodney's analysis of what it should do was strikingly achieved as well.

True to his own advice, while at the university Rodney launched a critique of TANU (Tanzanian African National Union), the ruling political party, and its program of UJAMAA (unity) in Tanzania.[29] This step angered some officials, and he decided to leave Tanzania and return to his native Guyana in 1974 to accept a position at the university there in African history. He did not participate in the Sixth PAC, but was subsequently critical of its leadership because of the exclusion of some progressive delegations from the Caribbean such as ASCRIA in Guyana, the New Jewel Movement in Grenada and NJAC (National Joint Action Committee) in Trinidad.[30] Essentially, despite the fact that the congress produced some progressive position statements, this confirmed his view of the negative effects of the collusion of petite bourgeoisie class interests among leaders in Africa states and the Caribbean.[31] Most important was Rodney's view of Pan Africanism in the Caribbean. Again, Hill tells us Rodney felt that the role of Pan Africanism was to liberate the West Indian masses from the dependency grip of the petite bourgeoisie. However, Rodney was a scientific socialist, and his challenge was to "effect the merger of the political with the cultural determinants of popular struggle in the Caribbean." This was the significance of his "groundings" in Jamaica with the Rastas or in Guyana with the working classes.[32]

There is, then, in Rodney's action and in Hill's interpretation of his Pan African philosophy the germ of an explanation for the perception among the leaders of Caribbean states that strong manifestations of theory and actions based on Black Nationalism and Pan Africanism were a threat to their stability. Indeed, as we have seen with the Black Power movement in Trinidad, the incident of social instability was produced because it was directed toward the examination and correction of critical social problems among the masses. This suggests that beyond whatever weaknesses of theory or practice may be involved in the attempt to implement Pan African programs in any given place in the Diaspora, fundamental problems may be unearthed, since the concept addresses itself to basic social conflicts between the condition of the masses and the direction of the leadership—whether the race of the leaders be Black or white. This, in turn, suggests that there is an "objective" sense of Pan Africanism where political unity may be forged with respect to the solution of problems which have either race or class at the center. Trinidadians were able to find flexibility in the cultural definition of Blackness when they, for example, interpreted "Black" to cover strategies of militant actions by both "groups of Black peoples"—Africans and East Indians—and were able to deal with economic questions by using the resource of revolutionary race consciousness to push the government to adopt reform measures with clear socialist intent.

Such flexibility in the application of pan Africanism to the Caribbean has been important. A case study emerges from Guyana, Rodney's native country, where a Pan Africanist organization known as ASCRIA (African Society for Cultural Relations with Independent Africa) was founded in 1963 by Eusi Kwayana. Ascria convened the Seminar of Pan Africanist and Black Revolutionary Nationalists in Georgetown in 1970, and its creation eventually led to the establishment of the Pan African Secretariat on African Solidarity Day, May 25, 1971.[33] Through the seminar Forbes Burnham, the prime minister of Guyana, seized the opportunity to project himself as a supporter of the African liberation movement. Gradually, on several issues involving housing, the use of land, and the establishment of enterprises, Kwayana found Burnham's socialism to be the "bridge between imperialism and the peoples' mass movement . . ."[34] In addition, Kwayana suggested that Burnham had appropriated Pan Africanism essentially as a tool for racial competition.

On the other hand, Burnham saw his government as favoring "emancipation of the black man wherever he may be, whether he be in North America, or in Africa, or elsewhere." He cited the refuge he had given to Black writer Julian Mayfield and to artist Tom Feelings after they were deported from Ghana following the coup against Kwame Nkrumah.[35] It was for these sharp differences of perception of his government's role and other reasons that the split eventually occurred between ASCRIA and the Burnham government in 1971.

As Black Power was used in Trinidad in 1970 to solidify multiracial politics, so Kwayana saw a role for Pan Africanism in a society that was almost equally divided between African-origin and East Indian working-class peoples. In January of 1973, ASCRIA protested the sale of 200,000 acres of the best coastal lands to the sugar companies. ASCRIA held that racial competition was in the interest of the sugar companies since it kept both sets of peasants landless and at the mercy of "feudal capitalism." ASCRIA's campaign for working-class access to these lands drew a government promise of action against the sugar plantation owners and land agents, but no action was ever taken.[36] This problem of racial competition was probably why in the formation of the Working Peoples Alliance in Guyana, Walter Rodney and his compatriots found a class analysis more compelling as a tool to build cross-racial solidarity and to clarify the evils of the government they were attempting to change.[37]

The Caribbean Revolution

If the 1970s was the era of the African revolution, in which independence was won on the battlefield by Zimbabwe, Mozambique, Angola, Guinea-Bissau, and Cape Verde, and the struggle continued in Namibia and South Africa, then the early 1980s was the era of hope for fruition of the Caribbean revolution. The period saw the coming of the New Jewel Movement in Grenada and the regime of Michael Manley in Jamaica. These regimes sported charismatic leaders in Manley and Maurice Bishop, who were spellbinding articulators of Third World problems. They daringly forged warm relations with Cuba's Fidel Castro, a pariah to the United States, the dominant power in the region. These elements made for the creation of a constituency in the United States among the Pan Africanist community and the Black middle class alike, reaching to the Congressional Black Caucus.[38] As Marxist regimes, they had to confront the reality that the basis of this external support, although they might have wished it to be aligned with and originating from the working class, in fact was distributed among all classes and especially within middle classes.

Grenada's New Jewel Movement constitutes a case of "objective Pan Africanism" since, as a government with the intent to fashion a socialist society, it did not utilize a theory of race unity, but sought unity and support from among all socialist and progressive states and peoples. Racial unity, both domestically and internationally, was nevertheless, a resourceful element in the government's attempt to implement its strategy.

Indeed, one strain of what became the New Jewel Movement began as an organization called Forum, created by Bishop in 1970, which held several demonstrations against the government of Eric Gairy as a response to the force of Black Power sweeping other Caribbean territories.[39] This organization became known as MACE (Movement for the Advancement of Community Effort) in 1972, and then the more progressive elements formed MAP (Movement for Assemblies of the People) which merged with the Jewel (Joint Enterprise for Welfare, Education and Liberation) Movement in the New Jewel Movement in 1973. In 1974, Bishop would be a delegate to the Sixth Pan African Congress.

Otherwise, it is difficult to identify the variety of pan Africanism that is the subject of our inquiry in the Caribbean after the advent of the Black power movement which finds people of African origin within the Caribbean involved in a specific common political enterprise or project. Perhaps, as we consider states such as Jamaica under Manley in the 1970s or the regime of Bishop from 1979–1984, we observe that these Black-led socialist regimes had elevated the level of politics from either countering policies of the state or obtaining independence from a ruling expatriate colonial power to using state power in order to obtain progressive results for all citizens. In this scheme of things, although it was possible for those outside of these countries to

sympathize with and support the leaders and their governments, their needs were so great and their strategy so ambitious
such that a Diaspora community of African origin could contribute little else.

Still there was an acknowledgement that at the base of even
the revolutions they sought to make, people might be stimulated by and would respond to a program that not only gave
them cultural dignity but also attended to their class interests
from the perspective of their place in the world, both as workers
and as part of an historical and cultural continuum. This was the
problem noted by Trevor Monroe, a Jamaican economist at UWI
(Mona), who said that as Marxists who had been trained to ap-
preciate the task of elevating the condition of the working class,
they had not sufficiently appreciated the dynamic of race in that
operation—or the problem of uniting the "red and the Black." [40]

Within the New Jewel Movement, there was an ideological
debate over whether the cultural character of the movement was
primarily working class or oppressed African people. [41] Key actors such as Unison Whiteman were openly pan Africanist and
humanistic; however, there were others who were expelled from
the party for displaying excessive "black nationalism" rather
than exhibiting an identity with the working class. [42] Given Bishop's sympathetic inclinations toward a politics of Pan Africanism, some observers suggest that in the inter-party conflict that
ultimately led to his untimely death, the essence of the ideological struggle was between Bishop's concept of "power to the
people," a socialist concept and American Black Panther party
slogan, and that of Bishop's rival in the organization's leadership, Bernard Coard's "power to the central committee." [43]

Representatives of U.S. Black progressive organizations such
as the Black United Front, the National Black Independent Party,
TransAfrica, and others visited Grenada in the late 1970s and
early 1980s. These were mixed ideology and mixed class organizations, with a strong component of Pan Africanist (Black Nationalist) intellectuals in their leadership, that were seeking to
establish solidarity with the revolution and to contribute material support as well. There is some evidence that this activity,
presumed to be against U.S. policy, was not only counter to U.S.
policy in fact, but was also contrary to a policy specifically designed to thwart the establishment of Pan African relations be-

tween African American and Afro-Caribbean peoples. Speaking at Hunter College in New York during a tour in 1983, Bishop suggested (in a reference to a report of the U.S. Foreign Broadcast Information Service on CIA activity in Grenada) that an important motivation for American opposition to the revolutions in Cuba, Nicaragua, and especially Grenada was that "the people and the leadership of Grenada are predominantly Black. They said that 95 percent of our population is Black—and they have the correct statistic—and if we have 95 percent of predominantly African origin in our country, then we can have a dangerous appeal to 30 million Black people in the U.S. Now that aspect of the report is clearly one of the most sensible."[44] Obviously, then, this evolving pan African relationship constituted a "second front" for U.S. policy makers in opposition to the spread of Caribbean Marxism and social revolution.

However, in the main, Africa became the defining feature of Caribbean pan Africanism among progressive states, rather than "Diasporic" pan Africanism. Perhaps because of the early connection with Tanzania, the major model for the development of the Bishop government was the Nyerere model.[45] However, in 1983, several heads of state from Africa such as Samora Machel of Mozambique and Robert Mugabe of Zimbabwe were invited to Grenada by the Bishop government, and before he was assassinated, Bishop was preparing a return visit to Africa. In particular, he was touched by the plans of Machel and wanted to learn more about the Mozambique system.[46]

The main source of external support for Jamaica or Grenada, outside of Cuba and other socialist countries, was the expatriate community of citizens or former citizens who still possessed residual influence through their retention of voting rights, through the remittance of taxes or through various associations with families resident in the country. This linkage might be conceived broadly as Diasporic in nature and, thus, pan African in content, although few writers have expressed this thought. Nonetheless, there is a Diaspora of expatriate Jamaicans, Antiguans, Barbadians, and others in the Caribbean and elsewhere who maintain relations with their places of origin in one form or another. Expatriate communities, however, are often viewed by the existing governments not only as a positive resource but as communities of mischief and sites for the hatching of conspiracies for destabilization and collusion with foreign governments. Manley, like other Caribbean leaders, was sensitive to this problem because he understood that there was dissatisfaction among those expatriates who found the socialist direction of his government distasteful.[47] For the politically oriented among Blacks in the United States, the politics not only of Jamaica, Grenada or Guyana were of interest, but likewise the politics of Nicaragua or Cuba. In the late 1980s, delegations of African Americans visited the Black community of Greenfields on the coast of Nicaragua and Cuba in an effort to assess the progress not only of the revolution in general, but that of people of African descent in particular. Through this connection, the Nicaraguans gained a sympathetic position in the American Black community on a human level among progressive activists, and the same extended to Cuba, but more fundamentally to Cuba because of its significant Black population.[48] The Cuban situation became a source of pride both for the achievement of the revolution on the social level and for the early leadership Cuba provided in support of the African independence movement through the activities of Ché Guevara. Although Cuba was admired by progressives and pan Africanists alike, the persistence of racism was problematic.[49] The delegations of African Americans who went into Cuba in the "brigades" of Black socialist intellectuals in the early 1980s examined the race question as well. The Cuban government, which once declared that the revolution had made racism almost insignificant, now adopted the more mature position of admitting that racism was still a problem within the country. As Professor Manning Marable explained it:

> Cuba's commitment to destroy racism, and to eradicate the material foundations for its perpetuation, is unequaled in the socialist world. But the weight of the racist superstructure of the past, the conscious and subconscious ideological assumptions, and cultural patterns and social relations, transcend the particular social formation which gave it life. With notable exceptions . . . most black North American radicals have been reluctant to pursue the difficult question of race relations in a post capitalist society, within a political context of solidarity.[50]

Official Cuban attitude toward race made race consciousness illegitimate within the theory of Marxism, which opposes racial chauvinism in practice. Thus, while Black Power acted as a basis of Pan Africanism in other Caribbean states, "Black identity groups" were frowned upon by Cubans.[51] This attitude, which promoted an orthodoxy in the use of Marxian theory, doubtless spilled over into Cuba's relations with other regimes such as the Manley government in the Jamaica of the late 1970s, where state Pan Africanism was practiced but where there was an ambivalence toward the cultural Pan African movement at the mass level. Nevertheless, as indicated, Fidel Castro practiced a form of objective "state pan Africanism" in his foreign policy by supporting Angola's military defense against South Africa in 1974 on the theory that "African blood runs deep in Cuba."[52] Thus, a kind of political solidarity based upon mutual national interests was possible which took into consideration the context of racial solidarity.

Conclusion

Part of the challenge of the relevance of Diasporic Pan Africanism in the Caribbean appears to be the development of a variety of the concept that is compatible with the real cultural foundations of the people in the various countries, yet revolutionary enough to attract the attention of the progressive intellectuals and activists who might utilize it as a tool of liberation. This is the problem of racial pluralism, set within a post-colonial framework, where most of the people are still oppressed and, therefore, contesting for development, while the ruling elite often use the symbols of African heritage for control rather than development. In Jamaica under the Seaga government, the symbols of Marcus Garvey were appropriated openly and extensively in an effort to distract the masses from the failure of Seaga's alliance with the Reagan Administration's Caribbean Basin policy, a policy that yielded little for the masses of Jamaicans or other Caribbeans who were Black.[53] Still, "state pan Africanism" was also obviously being utilized; for example, Seaga hosted the visit of Oliver Tambo, president of the African National Congress, who led a delegation to Jamaica in 1988.

One of the most important of the "African" heritage events in Caribbean society is Carnival. The festival is often a transmission belt of political messages through songs and bands. In fact, in 1970 in Trinidad, protest bands appeared at Carnival to signal the dawning of the new Black Consciousness.[54] Still, as an opportunity for the gathering of African-origin peoples, Carnival does not have an explicit political role in a society that is Black-dominated and where African-origin people often run the government. This leaves the Rastafarians as the most explicitly political force with a pan African expression in most Caribbean countries today, but the organized force of the Rasta, while making an important impact on the popular cultural consciousness of Africa and the African Diaspora, is not powerful enough to intervene in the politics of the state. Thus, the politics of the people in the Caribbean is mostly driven by an absence of explicit references to the Black or cultural dimension of politics, except in the narrow field of foreign policy. Given the example of ASCRIA and the regime of Forbes Burnham, the major contradiction in a multiracial society appears to be how to use the vital cultural force of the African-origin masses for positive change without alienating other ethno-racial groups or being co-opted into alienating them by the political elite.

In any case, we agree with Hill's conception that Rodney's view of the function of Pan Africanism in the Caribbean performs three functions: (1) strengthening the linkage among the masses of Africa and the Caribbean in popular struggles to liberate the African continent; (2) participating with other progressive forces in the African Diaspora in similar activities such as in the United States, Canada, England, and other countries, and (3) forging a coalition between the working classes and the progressive elements of the bourgeoisie to redirect state power to the benefit of the masses. These functions have been substantiated by our brief review of Pan Africanism in the Caribbean and in other parts of Latin America as well.

Finally, it has been theorized in some of the other cases that the Afro-American Pan African movement has had an important impact upon other African-origin peoples within the African Diaspora. In the case of the Caribbean, it should be understood that one of the elements shaping the official American attitude toward the more revolutionary states and, by extention, toward a revolutionary brand of Pan Africanism, is concern as to its effect upon the Black American population. For while it is true that revolution within the Caribbean could disrupt capitalist ties and profits for firms representing developed countries, it is also true that the currents of revolution could travel from that region into these very United States. Those who worry about this are aware of the past influence of the Caribbean peoples upon American history in a relationship that confirms our view of the "organic" nature of the relationship between Caribbean and Afro-American peoples. Nothing is more confirming of this than the knowledge that others also understand the potential for these organic social and political relations to flow in the reverse direction. The Caribbean is, then, not only an important pan African center because it is a midway station between Africa and the United States; it is also an area where Afro-Caribbean and Afro-Latin American currents wash upon the shores of the United States and find a place in the African community within the country.

12
The Structure of Pan African Unity in the African Diaspora

I have attempted to argue, given the quality of the evidence, for the significance of the extracontinental dimension of the Pan African reality as a vital phenomenon not only in the genesis of the early movement but in its continuing evolution in varying forms and as a necessary compliment to continental Pan Africanism. In doing so, I have utilized two methodologies: comparative "race" analysis and the Pan African method in an effort to define more carefully the relevant aspects of the persistence of Pan Africanism in the Diaspora. Accordingly, I will summarize the evidence within the framework of the broad conclusion that the Pan African movement persists and will continue to persist both because of continental necessities and because of the increasing importance of the extra-continental dimension in world affairs.

Comparative Race Analysis

In this regard, the evolution of an African Diaspora is critical. Other writers have indicated that part of the reason why so much of the initial impetus for the conceptualization of Pan Africanism came from the African Diaspora was the need (for the Black man) to "attach himself to an identity" or other such rationalizations. However, little understood are the facts that: first, the diversity of the Diaspora was a natural response to world events that resulted in the evolution of African communities in many places in the world; second, Pan Africanism was the most effective organizing principle (although it was often not recognized by this concept) in the survival of African peoples in the new communities.

But just as Pan Africanism serves as an organizing principle within African-origin communities outside the African continent, it serves the same function between or among such communities. This function, the key concern of this study, is a crucial aspect of the Diaspora illustrating to us that Pan Africanism is an evolving, persistent phenomenon. It rests essentially upon the recent maturation of the African community in various countries, most of which were former colonizers of African peoples. But in the maturation of African communities such as that in the United States we also have experienced an important adaptation process taking place where Black institutions endure as resources for Blacks to take their place in new majority white societies.

We conclude here, from a comparative analysis, that the extent of the persistence of Pan Africanism is therefore dependent upon such factors as racial progenesis, or the way in which the African communities were created in the Diaspora and what factors have opposed or facilitated their attempt to establish community. This view is similar to that of Professor Locksley Edmondson, in two respects. The first aspect of our agreement with Edmondson is that, in his words, "Negro America was one of the first black communities to gain legal political freedom and equality, but after a century the American political system has failed to convert this nominal freedom and equality into actuality." And, secondly, "in articulating his [the Black American's] needs and strivings, he was strategically positioned to attempt to effect a linkage of ideas and aspirations with others of his race who were in large measure similarly situated in terms of white domination."[1] Edmondson proceeds to tell us also that given the viciousness of white racism, the Black reaction in the form of Black Nationalism or Black Power was inevitable. Here, he supports the view of Professor James Turner who, in his article "Black Nationalism: The Inevitable Response," earlier made the same case for the necessary development of a strong response by the African-American community to its subordination.[2] Then, as we have seen in our chapter on the Pan African movement in the United States, Pan Africanism is viewed as the highest form (international expression) of Black Nationalism, so that it, too, logically constitutes an "inevitable response" to the similar oppression of African peoples around the world. This development was inevitable in that the common experience of Black people at the bottom of most societies around the world has given a "liberative" content to the concept of Pan Africanism which defines its overall mission.

Obviously, then, from the evidence above, one of the most important of these factors in the character of the Diaspora African community is the white-dominant state's response to the insertion of an African people into its social structure. We have seen that the existence of a common European-origin culture among the white majority nation states has made possible a relatively similar treatment of racial problems, beginning with the existence of certain racial attitudes and ending with the adoption of similar racial policies and similar agencies to manage race relations. We have found that there is an empirically provable pattern in that the first response of whites is rejection of the African-origin community, both in terms of the social response and the formal policy response of the state. After a period of social conflict, the most intensive aspects of the rejection pattern are moderated and adjustments are made by both racial groups to the fact of the permanent presence of the African-origin community, again as reflected in social behavior and in public policy. Critical forms of racial subordination on both the collective and individual levels persist and evoke mobilizational responses from the African-origin community in an attack-response pattern.

The next stage is the emergence of a Black middle class from among the relatively homogeneous working population, a middle class that begins to challenge whites for public-position resources—middle-class jobs, middle-class housing, modest forms of material accumulation, official standing in politics, and legitimation of the culture. The last stage represents not the resolution of the racial crisis but an expansion of the crisis along the considerable fault line of racial cleavage in society. Thus, there are still daily struggles with the police, poverty and other manifestations of raw racism at the mass level, while more subtle forms of oppression are experienced by other middle-class Blacks and those few in the upper strata of society.

Next, I will say a word about the cases upon which these assumptions are based and the methodology used in this study. The cases were initially selected because they represented structurally similar situations in many respects. This enabled me to make generalizations about other such potential cases that I did not study, for example, in Canada, France, and other countries. Even South Africa, despite its location on the African continent, has distinctive European characteristics because of the origin of the white minority and its management of the process of internal colonialism. This means that the relative experiences of African peoples with European-origin peoples in a subordinate-superordinate power relationship is a critical element in the empirical pattern of racial relationships observed. The central ingredient, then, in the pattern of race stratification is the distribution of power and the fact that universally in white host states, African-origin peoples are relatively powerless. Other factors are the process of the development of an African Diaspora and the rationale for African-American initiative in the cases examined.

With regard to some additional common characteristics found in these cases, we return to a rough paradigm set forth in chapter 1 on the comparative role of African communities in the Diaspora. We suggested that there was first the struggle to achieve community, then the struggle to maintain it, and finally the struggle to use its resources in the achievement of personal and collective social (inclusive term) objectives. This developmental paradigm comes close to what we meant earlier when it was suggested that the Diaspora was "evolving" outside the African continent. We could, then, consider each of these three objectives as discrete stages in the growth and maturation of each African community, except for the fact that as we move from Africa into the Diaspora, there is a tendency to objectify African identity and to refer to problems presented by the presence of African peoples as "race" problems or to peoples of African descent as no longer African but as "Black" peoples.

The use of "race" as a synonym for Black people and other nonwhite minorities characterizes a way in which the majority perceives the problem. They are the objective majority and, therefore, raceless and blameless as the original inhabitants, while the visible minority constitutes an unwanted intrusion and even a possible contestant to the use of power or the maintenance of power by the majority in the pursuit of its objectives. I discovered that "race" is as problematic a concept in Britain as it is in Brazil and the Caribbean. In the Caribbean and Latin America there is the added complexity that "race" does not have as sharp a delineation as class, as a social phenomenon, so that racial problems are more contentious as social targets around which to organize and, thus, more difficult to solve as racial problems. The racial formulation of social problems is disputed in many Latin American countries as a way of containing another volatile ingredient of social (and cultural) difference, while in English-speaking societies, there is not only an explicit acknowledgment of "racial problems" and in most cases a racial bureaucracy established as a method of containing them.

Also, as suggested, the denial of racial problems is also a way of positing the superiority of the national identity and of subordinating any threat to the hegemony of the dominant culture. In Brazil, there is not only the merging of but the tension between Portuguese and African culture, with the African culture often being defined as "folkloristic" while the superiority of Portuguese culture is reaffirmed by its functional imposition upon the people. There, the affirmation of an African identity by "Black" people constitutes a challenge to the dominant cultural fusion and builds the *inevitable* linkage to a politics of Black self-determination.

In the Caribbean, the Pan African movement has been only episodically initiated because of the dominance of Blackness or nonwhiteness, both of which have produced an emphasis upon class as the most critical social problem. Progressive racial politics there is the struggle to prevent racial antagonisms from dividing the movement to build a multiracial society where power and resources are distributed equitably among all cultural groups. Here, race relations involve Pan African consciousness and programs involving African countries where state interests are concerned. Otherwise, the fundamental relations between the African-American community and Afro-Caribbean Blacks finds its expression not necessarily as the acknowledgement of the need to forge links between dissimilar peoples, but often as the mere extention of the African-American struggles within which Afro-Caribbean peoples have participated freely as both leaders and followers for decades.

This study has shown that in the attempt to achieve the various objectives of the African-origin community, the political ideologies of Black Nationalism and Pan Africanism have been used by various communities in the Diaspora. First, they were used in an effort to recapture the sense of an African identity and to utilize it as a resource for the linkage of Black people to the essential unity of African history and culture. This was a precondition to seeing themselves as an extention of the African phenomenon and of accepting a sense of African obligation.

Then, in our two types of extra-continental communities mentioned above, we have seen that Blacks in Britain, while attempting to use Pan African strategies in order to have mobility within the larger social environment, nevertheless exhibited certain features that were very similar to the older African communities such as that in the United States. Also, we theorized that such leadership in the use of Pan African-oriented strategies exercised by Black peoples in the United States may have occurred because (1) the Black community is of several centuries in duration; (2) therefore, it experienced the negative influences of racism, capitalism, technology, and the other features of an advanced European society earlier than did Africans in South Africa or Britain; (3) it had access to a different political milieu created by a different constitutional history; and (4) it responded by adopting a variety of Pan African strategies of survival, thus influencing other African communities in similar circumstances.

In fact, we might suggest that the Black American Diaspora might constitute the "old African Diaspora" model, since many of the early studies were based on African-American "linkage" with Africa. The "new Diaspora," however, is characterized by the emergence of a substantial heterogeneous Black population in the United States, as well as the emergence of new Black communities in other Western countries. As such, this phenomenon deserves a new conceptualization.

It is logical for us to posit the veracity of this rough method, to which we will now give explicit form in order to evaluate each of these developmental stages in the paradigm with reference to what we have called "the ideologic criterion of African unity," as suggested by St. Clair Drake. As we have used it in this study, the ideological criterion had only one dimension—the quality of unity achieved in the attempted or accomplished relationship between or among communities in the Diaspora. But in trying to work through our cases, we discovered that it would be useful to construct two dependent variables—(1) the nature of the opposition to the achievement of the objectives of African communities, and (2) the response of the African community in terms of the utilization of Pan African strategies to overcome that opposition. This fortuitous conclusion has also given us a way to rationalize the juxtaposition of the two methodologies used in our study, since most of what we discovered about the opposition to the African community was contained in its environment—the subject of the comparative method. We will use this theoretical formulation in a brief discussion of our cases and the significance of our findings.

One should recognize that, in effect, although I have capitalized the concept of Pan Africanism and the Diaspora, I am aware of the distinction made by both Shepperson and St. Clair Drake: the capitalization makes reference to a specific movement and the lowercase use of the terms illustrate the general phenomenon in the generic sense of its reference to the political or cultural characteristic of a social event.[3] However, I do not agree with Dr. St. Clair Drake's 1979 observation that within the context of pan Africanism (small p) "racial Pan Africanism will never occur again."[4] In fact, it may occur in one place more than once, as we have seen in the United States where two cycles have already been identified, and in other countries where the Diaspora continues to expand and where the foundations of racial Pan Africanism as being laid by the growing intensity of the race relations dynamic.[5]

Thus, we may summarize the following typology of potential unifying relationships:

1. unity among peoples within an African-origin community;
2. unity among African-origin peoples within a predominantly Black, culturally heterogeneous state;
3. unity between or among African people in African-origin communities in the Diaspora;
4. unity among African people in African-origin states;
5. unity between or among peoples in African-origin communities and African-origin states.

Now, perhaps one may understand the previous assertion with reference to the role of the Black community in the United States in its Pan African relations with other African communities in the Diaspora. It was that the American African community had an inordinate impact upon Pan African relations with other African communities, and I attempted to rationalize this fact by stating, in essence, that the community is older than other Diaspora communities or has overcome certain opposition to its presence by the use of Pan African strategies. In terms of the developmental paradigm of the Black community, therefore, I may say that it has mastered the first stage of struggle to achieve community. By saying this, I do not suggest for one moment that the kind of community that has been achieved is ideal, but rather that it is the kind of community which enables individuals and groups to function within the society in order to achieve their objectives *in a limited sense.*

I suggest also that the second stage has been reached by which Blacks have been able to maintain some of their communities through the achievement of political power and a relatively much smaller amount of economic power. But the final stage, where there is the freedom to use the resources of the community to achieve objectives without severe limitations, that stage has not been reached. This is so because the impact of objectives of the dominant culture is so strong that its broad (racial and nonracial) objectives take precedence over the condition of the Black community and, consequently, through neglect as much as through racism, economic exploitation, and cultural and technological hegemony, it influences the character and limits the quality of the evolution of the Black community. Nevertheless, it is in an advanced stage of the struggle for community relative to other communities in the Diaspora.

Diasporic Pan African Linkages

Now if we utilize the "criterion of unity" to examine the Pan African relations of the African community in America with those on the African continent, for example, we would find that there has been progress in achieving a substantial amount of unity, but the basis of this unity has primarily been controlled by the similarity in the status of the all Africans relative to Europeans. Since Africans on the continent are in transition from colonialism and neocolonialism to genuine independence, the basis of Pan African unity is also in transition. Most important, I argue that since a major dimension of the agenda for Pan African unity within the Diaspora comprises continental politics, these stages are fundamentally important to understand. In fact, there the author has posited two simultaneous stages occurring, the transion stages on the African continent and the developmental stages of African communities in the Diaspora. Perhaps the key to fruitful Pan African relations resides in recognizing the place of African peoples within these stages.

Continental Africa	*Extra-Continental Africa*
colonialism	proto-Community
neocolonialism	Community development
independence	Community capacity

Given this set of stages, the criterion of unity may be used to ask whether or not certain kinds of unity are possible, for ex-

ample, between a "colonial state" and a "proto-community."
How functional are their resources, how similar are their problems, are people able to be of assistance to one another based on
models of development or upon the transfer of resources or
from sympathetic assistance to a movement? It is clear that in
answering these questions, and in using these categories, we
need to know more about their particular characteristics in order
to make more than surface-level generalizations. The question
is: can functional Pan Africanism occur between states or
peoples located in any of the categories?

The problem is complex, for the nature of the opposition
to a functional Pan Africanism, we pointed out, will often involve such factors as ideologues who perpetuate the "two-line
struggle," Black leaders and Black foreign affairs professionals
who have cast their lot in with the state and its objectives, African leaders who are excessively xenophobic or politically vulnerable and therefore exploit the potential of Pan African strategies and, of course, the dominant opposition of the European
Diaspora attempting to achieve its own objectives through strategies of Pan Europeanism. I attempted to say that the substance
of Pan African unity on the African continent increasingly must
consider problems relevant to achieving genuine independence
and development and must be improved by Pan African strategies that provide opportunity for the Black community in America and other places to contribute to it, by (1) challenging
African-origin peoples to make the cognitive transition to the
practical bases of unity, (2) supporting African and Caribbean
states in various ways as they seek to achieve their objectives,
and (3) continuing to emphasize the development of Pan African
institutions to supplement national institutions as the vehicles
through which Pan African relations become routinized.

The African community in Britain is lodged between the
stages of the struggle to achieve community and the struggle to
maintain community, primarily because it is of more recent vintage as a community within British society. This was determined
by our case study of community objectives which, although different from the American case, are also designed to achieve a
similar rudimentary legitimacy of individuals as citizens and the
ordinary rights to social resources such as employment, housing, education, and other social services. This stage may also be

confirmed by the opposition of the British whites to the presence of Blacks, by their promulgation of new citizenship criteria, and by the racist and ineffectual handling of race relations by the officials of the state, including the police, the legislators, and the various agencies in the race relations industry.

The most important confirmation of our conclusion about the stages of the development of Black British society is derived through the use of the "criterion of unity." Pan African relations between the Black communities in America and Britain were such that a unity was achieved by the acceptance of certain strategies of social change that were operative in America, including the Black Power movement, the Black Muslim movement, the Black Panther movement, the civil rights movement, the Pan African movement, and other such phenomena. Individuals from these various American political movements were welcomed into a relationship with the Black community in Britain, and that community adopted the ideology and tactics of these movements as valid for its own circumstances. We attempted to illustrate that these "first-stage" tactics were useful in assisting the African community in Britain to posit its right to residence in Britain, as a community and as British citizens, and the right to be treated in a nonracist manner.

The question we pose, however, is whether or not the quality of the Pan African relations between the two African communities will improve over time. We have noticed that in the past two decades the nature of the Pan African relations has been of a more episodic rather than a systemic nature. Also, it appears that the similarity between racial problems in the social, economic, and political sectors of British society and those in the United States, especially those culminating in the rebellions in Britain, suggest a similar pattern of evolution of the African community, which may be more amenable to continuing comparative treatment. Perhaps the basis for enhanced systematic relations resides in more recent parallel developments we have noted such as the Black Sections initiative in the Labor party and the coming of the first generation of Blacks to the British Parliament.

The pan African element in this latter case above was explored, and I discovered the pursuit of similar patterns of public policy by Black British legislators, no doubt stemming from a similar socio-economic condition and status to African Americans. If this is true, one might expect that they represent empirical proof of the need to adopt similar political strategies for the defense and development of their communities.

Continental Linkages

The second type of continental Pan African relations involves those that find the African community in the United States attempting to make a fundamental linkage with a community or state on the African continent. The case studies presented here concern South Africa and Ghana. Here, the most immediate similarity one finds between the two case studies is the existence of historically parallel movements on the African continent and in America. In America, the civil rights movement, begun in 1957, gathered force in the early 1960s, providing a dynamic context for a modern reconceptualization of a positive relationship between African Americans and Africa. Simultaneously, the development of the Independence Movement in the Gold Coast had begun in the 1950s and reached the consummation stage with the independence of Ghana in 1957. Thus, free Africans might have the possibility to establish new relationships with newly motivated African Americans wishing such a relationship.

African Americans attempted, in both case studies, to utilize the African linkage for the dual purposes of supporting the objectives of the African state/people in Ghana and South Africa and in fighting American racism. In the case of Ghana, this dual purpose was clear as the Black American community in general sought both to uphold the objectives of the Nkrumah government and, in doing so, to establish a "safe house" where they might also point to the evils of racism and rally support for its condemnation from abroad.

The South African case represents one type of Pan African linkage where a Black community in the Diaspora has influenced a continental African community. In South Africa, as we have said, the African community possesses the features of a Diaspora society where power relations are concerned, and an African continental situation where the questions of culture, colonialism and majority status in society are concerned. There, we found that the African community is very much at the stage of the struggle to achieve community in the sense that its objectives are to gain control over its own land. The current status of the African community as powerless people, relegated to a small portion of barren land, labor reserves, and hovels, in no way constitutes its existence in the kind of community through which it may achieve humane social objectives. Even where the Africans live and work in the bustling cities of Johannesburg, Cape Town, and Durban, they live in a total community of oppression. Still, the objective of the Africans is to go beyond community to the achievement of equal status with all peoples within the framework of leading an independent nation.

The objectives of the white South African minority, however, are to contain the potential African nation within the framework of a new political regime where Africans have citizenship within a corporate State of South Africa where the erection of a regime of "equality" between the races politically gives functional control over society to whites because of their superior economic power. This strategy adopted by the white minority serves the objectives of maintaining the life of privilege they have created through the exploitation of Black people, while maintaining control over the process of the exploitation of Black labor and fashioning their version of a response to the Black demand for political rights and full participation.

Under such circumstances, the degree of unity achieved in the implementation of Pan African strategies has been primarily a unity of support and ideas transmitted from America and from other parts of the African continent to the Black community in South Africa, where the objective situation found fertile ground for their application to Apartheid. This in itself is testimony to the power of the ideas of Black self-determination, such as Black Power and Black Theology, but it is also evidence of the receptivity that exists inside the Black community for similar strategies of liberation. One unique aspect of this situation is that, whereas the potential liberating force of the Black Power in America is reformism because of the objective problem of white monopoly of power and Black minority status, in South Africa this philosophy can reach its full national potential even beyond the way that it has in many other African societies (understanding the considerable qualifications to this notion).

I have suggested that in such a situation as that in South Africa, both Black power and Pan Africanism were revolutionary because the aim of the Black community is to reach the status of nationhood. Thus, in order to achieve its objective, the community must radically change its present status and, either through the revolutionary process or negotiation, successfully challenge those who keep the community in subjugation. To posit the goal of "one-man one-vote" without realizing that it means a political revolution in the status of Blacks inside South Africa is to misunderstand Black objectives as integrationist only or "participationist" only. So, one must clearly understand that while it is white oppression which keeps the African fixed in his/her relationship to the power of the white minority in a manner that makes his/her situation appear to resemble the Black situation in America, the stakes are substantially different.

In one sense, there will be a continuing basis for Pan African relationships between the two African cultures which have been shaped to such a fundamental degree by their relationship with white power and European culture. But if one assumes that the South African blacks will ultimately be victorious in the struggle for nationhood and independence, then one must realize they will live in an advanced industrial state and their ability to grapple with the problems of technology, industry, communications, and other world dynamics will provide the opportunity for the exchange of perspectives on similar problems and the employment of the skills of other African peoples.

In Ghana, however, American Blacks were unable to connect culturally with indigeneous people, since their base culture was qualitatively different. Ghanaians lived in a racially homogenous society where they were not only the majority but also entirely Black; Black Americans, by contrast, lived in a racially heterogeneous society where they were a minority. In addition, Black Americans lived in a large Western country with an advanced industrial base and had socialized to the point of possessing ways of behaving and skills that Ghanaians did not possess and ways of behaving socially that Ghanaians often considered to be different or even offensive.

As a result, there were severe limitations placed on the ability of African Americans, because of their inaccessibility to the indigenous culture, to influence the Ghanaian situation. They in turn were absolutely vulnerable to the leadership of Kwame Nkrumah and his program for the development of Ghana and the propagation of continental Pan Africanism. These factors limited the extent to which Blacks might have played a more balanced role, serving to moderate the negative features to which C.L.R. James points in Nkrumah's program by playing the role of mediating advisers rather than only as committed supporters. The role Black Americans played both in Ghana and in the United States in support of Ghana and of Nkrumah might have been historically inevitable. In this sense, "historical necessity" takes on more than an objective meaning, suggesting that the subjective content of both movements might have required just such a response. In the South African case, the influence of African Americans was felt through the force of their own Black Power movement which struck a sensitive cord in the Black Consciousness movement within South Africa, thus helping to legitimize the concept both within South Africa and abroad.

Differences in the Ghana and South African case studies as attempts by African Americans to forge continental Pan African linkages illustrate themselves in two ways. First, the cultural basis as the foundation of political linkage between African Americans and Black South Africans was similar in that the political movement for Black Power arose, in both cases, from the cultural conflict between Blacks and white power. This historical phenomenon has resulted in the production of a range of social characteristics that are shared by Black Americans and South Africans in their relationships with whites in both societies. The following similar elements can be noted: the bicultural perspective of Blacks, the evolution of a distinct mulatto class, the shared tactics of a nonviolent, civil disobedience internal struggle, a similar social structure and function in relation to the economic system.

It is, of course, possible to conclude that continental linkage of the type illustrated by the South Africa case will be far more prevalent in the future than that represented by the Ghana case. That is to say, there will be a far more constructive bedrock of unity among African peoples in the Diaspora to have influence in a given political situation or movement if they do so from a base in the Diaspora, rather than inject themselves into an African continental socio-political system in a modern "back-to-Africa" movement. In fact, perhaps, this is one of the most important distinctions within a "Pan" cultural movement that is based on the explicit privilege of "the return" and Pan Africanism; other cases may not involve the level of cultural complexity found in the African return.

And yet, one must qualify the sense that a type of Pan Africanism based on the return to Africa will never be successful, because the baseline of culture between Africans on the continent and those in the Diaspora is narrowing as a result of the increasing adoption by continental Africans of a Western material culture that, thus far, has been synthesized with African traditional culture. When the scales of culture tip more decidedly toward the world material culture, then perhaps the traditional culture will not be the impediment that it is today. In such a case, "race" may still not act as the primary basis for a functional pan African relationship, because race is not the sole basis of continental African alienation and hence cannot be the only basis for unity. Instead, other factors such as economics might serve as a more influential basis for a lasting relationship. This may be especially true with the waning of the independence struggle that had previously been the most consistent basis for Pan African linkages between continental and Diaspora Africans.

The Ideology of Pan African Unity

It has been discovered in the course of this study that ideology has played an important and often troubling role in the attempt of African peoples in the Diaspora to achieve community or nationhood. Whereas one may be led, in the early stages of an effort to understand the dynamics of political movements, to feel that the discipline of ideology is a necessary ingredient to the success of a movement, in subsequent stages it is also possible to come to feel that an explicit ideology, while a necessary reference for the faithful, may be an occasional hindrance to the political unity to which many movements are directed. In this sense, I have not been overly exorcised about the necessity to conform to a particular regimen of Pan African ideology, for a vast potential exists for achieving Pan African objectives by contributions from people involved in activities in the Diaspora who do not have an explicitly conceptualized ideology.

On the other hand, we have referred to the inevitable problems of ideology that accompany the struggle for community within the context of the necessity for substantial social change. We have seen, for example, that Diaspora Pan Africanists have attempted to project the "two-line struggle" on the African continent back into their activities in the Black community in the United States. But we also recognized that the nature of the ideological struggle on the continent of Africa itself is part of qualitatively different political processes and is connected to other unique processes such as the independence movement and the subsequent process of national reconstruction.

Thus, without taking sides or blaming the ideologues, we view the emergence of the "two-line struggle" as a natural phase of the post-independence era in which African states (and Caribbean states) are sorting out their political direction and ultimately their approach to satisfying social needs through the management of the productive process. The problem is that the force and charisma of ideology as a substance that promises to satisfy these needs by itself is at first seductive, and supporters of one side or another are led to adopt ideological positions with fury and inordinate devotion rather than with an historical perspective and a rational outlook in mind. So the problem is not with the "two-line struggle" itself, but with the degree to which those supporting each side see it as the *only answer* (or at least the only way to begin the answer) to the problems of the underdevelopment and subordination of African peoples in Africa and in the Diaspora.

The historical perspective, on the other hand, would lead partisans to understand that all revolutions change their course. Part of the reason for this is that as the revolution passes and the seizure of power brings responsibility for governing, this new stage requires flexibility. For the most potent impediment to the achievement of objectives is often not the lack of resources but the presence of the uncertainty of direction within the new dynamic and interactive global environment. Thus, the other part of the reason is that the new states and new communities do, in fact, lack competitive resources and are most often opposed by those holding superior resources and formulating the rules which govern the attainment of economic viability. Dogmatism under these circumstances is a luxury that only the powerful can afford.

At the same time, one must not underestimate the value of an explicit cultural referent. For example, to clarify an earlier discussion that introduced the question of African identity within the context of various types of social situations in the Diaspora, a "Black" identity must be constantly understood by Black peoples not just to signify the coloration of a people, but to be fundamentally grounded in an appreciation of an African identity and relationship and, therefore, carrying an implicit Pan African obligation.

The challenge is to identify with the society in the new state. It is the pragmatic challenge of acquiring full citizenship as a legitimizing factor to full participation in society. The pragmatic goal is to become not African, but African American, Afro-British, Afro-Canadian or simply "French" or "South African." Although the question of national identity is paramount, it is also true there are various levels of identity. There is identity to the state, to the nation, to the locality, and to the more basic features of race and original place of origin. The political task of the African in the Diaspora is often to resolve the contradictions presented by the old identity and the new. In this regard, one must confront the question of whether the new society is racially exclusive, a factor that will shape the character of political objectives which are related to the possibility of changing the status of a community. Resolving these contradictions will rarely be done manifestly (or consciously) in the name of a distinctly "African" or "Pan African" concept; it will more likely be done in terms that fit the conscious and pragmatic reality with which peoples are confronted. However, this does not obviate the theoretical observation that the character of such responses are in fact "African" or "Pan African" in character. The use of the term "African" as a categorical identity is meant in this work to signify reference to "African-origin" people or peoples of African descent, generally to Black peoples south of the Sahara Desert. It also allows for, besides the historical dimension, the persistence of a physical, psychological, and, depending on the circumstances, cultural, claim upon Black people all over the world. This claim is the basis upon which the theoretical and practical permutations of the Pan African phenomenon are founded. Furthermore, the Pan African category is marked by the definition of "unifying activity" as the basis of the analysis in this work. However, it should be clear that we do not mean "unity" in its mechanical sense, but rather a rough mutuality of purpose that forges an interaction among Black leaders that results in sharing concepts which guide the application of common strategies to similar problems. More will be said later about this subject, the relationship between politics and culture, than is appropriate to include in this section.

Given the importance of a categorical identity, there remains the question of whether the cultural referent to politics within the Black struggle for community, a natural struggle as we have posed it, is also a progressive struggle. I view the struggle for unity within African communities around the world and upon the African continent as a progressive struggle because it is a struggle for self-determination that forces change in the global distribution of power for other Third World peoples. Without self-determination, the natural predisposition of a colonized or oppressed people, it is impossible for people to realize their own human aspirations; otherwise, they must constantly assist in the realization of the dreams and projects of others. That is why any progressive struggle begins somewhere specific, with a particular group, but can be related to the struggles of other groups, especially if the patterns of subordination are similar and emanate from the same source.

Thus, the struggle for Pan African self-determination is a *sine qua non* to the possession of the necessary resources and disposition to enter into larger struggles for change and to rid the world of those forces that stand against the movement toward an enlightened living situation for humanity. Thus, while the cultural nationalism implied in the philosophy of Pan Africanism may be considered parochial or "narrowly" directed toward peoples of African descent, in fact, it is very broad, both because Africans are global people and because by helping themselves they position themselves to be of the greatest service to others. In fact, part of the task of demystifying the "progressive" pretentions of a political struggle is to admit that no struggle is largely altruistic, that all struggles are, in the first instance, local and particularistic in nature, and that whether they have wider significance depends not alone upon ideological declarations, but upon the character of the struggle—whether or not those involved have the resources to utilize in that manner.

Secondly, whether or not the Pan African struggle in each place in the Diaspora is a progressive struggle depends upon its mass character. The struggle for self-determination cannot be to empower only the state and its managers, but through the state, to empower its citizens and provide for their basic needs. This is where one agrees with the analysis of Professor Claude Ake and writer A. M. Babu and others who observe that in the post-independence period the integrity of the struggle for self-determination has been derailed by corruption and self-gratification by the agents of the African state, and, therefore, they lack either the discipline or the will to pursue fundamental strategies and tactics of change.[6] So the preoccupation with elite interests to the detriment of obtaining benefits with the broadest impact upon the community or state defines African leaders as agents of the colonial state (not simply its economic system) and, thus, perpetrators of neocolonialism. My agreement with this observation is not so much a question of ideological solidarity as of common sense. How is it possible for the Pan African struggle to contribute to the achievement of local objectives or to contribute to human progress—as a progressive project—if the local African community or state is managed for the benefit of a few and their models in the Western or Eastern colonial state? It would appear, logically, to be impossible.

Unity, Pan African Obligation and the State

In this study, I have proceeded under the assumption that a Pan African methodology of analysis could be useful in studying the Pan African political phenomenon. This process has facilitated a description of the operation of the "criterion of unity" in several case studies. We now know that both in an historical sense as well as in the present, Pan Africanism has meant African unity—and hence Pan Africanists have attempted to achieve a unity either with Africa or among peoples of African descent in the Diaspora with respect to some common project. For the purpose of a study substantially concerned with the Diaspora, we have adopted the pragmatic formulation of Maulana Karenga in suggesting that Pan Africanism can only be functional within the context of a struggle for community or the struggle to develop the capacities of the African communities in the Diaspora to the point where they are able to have real influence within the Pan African world dialogue on questions of survival and development, either directly or indirectly.

This implies that the "twoness" of which W. E. B. DuBois spoke is not only an internal question of African and European cultural symbiosis, but is also perpetuated by the twin obligation of the African in the Diaspora both to his immediate circumstance and the other African peoples. But increasingly, we realize that the priority becomes his immediate circumstance and the other a secondary though strongly influential part of his total African obligation. In my view, this obvious situation does not diminish the overall cultural framework of "African unity" because we have shown that in a political struggle for community the use of Pan African strategies does not require "cultural synchronization." It does mean that attention to the obligation to improve one's immediate community is a *necessary precondition* to effective Pan Africanism because it is there that the resources are developed for strategies directed to both aspects of African survival. In theoretical terms, it is the "national question" that is primary and that affects the way in which Pan African relations evolve among peoples and states in the Diaspora.

For example, I have suggested that the mobilization of all

Americans to oppose South African Apartheid in 1985 was initiated by African Americans who had developed a resourceful organization and strategies, the result being the passage of national anti-Apartheid legislation. This model has been often replicated in other instances. The civil rights movement produced the Voting Rights Act. That act produced Black elected officials. In turn, that led to passage of anti-Apartheid legislation as well as legislation resulting in millions of dollars in appropriations to deal with the African drought and famine.

One can also recognize from my analysis of the comparative framework of the case studies that the state in America or Britain is a powerful impediment to the achievement of an authentically viable African community. One symptom is that the cultural conflict is endemic in the form of the struggle between aspects of the African and European Diasporas within the state because of the structural inquality between the races. The state, more often than not, is not merely a passive political authority, but the repository of the power of the majority culture and, therefore, the state mediates the social struggle as the political agent of the majority. Rarely, then, does struggle take place directly between peoples, but generally between Blacks and agents of the state.

The state usually is able to subdue the conflict over racial demands by institutionalizing it, by demanding that the African community resolve problems through the institutions set up to represent the cultural interests of the majority in the first place. That is why Blacks often object to the mystification of the state and its various apparatuses, and that is equally the reason we see the process of *community building* as a necessary activity through which to develop competitive and protective resources. The state has attempted to objectify the endemic conflict and to force everyone to conceptualize it within the framework of its agencies and institutions. Hence, the conflict is one of "police-community" relations; it is one of "minority unemployment"; it is one of "inadequate housing" and other such objective referents of public policy. But the totality of this conflict should lead any rational individual to conclude that if it is pervasive, encompassing the sum of the social activities all along the fault line of racial stratification, then it is a basic conflict essentially between the peoples and the culture they represent, not merely a conflict within the intermediary structures of government.

Therefore, I do not conclude that the state is unimportant, but that the struggle for community is legitimate and progressive because it understands the nature and function of the state and is pursued *regardless of the state*—but with due consideration for its power—to help establish *areas of autonomy* in the lives of African peoples. This gives to the nationalism of the African community its character, even though a substantial aspect of that character is to be like the dominant community in many respects. Nevertheless, the necessity to challenge the state in order to achieve both autonomy and open access formulates the understanding that social change is an implicit objective in the Pan African struggle inasmuch as the majority culture did not invent institutions to empower Black people but to enhance their own control.

The state, as we have seen, may also be an impediment in the development of linkages from the African Diaspora to the African continent because of the inequalities of status between those who represent states and those who represent peoples or communities in the Diaspora. This has been illustrated in many of the cultural and political Pan African conferences where African or Caribbean government representatives interfaced with delegates from Diaspora communities, attempting to achieve communication, understanding, and the drafting of programs. The evidence for this assumption is the long record of the intelligence agencies of the American government and European governments of both the West and the East in seeking to subvert a constructive dialogue among African-origin peoples by infiltration, assassination, economic control, control of communication, and outright disinformation.

As suggested, the solution is to sponsor conferences and projects on two levels: among parallel government officials in the Diaspora where they are now developing, and among *all African peoples.* The latter model was popularized by Kwame Nkrumah, beginning in 1958, but was also prevalent in the formal period of the Pan African movement from 1900 to 1945. Although the reality in many African and Caribbean states is that not much may be accomplished without the support of the government, still there are subnational forces with considerable resources among women's groups, churches, social clubs, professional associations, the business and education communities. There would appear to be much opportunity for parallel linkages to occur among such groups in various places of the Diaspora.

Unity and Economics

Many Pan Africanists in the Diaspora have had a difficult time approving of capitalism as the most desirable economic model in their struggle to build community. And so we have suggested that most would prefer some form of socialist system or set of activities. Even Africans who probably would not approve of adopting pure "scientific socialism" as an organizing principle for their economy would nonetheless view unbridled capitalism as negative, because: (1) Capitalist values stress individual profit and possession of private property counter to the need for shared resources in a resource-poor and oppressed community. (2) The traditional African heritage of communalism emphasizes shared resources such as land and wealth. (3) In the Diaspora, Blacks have been prevented from accumulating large sums of capital so that the community does not have large-scale capitalists, being supported largely by wages from the capitalist system and transfer payments from the government. (4) The result of the actual functioning of capitalism in states which contain Africans in Diaspora are: (a) class cleavages that develop with the creation of a small middle class with vastly greater material resources than the much larger lower classes, (b) the Black community is kept essentially as a labor reserve appended to the dominant white capitalist enterprises, and (c) chronic dysfunction of the community structure, due to overburdened institutions and social deterioration.

The suspicion is that, although lip service is often paid to the myth of boundless opportunity, whites would not prefer to experience the rise of a significant class of large-scale Black capitalists able to provide a basis of political and economic support for the Black community and to participate with power in the larger economy; for that would ultimately raise questions of control (autonomy/dependency) and competition as it has with the Japanese. The effect of the exclusion of African peoples from significant involvement in capitalism has meant that there is less of a symbiosis between Black culture and capitalism than exists in white Western communities.

So, while some form of collectivism has always been a necessity among African peoples in the Diaspora, the demand by progressive thinkers that they adopt "scientific socialism" as an explicit ideology is equally and obviously flawed. Thus, in the early stages of the establishment of a Black community in Britain, Blacks were often being told that it was folly for them to organize in their own racial interest, that they had no choice but to adopt scientific socialism because their paucity of numbers made necessary a common political coalition with the British working class. But the notions of national class or interracial class solidarity has been tenuous at best in each case because of the differences in objective conditions between the races regardless of the class position. What appears to be occurring in Britain and in other Diaspora communities is a closure on the question of racial solidarity that does not mitigate against class solidarity. This conclusion emerges from the analysis, not predominant in Diaspora communities, that race and class are issues which the state has problems digesting simultaneously and which must, therefore, be integrated into a common Black political strategy.

It is, therefore, impossible for Africans in the Diaspora as well as Africans on the continent to be pure socialists in ideology as long as they have to deal with the global capitalist system for their survival. If Africans in the Diaspora are socialists, their socialism will obviously be "mixed" since it will be impossible to practice "scientific socialism" within the bowels of a capitalist state. So there will be many (as there are at the moment) "sympathetic socialists" who have adopted the identity and the humane goals of various kinds of socialism and Marxism but who, in a thorough-going fashion, yield to the perquisites of living in a capitalist state by being practical capitalists.

The pursuit of community "collectivist" values, therefore, is probably the most advanced form of socialism possible within a Western state, because these values ironically are the basis of both Black Marxist and Black Cultural Nationalist social movements. These "islands" of semisocialism, represented by groups such as the Black Muslims, have one thing in common; they are externally structured to relate to the capitalist economic system in the most efficient way possible, as capitalists, while using the profits from that economic activity internally in a socialist fashion to meet the needs of the group. This mixed system has potential throughout the Diaspora to contribute to Pan African values and objectives in ways compatible with the struggle for community.

Of course, I hope that the sheer weight of the evidence marshalled in the description and analyses of the cases presented is enough itself strongly to suggest to the reader that Pan Africanism is a living and important phenomenon. To end this discussion, however, I make this explicit point with reference to the many manifestations of Pan Africanism currently in existence in the Diaspora, on the continent and on several different levels of global relationships, both among African peoples and between them and other peoples.

In the Diaspora, the continuing manifestations of Pan Africanism persists on two levels, with respect to the traditional role of influencing community development and survival strategies in other African-origin communities, as well as through linkages with African states. In the first case, the development of the Black British community is critical, not only for its own sake, but for the extent to which the community is able to provide political leadership for similarly situated communities in all of Europe. For its sake, the maturity of its political leadership has meant that it is coming to grips systematically with the necessity for economic development. Thus, former cultural events such as the Notting Hill Carnival have increasingly been perceived by some as vehicles for economic development as well as a cultural legitimizing instrument for the community.[7]

The concentration on economics has bred a concern with the way in which European economic integration in 1992 will impact on the economies of Africa and the Caribbean, areas from which many of the Black leaders of Britain originated. Just as important, as these Black leaders have fought racism within the context of Britain, they will have to take into consideration that the new Europe will have few provisions to fight racism through public policy on a continent-wide basis. European racism developed as a consequence of the immigration of African-origin and other non-European peoples to that continent in search of a viable life-style.

An assault on European racism is important; France has begun to debate and adopt the restrictions on immigration and the expulsion tactics vis-à-vis non-French Third World peoples that were tested in Britain. French actions had particular consequences for Arabs, Africans and Afro-Caribs from former French colonies. While the Middle Eastern guerillas and Basques revolutionaries of Spain have ostensibly served as cases-in-point that the French have used to fight "terrorism" and to adopt more strenuous immigration policies, the rise of internal racism against Jews, Arabs and Blacks drew scant attention on the part of the conservative government of Jacques Chirac.[8] In 1987, strong racial tensions developed in Pont-de-Cheruy as the result of the murder of a local policeman by an Arab.[9] The French responded with reactionary measures such as transferring to the local authorities the power to initiate expulsions from the country.

In reaction to such steps and the racism preached by Jean-Marie Le Pen, head of the National Front, a new movement called "SOS Racisme" was formed by Arabs, Jews and Blacks and led by Harlem Désire, a Guadeloupean emigré. Désire, who openly says that Martin Luther King, Jr. was the most important inspiration for this movement, conceived of himself culturally as a "cross-breed" and as having "old roots and no roots, Black without being African."[10] Désire also considered himself to be the new Black European and so oriented his movement toward the largest segments of French society affected by racism—Arabs, Jews, and Blacks.

In Spain, the bulk of the Black population lives in Catalonia and comes from Gambia and Senegal to work as migrant laborers picking fruit and vegetables. Racism exists there to the extent that a defense organization has been formed, the Jama Kafo, or "Peoples Organization" in the Mandingo language. Momodou Cham, head of this civil rights organization in 1987, said that "Spanish people are real racists, the authorities more so than the common people."[11] This opinion, which is shared by a number of Spanish intellectuals, is denied by government officials who say they have no reports of serious racial difficulties. The African population is tiny, 151,000 out of 40 million, and current indications of the level of racism are confined to the existence of graffiti saying "Africans go home" or alluding to the Ku Klux Klan. However, observers wonder whether more serious manifestations of racism will occur if the African and non-Spanish population grows much larger.[12]

Italy has for some time cooperated with the United Nations High Commission on Refugees by granting asylum to refugees fleeing persecution as a matter of national law. In fact, the extradition of foreigners for political reasons is not admissible, and Italy provides sanctuary for individuals who do not have access to democracy. Three thousand asylum seekers were received in Italy over the past few years.[13] In addition, Italy has been a country of transit for refugees, processing at least one million persons, many from Northeast Africa over the past decade. The link to the Horn of Africa is well established, inasmuch as Italy was the colonial power ruling Ethiopia and Eritrea, a status that ended when the British helped Ethiopia drive out the Italians in 1941.

With this flow of refugees and legal immigrants, obviously a sizeable non-Italian, African-origin population is building in Italy, a country of sixty million people. Predictably, racist incidents began occurring. Before Jerry Essan Masslo, a South African refugee was slain for a few dollars in a tomato field in southern Italy, he said: "No black or South African can forget what racism is. I see it happening here in Italy, and I can't accept it."[14] In fact, near his body was a flyer proclaiming "permanent open season on Negroes." But there have been other incidents—Italian passengers compelling an Ethiopian woman to give up her seat on a bus amid insults, a gang of young toughs forcing a Black man out of a third floor window—indicating the rise of considerable animosity against Black people. Inevitably, pressures have arisen for tightening immigration, restrictions have been placed on the movement of nonwhite, non-Italian citizen immigrants who reside in Italy, and a policy of expulsion has been debated.[15]

As witnessed by the development of political struggle in Britain, the African-origin community organizes itself, then seeks allies among other oppressed communities. The strategy of Harlem Désire in France is symptomatic of this stage. Then, when the community grows large enough, the tensions within the coalition are exposed and each community begins to organize along the lines of its own basic interest, maintaining a loose coalition for specific purposes. It is highly conceivable that in the future, for example, just as the Black and Asian community in Britain struggled together as one "Black" community, and are now beginning to find their distinctive political interests, the question will be asked, "What ever happened to the coalition?" One opportunity for such a coalition might arise in the developing pan-European movement scheduled to culminate in economic union in 1992. Given the amazingly similar socioeconomic and political dynamics faced by the African-origin immigrants in Europe, it would be natural that as a pan-European movement develops, a pan African movement in Europe might develop in response.

Even where there are no Black communities, it could still be asserted that Pan Africanism is useful in playing a defensive role to the racial stereotypes which have emerged strongly from Asia. In China, for example, a violent confrontation broke out between Chinese and African students in early 1989 when an African student brought an Asian female student to a social affair.[16] That resulted in attacks against African students by thousands of Chinese students at the Beijing Languages Institute. Attacks against Africans occurred a week later in the eastern city of Nanjing and were replicated in four other cities. The 1,500 African students in China, suddenly vulnerable, sought to leave the country in the face of feeble attempts by African diplomats to stem the flow of violence against them. The Africans were scapegoats for student resentment over reports that foreigners were being accorded special privileges, but violence was not exercised against white foreigners.

In 1988–1990, there were a series of racist comments by high Japanese officials, that American test scores were low allegedly because Black students performed badly, that Blacks ruined neighborhoods by their presence, and so on. The Congressional Black Caucus reacted quickly, leading a delegation of business and civil rights leaders to Japan and drawing apologies from the government, but without securing economic amends. Following another insult, in the autumn of 1990, a task force of Black leaders made plans to boycott Japanese-made products. Meanwhile,

President Bush ignored the insult to African Americans, respecting the economic power of the Japanese. At the same time he signed into law a bill providing for $30 million in financial reparations to the Japanese Americans interned during the Second World War.

The second-level manifestations of Pan Africanism in the Diaspora are at *the community level* where, as suggested earlier, the concept has a promising usage, but where it has scarcely been attempted. For example, in Miami there is a sizeable Haitian community, created by a sudden flow of thousands of migrants, beginning in November 1977, as a result of repression at home. After experiencing considerable racism in the immigration process, particularly in comparison to the treatment accorded Cuban immigrants, the movement of Haitians to Miami resulted in the establishment of a distinct Haitian community known as "little Haiti." A sizeable community of Haitians settled in Brooklyn and Harlem in New York City as well.[17]

Between 1957 and 1984, an estimated 900,000 Haitians left their country; more than two-thirds of them came to the United States, most residing in New York City.[18] Haitians who have attempted to come to America, are treated different than Cuban immigrants whose parallel migration has produced such numbers that they now dominate Miami politically. This has led to charges of racism in American immigration policy. American Blacks, who gained little relative advantage before the migration, have far less.[19] The animosity that exists between Haitian and African American at the mass level is rooted in the Haitian sense of optimism about life chances and the relative ability to overcome racism.[20]

The fact that the Haitians feel themselves hardworking people and see indigenous Blacks as lazy and lacking in pride may simply be what one observer calls the classic perspective between the old and the newer groups. Nevertheless, the obvious fact that both are of African-origin could be a basis for a unifying approach to problem-solving. If leaders of the African-American community took the responsibility for the political education of the Haitian immigrants, rather than leaving the task to the socializing agents of the larger community, a common alliance might be developed in obtaining much needed resources for both communities.

The same scenario is present in Washington, D.C., where there is a sizeable and growing nonwhite immigrant population, largely from Africa and Latin America. Surveys of the attitude of the predominantly white residents in metropolitan Washington—the District of Columbia, surburban Maryland and northern Virginia—about immigrants revealed that while the oldtimers generally had a positive attitude toward the newcomers, tension lay just beneath the surface. The critical factor was that in the District of Columbia, as elsewhere in the nation, Blacks viewed other immigrants, whether from African-origin countries or not, as potential competitors for employment. Then, too, the fact of differences in language made the immigrant appear extraordinarily alien. Even where language problems were not an issue, there was a feeling that there were too many immigrants in the area.[21] Again, there was no common organization in Washington through which large numbers of Africans (Nigerians and Ethiopians being the largest groups) in the majority African-American District were brought into a common framework of discussion and action with respect to social, political, or economic questions.

The stakes are important and the need is great. And many questions arise, both on the African continent and in the Diaspora, with respect to the responsibility of the African-American community. For example, in response to the drought in the African Sahel in 1985, the NAACP held a meeting in New York and developed a short and long-range strategy for addressing the problem. A statement issued after the meeting said: "The Black community should work effectively with African governments to enlist support among Americans to assist with African development."[22] The statement then asked for cash donations and said the NAACP would be responsible for distributing the funds. In that same period other Black communities attempted to respond to the drought through local fund-raising campaigns. The city of Atlanta, for example, was assigned a goal of $300,000 in a nationwide campaign, but only $50,000 was raised.[23] However, it should be noted that Atlanta, like other cities, lacks a common vehicle for mobilizing African Americans on a systematic basis for such purposes.

Despite these lapses in the building of local Pan African organizations to handle clearly pan African problems, traditional

African-American linkage projects have continued. TransAfrica, the Black American lobby for Africa and the Caribbean, has continued to maintain good relations and communication with the leaders of the Black South African freedom movement. In January 1989, for example, TransAfrica arranged a meeting between such Black South African leaders as Bishop Desmond Tutu, Rev. Alan Boesak, and Beyers Naude with U.S. political leaders and policy officials. In addition, the Commission for Racial Justice of the United Church of Christ, led by Rev. Benjamin Chavis, Jr., led an extraordinary series of investigatory groups into Angola in an effort to expose the extent of the human suffering caused by the activities of the rebel group UNITA (Union for the Total Independence of Angola), led by Jonas Savimbi. On one such mission in October of 1988, Paulino Pinto Jaoa, Angola's director of information, said, "Our goal is to have good relations with all Americans, but Black Americans are often more aware and more interested in Africa."[24]

In Africa, there is a curious situation; one senses from scholars, such as Claude Ake, that while the theory of Pan Africanism is often denounced as irrelevant and Nkrumah, Nyerere, and other Pan Africanists condemned as "reactionaries," the landscape of economic development strategies is increasingly littered with attempted Pan Africanist solutions. That these strategies in the main have not worked has something to do with what scientific Marxist theorists consider the process of "embourgeoisment" of African elites.[25] But this analysis fails to take into consideration the fact that these countries came into the international system as independent entities at a time when real possibilities for alternative economic futures were not as great as when the European state system was born.

When the economies of Western states were formed the international system was a relatively open affair and only armed conflict stood in the way of money making. Today, resort to war is far less frequent; civil trade has flourished for the better part of the twentieth century; mechanisms of global finance have been routinized, and international financial institutions serving governments have been established along with the terms for participation. But African countries have not had access to the processes of world imperialism and the human slave trade which made monumental contributions to the accumulation of Western capital. African countries, independent for less than thirty-five years, emerged at a time when there was little room for global manueverability and little choice among specific economic models, particularly with Soviet Russia beginning to dismantle rigid structures of state socialism. In any case, I do not place a positive value on the failure of the socialist models, but only comment on it to illustrate the dilemma of African states in the declining choice of economic models.

As a result, African states have attempted to survive economically by mounting valiant struggles against the terms of participation in institutions such as the International Monetary Fund, then giving in, as in the case of Tanzania, because of the lack of real alternative sources of development capital. On the continent, African states have fashioned Pan Africanist principles and projects for economic development with the clear understanding that collective solutions were the key to their ability to mediate external economic influences upon their economies and develop some sense of relative autonomy. This was the undergirding of the Lagos Plan of Action, the Economic Community of West Africa, the Southern African Development Coordinating Conference (SADCC), and other such projects.

Perhaps the major problem with the concept of Pan Africanism in Africa and the contradiction of its presence without its adequate conceptualization is its primary association with the Organization of African Unity. There appears to be considerable substance to the criticisms of the OAU voiced by Elenga M'Buyinga, who speaks of the conflict between the two tendencies of "revolutionary Pan Africanism" and "demogogic Pan Africanism" in achieving Pan African unity.[26] On the one hand, he suggests that Nkrumah exemplified revolutionary Pan Africanism with his program to unify Africa under an independent and neutral banner, and on the other, he suggests that African political leaders stiffled this movement with essentially demogogic appeals to concepts such as "noninterference" in the affairs of each other's states.

Thus, M'Buyinga reaches the conclusion that the bourgeois state model in Africa has prevented the arrival of true Pan Africanism or the continental unity of Africa under a socialist economic model. Given the obvious problems of economies of scale in approaching the underdevelopment in countries with few of the elements that would provide opportunities for autonomous viability, African countries could well be driven to rethink the state system as a basis for Pan African continental unity in the future. An example of this trend was the Brazzaville conference of African scientists in 1987 which called for a "nongovernmental Pan-African Union of Science and Technology," a network and federation of African scientific and technological institutions working for African development.[27]

In a remarkable volume of essays honoring Kwame Nkrumah's contribution to the OAU, each of the writers, concerned with such topics as the African Development Bank, communications flows, the application of African common law, conflict resolution, and racial reconstruction, paid tribute to Nkrumah's original vision of Pan African unity.[28] In this work, Professor Thomas Nsenga Kanza writes, ". . . twenty-five years later, in 1988, the African continent has no union government, no unified defense policy, no common foreign policy, and to sum it up, no peace, no stability and no credibility. Twenty-five years later, independent Africa is not yet free. Independent Africa may never be free."[29] The amelioration of this circumstance, or the "African syndrome," as Edem Kodjo has called it, must come through pan African strategies which resurrect the need for common projects. Kanza sees the adoption of a "rationalized Pan Africanism" as urgent for African survival on the continent, utilizing the European model of centralized economic growth, as illustrated for example, by German unification for survival in the nineteenth century.[30] He also urges that other Pan African projects such as an "African Defense Community" be attempted.[31] He concludes: "At this stage of the 'African syndrome' it is necessary that the pan-Africanism that has served as a beacon to a whole generation of leaders overflows the small circles of intellectuals in order to penetrate the social segments constituting the entire African population. This precept of African unity, this 'rationalized pan-Africanism,' will trigger the immense upheaval of Africans for the reconquest of their territorial space, and the rebirth of Africa."[32]

I agree with Kodjo, as well as with Professors Locksley Edmondson, Elliot Skinner, and others, that Pan Africanism in the African diaspora, as an explicitly international phenomenon, must take into consideration the nature of *the global system.*[33]

While it is possible to discuss this issue as a problem of foreign policy and international politics on the one hand, we have eschewed that discussion here in order to deal with the subnational level, at which the Pan African activities of African Americans, Black South Africans and other Diaspora groups are more clearly seen. Nevertheless, there is in this study a strong illustration of the fact that one of the most important rationales for African unity is that the African world is arrayed against other, often more powerful, diasporas and "pan" movements.

African peoples are part of a "world system" and Professor Elliot Skinner has suggested that there is a dialectic between the African Diaspora and the status of other diasporas. He says, for example, that "many Afro-Americans concede that the decline of Europe or lessening of white power might be the antithesis to the thesis of racism and cultural chauvinism that attended Europe's control of the globe."[34] This view comes, no doubt, from the knowledge that global social movements like wars, the labor movement, economic trends and so on have played an important role in the "readiness" of nations to deal with racism within their borders and in other countries.

In his evaluation of the crisis of capitalism as a problem of the transition to socialism, Emmanuel Wallerstein, a leading theorist of "world systems" analysis, argues that one of the cultural premises of the world system is that "racism is not merely endemic to the modern world system, it is intrinsic to it," and that a crude system of privileges that finds some peoples on the top and others at the bottom of humanity is buttressed by the state system hierarchy.[35] Therefore, as the crisis of capitalism intensifies and the balance of power among the nations shifts, the prevailing hierarchy will shift as well. Wallerstein says social organization across national lines will facilitate the demand for reallocation of resources; while he rejects "pan-movement" organizing in this regard, he approves "anti-systemic" organizations.[36] Still, although his rejection of "pan-movements" is based on the view that they tend to be nationalist movements "defined more in terms of proto-state boundaries," he misses the point that the cultural base of the "Pan African movement" may facilitate such political organization, a point we have attempted to make here.

Finally, we realize that many strategies utilized in the struggle for community will not be Pan African strategies, since they are based upon the unique problems of the new environment in the Diaspora and require conformity to it. But to the degree that Pan African nationalism and Pan African socialism may contribute to defining the progressive character of the struggle for community in the Diaspora, such strategies have a fundamental role in the survival of African peoples. This contribution depends, as it always has, on the acknowledgement by individuals and groups in the African Diaspora of their African identity, their relationship to other peoples of African descent around the world, and their willingness to confront their identity, synthesize it, and utilize it in practical ways in localities where African peoples are found.

Most important, in this regard, is the ability to enhance the power of Pan African strategies and linkages by building Pan African institutions through which they can operate. This applies to the building of educational, political, social (religious, fraternal, and so on), economic, and other types of institutions, as well as recognizing the pan African possibilities in those that already exist. Ultimately, it is these "mediating structures" that will capture the hopes, the skills, and the future of African peoples and make the most decisive contribution to their survival.

Postscript:
Culture and Politics in
the African Diaspora

One of the most important things I have had
to face at the end of this work is the necessity to make clear to
the reader the primacy of culture in my construction of the political life of African people. Here I mean "culture" in the broad
sense in which the encompassing dynamics of the economic, social, and political components blend to form a comprehensive
way of being.[1] Therefore, although I have been concerned in this
work with the subject of "politics" in the African Diaspora, I recognize that in every act of politics it is the cultural precondition
which forms a constant subtextual theme and foundation. In
any case, the matter was brought home to me by Professor Willard Johnson, a political scientist at MIT, who, in a review of one
draft of this work, questioned a lack of clarity as to the extent to
which the Western Black man and woman can continue to be
regarded as "African." Thus, I felt the need here to be somewhat
more explicit about the cultural basis of politics in the context of
Pan Africanism.

This is a fair question because for other diaspora groups, the
substance of politics is informed by the rather explicit basis of

culture, maintained either by their religion (as is the case for the Jews) or by an unbroken relationship with the mother country (as with many European or Asian immigrants). But for Blacks, having maintained neither their indigenous religious identity nor an unbroken relationship to the mother country, it is necessary to suggest the ways in which Africa still informs Black identity in the Diaspora and so to understand the longevity and force of the Pan African idea.

Africa endures in Black people of the Diaspora not only in the surface physical manifestations of skin color and physiognomy and the remnants of cultural practices, but most powerfully *in the imagination*. In the United States, for example, in an unbroken line from Henry Highland Garnett, Rev. Alexander Crummel, and especially Martin Delaney and Bishop Henry McNeal Turner to present-day advocates of Pan Africanism, what fired the imagination was the incongruity of the European perception and treatment of Africans and the African's own perception of his native continent as an option for liberation. The longing for Africa created by distance, by being deprived of and brutally torn from its bosom drove the Black poets of the early twentieth century to express their love of Africa in songs of remembrance and praise. They said once again—this time with pride—the names of the rivers, evoked the myths of the people to construct useful parables for living. They called out the pain of the centuries of oppression and, in doing so, communicated the sustained feeling and knowledge of being African. This was the essence of W.E.B. DuBois' *Souls of Black Folk*. One can almost feel DuBois searching the catacombs of his mind for bits and pieces of memory with which to construct a lyrical explanation for his own Africanness and that of the so-called Negro.

Of course, at the turn of the century when DuBois was writing, there were many African people still alive in America who had been born in Africa, for Africans were still being imported into the United States as late as the 1850s, long after the legal ending of the slave trade. So among the four million people released from slavery in the early 1860s there were many who did not have to depend upon second-hand memory of Africa and who were regarded as (and called) Africans by the Europeans who made America until the late nineteenth century. Yet it was and still is impossible to declare that the African identity is the whole of the Black identity because of the recognition by both Black and white alike that the process of one-way acculturation, dominated by Europeans, had created a hybrid, a "colored" person. This is the essence of the well-known metaphor coined by DuBois called the "twoness," or as William Ferris, a Black contemporary of DuBois, said, in being forced to live among the Anglo-Saxons, the Black man had become a "Negro-Saxon."[2] We are concerned here with the African dimension of the "twoness."

In any case, there is still a predominant African dimension to the identity of the Black man and woman in the Diaspora today that overwhelms the other dimensions of birth, physical make-up, language, and even nationality. The African personality in the imagination has thrived because African life was a subject of the first-hand experience of many Blacks who survived slavery and lived on into the twentieth century; their associates and first-generation relatives passed down African customs, names, and languages, and an unshakable African kinship was formed. Indeed, the question should be rather put in reverse: when did we stop being African?

Empirical proof of the power of the "African imagination" within Black people was provided by the Négritude poets in Europe at the turn of the century who, facing the push of racism and oppression and the pull of the substance of African culture, also created an expression of the new "African personality" as a way of rehabilitating and defending African culture and using it as an alternative model for their psychological liberation. It is ironic that in the attempt to create a universal basis for the African identity, some generalized an anthropological view that drew sharp dichotomies between European and African personalities. Attempting to liberate the African personality from the death grip of European negative perceptions of Blacks, especially the perversities of Hitlerian Nazism of that day, they went too far and adopted elements of their colonial education to explain the difference.

Thus, Léopold Sédar Senghor, a student at the Sorbonne in the 1930s and former president of Senegal, in his explication of the philosophy of Négritude, struck a difference between the Anglo-Saxon's use of reason or the "Dieu de raison" and the African's spirituality. He also held that the differences in the values of Africans and Europeans emerged as a by-product of their environment; Africans existed in a tropical and agricultural environment, while Europeans emerged in an environment of scarcity of resources and aridity. With regard to politics, he suggested that the construction and operation of African traditional political systems were distinguished by their essentially "humanistic" approach. For, while the European had elevated law over custom, the African valued custom over law, with the power of the king (or other royalty) being used to maintain the balance between them. These differences emanated, he suggested, as in other things, from the different rhythms of life observed by the two peoples.[3] The anthropologist Dr. Basil Matthews of Trinidad has coined the concept of the "feeling intelligence" to explain how African people process information and assign meaning to their external environment.[4]

On the other hand, many have taken exception to this concept. Sékou Touré, former president of Guinea and perhaps Senghor's most bitter critic while he was alive, condemned Senghor for engaging in mysticism for suggesting that even socialism should yield to the vagaries of African traditional culture. Indeed, the debate over Négritude on the African continent, long since abated, appeared to be over whether the basic content of African culture should be revolutionary or traditional. This debate no doubt was influenced by the independence movement and the necessity of African leaders to work out an ideology that would guide the construction of the state.

Nevertheless, it is fitting to pose the question whether a purely cultural theory of Pan Africanism is not only appropriate but necessary in order to understand the value of traditional African civilization and the way it has evolved. Factors such as imperialism, colonialism, and local politics have shaped African culture, but that culture should have an explanation which begins with the terms of its own integrity. What is the baseline of African culture? How was it changed by forces on the continent, both African and foreign? How have its manifestations emerged in other places in the world? Is there a universal African dimension to the cultural life of African-origin peoples in the Diaspora? These are important issues that must begin where the Négritude poets began—with an attempt to project and establish the African personality in the world. For such an effort, it is not necessary to throw out the baby with the bath water or to declare the philosophy of Négritude null and void, especially in the absence of a cultural theory to the contrary. Rather, it would appear that the philosophy of Négritude, the cultural theory of Pan Africanism, must be rehabilitated, and it must be considered as a place to begin, rather than as a place to end this critically important discussion.

The search for the unifying elements of African culture has taken place in various international conferences of intellectuals, especially meetings of Black artists and writers. Perhaps the first of these meetings in the modern era was the Conference of Negro-African Writers and Artists, held in Paris in 1956, under the sponsorship of a group of Black French-speaking intellectuals from Africa and the West Indies—Alione Diop and Léopold Senghor from Senegal, Aimé Césaire from Martinique, Dr. Jean Price-Mars from Haiti, and others—who would go on to create the Society of African Culture (SAC). Diop opened this conference with a statement about the relationship between politics and culture, saying the racial domination of Black people made Blacks incapable of creating an authentic culture and pulled them toward psychological alienation. Senghor attacked the perspective of (aesthetic) European culture, saying that in the African conception there was no difference between art and life, that as European art attempts to imitate nature, African art reached past the symbol to encompass that vital force (la force vital) which creates nature. Inevitably, this presentation led to the debate over what is culture. But in his presentation, Aimé Césaire forcefully returned to the theme of colonial control, saying that the essence of the crisis was that the culture with the strongest material base threatened the survival of all others, since no culture could survive without control of its own economics and politics in its own hands.

Senghor used this forum to resurrect the philosophy of the African symbiosis, or the belief that the cultural unity of African-origin peoples is rooted in their biological heritage and thus in their physical ("instinctive") as well as their intellectual approach to knowing the world. The African, Senghor said, developed a harmony with nature, a harmony that affected his psychic traits of strong emotionalism and heightened sensibilities, from two essential sources: the tropical environment and the agricultural nature of his work. These influences, over time, punctuated by strong and steady rhythms of the changing seasons, gave the African the potential for the adaptability to nature.[5] In making these points, Senghor even alluded to his belief that Richard Wright's writing was "African" in nature.

But Richard Wright, a socialist, criticized Senghor frontally, asking him: "Where are the instincts that enable me to latch on to this culture?"[6] He continued the attack by thanking "Mr. White man" for the "rot of my irrational traditions and customs . . . bravo for that clumsy and cruel deed."[7]

Nonetheless, the position of the American delegation, composed of Professors John D. Davis, Mercer Cook, William Fountaine, Horace Mann Bond, and James Ivy, was compromised first by a communiqué from W. E. B. DuBois stating he could not attend inasmuch as the U.S. government had denied him his passport.[8] Of course, this announcement raised questions about the status and posture of those who came to the conference to represent African Americans. Their position became clearer when the meeting, which was supposed to deal largely with the cultural aspects of the Black world, was shattered by the scathing political attack on colonialism by Aimé Césaire. The result, as James Baldwin noted, was "a rather sharp exchange between Césaire and the American delegation."[9] But nothing could stop the presentations in the meeting of cultural topics with strongly political implications. In the end, Wright emphasized the role of the Afro-Americans, saying that inasmuch as they were in "the technological vanguard, they would prove of inestimable value to the developing African sovereignties."[10]

It was the French Africans such as Senghor and Alione Diop who spoke directly of African-origin peoples as "the Blacks," a term describing Negro-Africans both physically and psychologically, at home, but especially in the Diaspora. Wilfred Cartey characterizes the concept thus: "the desire to be black arises out of the [poetic] assertion of blackness"; "the assertion of blackness of naturalness—implicitly then, of the human—is, in this poetry, but one manifestation of a revolt that receives a charge from the combustive powers of memory. One can feel the force of memory, of race, and of racial suffering in Tchicaya U Tam'si's 'Fe de Brousse.' " He then quotes from the poem:

> je vous ai dit ma race
> elle se souvient
> de la teneur du bronze bu chaud [11]

It is this memory that revived the trembling emotions of a Black man named Césaire (not Aimé) in this meeting who said, "Nothing will ever make us believe that our beliefs are merely frivolous superstitions. No power will ever cause us to admit that we are lower than any other people." [12] This emotion rekindled the debate about the nature of the African personality let loose through the political processes of the African liberation movement.

James Baldwin, the noted African-American writer, observed, however, that Aimé Césaire had left out the answer to the position he had taken: what had the colonial experience made of men like him and what would they do now? But George Lamming, an outstanding West Indian writer, responded by referring to the variation in African culture as contained, for example, in the Nigerian writer Amos Tutuola's *Palm Wine Drinkard*. He observed that because of the colonial experience, the Englishman felt he was close to the African and the African felt close to the Englishman, so that a great part of the Negro experience was its "double-edgedness." Reaffirming the popular DuBoisian insight, he continued: "there is a painful contradiction between being a Western and a Black man. I see both worlds from another, and third point of view." [13]

Baldwin's seminal question was important because it opened the door to a discussion of the specific impact of the imposition of European culture upon African-origin peoples, a door that led back to the answer of politics. The point of the discussion initiated by Baldwin and Lamming was that the West had reshaped continental African culture to a considerable extent, just as it had obviously influenced those Africans born and living in Western countries. The challenge, therefore, was to understand this impact in terms of the changes and influences in the hope of reconstructing an African culture that has universal validity, most importantly among African peoples, but among others as well.

The Second International Conference of African Artists and writers was held in Rome in 1959 by SAC, which by this time had established the journal *Présence Africaine*. The goal of this meeting was to affirm the values of African culture as the basis for unity or as a fundemental aspect of Négritude, then to elaborate the various elements that give significance to modern life. Senghor elaborated these elements: psychic traits, strong emotional quality, heightened sensibilities of nature, and intuition. Ignazio Silone, the distinguished Italian novelist, told the meeting it was not unusual for oppressed people to find value in those elements whose nature was most condemned by others. Alione Diop expressed an often repeated theme of these conferences, that it was sad to have to affirm the value of one's culture in the world, while Jacques Rabenmananjara, a poet from Malagasy, defined the unity of African culture at that stage as an "act of faith." Otherwise, many themes of the previous conference were repeated.

The Paris Conference of 1956 initiated the founding of SAC in Paris, and the following year, the nucleus of the American delegation to the Paris conference founded the American Society of African Culture (AMSAC). In June of 1960, AMSAC sponsored a conference in Philadelphia which brought together 350 scholars, artists, and writers to assess the implications of African culture in the context of "The Independence Movement," a much more specifically political subject than the themes of the earlier conferences. Several leading African intellectuals and diplomats attended, and Haiti had a strong delegation. There were many panels and workshops on themes focusing on the role of the state system in international affairs, but the panels on culture essentially repeated the discussion held in Paris. The delegates were fascinated with the idea of the unity of African culture, or the concept of Négritude as propounded by Senghor, and especially with his view that so much of American Negro artistic expression in art, music, and literature was characterized by an emotion and intuition derived from the artist's African personality. To the extent that it did not, Senghor held, the cause was the deliberate attempt by Blacks over time to subordinate their African instincts to achieve integration into American life.[14]

J. Newton Hill, an artist from Lincoln University, and Ezekiel Mphalele, a writer from South Africa, attacked the concept of Négritude on the grounds that the universal African personality derived from no biologically inherited characteristics and that Négritude, thus, was an "unscientific" concept.[15] The question of Négritude as an issue in Black American and continental African tension and dialogue about attitudes of superiority and inferiority was examined, and the concept was found to be somewhat useful. Still, the question of the content of African culture beyond the traditional continental culture and its relevance to the Diaspora was unresolved. The search continued for what Samual Allen, an African-American poet at Texas Southern University, called an "ensemble of African values" that comprised the "vital force" as the concrete expression of the African personality.[16]

In 1966, the first World Festival of Negro Art, sponsored by the United Nations Economic and Social Council (UNESCO), assembled African-origin writers and artists from all over the world. This conference did not emerge from a movement, but rather from a bureaucratic sense of the need for an examination of African art by artists and writers, moving from a discussion of the function and nature of African culture to specific consideration of more narrow professional concerns.

Then, in 1969, the First Pan African Cultural Festival was held in Algiers, with 31 African states represented. And although the African-American presence was almost nonexistent, the Soviet Union, Brazil, France, Czechoslovakia, and other countries were represented. At issue in the holding of cultural conferences on the continent of Africa was the extent to which Arab culture would be represented as culturally "African" or geographically African. Léopold Senghor held that Négritude and Arab consciousness were complementary concepts and that the Sahara had never been an obstacle to such unity. "*Africanity* is the age-old dialogue between Arabo-Berber and African Negro. It is the symbiosis of two complementary groups."[17]

On the other hand, Sékou Touré expressed the view that the necessity of cultural revolution negated the concept of Négritude, calling it "a false concept—an irrational furthering of racial discrimination . . ." He believed that all cultures had the universal objectives of liberty, democracy, and so on. While acknowledging the differences of color, religions, and nationalities giving expression to different living strategies, he said, "There is neither black culture, nor white culture, nor yellow culture. Neither is there a black civilization, a white civilization, or a yellow civilization." [18] He suggested that the humanist values of African culture would contribute to that universal culture. Appearing to be contradictory, he also suggested that in order to contribute to that culture ". . . they [Africans] will have to preserve their personality and assert the values a of their civilization . . ."[19]

Touré's statement illustrates the difficulty of developing conceptual generalizations about the function of African culture without having finally to acknowledge its specificity. What was striking about the dialogue on culture, however, was its insularity, that it excluded the African Diaspora as such. This omission was probably a function of the independence stage of history, an era when African states were self-absorbed with the question of continental unity and thus fostered a narrow view of the function of African culture.[20] We, therefore, have little emanating from this discussion to guide us to the place of African culture in the Diaspora.

In the foregoing discussion above, I viewed the Algiers Festival from the perspective of Dr. Nathan Hare, an African-American sociologist who was a principal in the Black Studies movement in this period.[21] Eldridge Cleaver was in exile in Algiers, heading a chapter of the Black Panther party, and Stokely Carmichael, as head of SNCC, was a guest of the Festival organizers. The presence and position of these two was ironic in that they mirrored the difference of opinion between Senghor and Touré on the question of culture. The deeper irony is that although Carmichael came to reside in Guinea and become an ally of Touré's, his views were closer to those of Senghor at the time, while Cleaver's views were closer to Touré's.

Also, as stated above, the Second World Festival of Black and African Arts and Culture took place in Lagos, in 1977, and the largest body of African Americans to return to visit Africa at one time since the nineteenth century was present. The symposium discussed the question of culture in the African world. An important theme was Maulana Karenga's position that the cultural crisis was central and that the essence of the problem of unity between Africans and Afro-Americans lay in the crucible of working out a concept of the mutuality of Pan Africanism as previously discussed.

This review of pan African cultural conferences explicitly addressing the problems of African culture illustrates the paucity of progress that has been made in such forums toward the clarification of the relationship between politics and culture in the context of Pan Africanism.[22] Such discussions have either been overwhelmed by the continental politics of the moment, in which case they have not considered the Diaspora as a part of the functional Pan African cultural symbiosis, or they have been restricted by the representational limitations placed on the official delegates representing nation states or international sponsors. Perhaps, the major use of such meetings was that they surfaced such questions and built a foundation of fraternity among peoples who knew each other, were aware of the problems of unifying African peoples, and had developed a legacy of experience in attempting to find solutions to pass on to the next generation.

Pan Africanism Within: Unity Within Diversity

The political movement of Black Power set in motion in 1966 a new ideology of Black thought and action in the United States that, as we have seen, had its ramification around the world. The concept would be ascendant for four years as the definition of the advanced movement for Black liberation in the United States and in other parts of the world where African-origin peoples were seeking national equity. By 1970, however, it was clear that the African dimension of the Black Power movement was growing more powerful as the movement sought a genuine definition of itself rooted in the history and culture of Black people. It was inevitable that this discussion would end with the rediscovery of Africa. The symbols of Africa began to appear with increasing frequency; pictures of

Africa were engraved on maps, on clothes, on leather amulets, on gold and silver, on everything that touched the personhood and collective identity of Black people. Swahili and other African languages began to be spoken, African clothes were worn, African hairstyles were adopted, and the mind turned to the relationship between African peoples in the Diaspora and Africa. The Black Power movement unleashed the desire for an indigeneous scholarship of Black peoples, scholarship initiated in the colleges and universities as "Black Studies." As Professor Sterling Stucky prophesized, with "the pressures emanating from the civil rights movement and carried to the universities by black students, scholars are likely to become increasingly interested in the relationships between Afro-Americans and Africans." [23]

This movement challenged the hegemony of white scholarship in all of the social sciences, and Black caucuses were created inside the major white scholarly organizations during this period. Among the first of these were the African Heritage Studies Association and the National Conference of Black Political Scientists, which became independent organizations in 1968 and 1971 respectively.

Many Black historians were members of the Association for the Study of Negro Life and History, already an independent organization since 1915; it was founded by Dr. Carter G. Woodson, who also founded the *Journal of Negro History* in 1916. This organization was challenged in October 1969 by a group of youthful Black scholars (The Black Academic Defenders) to become more ideologically Black in its name and leadership. It yielded by becoming the Association for the Study of *Afro-American* Life and History in 1975. The National Economic Association, born as an independent organization and with support from the Twentieth Century Fund, founded the important journal, *Review of Black Political Economy*. The Association of Black Sociologists became a caucus, becoming an independent organization only in 1989.

Most important, as the political character of the Black liberation movement of the 1960s changed to become more pan Africanist, so did the movement for Black studies. Indeed, so urgent had the question of African scholarship become as the anchor of Black studies that a political crisis was precipitated. In 1957, the African Studies Association (ASA) was founded as an organiza-

tion for the scholarly study of Africa. As the African independence struggle became more important to American foreign policy, ASA attracted more academic prominence and the
organization became a predominantly white organization of
nearly 2,000 scholars. In very little time, the organization had
established an impressive array of programs in the teaching and
research on Africa and exercised influence beyond the academy
into the foundation world and eventually into the U.S. government, as well as African governments. In a 1969 article in *Africa
Report,* Professor John Henrik Clarke of Hunter College asked:
"Why are so many Americans now studying about Africa? Why
are most of them white Americans? Why are there so few black
Americans with decision-making positions in present-day African studies programs?"[24]

At the annual meeting of ASA in Los Angeles in 1968, the
Black caucus was called together by Dr. P. Chike Onuwauchi, a
dynamic Nigerian anthropologist and director of African studies
at Fisk University. Perhaps Black studies saw the birth of a Black
caucus in advance of the other social sciences because this subject was more racially and politically sensitive, involving the
identity of the very people then engaged in an intense struggle
for their freedom in the streets of America.[25] Among the reasons
Black scholars elaborated for the Black caucus' development
within ASA were the need to control one's own history and culture, the need to participate in conferences in Africa, the need
to reduce the distance between Africans and Afro-Americans,
the need to contribute to the Black community, the need to form
a liaison to other Black scholars, the need to collaborate with
African countries and their embassies, and so on.[26]

On October 19, 1968, a statement from the Black caucus was
read in its entirety to the board of directors of ASA, making the
basic charge that too few Africans and Afro-Americans participated in the organization as leaders and that the body had not
worked for the inclusion of Black scholars. ASA responded by
creating a Committee on Afro-American Issues; that committee
then invested a year of work in an effort to attract Black membership in ASA and to expand Black participation in the 1969 annual meeting. In view of the intensity of the political movement,
however, this would not be nearly enough, and the African Heritage Studies Association (AHSA) was formed as a separate or-

ganization in the Spring of 1969. Clarke supported this action. It was not the original intent of the Black caucus to leave ASA, he said, but then he observed: "I think this revolt, which seemed minor on the surface, will have far-reaching repercussions on African studies programs in the United States because it is not unrelated to the growing revolt of Afro-Americans against the structured exclusion from matters relating to them and their culture."[27]

The 12th annual meeting of ASA convened as a joint meeting with the Canadian African Studies Association in Montreal, in October 1969. The meeting attracted a surprising number of delegates from the United States and many students from the United States and Canada, including students from the West Indies who had been active in the protest at Sir George Williams University. These delegates forcefully raised the issue of Black participation in ASA to the point of disrupting the proceedings.[28] Indeed, the first plenary session, featuring Gabriel d'Arboussier, Senegalese ambassador to Germany, as the main speaker, was so interrupted, setting the tone for the following three days of panel discussions, workshops and plenary sessions. In fact, the conference, which had attracted more than three thousand scholars from all over the world, was virtually shut down by the spontaneous militance of Black attendees; they prevented any sizeable meeting from occurring while negotiations were being conducted between the ASA and AHSA leaderships on the future of ASA.

The first meeting of AHSA had been held in New York City at the home of John Henrik Clarke in December of 1968; he chaired the session in the absence of Michael Searles of Washington, who had been chosen acting chairman. The decision was made to have a follow-up meeting at the newly created Federal City College in June 1969; this meeting developed the basis for many of the demands that would surface in Montreal as negotiating items. The "revolt," as it is referred to by Clarke, occurred in a context where the Black delegates in Montreal were unaware of the tentative steps taken by ASA to answer the Black caucus concerns. This was, nonetheless, fortuitous for AHSA because its leaders were thrust into key roles in the negotiations in Montreal.[29] Indeed, Clarke himself put forth the demands representing the Black caucus at Montreal.

The Montreal demands, closely resembling those of the Committee on Afro-American Issues of ASA, were expanded to include such matters as equal membership of Blacks on the board of directors and adoption of the Pan Africanist (or Afrocentric) perspective on African scholarship. Clarke explained, "This perspective defines that all black people are African people and rejects the division of African peoples by geographical locations based on colonialist spheres of influence."[30] Many in the leadership of ASA, both Black and white, took offense at these recommendations, which through the political action of Blacks had become demands. The negotiating team also included these AHSA members: Dr. P. Chike Onuwauchi, Dr. Nicholas Onyewu, both from Nigeria, Kenneth McIntyre, a music professor at SUNY Old Westbury, and Dr. Acklyn Lynch, West Indian from the Federal City College.

The negotiations were conducted in a democratic manner, with the leaders reporting back to the expanded Black caucus of conference delegates, and the discussions which often reshaped the demands were particularly intense. These discussions were useful, since some invited guests from Europe and Africa had an opportunity to be socialized into the political culture of opposition to ASA. They included, for example, Léon Damas of Paris, one of the key figures in the Négritude movement and a plenary speaker, who was at first confused, but later joined the Black caucus and finally issued a personal declaration of support.

The demand of the Black caucus at Montreal for racial parity on the ASA Board of Directors was rejected in a 104–to–93 vote. The subsequent vote on a resolution challenging the organization to restructure membership on the board by forming a thirty-member constitutional revision commission with 50 percent Black membership passed overwhelmingly. In addition, a resolution, presented to the ASA Board by Black professors Dr. Willard Johnson and Dr. Johnetta Cole, contained recommendations that: (1) a separate "liberation fund" be created by splitting the dues proceeds, (2) that AHSA organize one panel at every annual meeting, (3) that the board be directed to implement the agreement made in Montreal, including the resolution on restructuring the board to achieve racial equity.[31] This resolution, proceeding from an even more activist vision of the contribution

ASA might make to the liberation struggles then occurring in Southern Africa, was ultimately defeated.[32]

John Henrik Clarke, associate editor of *Freedomways* journal and adjunct professor at Hunter College, was elected first president of AHSA at the Washington meeting in June 1969. Clarke was a largely self-trained community scholar and expert on African history for many years in his adopted Harlem; his intellectual leadership and challenge to the ultra-academistic approach and Eurocentric interpretation of African scholarship by whites was an important source of direction for the new organization and an entire generation of younger Black scholars. His contribution complemented those of the more traditionally trained, but African-conscious scholars like Dr. Leonard Jeffries of San Jose State University, Michael Searles, Dr. Nicholas Onyewu of SUNY Albany, Dr. Shelby Smith of Atlanta University, Dr. Herschelle Challenor of Brooklyn College, Dr. Niara Sudarkasa, Dr. Inez Smith Reid of Brooklyn College, Dr. Elliot Skinner of Columbia University, Dr. Tilden Lemelle of the University of Denver, Prof. Keith Baird of Hofstra University, and Dr. James Turner of Cornell University, as well as attorneys Thurlow Tibbs and Richard Thornell of New York City.

Small wonder, then, that the concept of "Afro-centrism" emerged from this political struggle as a product expressing the need of this collection of Black scholars to articulate the ideology of Pan Africanism as applied to the study of the land of their parents. In fact, the first point made in the collectively crafted objectives of the newly formed AHSA would indicate that in the field of education, AHSA's purpose was the "reconstruction of African history and cultural studies along *Afrocentric* lines while effecting an intellectual union among black scholars the world over."[33] By 1970, the impact of the emerging Pan African movement was felt by AHSA directly; a loose association with the Congress of African People was formed. In 1970, Clarke and Yosef ben-Jochannan, a community activist/scholar and well-known expert in African history, attended the Atlanta conference and wrote the workshop recommendations on African history. Some of the recommendations were similar to those put forth by the ASA Black caucus and AHSA, especially in proposing the linkage among Black scholars worldwide, the need to control African history, the inclusion of Black colleges, and the

370 PAN AFRICANISM IN THE AFRICAN DIASPORA

connection of African history with the Black community.[34] In fact, the last recommendation suggested that CAP establish affiliation with organizations such as the Institute of the Black World and AHSA! Subsequently, Clarke was asked by Imamu Baraka to serve as the convenor of the history and culture council of CAP.

The highlight in the formation of AHSA, however, would be the May 1970 conference held at Howard University. A memorandum developed by the program committee for the second annual conference stated: "The African Studies Association is dedicated to the reconstruction of African cultural and historical studies along afro-centric lines. The A.H.S.A. takes the position that the study of African life must be undertaken from a Pan Africanist perspective. This perspective defines that all Black peoples are African peoples and negates the tribalization of African peoples by geographical demarcations based on colonialist spheres of influence."[35]

Thus, not only was AHSA's basic characterization put forth as "Pan Africanist," but the organization also began to evolve a philosophy of "Afro-centrism" as the ideology which would guide its work. This was also evident in the theme set for the conference, "Africanism: Toward a New Definition." The Howard conference was a special event, attracting a collection of African-conscious artists and scholars and, altogether, more than two thousand attendees from all over the country. The panels exhibited the interest in Africa at the community level; some presenters were challenged for being too academic, for using Western concepts, and for not connecting analyses to current events, such as the incarceration of Black Panther figure Mark Clark.[36] Professors such as Joyce Ladner, Elliot Skinner, and Mary Berry, activist-writer Imamu Baraka, and others called for a massive reappraisal of the culture of African peoples. This call was joined by the keynote speaker, Dr. James Cheek, president of Howard University. A highly emotional moment occurred at the Ujamaa Festival on the closing night; Barbara Ann Teer's performance of African spirituals captured the mood of the thousands of people who sang in a fever-pitched unison that they would "reclaim our strength and reclaim our power, right now!" Thus, not only was the African Heritage Studies Association born in Los Angeles, forged in Montreal, and christened at Howard University, but its character as the Pan African cultural parallel in Black scholarship to the political movement within the community was also recognized.

With every concept there are prototypical antecedents in evidence before the terms or concepts which become more widely accepted emerge. This was so with the concept of Afrocentrism. As part of the "Africanization" of the Black Power movement, Dr. Maulana Karenga in 1968 elaborated an Afrocentric system of belief known as Kawaida (meaning principle or custom in Swahili). This faith is composed of a series of rituals, supported by teachings and by a series of positive African-derived principles. In particular, the "Nguzo Saba" or seven principles have had wide exposure within the Black Nationalist community in the United States as the basis of the popular Kwanza observance held at Christmas time. Karenga has been a major cultural figure within the African-American community and interpretor of life in pan Africanist terms.[37]

Another major exponent of the concept of Afrocentrism is Dr. Molefi Asante, editor of the *Journal of Black Studies* and founder with Kariamu Welsh, an expert in African dance and culture, of Njia in Buffalo, New York, in the 1970s. Njia (meaning "the way" in Swahili), like Kawaida, contained its own ritual/philosophy which was similar in some respects to those of Kawaida and other African-oriented cultural organizations around the country. Asante, an expert on communication, produced a work entitled *Afrocentricity* (1980), in which he says, "Njia is the collective expression of the Afrocentric world view based on the historical experience of African people." He continues, "Njia represents the inspired Afrocentric embodiment of spirit and is founded in the tradition of African-Americans as the spirit of humanity meant to be an expressed symbol for the survival of African essence. Thus, it sees Afrocentricity as being possessed in the African population of the Diaspora and the continent."[38] Practicality initiates travel through several levels of consciousness before arriving at the stage of Afrocentricity where "the person becomes totally changed to a conscious level of involvement in the struggle for mind liberation," an imperative, Asante says, that dictates the rhythms of one's life.[39] His intellectual corollary to Afrocentricity is "Afrology," which he defines as "primarily pan Africanist in its treatment of the creative, political and geographic of our collective will to liberty."[40] Thus, Asante locates his system within the context of the pan Africanist tradition, using the value of the "will to victory" as the criteria for evaluating how events relate to the survival of African people.

It is important to mention at least briefly the formalistic beginnings of this concept, as we have done, because there are some indications that the concept of Afrocentricity has taken hold at a grass-roots level within African-American communities in the 1990s. This has happened largely as an antithesis to and as a result of the three-decade movement for racial integration within the schools and other institutions dominated by whites that control the socialization of Black youth. The current dysfunctional condition of urban Black educational institutions and the connection between this condition and the rise of serious youthful crime, drug involvement and other antisocial behavior have called for a response by Black people themselves. And Blacks have embarked upon an indigenous reinvention of aspects of their life encompassing such cultural artifacts as Rap music, break dancing, inventive language, and now the movement for the "infusion" of African and African-American studies in the schools.

This movement, which is called Afrocentric education, or "Africancentric" in the terms of John Henrik Clarke, is a manifestation of the continuing strength of the African ethic and ethos among Black people in the United States. As we suggested at the outset, the continuation of the African ethic in a society where African survivals do not constitute a major part of one's daily consciousness is a marvel. Yet Africa is truly within the African-American experience as witnessed by the various levels of activity.

Activities Dealing Directly with Africa

I considered the activities occurring in one community as indicated by the events placed in one newspaper, *The City Sun* (Brooklyn, New York), for the period June–October

1990 and selected those which appear to have been more explicitly concerned with African culture. The following events are listed below in order to indicate the richness of the variety of events involved.

- African dance classes, Idoda Entsha Society
- Harlem Black Cinema, South African Film
- Advertising travel to Togo, Ghana
- Odunde Festival, ancient Yoruba rite honoring the river god, Oya
- African dance, Dr. Kariamu Welsh (Asante), publisher of *Afrocentric Times Magazine.*
- Film showing, *Emiti*, Ousmane Sembene, African Poetry Theater
- Africa/Newark Cultural Festival, various events
- Skoto Gallery, Nigerian painting and sculptures, Harlem
- Fashion show to benefit the TV show, "South Africa Now"
- Carnival in New York, Caribbean Cultural Center, African Diaspora Institute, (festival—Africa, Trinidad, Brazil, Jamaica, Puerto Rico, Haiti, etc.)
- Fundraiser for student travel to Egypt
- Celebration of the African Diaspora: African Music and Dance, Pyramid Ensemble
- Traditional African beauty techniques, seminar
- Film, *Yaaba*, Burkina Faso, African Poetry Theater
- Jalal Sheriff, African percussion performance
- African craft and mask making, African Poetry Theatre
- African religion lecture series, Yoruba Theological Archministry, Babalorisha John Mason.
- Salute to African heritage, Nia Productions, art-making, poetry and literature readings, African Poetry Theater
- South African Reggae show, Lucky Dube, Kilimanjaro
- Video, Nelson Mandela Visit to the United States
- Workshop in Tie-dying and African mask craft, The Center for Culture, The African Poetry Theater
- Discussion of Chinua Achebe's Novel, *Anthills of the Savannah*, The Cultural Politics Discussion Group
- African origins of Yoga, Sonia Diaz, Yoga for Health and Beauty
- African Rhythms, music show, from Hip-hop to Reggae and African music

- Dance, Youssouf Kambasa, Guinea-Bissau, Mani Basse, Mali/Senegal
- Film, anti-Apartheid film series, *A Dry White Season, Place of Weeping*, etc.
- National Association of Kawaida Organizations, symposium, "Culture, Community and Struggle," featuring Dr. Maulana Karenga and others
- Travel, Journey to Zimbabwe/Zambia, International African-American Cultural and Research Association
- Weekend Festival, West African dance classes, Djembe Orchestra
- Queens Festival '90, continuous live performance of Afrocentric culture, including African events
- Symposium, "Cuba's Internationalism in Africa," 21st Contingent, Vinceramos Brigade
- African music concert, Central African Bakongo music
- "400 years without a comb," African cosmetology secrets
- Afrocentric shopping, day-long African market
- Symposium, End Apartheid, Vibes of Africa, Simalone, ANC
- Travel to Ghana and Togo, Africa '90, Black Men's Congress
- Travel, "Journey to The Motherland," Senegal/Gambia, African Poetry Theater
- Father's Day celebration, Spirit Ensemble, Kemet Orchestra, etc.
- "The African Village," Cultural Arts Committee, St. Marks Church (Fashion Show and Luncheon)
- Reception, Coumba Gaye of Senegal, hair stylist
- Workshop, African Heritage Society Orientation, Bethel Church Fellowship

A categorization of these events yields the following frequency of types:

A. Festivals	8	G. Dance	3
B. Film	5	H. Market,	1 each
C. Travel	5	Religion,	
D. Music	5	Benefit,	
E. Symposia	5	Reception	
F. Art	4		

It is well to remember that the categories above are directed to specific types of events, whereas the festivals increase the frequency of these specific events. Still, while acknowledging that the level of events focusing on the culture of Africa may be more intensive in Brooklyn than in many other urban areas of the country, this frequency of events is suggestive of the presence of an active Africa consciousness. It may also be inferred that the dynamic we illustrate is not bottled up in New York City and that many of these events travel to other parts of the country on a circuit that exposes indigenous African culture to literally millions of African Americans.

It is, of course, wrong to suggest that the appreciation, or attempted appreciation, of explicit forms of indigenous African culture is a preoccupation of only lower-income Blacks. In fact, the case might be made that the more knowledgeable population about Africa is precisely the educated middle class, a group that may be said to be more open-minded about the adoption of aspects of an explicit African cultural identity. I eschew any attempt at class analysis in this area, since it is clear that all classes of Blacks may be found close to the sources of African consciousness illustrated above. Rather, I believe that the appreciation of indigenous African culture is more a matter of consciousness than class and that, therefore, the question is how one comes to acquire an African consciousness in America. The answer is by being or becoming predisposed to plumb the depths of one's heritage and becoming exposed to the elements of the culture.

Within the middle class there is an element that has access to resources and that, because of the extent to which indigenous African culture has steadily gained legitimacy, have given African culture a place (even if often a faddish place) in the scheme of its artistic pantheon. This involves a more stylized appreciation of "Africa" consciousness; for example, the wearing of Kente cloth, the acquisition of African art or sculpture, and the display of such works in one's home marks the definition of kinship. This is quite normal in America. Because of the inaccessibility of Africa and African culture to many, there is often a "groping" that results in a half-understood, distorted and eventually stylized presentation of Africa. In any case, the African imagination is there, almost as if, against the will of their Europeanization, these middle-class Blacks must possess some icon

which reminds them of themselves, seeking a fundamental anchor for *their real selves!*

The evidence is present often without experiential references
or final understanding. For example, while reading a list of
Black debutantes in the *Washington Afro-American* newspaper, I
became aware that their names evoked the heritage of Africa.
Out of the 17 young African-American women shown, some
had such names as Tia, Tiya, Dasha, or Rajem, and Kenya's es-
cort was a young man named Kofi.[41] I understood at once that
some of these young people with explicit African names were
products of Afrocentric parents. But how does one explain the
names that have captured the sounds of recognizable African
words, but not the spelling? It may be that those who used the
near-misses are ultimately as important to preserving the African imagination as those who know the explicit references, because the former, like the latter, will continue to reproduce the
original sounds of the culture long after the fads have disappeared.

Finally, the power of culture as both the womb and parallel
supportive system of politics must be understood as a contribu-
tory factor to the tremendous success of the anti-Apartheid
movement in the United States. The value of South African artists such as Hugh Masekela and the previously noted Miriam
Makeba as residents in the United States in the modern phase of
the struggle cannot be underestimated in helping to educate and
"conscientize" people to the problem of Apartheid. Hugh Masekela, in particular, had long acknowledged the influence of
American jazz musicians upon his own development, and Miriam Makeba sealed this union by marrying one of the most dynamic black leaders of the 1960s, Stokely Carmichael.

In the 1970s and 1980s, a veritable cultural industry sprouted
in the United States along with the popular political phase of the
anti-Apartheid struggle. Nelson Mandela paraphernalia, brace-
lets commemorating the Robbin Island prisoners, plays, books,
film, and music were all part of a national outpouring of culture
addressed to this issue. Perhaps the zenith of the cultural movement was reached in the period 1989–1990 when the Broadway
musical *Sarafina* had its successful run and Paul Simon released
the album *Graceland* featuring both folk music and variations of
township jazz. Through these media, millions of people, includ-

ing the many Blacks who attended many of the performances, were socialized into the world of South African Apartheid from the perspective of the victim.

Nommo: A Cultural Offensive?

The new movement to adopt the name "African American" as the most accurate description of the people of African descent living in America is yet another positive cultural initiative that illustrates the power of the African imagination in the Diaspora. In December of 1988, a Black leadership meeting was held in Chicago by the National Rainbow Coalition to assess the strategy of the Black community after the 1988 presidential elections. Dr. Ramona Edelin called for a "cultural offensive" as part of the strategy, beginning with the idea that Blacks should move toward the adoption of the name "African Americans." When Rev. Jesse Jackson agreed to this recommendation and communicated it to the news media following the meeting, the movement began.[42]

The straightforward application of the term *African* connects Black people here and elsewhere to a past that is beyond slavery and that is related to the birth of man, to the grandeur of the pyramids, to the kingdoms of the Sahel, the Savannah and Southern Africa. In the American context, the movement to return to the original nineteenth-century concept of African identity comes "full circle," but that is not a negative; rather it should be a desired objective. Since we have never stopped being one of many African peoples on the globe, part of the process of throwing off the mind of slavery finally and becoming a whole people after centuries of humiliation and degradation is to continue to reject the inferiorization of our birthright and to validate our original identity. In this sense, the adoption of the name "African American" also presents the opportunity to revitalize the fundamental linkage between the question of identity and the ongoing struggle for justice and equality in this country in order for this act to have any real significance.

Part of the challenge is to embue the term African American with a potent cultural integrity beyond the adoption of the actual words. One must begin by recognizing that this "new" designation is the fundamental bedrock of who we are. When the Free African Society was founded in 1793, its rules began by stating the obligations of "we the African members . . ."[43] This was a natural appellation inasmuch as the society's members were still consciously and culturally, for the most part, Africans. The fact is, of course, that we have not become American by the sheer dint of the longevity of our residence or by some political or cultural transmigration. "Americaness" may imply a level of our adoption of the culture, but "Americanhood" also implies both our adoption and a process of wider social acceptance. As much as the positive imagination of Africa is implicated in the continuance of the African side of our identity, the ambiguity is also created by the often violent rejection of Africans by European Americans, a fact which has maintained the distance in our becoming fully "American." Witness the fact that 60 percent of the white population of Louisiana voted for David Duke, a "former" Klansman and Nazi, in his losing bid for both the GOP Gubernatorial and earlier the nomination for U.S. Senate. One reporter asked a citizen of the state to explain his vote for Duke and he replied that "if you give Blacks an inch they will take a mile; they should still be in chains."[44] Under the circumstances, this could not have been an isolated feeling.

In the early 1960s, Malcolm X adopted the term "Afro-American" in naming his Organization of Afro-American Unity, but the phrase "Americans of African descent" is sprinkled through the organization's charter: "Conscious of the fact that freedom, equality, justice and dignity are essential objectives for the achievement of the legitimate aspirations of peoples of African descent here in the Western Hemisphere, we will endeavor to build a bridge of understanding and create the basis for Afro-American Unity." Yet, the "Afro" identity was considered by many to be a partial adoption of the term African that communicated a continuing shame. Later on in that decade, the adoption of the "Black" identity was forged as the heat of our grand political encounter with America produced the "Black Power" movement. In this context, the adoption of a "Black" identity

represented a certain self-affirmation by claiming a term that for
so long had carried derogatory connotations.[45]

Although when Blacks were referred to as such in the nineteenth century the word connoted color, this new "Blackness"
was a concept which symbolized defiance, even audaciousness,
a forthright championing of the whole people of African descent
in America and their aspirations for liberation. Indeed, the use
of the became a term was an act of psychological liberation. Most
importantly, this term, which on the surface was color-oriented,
encompassed all colors of Americans of African descent, and the
concept ultimately came to embrace original African values
more fiercely than even the current resurrection of the name African American is likely to achieve.

As the Black Power movement became more international in
scope, as has been noted, it became more Africanized, and simultaneously there emerged the practice of "Blacks" being
called "Africans" in recognition of the basic distinction between
the Americanization of our identity and the attempt to recapture the original identity. On one occasion in 1969, Stokely
Carmichael of SNCC said: "One of the most important things we
must now begin to do is to call ourselves 'African.' No matter
where we may be from, we are first of all and finally Africans,
Africans, Africans."[46] What led him to this view was his recognition that Black people were involved in "a struggle for cultural
integrity" and that, given this struggle, they could not align
themselves with the capitalist system because racism was implied in its structure.[47] Thus, the only alternative was to adopt,
both in name and political strategy, the most valid fundamental
identity and alternative.

The central question is, what will give to this new act of
"naming" a cultural integrity that has a powerful liberative content? Fundamentally, the attempt to dignify Black identity has
always symbolically been a call for cultural unity that is more
comprehensive than the simple act of naming. This idea is
grounded in the fact that the name is not new and, indeed, that
all the other names—African, colored, Afro-American, Black,
African American, and so on—exist at various levels within our
society, being used interchangeably and surfacing with the historical tides of necessity. As a practical matter, people will indi-

vidually adopt the name or not, depending upon other concep-
tions they might hold of the destiny of peoples of African
descent. For instance, if they have a strong view of the necessity
for people of African descent in America to have a core set of
common values, objectives, and strategies, then it is more likely
that they will adopt the new name as an act of unity and a genuine appreciation of its cultural, political, and social significance. If not, they will temporize on this question and yield to
the temptations of the popular culture to project a raceless diversity on the strength of a naïve individualism that they can successfully "be anything" they choose. The ability to "be anything" is initially attractive in a society where "pop" culture
promotes the adoption of artificial identity and where they are
available especially for many in the affluent class. However,
neutered identity is dysfunctional for political organization
where the requirement is for a strong group identity in the process of mobilizing people and attempting to achieve mass gains.
So, it is more important that there exists an a priori Afrocentric
conception of life that makes the adoption of this name a natural
extention of one's belief, indeed an enthusiastic event along the
never-ending road to self-discovery in each new age—and at the
same time politically useful.

Symbolic of the tendency to adopt noncontroversial and raceless characterizations of Black identity is the ease with which we
have allowed the "minoritization" of our ethnicity. The term
"minority" was a proportional concept coined by sociologists
early in this century to describe the social composition of America as being stratified between a smaller disadvantaged nonwhite group and a larger advantaged white group. But as the
number of recognized disadvantaged groups grew, the concept
quickly became a convenient way to discuss, package, and distribute public policy benefits. The most prominent aspect of this
development was in the area of affirmative action policy; African
Americans pioneered in fighting for affirmative action but it was
extended to protect every conceivable social class to the point
that we have benefited from it less perhaps than any other
group. Early on, the major protected classes were referred to as
"minorities and women"; then, since "Blacks" constituted 90
percent of the "minorities," the term began to be used interchangeably by both African Americans and others alike as a syn-

onym. Indeed, in an age when it became less efficient to refer to one's ethnic heritage because of our widespread entry into a variety of majority-controlled institutions in the 1970s, many African Americans even preferred the racially neutral identity. The problem is that the "minoritization" of our identity has continued to confer upon the group an inferior social status of powerlessness and, the most dehumanizing characteristic of all, a rootless negation of culture.

"Minorities," however, have no common history, no real social culture, no uniqueness within American society, except for their role in balancing out the equation for the majority. African Americans reaffirm their uniqueness by endowing the act of naming themselves with the specific names that flow from their own historical and cultural experience as authorities for their actions and as models of strategy with which to address current problems. For example, *Frederick Douglass* probably would have said about the Supreme Court's recent Richmond v. Croson decision on affirmative action what he said about the Dred Scott Decision of 1854, that it was decided by the "slave-holding wing of the Court." *Booker T. Washington* would probably have said that Black enterprise needs to be built on the back of the business talent of our community and the continuing need for Blacks to patronize these businesses whether they live in the major metropolitan centers or not. *W.E.B. DuBois* would probably have said that beyond the struggles in Southern Africa, our world vision needs to be shaped by an analysis of the new relationship between African peoples and the West, especially as the West appears to seek political and economic rapproachment with the East. *Marcus Garvey* would probably have wondered why we had not institutionalized the talent that exists in all fields among African Americans to assist Africa and the Caribbean with their economic and technological development. *Malcolm X* would have proposed the liberation of South Africa "by any means necessary"; and he would have wondered why the African-American leadership did not mobilize mass demonstrations to oppose the policies of the Reagan Administration at every building and street corner where the impact of these policies contributed to the devastating poverty in our communities; and he would have made us listen to the rebellious voices of Shreveport and of Liberty City in Miami. It is still possible to hear *Martin*

Luther King, Jr., in explaining the magnetism of his own and of Nelson Mandela's personality, say that any movement we launch in the name of our people should be done with dignity and integrity as the moral keys to the allegiance and follower-ship of the masses. Then, at this moment in history while the Democratic party takes Black votes for granted, we should re-member that *T. Thomas Fortune,* publisher of the *New York Age,* said in 1932 that "Negroes" should increase their political inde-pendence, should switch to Roosevelt and "should go home and turn their pictures of Lincoln to the Wall." Perhaps it is now Roo-sevelt's turn to face the wall of history.

The question has been asked that if an African born on the African continent comes to America and takes out citizenship, is he/she, then, an African American? Why not? It would appear that the one born in America is old and the one born in Africa is new, and that there are the attendant cultural differences be-tween them which represent this cultural and historical transi-tion. But the name binds both old and new into a new reality with the obligation shared by both types of African Americans to the African continent and to the wider grouping of African-origin peoples elsewhere in the Diaspora. Yet, there are those who have argued that affirming the uniqueness of Black people and adopting the name "African American" at this moment in history heightens the emphasis upon ethnicity and detracts from the process of social inclusion. So be it. The name consti-tutes a most telling critique upon the present state of the notion of social integration. On the other hand, this concept of the Af-rican American holds out the possibility of validating the posi-tive aspects of the American dream as well, because it is ironi-cally the only one of the names among colored, Negro, Black, Afro-American, and so on that has the capacity to dignify both the African and American parts of this identity. And yet, for one to be able to adopt both terms at this moment in history may represent more of an aspiration than a fact. In this sense, the name does not carry the connotation of equal power and dignity of Italian-American or Greek-American or other forms of hy-phenated American identities.

The idea of a cultural "offensive" implies at its core the call for the initiation of a social movement that has both cultural and political significance. It is an open question whether or not the source of such a movement might be generated from the mere adoption of the name African American. In fact, one of the central questions is, why does such a phenomenon as Black people attempting to adopt a new name again, beginning to wear the symbols of African identity again, searching for the meaning of Malcolm X's message again, and other signs of a reawakened political consciousness, arise outside the context of any Black social movement existing at this time in history?

It is because there is a need for direction and, in times past, we have found that direction in the wellspring of the values that emerge from our experience in confronting the impediments to our achievement of the promise of full American citizenship and democracy. Professor V. P. Franklin has delineated some of the core cultural values of the Black experience as the desire for freedom, resistance to oppression, the desire for self-determination, and the construction of a culture (in the form of religious and educational institutions).[48] Among these, unity is the premier value which dignifies our peoplehood and provides the basis for an equitable relationship to all humanity because without it we could not have contributed to humanity the gifts of life and of African civilization.

Culture and Politics

It should be clear, then, that an underlying challenge in this work has been to understand how varieties of African culture has been used to inform political struggle in the Diaspora. Politics emerges not as a unique product of social life apart from culture, but as part of the challenge of everyday living. It is the organized way in which people respond to their environment by seeking to protect and advance their overall cultural interests. Thus, where people organize, plan strategy, and implement action, politics is the core of this activity, and it can be expressed either within the context of a formal system of action or in social circumstances as informal as the bedroom.

A unique form of politics is related to Pan Africanism where the activity is directed toward protecting and advancing the cultural heritage of African-origin peoples, where they are engaged in protecting and advancing the interests of African continental peoples, and where the activity is based on protecting and advancing the linkages of kinship among African-origin peoples in the Diaspora. Given this, one can see that culture not only informs the substance of politics, but is absolutely fundamental to its nature.

For example, the quest for self-determining the interests of African peoples everywhere faces a challenge that is not as much political as cultural. If people are satisfied in terms of the resources that make it possible for them to participate in the culture of their choice, then they are easily led politically. In fact, it is possible to argue that even after achieving political "independence," what has kept African and Caribbean countries from becoming self-determining is not only their continuing dependence on the former colonial power, but also the fact that they have nothing better culturally to offer the people. People want to consume Western products, and the terrible seduction of this technological aspect of Western culture has been a major source of political instability in the Third World. The political elite consumes Western education because it understands that the entry point to power and security is to become proficient in the culture; but once it becomes connected to Western culture, lacking power it is subject, ironically, to the exploitations of powerful Western interests. In this scenario, culture is both the seductive substance and the transmission belt of dependency.

How to break out of the process of internal colonialism, then, has always been determined by the degree to which the insurgent has broken with the culture of the colonizer. Khomeni stopped the Westernization of Iran and imposed the supremacy of orthodox Islam as the basis upon which the revolution would be waged. Similarly, the most revolutionary force in the Middle East today is Islamic fundamentalism. It is the key to the antithetis of Western thought and politics in that region. Africa likewise must break out of the process of neocolonialism through the revitalization of African culture because the values implicit in the Western dominance of African culture will keep the people subject to external criteria of their destiny.

There is a corollary to the question of "breaking out" of the process of neocolonialism either in the classic sense or the internal colonial sense. The colonizer wants the colonized to attempt to break out of the process of dependency as *individuals*. Individuals are often utilized, then, to destroy the unity of the group. Breaking out as a group threatens the unity of the colonizer in the process of controlling the destiny of the colonized. The process of developing individual African consciousness, then, is important, but it is only powerful if it acquires group strength. If the identity of the group is stable, then it serves as a resource through which politics then becomes possible. That is the lesson of Marcus Garvey, W.E.B. DuBois, Malcolm X, Martin Luther King, Jr., and others who possessed a certain vision. They may have acquired that vision as individuals, but they quickly sought to develop group consciousness because of their understanding of the inherent power involved.

So, with respect to the question of the role of African identity, African people in the Diaspora do not share the specificity of the African personality as it emerged from the colonial era into the nation state, seeking to establish its national and continental integrity. This is simply another way of saying that Africans in the Diaspora are not a part of the daily particularities of African history and so cannot possess the identity which flows from these experiences. However, they do share certain aspects of this history, and the basis upon which they do so is (1) their affirmation of an African heritage; (2) their participation in the Diasporic aspects of pan African political struggles; (3) their continuing concern with the status of Africa and their efforts to improve it, and (4) their relationship to other hyphenated Africans in the Diaspora.

In general, African-origin peoples do experience certain similarities of culture—the broad experience of racial subordination, including racial prejudice and discrimination; economic exploitation, political exclusion and marginalization, one-way acculturation. Only the form of these experiences is different. And yet, the level of this shared experience is so general and amorphous that it does little to facilitate the understanding of concrete problems. For instance, Africans on the continent and in the Caribbean are often perplexed by the emphasis of African Americans on race in their formulation of social problems, while their own reality is more apparently class conflict. African

Americans, however, see behind the class problems of homogeneously Black nations and peoples; though whites are absent, the abiding hand of racial dominance is the key to their subjugation. These cultural differences have been responsible for what emerges as different political ideologies addressed to the solution of problems.

In any case, the question of culture as a basis for political action in the Diaspora is complex, as we have seen, in part because of the fact that the imposition of European culture upon Africans changed and distributed African culture into many different cultural frameworks, a development compounded by the fact that the Africans were not historically monolithic to begin with. Add to this an additional complexity, that in many geographical regions with even rough similarity to the Euro-African cultural synthesis there are different baselines of culture, from ancient Africa to modern Europe, and the problem of politics is again compounded. This is one of the reasons why some political activists have opted for a definition of culture that avoids the historical problem and starts from a modern baseline of opposition to further encroachments of European imperialism. It simplifies, but it is also far too simplistic.

What we know is that identity is a key to political action in that it identifies the group that is the subject and object of that action. We also know that whatever the nature of the grievances, goals, or objectives, they are shaped by the cultural conflict between dominant and subordinated peoples and, therefore, the political nature of the conflict that emerges is defined by the history of that conflict and the substantive permutations of its issues. We know also that the way in which people attempt to resolve their political conflicts are shaped by "the way" of their culture. In a subordinated state "the way" of a people is always subject to attack in a variety of particulars and, therefore, the substance of politics must be directed toward defending the culture elements—music, art, education, and the like. In this process, if the people are powerless but have access to more people power than other sources, they will use the strength of their numbers; in their organizational activities, they will use the symbolism of their heroes to inform their strategies, the uniqueness of their culture to enhance mobilization. They will also evaluate success with reference to the historical condition of their situation and their position in society relative to others. In any case, the process of informing the individual or the group that the culture is in danger, that a defense or offense is warranted, begins with a keen understanding of who one is in the world and in a given situation. It is the question of clarifying particular cultural identity. And though this is no new insight, it is amazing that this thought must be constantly reinforced within the Pan African context because of the superior forces which challenge the identity of African-origin peoples at every turn.

In the Diaspora, the contradiction of possessing more than one identity has never been resolved and will not be as long as the basic identity of Africa continues to be the footstool of the world and African people (as Professor Mack Jones once said) are everywhere subordinated.[49] The "twoness" is not yet one—if it ever will be; the concepts are still at war, and in this war, many have chosen the "flag of convenience," either the African identity or the American. Nevertheless, no matter which is chosen, the other still continues fundamentally to color the essence of life in a way that makes "Black" culture uniquely different in the world.

It would seem that the influence of indigenous African culture, though present, is also largely absent, and yet it is so self-evidently real that one must take that culture into consideration as an element of each choice, either knowingly or unknowingly. Every now and then, the awareness can rise to the point of possession—the possession of both spirit and of contemplation—in any conceivable situation. For here I sit, dressed in a three-piece-suit, in the window seat of a jet airplane, headed to New York City very much like the young white lawyer beside me—except that in our splendid sameness, after the distance of thousands of miles of ocean, and several generations of families, and millions of attempts to rob me of my cultural sensibility, Africa is in my imagination.

Notes

1. A Theory and Method of the Relationship

1. Joseph E. Harris, ed., *Global Dimensions of the African Diaspora* (Washington, D.C.: Howard University Press, 1982), 59.
2. John Hope Franklin, *From Slavery to Freedom* (New York: Alfred Knopf, 1967), 58–59.
3. David Brion Davis, *The Problem of Slavery in Western Culture* (Ithaca: Cornell University Press, 1966).
4. Franklin, *From Slavery to Freedom*, 120.
5. Gustav Spiller, ed., *Inter-Racial Problems: Papers From the First Universal Races Congress Held in London in 1911* (New York: Citadel Press, 1970), 249.
6. Robin Winks, *The Blacks in Canada* (New Haven: Yale University Press, 1971), 9.
7. Manuel Maldanado-Dennis, *Puerto Rico: A Socio-Historic Interpretation* (New York: Random House, 1972), 45.
8. James G. Layburn, *The Haitian People,* (New Haven: Yale University Press, 1941), 15. Also, Eric Williams, *Capitalism and Slavery* (Chapel Hill, 1944), 33.

9. Spiller, *Inter-Racial Problems*, 335.
10. Laura Foner and Eugene D. Genovese, eds., *Slavery in the New World* (Englewood Cliffs, N.J.: Prentice-Hall, 1969), 3.
11. Michael Cohn and Michael K. H. Platzer, *Black Men of the Sea* (New York: Dodd Mead, 1978), 1.
12. Paul Edwards, ed., *Equiano's Travels* (New York: Praeger, 1967).
13. Esther M. Douty, *Forten the Sailmaker* (New York: Rand McNally, 1968).
14. Cohn and Platzer, *Black Men of the Sea*, 92.
15. Interviews, "United Brothers" (male welfare house), Syracuse, New York, spring 1969.
16. Lewis H. Gann and Peter Duignan, eds., *Colonialism in Africa*, vol. 2 (New York: Cambridge University Press, 1970), 8.
17. Ibid., 19.
18. Ibid., 21–22.
19. Benjamin Quarles, *The Negro in the Making of America* (New York: Macmillan, 1969), 178.
20. Erwin Salk, ed., *A Layman's Guide to Negro History* (New York: McGraw-Hill, 1967), 63.
21. Jay David and Elaine Crane, eds., *The Black Soldier: From the American Revolution to Vietnam*, (New York: William Morrow 1971), 13.
22. Ibid., 14.
23. The data with regard to the migration of Black Africans were often subject to the treatment as described with reference to the figures for 1900–1924 involving South Africa: "The Official Year Book of the Union of South Africa" publishes for 1910–1923 statistics of arrivals and departures by sea. New arrivals and permanent departures after 1913 (including visitors, transit passengers, and others) are given separately. "Tables VI–XIII since 1918 include migrants passing the land frontiers. These relate to Europeans, Asiatics, and colored persons of mixed race, the aboriginal natives of the Bantu race being *excluded*" (my emphasis). Source: Official Year Book of the Union of South Africa, No. 6, 1910–22, Pretoria, 1924, 165. Cited in *International Migration Statistics, 1900–1924*, 1051.
24. Kenneth Little, *Negroes in Britain* (Boston: Routledge and Kegan Paul, 1972), 209.
25. Shalby T. McCloy, *The Negro in France* (Lexington: University of Kentucky Press, 1961), 204–5.
26. Adel Paton, for example, shows that while a few African students came for medical school study in the late nineteenth century, by the early twentieth century such study had become much more commonplace. See *Global Dimensions of the African Diaspora*, 149–155.
27. *The Washington Afro-American*, newspaper, Washington, D.C., August 11, 1973, 13.

28. "African Students and Study Programs in the United States," Report and Hearings, Subcommittee on Africa, House Foreign Affairs Committee, August 15, 1965, Government Printing Office, Washington, D.C., pp. 13, 25.

29. Statement of John Spenser, professor emeritus, Fletcher School of Law, Hearings, Subcommittee on Human Rights and International Organizations and the Subcommittee on Africa, Committee on Foreign Affairs, House of Representatives, 98th, June 21; August 9, 1984 (Washington: U.S. GPO, 1985), 155.

30. E. Franklin Frazier, *Race and Culture Contacts in the Modern World* (Boston: Beacon Press, 1957), 92.

31. Ibid.

32. Alain Locke, ed., *The New Negro* (New York: Atheneum, 1969), 359.

33. Melville Herskovits, *The Myth of the Negro Past* (Boston: Beacon Press, 1958), 298.

34. Robert Hill, lecture, Institute of the Black World, Atlanta, Georgia, spring 1969.

35. Richard Price, ed., *Maroon Societies: Rebel Slave Communities in the Americas* (Garden City, N.Y.: Doubleday/Anchor, 1973).

36. Ibid., p. 392.

37. S. Allen Counter and David L. Evans, *I Sought My Brother* (Cambridge: MIT Press, 1981), 49–50.

38. Walter Rodney, *How Europe Underdeveloped Africa* (London: Bogle-L'Ouverture Publications, 1972; Dar es Salaam: Tazania Publishing House, 1972, Washington: Howard University Press, 1974, 1981).

39. H. Hoetink, *Caribbean Race Relations: A Study of Two Variants* (New York: Oxford University Press, 1967), 4–5.

40. John Blassingame, *The Slave Community: Plantation Life in the Ante-Bellum South* (New York: Oxford University Press, 1972), 1–75.

41. Frazier, *Race and Culture Contacts*, 94–95.

42. Richard Wade, *Slavery in the Cities: The South, 1820–1860* (New York: Oxford University Press, 1964), 20–23.

43. John Henrik Clarke, ed., *Harlem: A Community in Transition* (New York: Citadel Press, 1969), 22.

44. Ibid., 24.

45. W.E.B. DuBois, "The Black North in 1901," *The New York Times*, November 17, 1901– December 15, 1901.

46. Frazier, *Race and Culture Contacts*, 95.

47. Marion D. de B. Kilson, "Afro-American Social Structure, 1790–1970," in Martin Kilson and Robert Rotberg, eds., *The African Diaspora: Interpretive Essays* (Cambridge: Harvard University Press, 1976), 445.

48. "Family Income in 1947, 1950, 1960, and 1970 to 1980—Families, by Total Money Income, Race and Spanish Origin of Householder,"

Bureau of Labor Statistics, Table 3, Current Population Report, Money Income and Poverty Status of Families and Persons in the United States, Advance data for March, 1981, Series P-60, No. 127.

49. Ibid.

50. Dilip Hiro, *Black British, White British* (London: Eyre and Spottiswoode, 1971), 107.

51. E.J.B. Rose and Associates, *Colour and Citizenship: A Report on British Race Relations* (London: Oxford University Press, 1969), 97.

52. John Rex, *Race, Colonialism and the City* (Boston: Routledge and Kegan Paul, 1973), 81.

53. McCloy, *The Negro in France*, 52–53.

54. Ibid.

55. Roger Bastide, *African Civilization in the New World* (New York: Harper and Row, 1971), 199.

56. G. Franklin Edwards, ed., *E. Franklin Frazier: On Race Relations* (Chicago: University of Chicago Press, 1968), 294–95.

57. William K. Tabb, *The Political Economy of the Black Ghetto* (New York: W. W. Norton, 1970), 24.

58. Michael Lipsky, "Rent Strikes: Poor Man's Weapon," in August Meier, ed., *The Transformation of Activism* (New York: Transaction/ Aldine, 1970), 40.

59. Anthony Downs, *Urban Problems and Prospects* (Chicago: Markham, 1970), 34.

60. Ibid., 50.

61. Ibid., 60.

62. William A. Gamson, "Rancorous Conflict in Community Politics," in Willis D. Hawley and Frederick M. Wirt, eds., *The Search for Community Power* (Englewood Cliffs, N.J.: Prentice-Hall, 1974), 199.

63. Philip S. Foner, ed., *W.E.B. DuBois Speaks* (New York: Pathfinder Press, 1970), 79.

64. W.E.B. DuBois, *The Suppression of the African Slave-Trade to the United States of America, 1638–1870* (New York: Schocken, 1969), xxxv.

65. W.E.B. DuBois, *The Negro* (New York: Oxford University Press, 1970), xxi.

66. George Shepperson, "The African Abroad or the African Diaspora," in T.O. Ranger, ed., *Emerging Themes of African History* (Nairobi: East Africa Publishing House, 1968), 153.

67. Vincent Bakpetu Thompson, *Africa and Unity: The Evolution of Pan-Africanism* (London: Longman, xxiv.)

68. Shepperson, "The African Abroad," 60–68.

69. Harris, *Global Dimensions of the African Diaspora*, 62.

70. Ibid., 353.

71. Ibid., 355.

72. Ibid., 358–59.
73. St. Clair Drake, "West Africa and Cross Currents with the New World," Studies of Afro-American Backgrounds and Experiences, Martin Luther King Distinguished Visiting Lecture Series, Brooklyn College, September 26, 1968, 8.
74. Richard L. Meritt, *Systematic Approaches to Comparative Politics* (New York: Rand McNally, 1970), 3.
75. W.E.B. DuBois, *An ABC of Color* (New York: International Publishers, 1969), 104.
76. St. Clair Drake, "West Africa and Cross Currents," see note 73.
77. Ofuatey Kodjoe, *Pan Africanism: New Directions in Strategy* (Lanham: University Press of America, 1986), 385.
78. Olisanwuche Esedebe, *Pan Africanism: The Idea and the Movement, 1776–1963* (Washington, D.C.: Howard University Press, 1982), 1
79. Ibid., 3.
80. Kodjoe, *Pan Africanism*, 385–407.
81. Ibid., 388.
82. Thompson, *Africa and Unity: The Evolution of Pan-Africanism*, xxiii.
83. Floyd J. Miller, *The Search For a Black Nationality* (Chicago: University of Illinois Press, 1975); Rodney Carlisle, *The Roots of Black Nationalism* (Port Washington, N.Y.: Kennikat Press, 1975); Hollis Lynch, *Edward Wilmot Blyden: Pan-Negro Patriot, 1832–1912* (New York: Oxford University Press, 1967); James Turner, "Pan Africanism and the Black Struggle in the U.S.A.," in Kodjoe, *Pan Africanism*, 165–66.
84. Esedebe, *Pan Africanism: The Idea and the Movement*, 46.
85. Philip S. Foner, ed., *W.E.B. DuBois Speaks: Speech and Addresses, 1890–1919* (New York: Pathfinder Press, 1970), 79.

2. The Pan African Movement in the United States

1. St. Clair Drake, "Negro Americans and the Africa Interest," in John P. Davis, ed., *The American Negro Reference Book*, vol. 2 (Englewood Cliffs: Prentice-Hall, 1966), 650.
2. This is especially evident in a series of articles by Tilden LeMelle, Locksley Edmonson, W. A. Jeanpierre, and St. Clair Drake, appear-

ing in a special issue of *Africa Today,* "Black Power and Africa," 14, 6 (December 1967).

3. "Africans and Afro-Americans," *Negro Digest,* September 1965. See also Jacob Drachler, ed., *Black Homeland, Black Diaspora: Cross-Currents of the African Relationship,* (Port Washington: Kennikat Press, 1975), 249. Also, these references to African Americans as anything less than "brothers" or "sisters" provoked sometimes violent outbursts in the late 1960s. For example, Tom Mboya, Kenyan Minister of Economic Planning and Development in 1969, made a one-hour speech in Harlem on March 18 of that year. He referred to American Blacks as "cousins" and rejected any movement of Blacks back to Africa. He said, "I was noisily interrupted by two or three people, one of whom projected four or five eggs in my direction. His aim was as bad as his manners." *The New York Times Magazine,* July 13, 1969, p. 30.

4. John O. Killens, "Brotherhood of Blackness," *Negro Digest,* 15, 7 (May 1966): 7.

5. Ibid., 10.

6. Drachler, *Black Homeland, Black Diaspora,* 126.

7. Ibid., 127.

8. Alex Haley, *The Autobiography of Malcolm X* (New York: Ballantine Books, 1965), 350.

9. George Breitman, ed., *By Any Means Necessary* (New York: Pathfinder Press, 1970), 37.

10. Ibid.

11. Peter Goldman, *The Death and Life of Malcolm X,* (New York: Harper and Row, 1965), 226.

12. Ibid., 227.

13. See Herschelle Challenor, "The Influence of Black Americans on U.S. Foreign Policy Toward Africa," in Abdul Aziz Said, ed., *Ethnicity and U.S. Foreign Policy* (New York: Praeger, 1977), 239–74. Also, Ronald Walters, "Black Organizations in International Perspective," in Leonard Yearwood, ed., *The Survival of Black Organizations* (Lanham, Md.: University Press of America, 1980).

14. James Forman, *The Making of Black Revolutionaries* (New York: Macmillan, 1972), 487.

15. Ibid., 504–8.

16. Stokely Carmichael, *Stokely Speaks* (New York: Vintage/Random House, 1971), 130.

17. Ibid., 87.

18. Ibid., 97.

19. Forman, *The Making of Black Revolutionaries,* 508.

20. Carmichael, *Stokely Speaks,* 98.

21. Such a meeting was arranged at American University in 1965 by Dr. Darrell Randall, a professor there, and I, then a graduate student, was present.
22. I was then a faculty member of the Maxwell School, Department of Political Science at Syracuse University, and was present at this lecture.
23. Africa Information Service, eds., *Return to the Source: Selected Speeches of Amilcar Cabral* (New York, 1973), 43.
24. Ibid., 52.
25. I will always be grateful to Ruwa Chiri, a Zimbabwian (now deceased) who lived in Chicago, and who told me of this meeting, met me there and broadened my understanding of Cabral and his circumstances.
26. Africa Information Service, *Return to the Source*, 63.
27. Ibid., 74.
28. Ibid.
29. Ibid., 90–91.
30. Nkrumah was a mentor of Cabral's and had told him this on the occasion of one of their frequent meetings in Guinea.
31. See Kwame Nkrumah, *Handbook of Revolutionary Warfare, A Guide To The Armed Phase of the African Revolution* (New York: International Publishers, 1969).
32. African Information Service, *Return to the Source*, 71–72. He said: "Naturally if you ask me between brothers and comrades what I prefer—if we are brothers it is not our fault or our responsibility. But if we are comrades, it is a political engagement. Naturally we like our brothers but in our conception it is better to be a brother and a comrade." Cabral overlooked, however, the fact that brotherhood does carry with it an implicit obligation and responsibility stronger than lack of kinship. For it is there that the act of comradeship most effectively is nurtured and developed.
33. *Arusha Declaration*, The United Republic of Tanzania (Dar es Salaam: Government Printer, 1967).
34. "Education For Self Reliance," United Republic of Tanzania, Embassy of the United Republic of Tanzania, 1967.
35. Ibid.; see also Robert Malson, "The Black Power Rebellion at Howard University," *Negro Digest* 17, 2 (December 1967): 20–30. It is also historically revealing to peruse the demands made by students in subsequent documents. Many of these demands became standard even at white college campuses.
36. The account given by Leslie Lacy, for example, of the American Black community in Ghana in the early 1960s is a rare such account, and should be complemented by others, especially the Tanzanian

group and others in Nigeria and elsewhere. Such research would undoubtedly uncover the interesting specter of linkages among African Americans on the African continent during the high point of Pan Africanism in the 1960s. Malcolm, it will be remembered, attempted to bring some coordination to these communities through establishing the OAAU on the continent.

37. As a delegate to the Conference, and understanding Swahili, I witnessed this unexpected and fascinating spectacle.

38. Kwame Nkrumah, *Revolutionary Path*, (New York: International Publishers, 1973), 421–28.

39. Ibid., 426.

40. I participated in these debates at the Black Power Conference in Philadelphia, August 29 to September 1, 1968.

41. Imamu Amiri Baraka (LeRoi Jones), ed., *African Congress: A Documentary of the First Modern Pan-African Congress* (New York: William Morrow, 1972), xi.

42. Ibid., 57.

43. Ibid., 108; also, Ronald Walters, "African American Nationalism," *Black World* 22, 12 (October 1973): 9–27.

44. Letter from Owusu Sadaukai to Ronald Walters (general mailing), February 17, 1972, Washington, D.C. In 1973 I became a member of the Executive Committee of The African Liberation Support Committee (ALSC), but resigned in the spring of 1974 after the Frogmore meeting.

45. Ronald Walters, "The New Black Political Culture," *Black World* 21, 12 (October 1972): 4–17.

46. Ibid. See also articles by William Strickland, "The National Black Political Agenda," and Imamu Amiri Baraka, in this special issue.

47. Baraka, *African Congress*, ix.

48. I attended this session. Tape, May 24, 1972.

49. Haki Madhubuti, "The Latest Purge," *The Black Scholar* 6, 1 (September 1974): 46.

50. Ibid.

51. "A Black Scholar Debate: Responses to Haki R. Madhubuti (Don L. Lee) by Ronald Walters, S. E. Anderson, Alonzo 4X (Cannady)," *The Black Scholar* 6, 2 (October 1974): 47–53. But see also Haki R. Madhubuti, "Enemy: From the White Left, White Right and In-Between," *Black World* 23, 12 (October 1974): 36–47; and Kalamu ya Salaam, "Tell No Lies, Claim No Easy Victories," Ibid., 18–34.

52. Amiri Baraka, "The Congress of African People: A Position Paper," *The Black Scholar* 6, 5 (January–February 1975): 3.

53. Nathan Hare, "A Report on the Pan African Cultural Festival," *The Black Scholar* 1, 1 (November 1969): 2–11. Here Nathan Hare relates

the differences at the time between the Black Panther leader Eldridge Cleaver, in exile in Algeria, site of the First Pan African Cultural Festival, and Stokely Carmichael, who was attending the Festival, concerning the two-line struggle. This first issue of *The Black Scholar* is not only important as the beginning issue of the periodical, but also because it includes articles by Sékou Touré, Stanislas Adotevi, Stokely Carmichael, Amiri Baraka, and John Killens providing a "snap shot" of the various tendencies of political ideology in the American Diaspora and on the continent.

54. Amiri Baraka, "Why I Changed My Ideology: Black Nationalism and Socialist Revolution," *Black World* 24, 9 (July 1975): 31.

55. Gerald Bender, "Kissinger in Angola: Anatomy of Failure," in Rene Lemarchand, ed., *American Policy in Southern Africa: The Stake and the Stance* (Washington, D.C.: University Press of America, 1978).

56. I was co-convenor of the conference which met in June of the year. At a high point in the conference, those supporting UNITA withdrew and the conference was taken over completely by those supporting MPLA.

57. Abiola Irele, "Negritude of Black Cultural Nationalism," *Journal of Modern African Studies* 3, 3 (December 1965): 347.

58. Léopold Sédar Senghor, "The Problematics of Négritude," *Black World* 20, 10 (August 1971): 18. See also, Léopold Senghor, "In Defense of Négritude," *Negro Digest*, 15, 11, (September 1966): 4–9. Also, Négritude was the basis upon which Senghor and other Africans leaders would attempt to fashion and practice an "African socialism." For example, Mercer Cook, in the introduction of Léopold Sédar Senghor, *On African Socialism* (New York: Praeger, 1964), said, "The integration of *Négritude*—defined in the third essay as the common denominator of all Negro Africans—and socialism requires special directives that only the theoretician of *Négritude* and African socialism can furnish." (vi).

59. Sékou Touré, "A Dialectical Approach to Culture," *The Black Scholar* 1, 1 (November 1969): 15–16.

60. Léopold Sédar Senghor, "The Problematics of Négritude," 19–20.

61. *Africa* 25 (September 1973): 24.

62. *The Call*, Sixth Pan African Congress Temporary Secretariat, Washington, D.C., February 5, 1972.

63. Ibid.

64. "Pan-Africanist, C. L. R. James," *Africa* 30 (February 1974): 25–26. Also, "Interview with C. L. R. James," Sixth Pan African Congress, 1, 1, October 1973, pamphlet.

65. James Garrett, "A Historical Sketch: The Sixth Pan African Congress," *Black World* 26, 5 (March 1975): 18.

66. *The Black Scholar* (October 1974), 43.
67. Letter, Owusu Sadaukai to Courtland Cox, October 16, 1973, Washington, D.C.
68. Letter, Courtland Cox to Owusu Sadaukai, October 18, 1973.
69. Imamu Amiri Baraka, "Some Questions About The Sixth Pan African Congress," *The Black Scholar* 6, 2 (October 1974): 44. In addition, the Western district-region of the North American delegation had developed a position paper which was compiled and distributed in April 1974. "The Position Paper of the Western District-Region of North America (U.S.A.) as compiled through district conferences and consultations," April 1974.
70. I was asked to be a part of the original group that fashioned such questions to send to President Nyerere, but felt that such an approach was not only politically unproductive but also potentially dangerous to the conduct of the entire meeting. In a letter to Turner prior to the above questions being sent to President Nyerere, I said in part: "It should be said that the historical context of this Conference is radically different than that of thirty years ago. In such a setting, it was relatively easy (from outside the continent) to deal with progressive issues which were important to Africa and anti-thetical to the interests of the European powers. Today, unfortunately the concept of Pan-Africanism as it is known on the continent is primarily embodied in the political dynamics of African governments, and it must be weighted whether or not raising divisive issues within this context may or may not be a productive exercise on the whole. I am aware of the vital need for mutual respect which must exist between Africans on the governmental and especially non-governmental levels, and for reciprocal relations all around. But here the question of the context within which this takes place is important. I happen to believe that the most legitimate context (or base) from which we might make statements about the quality of African and Caribbean governments would be from where we are, emanating from the development of our own politics and our own conception of Pan-Africanism. I am not averse to raising questions about the progressiveness of certain governments in Africa and in the Caribbean, from our base, but I would be extremely reticent to do so where it would trouble the host governments, and raise questions about the legitimacy of those making such statements and indeed the entire Conference. I do not believe that it would be productive for us to force those issues in that context, just as I do believe that it would be presumptuous of a group of brothers from the continent to force certain issues on us without a correct understanding of the nature of our indigenous situation

and in respect for our views." Having stated my case, then, I went on to suggest a series of questions more positive in tone, directed to the question of the nature of a mutual agenda which could be supported by the African American community as the main set of questions to be posed as a prelude to the Congress and as preparation for the delegation. Letter, Ronald Walters to Professor James Turner, April 16, 1974.

71. Garrett, "A Historical Sketch"; Sylvia Hill, "Progress Report on Congress Organizing," *The Black Scholar* 5, 7 (April 1974): 35–40.
72. Hoyt Fuller, "Notes From a Sixth Pan-African Journal," *Black World* 23, 12 (October 1974): 75.
73. *Resolutions and Selected Speeches From the Sixth Pan-African Congress* (Dar es Sallam: Tanzania Publishing House, 1976), 15–16.
74. Hoyt Fuller, 80.
75. *Resolutions and Selected Speeches From the Sixth Pan-African Congress,* 211–12.
76. Ibid., 88.
77. Ibid.
78. Ibid., 218.
79. I was a participant in the International Colloquium. See also "The FESTAC Colloquium: A Black Perspective," *New Directions,* Howard University, June 1977.
80. Discussions with delegates to this conference.
81. *Black Books Bulletin,* Interview: "Maulana Ron Karenga," (1976).
82. Abdias do Nascimento, a prominent Black intellectual, was not permitted to be a part of the official Brazilian delegation because of his outspokenness about the extent of racism in Brazil. See his *Racial Democracy in Brazil.* At this meeting, he was excluded from the official program of FESTAC because of his status, but the delegates demanded that he be allowed to speak and this demand was granted. An exile for a considerable period of time in the United States, he is now a member of the Brazilian House of Representatives representing a district in Bahia.
83. I was a participant/observer of these events.
84. June Milne, Nkrumah's publisher, in a letter to Dabu Gazenga, denies that Nkrumah started AAPRP and felt that Touré was an inappropriate model for Nkrumah's ideas of Pan Africanism. This view appeared to be based on Gazenga's report that AAPRP was actually a Black Nationalist organization.
85. I am indebted to Dr. Sylvia Hill, an organizer of the Sixth PAC and professor at the University of the District of Columbia, for her insight about the difference in the material reality between the American delegation to Sixth PAC and African delegations.

86. James Garrett, "A Historical Sketch."
87. The Southern African Support Committee is a Washington, D.C.-based organization headed by Dr. Sylvia Hill and Saundra Hill that raises thousands of dollars annually for African projects.

3. Black American Pan Africanism in Africa: Going Home to Ghana

1. Elliot Skinner, "The Dialectic Between Diasporas and Homelands," in The Black Diaspora Committee of Howard University, ed., *The African Diaspora: Africans and Their Descendants in the Wider World to 1800* (Lexington, Mass.: Ginn Press, 1986), 6.
2. Ibid., 20.
3. Ibid., 21
4. Edward W. Blyden, "Progress is Difference," in Jacob Drachler, ed., *Black Homeland: Black Diaspora* (Port Washington, N.Y.: Kennikat Press, 1975), 56.
5. Floyd J. Miller, *The Search for a Black Nationality* (Chicago: Univ. of Illinois Press, Chicago, 1975), 192.
6. William E. Bittle and Gilbert L. Geis, "Alfred Charles Sam and an African Return: A Case study in Negro Despair," *Phylon* 23, 1 (Spring 1962), 178–94.
7. St. Clair Drake, "Negro Americans and the Africa Interest," in John P. Davis, ed., *The American Negro Reference Book* (Englewood Cliffs, N.J.: Prentice-Hall, 1966), 693.
8. Ibid.
9. Kwame Nkrumah, *Africa Must Unite* (New York: International Publishers, 1963), 136.
10. Benjamin Mays, "A Plea for Straight Talk between the Races," Leslie Fishel, Jr. and Benjamin Quarles, eds., *The Black American: A Documentary History* (Glenview, Ill.: Scott Foresman 1970), p. 509.
11. Hoyt Fuller, *Journey to Africa* (Chicago, Ill.: Third World Press, 1971), 80.
12. Ibid., 81.
13. Louis Lomax, "A Demand for Dynamic Leadership," in Fishel and Quarles, *The Black American*, 505.

14. Richard B. Moore, "Africa Conscious Harlem," in John Henrik Clarke, ed., *Harlem: A Community In Transition* (New York: Citadel, 1964), 91.

15. See George Padmore, *Pan-Africanism or Communism* (New York: Doubleday/Anchor, 1972), 130–63; also, Vincent Bakpetu Thompson, *Africa and Unity: The Evolution of Pan-Africanism* (London: Longman, 1969), 42–63.

16. The best account of this is by Ras Makonnen, *Pan-Africanism: From Within*, with Kenneth King (Nairobi: Oxford University Press, 1973), 211–25.

17. Kwame Nkrumah, *Africa Must Unite*, 137.

18. Ibid., 138–39.

19. Ibid., 140.

20. Basil Davidson, *Black Star: A View of the Life and Times of Kwame Nkrumah* (New York: Praeger, 1973), 36–38.

21. David L. Lewis, *King: A Biography*, 2nd. ed. (Urbana: University of Illinois Press, 1978), 90.

22. Marguerite Cartwright, "Travel Diary," *The Negro History Bulletin* 24, (Oct, May, 1960–1961), 35–36.

23. Peter Kihss, "Harlem Hails Ghanaian Leader as Returning Hero," *The New York Times*, July 28, 1958, 1.

24. Ibid., 4.

25. "U.S. Negroes Seek Ghana Livelihood," *The New York Times*, December 1, 1959, 11.

26. "Nkrumah Praises Ghana's Ties Here," *The New York Times*, July 29, 1958, 10.

27. *The Crisis* 65, 7 (August-September 1958), 411.

28. Ibid., 408.

29. "Nkrumah Urges Racial Equality," *The New York Times*, July 30, 1959, 4.

30. "Nkrumah in Chicago: Crowds Hail Ghana Leader—City Bestows Honor," *The New York Times*, July 31, 1958, 3.

31. Kwame Nkrumah, *Revolutionary Path* (New York: International Publishers, 1973), 125–35.

32. Ibid., 271.

33. Ibid.

34. Interestingly, in the biographical volumes produced by both women about their husbands, *His Day Is Marching On*, by Shirley Graham DuBois, and *Unsung Valiant*, by Dorothy Hunton, there is little or no reference to the expatriate community, but the focus is almost exclusively on President Nkrumah, the global significance of Ghana, and the worldwide activities of their husbands.

35. Maya Angelou, *All God's Children Need Travelin' Shoes* (New York: Vintage/Random House, 1987), 3.

36. Leslie Lacy, "Black Bodies in Exile," in Drachler, ed., *Black Homeland, Black Diaspora*, 147–49.

37. Angelou, *All God's Children*, 18–19; Julian Mayfield Papers, Box 1, Schomberg Library, New York City.

38. Julian Mayfield Papers, Box 1, Schomberg Library, New York City.

39. Lacy, "Black Bodies in Exile," 151.

40. Angelou, *All God's Children*, 19.

41. Ibid.

42. David Jenkins, *Black Zion: Africa Imagined and Real, As Seen By Today's Blacks* (New York: Harcourt, Brace Jovanovich), 1975, 158.

43. William Gardner Smith, *Return to Black America* (Englewood Cliffs, N.J.: Prentice-Hall, 1970), 96.

44. Richard Wright, "Blueprint for Negro Literature," in John A. Williams and Charles F. Harris, eds., *Amistad 2* (New York: Vintage / Random House, 1971), 3.

45. Smith, *Return to Black America*, 101.

46. Ingalls, "U.S. Negroes Seek Ghana Livelihood."

47. Lacy, "Black Bodies in Exile," 128.

48. Angelou, *All God's Children*, 101.

49. Ibid., 76.

50. "William Sutherland," Interview, in Drachler, ed., *Black Homeland, Black Diaspora*, 164.

51. St. Claire Drake, "Negro Americans and the Africa Interest," in Davis, ed., *The American Negro Reference Book*, 701–3.

52. Pauli Murray, *Proud Shoes* (New York: Harper and Row, 1978), xvi.

53. Alex Prempeh, "Negro Stooges Bid for Africans Challenged," *Voice of Africa* 3, 1 (January 1963): 17.

54. Lacy, "Black Bodies in Exile," 152–6.

55. Julian Mayfield Papers, notes on Saunders Redding, Box 2.

56. Ibid.

57. Julian Mayfield Papers, "Tales of the Lido," unpublished manuscript, Box 1.

58. Lacy, "Black Bodies in Exile," 147–49.

59. Ibid.

60. Smith, *Return to Black America*, 106.

61. George Padmore, "The Press Campaign Against Ghana," *The Crisis* 64, 10 (December 1957): 607–12.

62. Julian Mayfield Papers, Ghanaian Times, n.d.

63. Ibid.

64. Hunton, *Unsung Valliant*, 81–90.

65. Fuller, *Journey to Africa*, 93.

66. Basil Davidson, *Black Star*, 173.

67. "Dodd Says Ghana is Red Satellite," *The New York Times*, July 15, 1963, 9.
68. St. Clair Drake, "Where Nkrumah Stands," *The New York Times*, letters to the editor, July 30, 1963, 28.
69. Nkrumah, *Revolutionary Path*, 372.
70. Martin Kilson, "Politics of African Socialism," *African Forum* 1, 3 (Winter 1966).
71. Ibid., 22.
72. John A. Davis, editorial, *African Forum* 2, 1 (Summer 1966): 3.
73. See Shirley Graham Du Bois, "What Happened in Ghana?: The Inside Story," *Freedomways* 6 (1966): 201–23.
74. "Governor Folsom Saves Negro From Chair," *The New York Times*, September 30, 1958, 1.
75. Frank Lee, "Changing Structure of Negro Leadership," *Crisis*, 65, 4 (April 1958): 197; Dr. John Morsell, assistant to NAACP executive secretary Roy Wilkins, answered Lee's article, claiming that "it is a curious hodgepodge of inaccuracies, omissions, and logical distortions . . . ," John A. Morsell, "Comment on Frank F. Lee's 'Changing Structure of Negro Leadership,'" *The Crisis* 65, 5 (May 1958): 261.
76. Richard Moore, "Africa Conscious Harlem," in Clarke, ed., *Harlem*, 94.
77. Ibid.
78. George Brietman, ed., *Malcolm X Speaks* (New York: Grove Press, 1965), 6.
79. Alex Haley, *The Autobiography of Malcolm X* (New York: Ballentine Books, 1965), 354.
80. Angelou, *All God's Children*, 131.
81. Ibid.
82. Haley, *The Autobiography of Malcolm X*, 353, 355.
83. William Atwood, *The Reds and the Blacks*, (New York: Harper and Row, 1967), 188.
84. Angelou, *All God's Children*, 121.
85. Hunton, *Unsung Valiant*, 135.
86. Thomas M. Franck, "European Communities In Africa," *Journal of Negro Education* 30 (1961): 223–31.
87. Ibid., 224.
88. DuBois, *His Day Is Marching On*, 335.
89. See a remarkable survey of Ghana's first year by Marguerite Cartwright, "Ghana First Year: A Summing Up," *Negro History Bulletin* 21 (April 1958): 147–52.
90. Franck, "European Communities in Africa," 226.
91. C.L.R. James, *At the Rendezvous of Victory* (London: Allison and Busby, 1984), 175–79.

4. The Anglo-Saxon Diaspora: Britain and the United States

1. A. E. Eisenstadt, "The Special Relationship: Britain Through American Eyes," *Massachusetts Review* 18, 4 (Winter, 1977): 824–43.
2. Ibid., 827.
3. Peter Howells, "Mrs. Thatcher's Theory of Human Nature," *Contemporary Review* 237, 1377 (October 1980), 183.
4. Norman Yetman and C. Hoy Steele, eds., *Minority and Majority: The Dynamics of Race Relations* (Boston: Allyn and Bacon, 1971), 258.
5. Howard Odum, *Social and Mental Traits of the Negro* (New York: AMS Press, 1971).
6. Gunnar Myrdal, *An American Dilemma: The Negro Problem and Modern Democracy* (New York: Harper and Brothers, 1944).
7. Yetman and Steele, *Minority and Majority*, 266.
8. Brown V. Board of Education of Topeka, Kansas, 347 U.S. 483 (1954).
9. David L. Lewis, *King: A Biography*, 2nd ed. (Urbana: University of Illinois Press, 1978).
10. Voter Education Project, "Black Elected Officials in the South," Atlanta, Ga., 1973.
11. *National Roster of Black Elected Officials*, 9, Joint Center for Political Studies, Washington, D.C., 1979.
12. Even today, many city and county councils are filled by "at-large" elections, rather than through smaller single-member districts corresponding to racial make-up of the majority population in that district. Such at-large electoral systems destroy the equal opportunity for the black vote to elect a representative.
13. E.J.B. Rose and Associates, *Colour and Citizenship: A Report on British Race Relations* (London: Oxford University Press, 1969), 15.
14. The data are from a study by Prof. A. H. Richmond, *Color Prejudice in Britain*, London, 1954. See Kenneth Little, "Some Aspects of Color, Class, and Culture in Britain," in John Hope Franklin, ed., *Color and Race* (Boston: Beacon, 1968), 235.
15. Paul Sheatsley, "White Attitudes Toward the Negro," in Talcott Parsons and Kenneth Clark, eds., *The Negro American* (Boston: Beacon, 1966), 308.
16. "The Kerner Commission—Ten Years Later," CBS/New York Times Poll, 1978; 55 percent of whites would prefer to live in an "all white" or "mostly white" neighborhood, and only 66 percent would not mind if a black of equal income or education moved next door (p. 12).
17. Rose and Associates, *Colour and Citizenship*, 553.

18. In fact, E. Franklin Frazier maintained that this "indirect rule" was also a feature of American race relations. See G. Franklin Edwards, ed., *E. Franklin Frazier: On Race Relations* (Chicago: The University of Chicago Press, 1968), 11–12.

19. R. B. Davison, *Black British: Immigrant to England* (London: Oxford University Press, 1966), 60.

20. Rose and Associates, *Colour and Citizenship*, 208.

21. John Rex, *Race, Colonialism and the City* (London: Routledge and Kegan Paul, 1973), 95–96.

22. Dilip Hiro, *Black British, White British* (London: Eyre and Spottiswoode, 1971), 227.

23. Paul Foot, *The Rise of Enoch Powell* (Hammondsworth, England: Penguin, 1969).

24. Edward Scobie, *Black Britainia: A History of Blacks in Britain* (Chicago: Johnson Publishing Company, 1972), 302.

25. A. Sivanandan, "From Immigration Control to 'Indiced Repatriation,'" *Race and Class* (pamphlet), no. 5, Institute of Race Relations, London, 1978, 1.

26. Davison, *Black British*, 5–6.

27. Rose and Associates, *Colour and Citizenship*, 618.

28. Hiro, *Black British, White British*, 269–78.

29. Michael Hill and Ruth Isaacacharoff, *Community Action and Race Relations: A Study of Community Relations Committee in Britain* (London: Oxford University Press, 1971), 283.

30. Sivanandan, "From Immigration Control," 408.

31. Ibid., 405.

32. See *Searchlight*, London, March 1981, 17–18. Also *The Thin Edge of the White Wedge: The New Nationality Laws, Second Class Citizenship and the Welfare State*, Manchester Law Center Immigration Handbook, no. 5, spring 1981.

5. Comparative Linkages in the African Diaspora: Britain and the United States

1. John Rex, *Race Relations in Sociological Theory* (New York: Schocken, 1970), 121.

2. R.B. Davison, *Black British: Immigrants to England* (London: Oxford University Press, 1966), 80–81.

3. E.J.B. Rose and Associates, *Colour and Citizenship: A Report on British Race Relations*, (London: Oxford University Press, 1969), 407–15.

4. Hans Spiegel, ed., *Citizen Participation in Urban Development*, vol. 2: Cases and Programs (Washington, D.C.: NTL Institute for Applied Behavioral Science, 1969), 71–86.

5. J. David Greenstone and Paul E. Peterson, *Race and Authority in Urban Politics: Community Participation and the War on Poverty* (New York: Russell Sage Foundation, 1973), 94, 170.

6. Reginald E. Gilliam, Jr., *Black Political Development: An Advocacy Analysis* (Port Washington: Dunellen, Kennikat, 1975).

7. Robert Moore, *Racism and Black Resistance in Britain* (London: Pluto Press, 1975), p. 111.

8. Chuck Stone, *Black Political Power in America* (New York: Bobbs-Merrill, 1968), 230–42.

9. N.D. Deakin, Daniel Lawrence, Jonathan Silvey, M.J. Lelohe, "Colour and the 1966 General Election," *Race* 8, 1 (1966): 16–42.

10. Ferdinand Dennis, "Black Sections Debate," *Race Today* 17, 5:118.

11. Ibid.

12. Darcus Howe, "Black Sections for the Black Middle Classes: I Say 'Yes,'" *Race Today* 16, 5 (August/September 1985): 10.

13. "Darcus Howe on Black Sections in the Labor Party," *Race Today Collective*, pamphlet, London, 1985, 15.

14. Lorraine Griffiths, "The Debate on Black Sections," *Race Today* 17, 7 (July 1986): 18.

15. "Darcus Howe on Black Sections in the Labor Party," 9.

16. "Labour's Black Rebellion," *Daily Mail*, London, May 19, 1989, 1.

17. Darcus Howe, "As I See It," *Race Today* 17, 4 (1989): 15.

18. Report of the National Executive Committee working committee on Black Sections, July 31, 1989, Joyce Gould, Director of Organization, June 19, 1989.

19. "The Black Agenda," The Labour Party Black Sections, 1988.

20. "The Black Agenda," 30; "The Peoples Platform," The National Black Coalition for 1984 and the National Black Leadership Roundtable, Washington, D.C., 1984, 24.

21. "The Black Agenda," 31; "The Peoples Platform," 48.

22. *National Roster of Black Elected Officials 1979*, Joint Center for Political Studies, vol. 9, 1979.

23. Deakin, et al., "Colour and the 1966 General Election."

24. *The Parliamentary Debates*, Hansard, vol. 124, House of Commons, Session 1987–1988, December 7–December 18, 1987, Her Majesty's Stationary Office, London, 436.

25. Ibid., 1367.

26. Ibid., March 10, 1987, 618.

27. Ibid., May 23, 1987, 64–65.
28. Ibid., 626.
29. Moore, *Racism and Black Resistance*, 72–103.
30. Hugh Graham and Ted Gurr, *Violence in America*, vol. 2 (Washington, D.C.: U.S. Government Printing Office, June 1969).
31. William J. Bopp and Donald O. Shultz, *Principles of American Law Enforcement and Criminal Justice* (Springfield: Charles C. Thomas, 1972), 146.
32. E. Cray, *The Enemy in the Streets: Police Malpractice in America* (Garden City: Doubleday/Anchor, 1972).
33. Joe R. Feagin and Harlan Hahn, *Ghetto Revolts: The Politics of Violence in American Cities* (New York: Macmillan, 1973), 268.
34. Ibid., 145.
35. *Report of the National Advisory Commission on Civil Disorders*, (New York: Bantam, 1968), 302–5.
36. *Criminal Justice Issues*, Newsletter of the Commission for Racial Justice of the United Church of Christ, New York, 6, 2 (June 1981).
37. Ibid.
38. Nelson Blackstock, ed., *COINTELPRO: The FBI's Secret War On Political Freedom* (New York: Vintage, 1976).
39. Rose and Associates, *Colour and Citizenship*, 356.
40. Ibid., 356, or see Michael Banton, *The Politics and the Community* (London: Tavistock, 1964), chapter 4.
41. Stuart Hall, Chas. Critchen, Tony Jefferson, John Clarke, and Brian Roberts, *Policing the Crisis: Mugging the State, and Law and Order* (London: Macmillan, 1978), 44.
42. Ibid.
43. Ibid., 284–85.
44. Report of the Working Party on Community/Police Relations in Lambeth, Public Relations Division, London Borough of Lambeth, Brixton Hill, January 1981, 14.
45. Ibid., 6.
46. Ibid., 10.
47. *Police against Black People*, Race and Class Pamphlet no. 6, Institute of Race Relations, 1979, 30.
48. Hall et al., *Policing the Crisis*, 360.
49. Roy Sawh, speech at Hyde Park Conrner, London, January 28, 1972.
50. Moore, 62.
51. *Black Voice* 12, 1 (Spring 1981).
52. "Strategy for 1977," in "The Road Made to Walk on Carnival Day: The Battle for the West Indian Carnival in Britain Race Today," 1977, 17.

53. Ibid.

54. Louis Chase, "Notting Hill Street Festival," April 20, 1978, 26.

55. Interview Len Garrison, April 2, 1981; see also Len Garrison, *Black Youth, Rastafarianism, and the Identity Crisis in Britain*, A.C.E.R. Project, 1979.

56. William A. Gamson, *The Strategy of Social Protest* (Homewood: The Dorsey Press, 1975).

57. This is my estimate, since initial estimates of a study based on 1967 data were as high as $500 million and the rebellions continued until 1971, with the greatest number occurring in 1969. *Report of the National Advisory Commission on Civil Disorders*, 15.

58. Feagin and Hahn, *Ghetto Revolts*, 101–8.

59. William Ryan, *Blaming The Victim* (New York: Vintage/Random House, 1976), 236.

60. I share the concern of Ira Katznelson regarding the role the race of the observer plays in the study of race relations and suggests that logically the social scientist most often shares the class and racial perspective of his or her group in the interpretation of race phenomena. See *Black Men, White Cities: Race, Politics and Migration in the United States, 1900–1930, and Britain, 1948–1968* (Chicago: University of Chicago Press, 1976), 4–5.

61. Ryan, *Blaming the Victim*.

62. Floyd R. Barbour, ed., *The Black Power Revolt* (Boston: Porter Sargent, 1968).

63. Gerald Pomper, *Voters' Choice: Varieties of American Electoral Behavior* (New York: Dodd, Mead 1975), 126–36.

64. Gamson, *The Strategy of Social Protest*, 130–31.

65. Robert M. Fogelson, *Violence as Protest: A Study of Riots and Ghettos* (Garden City: Doubleday/Anchor, 1971).

66. Alan March, *Protest and Political Consciousness* (Beverly Hills: Sage Publications, Sage Library of Social Research), 9.

67. Ibid., 96–97.

68. *The Washington Post*, April 12, 1981; *The New York Times*, April 13, 1981.

69. *The Economist*, London, April 18, 1981, 11.

70. *New Statesman*, April 17, 1981, 3.

71. *The Economist*, April 18, 1981, 54.

72. *The Sunday Times*, July 12, 1981.

73. At the same time, it was interesting to note an article which suggested that "Disabled 'quota' may be scrapped." Ibid.

74. The Social and Economic Status of the Negro in the United States, 1970, Bureau of Labor Statistics Report No. 394, Current Population

Reports Series 23, No. 38, U.S. Department of Commerce, Bureau of the Census, July 1971, 23.

75. Oversight on Federal Enforcement of Equal Employment Opportunity Laws, Subcommittee on Employment Opportunity, Committee on Education and Labor, House of Representatives, November 28–29, 1978.

76. Social Indicators 1976, U.S. Department of Commerce, Office of Federal Statistical Policy Standards, Bureau of Census, December 1977, Chart 8/5.

77. The five-day Miami rebellion was the largest of these, occurring in May 1980 when the courts acquitted four white policemen for the alleged beating death of a prominent Black insurance executive. In the most recent incident, three hundred residents of a housing project rebelled with guns, bottles and rocks when a police officer arrested a youth who had opened up a water hydrant and was throwing water on passing cars. *The New York Times*, July 11, 1981.

6. Pan African Linkages in Britain and the United States

1. George Shepperson, "Pan Africanism and Pan Africanism: Some Historical Notes", *Phylon* 23, 4 (Winter 1962).

2. Cited in Stokely Carmichael, *Stokely Speaks: Black Power Back to Pan Africanism* (New York: Vintage/Random House, 1971), 179.

3. Dilip Hiro, *Black British, White British* (London: Eyre and Spottiswoode, 1971).

4. *The Observer*, London, December 24, 1965; *The Times*, December 7, 1964.

5. Hiro, *Black British, White British*, 58–59.

6. Ibid., 61–63.

7. Pamphlet, CARD, Campaign Against Racial Discrimination, n.d.

8. Secretary's Report, Campaign Against Racial Discrimination, 1967.

9. Ibid., 3.

10. Rose and Associates, *Colour and Citizenship*, 526.

11. Ibid., 527.

12. *Secretary's Report*, 5.

13. Rose and Associates, *Colour and Citizenship*, 527.

14. *Secretary's Report*, 6.
15. *The Sunday Telegraph*, London, September 11, 1966.
16. One picket in September 1966 is described in a CARD 1967 newsletter that involved the refusal of a salon to treat the hair of some Asian women.
17. "The Bayard Rustin Meeting," Newsletter of the Campaign Against Racial Discrimination, No. 1, 1967, p. 7.
18. Rose and Associates, *Colour and Citizenship*, 546.
19. Press Interview Statement, Johnny James, Campaign Against Racial Discrimination, November 9, 1967.
20. Rose and Associates, *Colour and Citizenship*, 620.
21. Chris Mullard, *On Being Black in Britain* (Washington, D.C.: INSCAPE, 1975), 170.
22. *The Times*, London, February 12, 1965.
23. Malcolm's performance was awesome and his impact upon the youthful audience profound, as seen by an eyewitness observer, Lebert Bethune, "Malcolm X in Europe," in John Henrik Clarke, ed., *Malcolm X: The Man and His Times* (New York: Macmillan, 1969), 231–33.
24. Peter Goldman, *The Death and Life of Malcolm X* (New York: Harper and Row, 1965), 278.
25. Paul Lee, "Malcolm X: African-American Statesman," Panorama, Xerox, January 23, 1980.
26. Carmichael, *Stokely Speaks*, 78–79.
27. Ibid., 85.
28. Ibid., 87.
29. Ibid., 88.
30. Ibid., 92.
31. Ibid., 97.
32. Ibid., 89.
33. Carmichael had met with many Black Power adherents in Britain during his visit such as Michael Defrietas, Roy Sawh and others. He left Britain for North Vietnam on July 24. *The Times*, London, July 25, 1967.
34. Obi Egbuna, *Destroy This Temple: The Voice of Black Power in Britain* (London: MacGibbon and Kee, 1971), 16.
35. Ibid., 18–22.
36. Letter, Black Panther Movement to Police Authorities, London, October 3, 1968, 3.
37. *The Times*, London, February 22, 1970.
38. *The Times*, London, March 1970; *Stoke Newington and Hackney Observer*, June 19, 1970.

39. *The Guardian,* London, July 30, 1969; *The Daily Express,* London, July 30, 1969.

40. Gus Johns and Derek Humphrey, *Because They're Black* (Middlesex: Penguin, 1971), 89.

41. A Black community of some longevity and the subject of an early work on Blacks in Britain by Dr. Kenneth Little, *Negroes in Britain,* 1947. In the early 1960s Michael X headed the Colored Peoples Progressive Association.

42. In a speech February 24, 1967, Defrietas had such words as "filthy" and "nasty" to describe British people, and he was briefly jailed, being the first person charged under the Race Relations Act of 1965 for using words which would incite racial hatred. It was pointed out that the purple language of Enoch Powell might also have qualified him for similar treatment, but that was not to be. See Paul Foot, *The Rise of Enoch Powell* (Middlesex: Penguin, 1969), 111, 112.

43. *The New York Times,* December 1, 1969.

44. Lennon, for example, gave a lock of hair that was later auctioned off in New York for a considerable sum. Also Ali's appearance in Britain had been exploited by the National Front, a racist and fascist organization that supported his racial separatist views completely. Ali expounded his views on British television and at the London School of Economics. *Spearhead,* Publication of the National Front, n.d. (1970?).

45. *The Observer,* London, August 2, 1970.

46. *North London Press,* London, February 13, 1970.

47. *The Times,* London, August 14, 1970; *The Guardian,* London, July 28, 1970.

48. *The Sunday Telegraph,* London, August 2, 1970.

49. *The Daily Telegraph,* London, June 11, 1971.

50. "Police Raid on the Black House," RAAS, n.d.

51. *The Daily Telegraph,* London, June 11, 1971.

52. David Clark, "A Second Chance for Michael X," *Race Today,* March 1973, 73.

53. Protesting "White Domination of Aboriginal Affairs," two hundred Australian aborigines rebelled, smashing windows and writing "kill whitey" and "Black Power" slogans on the walls of buildings. *Washington Afro-American,* December 14, 1971. But see also, Locksley Edmondson, "The Internationalization of Black Power: Historical and Contemporary Perspectives," *Mawazo,* Kampala, 1, 4 (December 1968): 16–30; Also, Locksley Edmondson, "The Challenges of Race: From Entrenched White Power to Rising

Black Power," *International Journal*, Canada, 24, 4 (Autumn, 1969): 693–716.

54. Carmichael, *Stokely Speaks*, 130.

55. Ibid., 162.

56. Ibid., 177.

57. Ibid., 202.

58. Letter, Carmichael to Owusu Sadaukai, February 17, 1972.

59. Ronald Walters, "The New Black Political Culture," *Black World*, October 1972, 4–17.

60. *Black Voice*, London, 4 (1973).

61. Ibid.

62. *Resolutions and Speeches from the Sixth Pan African Congress* (Dar es Salaam: Tanzania Publishing House, 1976), 56–66.

63. Ibid., 143–44.

64. *Grass Roots*, London, June–July, 1979, 11.

65. *Grass Roots*, London, June–July, 1978, 13.

66. *Grass Roots*, London, May–June, 1980.

67. *Black Voice*, London, 4, 2 (1973): 5.

68. Speech, Paul Boateng, Member of Parliament, Howard University, Washington, D.C., April 1988.

69. Interview, Amelia Parker, Executive Director, CBC, June 28, 1989.

70. Michael Mattus, "Solidarity Across the Atlantic," *The Carribbean Times*, London, April 7, 1989, 1.

71. "Black Caucus: United We Stand," *Asian Times*, London, April 7, 1989, 1.

72. "We Can Learn From Our American Cousins," *The Voice*, April 9, 1989, 1.

73. "Black Caucus: United We Stand."

74. Ibid.

75. See my *Black Presidential Politics in America* (Albany: SUNY Press, 1988).

76. Marian FitzGerald, *Black People and Party Politics in Britain*, Runnymede Research Report, The Runnymede Trust, London, April 1987, 1.

77. See "Pioneers of Britain's Parliament," *Ebony*, March 1988, 84

78. "Darcus Howe Interviews Bernie Grant at the House of Commons," *Race Today* 18, 1 (January 1988): 8. See also Muhammad Anwar, *Race and Politics: Ethnic Minorities and the British Political System* (Tavistock, 1986).

79. Letter, Bernie Grant to Neil Kinnock, House of Commons, Parliamentary Black Caucus, May 12, 1989

80. Interview, Bernie Grant, August 11, 1989, London, England.

81. Ira Katznelson, *Black Men, White Cities: Race, Politics and Migration in*

the United States, 1900–1930, and Britain, 1948–1968, (Chicago: University of Chicago Press, 1976), 23.

82. Ibid., 197. See also Christopher Bagley, "Race Relations and Theories of Status Consistency," *Race* 12, 4 (1970): 286–87; also Katznelson, *Black Men, White Cities,* 205.

83. Rose and Associates, *Colour and Citizenship,* 538–39.

84. CARD Information Bulletin, 1, 1967.

7. The Environment for Race Politics in the United States and South Africa

1. George M. Frederickson, *White Supremacy: A Comparative Study in American and South African History* (New York: Oxford University Press, 1981).

2. See for example: Gail Gerhart, *Black Power in South Africa: The Evolution of An Ideology* (Berkeley: University of California Press, 1978); Bernard Magubane, *The Ties That Bind: African-American Consciousness of Africa* (Trenton: Africa World Press, 1987), 207–28.

3. James A. Kushner, *Apartheid in America: An Historical and Legal Analysis of Contemporary Racial Segregation in the United States* (Frederick, Md.: University Publications of America, 1981).

4. A. G. Russell, *Colour, Race and Empire* (Port Washington, N.Y.: Kennikat Press, 1973), 29.

5. Thomas Noer, *Briton, Boer, and Yankee: The United States and South Africa 1870–1914* (Kent, Oh.: Kent State University Press, 1978), 112.

6. "South Africa Economic Survey," *Euromoney,* London, July 1981, 10.

7. Ibid.

8. Mackler, 27.

9. Ibid., 28.

10. Ibid., 27–39.

11. "Apartheid and U.S. Policy," *Newsweek,* March 11, 1985, 31–33.

12. Frederickson, *White Supremacy,* 166–67.

13. "Gwendolen M. Carter, *Which Way is South Africa Going?* (Bloomington: Indiana University Press, 1980), 68–76.

14. See Gary T. Marx and Michael Useem, "Majority Involvement in Minority Movements," *Journal of Social Issues*, 27, (1971): 81–104.
15. David Halberstam, "The Fire to come in South Africa, *The Atlantic*, May 1980, 90.
16. U.S.–South Africa Relations, Hearings, Africa Subcommittee, Committee on Foreign Relations, House, March 24, 1966, 329.
17. Spiller, *Inter-Racial Problems*, 315.
18. James Baker, John de St. Jorre, and J. Danial O'Flaherty, "South Africa: The American Consensus," *Worldview*, October 1979, 12–16.
19. U.S. Department of Commerce, Bureau of International Commerce, South Africa Desk, August 1981.
20. "U.S. Corporate Interests in Africa," Report, Subcommittee on Africa, Committee on Foreign Relations, Senate, January 1978.
21. Gail Gerhart, *Black Power in South Africa*, 86.

8. Comparative Black Politics in the United States and South Africa

1. Robert Ernst and Lawrence Hugg, eds., *Black America: Geographic Perspectives* (New York: Anchor/Doubleday, 1976).
2. G. Franklin Edwards, ed., *E. Franklin Frazier: On Race Relations* (Chicago: The University of Chicago Press, 1968), 314.
3. Data are from *Black Enterprise Magazine*, April 1989.
4. *The National Roster of Black Elected Officials*, vol. 10 (Washington, D.C.: Joint Center for Political Studies, 1988).
5. June M. Thomas, "Urban Displacement: Fruits of a History of Collusion," *The Black Scholar* 11, 2 (November/December 1979): 68–80.
6. Robert Hill, "Benign Neglect Revisited: The Illusion of Black Progress," Research Department, National Urban League, Washington, D.C., July 24, 1973.
7. R.W. Johnson, *How Long Will South Africa Survive?* (New York: Oxford University Press, 1977), 181.
8. Ibid.
9. This is the estimate given by C.J. Jooste, Director of the South African Bureau of Racial Affairs, cited in Ian Robertson and Phillip Whitten, eds., *Race and Politics in South Africa* (New Brunswick: Transaction, 1978), 37.

10. Johnson, *How Long,* 179.
11. Robert M. Price and Carl G. Rosbert, eds., *The Apartheid Regime: Political Power and Racial Domination* (Berkeley: Institute of International Studies, University of California, 1980), 131.
12. Alan Brooks and Jeremy Brickhill, *Whirlwind Before The Storm: The Origins and Development of the Uprising in Soweto and the Rest of South Africa from June to December 1976* (London: International Defense and Aid Fund for Southern Africa, 1980), 181–82.
13. Price and Rosberg, *The Apartheid Regime,* 99–126.
14. Johnson, *How Long,* 184.
15. This Household Subsistence Level has also been known as the Poverty Datum Line.
16. *The New York Times,* August 12, 1981.
17. Henry Steele Commager, ed., *The Struggle for Racial Equality* (New York: Harper and Row, 1967), 19–20.
18. Ibid.
19. Carter G. Woodson, *The Mis-Education of the Negro* (Washington, D.C.: The Associated Publishers, 1969).
20. Ibid.
21. E. Franklin Frazier, *Black Bourgeoisie: The Rise of a New Middle Class in the United States* (New York: Collier, 1962), 95.
22. Ibid., 190.
23. James Forman, *The Making of Black Revolutionaries* (New York: Macmillan, 1972), 392.
24. Ibid.
25. Ibid., 395.
26. Bernard Magubane, *The Political Economy of Race and Class in South Africa,* (New York: Monthly Review Press, 1979), 82.
27. At this writing, three such "Homelands" have become "Independent." They are: Bophthataswana, Transkei, and Venda. When Bophthatswana accepted this status in 1977, the UN General Assembly voted 134 to 0 to declare this sham status invalid. The only country abstaining was the United States.
28. No Sizew, *One Azania, One Nation: The National Question in South Africa* (London: Zed Press, 1979), 80.
29. Hendrik W. van der Merwe, Nancy C. J. Charton, D. A. Kotze and Ake Magnusson, eds., *African Perspectives on South Africa* (Capetown: Center for InterGroup Studies; Stanford: Hoover Institution Press, 1978), 376.
30. Ibid., 385.
31. Ibid., 392.
32. Ibid., 403.
33. Ibid., 404.
34. Robertson and Whitten, *Race and Politics in South Africa,* 85.

35. No Sizew, *One Azania, One Nation*, 89.
36. Van der Merwe et al., *African Perspectives on South Africa*, 580.
37. Price and Rosberg, *The Apartheid Regime*, 111.
38. Brooks and Brickhill, *Whirlwind Before the Storm*, 130.
39. Price and Rosberg, *The Apartheid Regime*, 118.
40. Warren St. James, *NAACP: Triumphs of a Pressure Group 1909–1980* (Smithtown: Exposition Press, 1980), 245.
41. Ibid.
42. Joel Dreyfuss and Charles Lawrence III, *The Bakke Case: The Politics of Inequality* (New York: Harcourt, Brace and Jovanovich, 1979).
43. Benjamin Muse, *The Negro Revolution: From Nonviolence to Black Power* (New York: The Citadel Press, 1970), 30.
44. Ibid.
45. George Breitman, ed., *Malcolm X: By Any Means Necessary* (New York: Pathfinder Press, 1970), 41.
46. Ibid., 42.
47. Ibid., 79.
48. LeRoi Jones, *Home: Social Essays* (New York: William Morrow, 1966), 137.
49. Ibid., 238–45.
50. Gail Gerhart, *Black Power In South Africa: The Evolution of an Ideology* (Berkeley: University of California Press, 1978), 287.
51. Ibid.
52. Ibid., 293.
53. Van der Merew et al., *African Perspectives on South Africa*, 92.
54. Ibid., 93.
55. Millard Arnold, ed., *Steve Biko: Black Consciousness in South Africa* (New York: Random House, 1978), 261.
56. Price and Rosberg, *The Apartheid Regime*, 86.
57. Van der Merew et al., *African Perspectives on South Africa*, 330–32.
58. Arnold, *Steve Biko*, 133.
59. Price and Rosberg, *The Apartheid Regime*, 88.
60. *Report of the National Advisory Commission on Civil Disorders* (New York: Bantam, 1968), 35–37.
61. *Violence in the United States*, Facts On File, vol. 1, 1956–67, 77.
62. David L. Lewis, *King: A Biography*, 2nd ed. (Urbana: University of Illinois Press, 1978), 306.
63. George Vickers, *Dialogue on Violence* (New York: Bobbs-Merrill, 1968), 30.
64. Ibid., 31.
65. Ibid., 23.
66. Leo Kuper, *An African Bourgeoisie* (New Haven: Yale University Press, 1965), 13.
67. Cited in Johnson, *How Long*, 178.

68. Ernest Harsch, *South Africa: White Rule, Black Revolt* (New York: Monad Press, 1980), 280–81.
69. Ibid., 281.
70. Brooks and Brickhill, *Whirlwind Before the Storm*, 92.
71. Ibid.
72. Harsch, *South Africa*, 282.
73. Ibid., 292.
74. Brooks and Brickhill, *Whirlwind Before the Storm*, 87.
75. Harsch, *South Africa*, 293.

9. Pan African Politics of Black Communities in the United States and South Africa

1. Richard Gibson, *African Liberation Movements* (New York: Oxford University Press, 1972), 43–55.
2. Ibid., 45–47.
3. Gwendolen M. Carter, *Which Way is South Africa Going?* (Bloomington: Indiana University Press, 1980), 142.
4. Memo, Merriweather to Members of the Committee, January 18, 1972. The entertainers included Sammy Davis, Jr., Aretha Franklin, James Brown, Lea Roberts, Judy Clay, the Isley Brothers, Timothy Wilson, and Muhammad Ali. The Committee included Don Lee (Haki Madhudbuti), Mari Evans, Imamu Baraka, Hoyt Fuller, John O. Killens, Edmund B. Gaither, Askia Touré, Sonia Sanchez, Paula Giddings, S. E. Anderson, Saundra Towne, Addison Gayle, organizers Louise Merriweather, John Henrik Clarke, and others.
5. Letter, Merriweather to Wilkins, February 27, 1972.
6. Letter, Wilkins to Merriweather, March 14, 1972.
7. *The New York Times*, March 28, 1972.
8. Ibid.
9. *The Amsterdam News*, New York, April 15, 1972.
10. I was a member of the Polaroid Revolutionary Movement in Boston for a brief period of 1970–1971.
11. Gail Gerhart, *Black Power in South Africa: The Evolution of an Ideology* (Berkeley: University of California Press, 1978), 292–93.
12. Alan Brooks and Jeremy Brickhill, *Whirlwind Before the Storm: The Origins and Development of the Uprising in Soweto and the Rest of South*

Africa from June to December 1976 (London: International Defense and Aid Fund for Southern Africa, 1980), 64.

13. D50. *The New York Times*, July 24, 1979.
14. *The Washington Post*, July 30, 1979.
15. Arthur Ashe with Frank Deford, *Portrait In Motion* (Boston: Houghton Mifflin, 1975), 127.
16. Ibid., 128.
17. Stokely Carmichael and Charles Hamilton, *Black Power: The Politics of Liberation in America* (New York: Vintage/Random House, 1967), 44.
18. Hendrik W. Van der Merwe, Nancy C.J. Charton, D. A. Kotze and Ake Magnusson, eds., *African Perspectives on South Africa* (Capetown: Center for Intergroup Studies; Stanford: Hoover Institution Press, 1978), 99–100.
19. Gerhart, *Black Power in South Africa*, 276.
20. Barney Pityane, "Afro-American Influence on the Black Consciousness Movement." Paper presented at the Conference on African American—Relations with Southern Africans, May 27–29, 1979, Howard University.
21. Ibid.
22. Ibid.
23. Floyd B. Barbour, ed., *The Black Power Revolt* (Boston: Porter Sargent Publisher, 1968), 266.
24. Gayraud S. Wilmore, *Black Religion and Black Radicalism: An Examination of the Black Experience in Religion* (Garden City: Anchor/Doubleday, 1973), 262–329.
25. Albert Cleage, *The Black Messiah* (New York: Sheed and Ward, 1967); James Cone, *Black Theology* (New York: Seabury Press, 1969); Vincent Harding, "Black Power and the American Christ," *Christian Century*, January 4, 1967, 10.
26. Wilmore, *Black Religion and Black Radicalism*, 327.
27. Gerhart, *Black Power in South Africa*, 261.
28. Basil Moore, ed., *Black Theology: The South African Voice* (London: C. Hurst, 1973), vii–xii.
29. Ibid., 52.
30. Ibid., 55.
31. Ibid.
32. Ibid., 24.
33. Ibid., 63.
34. Ibid.
35. Imamu Amiri Baraka (LeRoi Jones), ed., *African Congress: A Documentary of the First Modern Pan-African Congress* (New York: William Morrow, 1972), 158.
36. See Lorenzo Morris, ed., *The Social and Political Implications of the*

1984 Jesse Jackson Presidential Campaign (New York: Praeger, 1990). Also, Frank Clemente and Frank Watkins, eds., *Keep Hope Alive: Jesse Jackson's 1988 Presidential Campaign* (South End Press, 1989), 189.

37. "Apartheid in Crisis," Washington Notes on Africa, Spring 1990, Washington, D.C., 1, 3.

38. Martin Gottleib, "Mandela's Visit, New York's Pride: Symbols of Black Political Attainment," *The New York Times*, June 24, 1990, 1.

39. Ibid.

40. "Times Mirror News Interest Index," Times Mirror Center for People and the Press, Washington, D.C., July 12, 1990.

41. Gottleib, "Mandela's Visit."

42. "Remarks of Nelson Mandela, at the White House," June 25, 1990, Washington, D.C.

10. Pan Africanism in Brazil: Comparative Aspects of Color, Race, and Power

1. Elisa Larkin Nascimento, *Pan Africanism and South America,* (Buffalo: Afrodiaspora, 1980), 155–62.

2. See *Afrodiaspora* 3, 5 (January–March 1985).

3. Abdias do Nascimento, *Racial Democracy in Brazil: Myth or Reality?* (Department of African Languages and Literature, University of Ife, 1977), 69.

4. Thomas Merrick and Douglas Graham, *Population and Economic Development in Brazil: 1800 to the Present* (Baltimore: The Johns Hopkins University Press), 50.

5. A.J.R. Russell-Wood, *The Black Man in Slavery and Freedom in Colonial Brazil* (New York: St. Martin's Press, 1982), 171.

6. Florestan Fernandez, *The Negro in Brazilian Society,* (New York: Columbia University Press, 1969), 137.

7. Jose Honorio Rodrigues, *Brazil and Africa* (Berkeley: University of California Press, 1965), 80.

8. Ibid., 81.

9. Ibid., 79.

10. Charles Wagley, *Race and Class in Rural Brazil* (New York: UNESCO, International documents Service, Columbia University, n.d.), 27–33.

11. "Rio de Janeiro," *Domingo*, Rio de Janerio, Brazil, May 13, 1990, 5.
12. Abdias do Nascimento, *Mixture or Massacre?: Essays in the Genocide of a Black People* (Buffalo: Afrodiaspora, Puerto Rican Studies and Research center, SUNY, 1979), 2.
13. Carl Degler, *Neither White nor Black: Slavery and Race Relations in Brazil and the United States* (New York: Macmillan, 1971), 102.
14. Ibid., 145.
15. Nascimento, *Mixture or Massacre?* 81.
16. Anani Dzidzenyo, "The Position of Blacks in Brazilian Society," Minority Rights Group, London, Report no. 7, 1971.
17. Fernandez, *The Negro in Brazilian Society*, 303.
18. Interview, R. Walters with Collares, Porto Alegre, Brazil, May 22, 1990.
19. Nascimento, *Mixture or Massacre?* 86.
20. Helga Hoffman, "Poverty and Property in Brazil," in Edmar Bacha and Herbert Klein, eds., *Social Change in Brazil, 1945–1985* (Alberquerque: University of Mexico Press, 1989), 198.
21. Ibid., 209.
22. *Veja Magazine*, Rio de Janerio, May 11, 1988.
23. Ibid.
24. Ibid.
25. Ibid., 203.
26. Hoffman, "Poverty and Property in Brazil," 215.
27. Tom Schierholz, "Victorious Collor Faces Major Economic Challenges" (*Infobrazil* 11, 2:1.
28. Ibid.
29. "The Social and Economic Status of the Black Population in the United States," Census Bureau, U.S. Dept. of Commerce, 1973, p. 24.
30. Nascimento, *Mixture or Massacre?* 88.
31. Pierre-Michel Fontaine, "Pan Africanism and Afro-Latin Americans," in W. Ofuatey-Kodjoe, ed., *Pan-Africanism: New Directions in Strategy* (Lanham, Md.: University Press of America, 1986), 272–73.
32. Fernandez, *The Negro in Brazilian Society*, 201–3
33. Ibid., 222.
34. Abdias do Nascimento and Elisa Larkin Nascimento, "Afro-Brazilian Organizations and the Congress Movement of Black Culture in the Americas," *Afrodiaspora* 1, 2 (May–September 1983): 42.
35. Fernandez, *The Negro in Brazilian Society*, 232.
36. Ibid., 233.
37. Lelia Gonzalez, "Namibian Support of the Namibian Cause: Difficulties and Possibilities," *Afrodiaspora* 1, 2 (May–September, 1983): 29.
38. Ibid., 31.

39. Nascimento, *Pan Africanism and South America*, 102.

40. "O 13 de Maio Nao E Nosso Dia"; "20 De Novembro Dia Nacional Da Consciencia Negra," *Nego*, Special. Various documents and issues of *MNU Journal*, the national journal of the Unified Black Movement, 1989.

41. Nascimento, *Pan Africanism and South America*, 86.

42. Ibid.

43. I lectured at IPCN, May 15, 1990.

44. I met with 14 representatives of these groups in Porto Alegre, May 24, 1990.

45. "Brazilian Support of the Namibian Cause," 27.

46. Nzinga Collective of Black Women, Group of Black Women of Rio de Janeiro, *Afrodiaspora* 1, 2 (May–September 1983): 49. Annex of Resolutions to the United Nations Regional Symposium in Support of the Namibian Cause in Latin America, August 13–16, 1986.

47. Interview, R. Walters with the acting head, Palmares Foundation, Brazilia, May 21, 1990.

48. *World Development Forum* 8, 12 (June 30, 1990).

49. Folha De S. Paulo, Terca-Feira, April 3, 1990, 1.

50. Author visited the organization and surveyed its programs, May 21, 1990.

51. "Universitario Negro Denuncia Racismo e Roubo," press accounts, n.d.

52. "Entidades negras: Encuentro para Reivindacar su Papel," press account, n.d.

53. Interview with Pedro Chaves, political editor, and Paul Rubenich, international editor of *Zero Hora*, May 25, 1990, Porto Alegre. This is the city's most important daily newspaper.

54. Mark Brown, "PT Presidential Candidate 'Lula' Speaks at SAIS on Brazil's Future," *Infobrazil* 10, 4 (May 1989): 7.

55. Tom Schierholz, "Victorious Collor Faces Major Economic Challenge," *Infobrazil* 11, 2 (February 1990): 12.

56. Degler, *Neither White nor Black*, 260.

57. Logan traveled to Brazil in 1966 and Frazier wrote several articles on the subject. See "The Negro Family in Bahia, Brazil," *American Sociological Review* 7 (August 1942): 465–78; "Brazil Has No Race Problem," *Common Sense* no. 11 (November 1942): 363–65; "Some Aspects of Race Relations in Brazil," *Phylon* (third quarter 1942): 284–95.

58. Cited in Nascimento, *Pan Africanism and South America*, 82.

59. Interview, R. Walters with Richard Long, Atlanta, Ga., July 31, 1990.

60. Richard Long, "The First New World Festival of the African Diaspora," unpublished paper, 9.

61. Ibid., 10. Long says that the delegation also included such groups as the Marie Brooks Children's Dance Theater, Voices of Black Persuasion, Billy Higgins Jazz Group, and others.
62. Ibid., 8.
63. Interview, R. Walters with James Hill, Founders Library, Howard University, June 24, 1990.
64. Degler, *Neither White nor Black,* 5 (legal exclusion practices).

11. Afro-Caribbean Pan Africanism

1. Melville J. Herskovits, *The New World Negro* (Bloomington: Indiana University Press, 1969). Also, G. Franklin Edwards, *E. Franklin Frazier: On Race Relations* (Chicago: University of Chicago Press, 1968).
2. George Lamming, *The Pleasures of Exile* (London: Allison and Busby, 1984), 161.
3. Ibid., 214.
4. Kortright Davis, *Emancipation Still Comin'* (Maryknoll, N.Y.: Orbis Books, 1990), 24.
5. Rex Nettleford, *Mirror, Mirror: Identity, Race and Protest in Jamaica* (William Collins and Sangster, Jamaica, 1970), 27.
6. Ibid., 60–61.
7. Ibid.
8. Horace Campbell, *Rasta and Resistance: From Marcus Garvey to Walter Rodney* (Trenton: Africa World Press, 1987), 2.
9. J. Mutero Chirenje, *Ethiopianism and Afro-Americans in Southern Africa, 1883–1916* (Baton Rouge: Louisiana State University Press, 1987).
10. St. Clair Drake, *Ethiopianism* (Center for Afro-American Studies, UCLA, 1978).
11. Nettleford, *Mirror, Mirror,* 101.
12. Ibid., 166.
13. Ibid., 161.
14. "Interview w/ Rodney," *The Black Scholar* 6, 3 (November 1974): 40; Ivar Oxaal, *Race and Revolutionary Consciousness* (Cambridge: Schenkman, 1971), 24.
15. Campbell, *Rasta and Resistance,* 177; also, interview, R. Walters with Tim Hector, Washington, D.C., July 10, 1990.

16. Oxaal, *Race and Revolutionary Consciousness*, 11.
17. Ibid., 30
18. Ibid., 32.
19. Ibid., 21–41. Trinidad is a racially divided country whose population is 43 percent of African descent and 40 percent of East Indian descent, with the remaining of European descent.
20. Francis Alexis, *Changing Caribbean Constitutions* (Bridgetown, Barbados: Antilles Publication, 1984), 101–6.
21. "Introduction, Richard Small," Walter Rodney, *In the Groundings with My Brothers* (London: Bogle-L O'verture, 1969).
22. Ibid., 14.
23. Ibid., 24.
24. They included Dr. Vincent Harding, director and then curator of the papers of Martin Luther King, Jr. at the Gammon Theological Seminary; William Strickland, former member of SNCC; Robert Hill, a brilliant Jamaican who was with Rodney when the latter was barred from reentering Jamaica; and others.
25. "Towards the Sixth Pan-African Congress: Aspects of the International Class Struggle in Africa," *Institute of the Black World*, Atlanta, Ga., 1974.
26. Robert Hill, "Walter Rodney and the Restatement of Pan Africanism in Theory and Practice," in Edward Alpers and Pierre-Michel Fontaine, eds., *Walter Rodney: Revolutionary and Scholar: A Tribute* (Center for Afro-American Studies and African Studies Center, UCLA, 1982), 86.
27. Ibid., 80.
28. "Towards the Sixth Pan African Congress," 10.
29. See Vincent Harding, "Education and Black Struggle: Notes from the Colonized World," Monograph no. 2, *Harvard Educational Review*, 1974, 98–99.
30. "The Black Scholar Interviews Walter Rodney."
31. Rodney was not the only one to make such a criticism. See Horace Campbell, a Jamaican professor who was also teaching and studying in Uganda at this time. "Socialism in Tanzania: A Case Study," *The Black Scholar* 6, 8 (May 1975): 50.
32. Alpers and Fontaine, *Walter Rodney*, 93.
33. Eusi Kwayana, "Burnhamnism, Jaganism and the People of Guyana," *The Black Scholar* 4, 8–9 (May/June 1973): 40.
34. Ibid., 44.
35. "Black Scholar Interview by Marvin X," *The Black Scholar* 4, 5 (February 1973): 29.
36. Ibid., 42–46.
37. Campbell, *Rasta and Resistance*, 172.

38. Interview, R. Walters with Congressman Mervyn Dymally, Washington, D.C., August 10, 1988.
39. Manning Marable, *African and Caribbean Politics: From Kwame Nkrumah to Maurice Bishop*, (London: Verso, 1987), 208.
40. Interview, R. Walters with Desima Williams, former ambassador of Grenada to the UN, Washington, D.C., July 10, 1990.
41. Ibid.
42. Ibid.
43. Interview, R. Walters with Tim Hector; see also Marable, *African and Caribbean Politics*, 234–35.
44. Cited in William Eric Perkins, "Requiem for A Revolution: Perspectives on the US/OECS Intervention in Grenada," *Black Studies* 7 (1985–86): 21.
45. Interview, Desima Williams.
46. Ibid.
47. Speech, Michael Manley, Howard University, spring 1983.
48. Although official estimates are 70 percent caucasian, 12 percent Mestizo, 14 percent African, and 4 percent other.
49. One Black Cuban observer of this problem is Carlos Moore. See his *Castro, The Blacks, and Africa* (Los Angeles: Center for Afro-American Studies, 1988).
50. Manning Marable, "Race and Democracy in Cuba," *The Black Scholar* 15, 3 (May/June 1984); 23.
51. Johnetta Cole, "Race Toward Equality: the Impact of the Cuban Revolution on Racism," *The Black Scholar* 11, 8 (November/December 1980): 18.
52. Interview, Desima Williams.
53. Author's visit to Jamaica.
54. Oxaal, *Race and Revolutionary Consciousness*, 22.

12. The Structure of Pan African Unity in the Diaspora

1. Locksley Edmondson, "The Internationalization of Black Power: Historical and Contemporary Perspectives," *Mawazo* 1, 4, (December 1968): 20.
2. James Turner, "Black Nationalism: The Inevitable Response," *Black World* 20, 3 (January 1971): 4–14.

3. George Sheperson, "Pan Africanism and 'Pan-Africanism': Some Historical Notes," *Phylon* 23, 1 (Spring 1962): 346; See St. Clair Drake, "Diaspora Studies and Pan Africanism," in Joseph E. Harris, ed., *Global Dimensions of the African Diaspora* (Washington, D.C.: Howard University Press, 1982), 351.

4. Ibid.

5. Ibid., 357–78.

6. Claude Ake, *Revolutionary Pressures in Africa* (London: Zed Press, 1978); A. M. Babu, *African Socialism or Socialist Africa?* (London: Zed Press, 1981).

7. Sheila Rule, "Fun or Profit? Black Festival Tries To Have Both," *The New York Times*, August 25, 1989, 29.

8. Richard Bernstein, "French Debating Immigration Laws," *The New York Times*, August 3, 1986, 11.

9. "Les tensions raciales d'une petite ville," *Le Monde*, December 14, 1987, 10.

10. Flora Lewis, "Harlem Desire's Message," *The New York Times*, September 25, 1987, A39

11. Paul Delaney, "'Real Racists,' Black Asserts of Spaniards," *The New York Times*, September 10, 1987, A15.

12. Ibid.

13. "Refugees," United Nations High Commission on Refugees, no. 60, January 1989, Geneva, 20.

14. Jennifer Parmelee, "'Italian Dream' Soured by Racism," *The Washington Post*, August 31, 1989, A46.

15. Ibid.

16. Nicholas Kristof, "China's Burts of Rage: A Show of Racism, and of Something More," *The Washington Post*, January 8, 1989, A4E.

17. "Hidden Exiles No More," *The City Sun*, Special Report, June 6–12, 1990, A1–A9.

18. Ibid., A8.

19. Marvin Dunn, International Conference on Immigration and the Changing Black Population in the United States, May 18–21, 1983, University of Michigan, Ann Arbor, Mi.

20. Jeffrey Schmalz, "Miami's New Ethnic Conflict: Haitians vs. American Blacks," *The New York Times*, February 19, 1989, p. 1.

21. Richard Morin, "D.C. Area Residents Look Favorably on Recent Immigrants," *The Washington Post*, December 13, 1987, A21.

22. *Atlanta Daily World*, January 6, 1985, 1.

23. *Atlanta Daily World*, February 7, 1985, 1.

24. James Brooke, "Blacks in U.S. Are Wooed by Angolans," *The New York Times*, October 3, 1988, A3.

25. Ake, *Revolutionary Pressures in Africa*, 89.

26. Elenga M'buyinga, *Pan Africanism or Neocolonialism?* (London: Zed Press, 1982), 44.

27. "Scientists Call For Pan-African Union," *African Concord*, July 16, 1987, 28

28. Kwesi Krafona, ed., *Organization of African Unity: 25 Years On* (London: Afroworld Publishing, 1988).

29. Ibid., 146.

30. Edem Kodjo, *Africa Tomorrow* (New York: Continuum Publishing 1987), 200–227.

31. Ibid., 258.

32. Ibid., 290.

33. Locksley Edmonson, "Black American Political and Diasporic Mobilization: Toward the Heightening of a Linkage," *CAAS Newsletter*, vol. 8, no. 1, UCLA Center For Afro-American Studies, Los Angeles, 1984, 1.

34. Joseph Harris, ed., *Global Dimensions of the African Diaspora* (Washington, D.C.: Howard University Press, 1982), 41.

35. Emmanuel Wallerstein, "Crisis As Transition," *Dynamics of Global Crisis*, (New York: Monthly Review Press, 1982), 28.

36. Ibid., 49.

Postscript: Culture and Politics in the African Diaspora

1. Here I agree with one writer who says: "The Black experience in history, religion, politics, law, social relations, philosophy, and the arts comprises the consortium of Black culture." W. H. McClendon, "The Foundations of Black Culture," *The Black Scholar* 14, 3–4 (Summer 1983): 20.

2. William Toll, *The Resurgence of Race* (Philadelphia: Temple University Press, 1979), 139.

3. Léopold Senghor, *Négritude et Humanisme*, (Paris: Le Seuil, 1964), 31–35.

4. Dr. Basil Matthews, a series of unpublished papers on "The Black Perspective," transmitted to me January 4, 1971, Howard University, Washington, D.C.

5. John A. Davis, ed., *Pan Africanism Reconsidered* (Los Angeles: American Society of African Culture, University of California Press, 1962), 315.

6. Cheikh Anta Diop, *The Cultural Unity of Black Africa* (Chicago: Third World Press, 1978), 222.
7. Davis, *Pan Africanism Reconsidered*, 311.
8. James Baldwin, *Nobody Knows My Name* (New York: Delta/Dell Books, 1962), 18.
9. Ibid., 37.
10. Ibid., 55.
11. Norman R. Shapiro, ed., *Négritude: Black Poetry From Africa and the Caribbean* (Stonington, Conn.: October House, 1970), 31.
12. Baldwin, *Nobody Knows My Name*, 53.
13. Jacob Drachler, ed., *Black Homeland, Black Diaspora* (Port Washington, N.Y.: Kennikat Press, 1975), 108–9.
14. Davis, *Pan Africanism Reconsidered*, 306.
15. Ibid., 308.
16. Ibid., 313.
17. *African Culture*, Algiers Symposium, July 21–August 1, 1969 (Algerian National Publishing and Distribution Company, 1969), 30.
18. Ibid., 32.
19. Ibid.
20. There is some support for this idea by Professor Ali Mazrui, *World Culture and the Black Experience* (Seattle: University of Washington Press, 1974), 107.
21. Other participants in the symposium for the Afro-American delegation were: Dr. Ronald Walters of Howard University and Dr. Abdul Alkalimat of Peoples Press, Chicago.
22. In 1981 a pre-colloquium was held in Senegal for the Third World Festival of Negro Arts. Note that in Senegal, the subject is "Negro Arts." However, the full festival has not been held at this writing. Harold Cruse continued to believe that although Négritude might be potentially useful as an explanatory concept in understanding the cultural content of Harlem, for example, the matter was unresolved, partly, he also believed, because there were few Black cultural philosophers who took the concept seriously in the United States. (Harold Cruse, "Négritude Reconsidered," n.d.)
23. Sterling Stucky, "Relationships between Africans and Afro-Americans," *Africa Report* 16, 2 (April–May 1969): 5.
24. John Henrik Clarke, "African Studies in the United States, An Afro-American View," *Africa Report* 16, 2 (April–May 1969): 10.
25. Some support for this is found in the fact that in the 1968 first plenary session, the speaker was Dr. Charles Hamilton, whose topic was "Black Africa and Black America," *African Studies Newsletter* 1, 3 (May–June 1968): 1.
26. *African Studies Newsletter* 2, 1–2 (February–March 1969): 2.
27. Clarke, "African Studies in the United States," 12.

28. For a picture of this event, see C. Gerald Fraser, "Black Caucus Deliberations at Montreal: Who Should Control African Studies and for What Ends," *Africa Report* (December 1969): 20–21. The Black Canadian contingent was also motivated by the crisis of race, characterized as a cultural crisis. See a special issue, "Black Cultural Crisis in Canada," *Black Images*, Toronto, 1, 1 (January 1972).

29. Clarke himself said that since "the main aims and objectives of A.H.S.A. had not been made known to any appreciable number of the attending black intellectuals, who could have explained these objectives to the students, . . . the revolt against the domination of the Conference by white 'scholars' might still have occurred, but . . . would have been more orderly and constructive." *African Studies Newsletter* 1, 6–7 (November–December 1969): 10.

30. Ibid., 11.

31. "Resolution on the African Studies Association's Commitment to the Liberation and Dignified Survival of African People," *African Studies Newsletter* 3, 7 (November–December 1970): 3.

32. This is clear from the background paper written by Johnson, which explains the intent of the resolution.

33. Letter, AHSA Membership Form, Nicholas Onyewu, December 15, 1969.

34. Amiri Baraka, ed., *African Congress* (New York: William Morrow, 1972), 446–67.

35. Memorandum from the program committee for the second annual conference of the African Heritage Studies Association, to be held At Howard University, Washington, D.C., May 1–3, 1970. The concept of "Africanism" might be traced to Dr. Chike Onuwauchi, who, in a later paper defined this term which would be used as the theme of the 1970 AHSA Conference. "In the ideological perspective of Africanism—which is Afro-centric—the fundamental issue is the knowledge of who we are. It is saying in essence that to be free the Black man all over the world must regain his Africanism based on his cultural heritage. Africanism is the process which operates with African spiritualism and communalism as a philosophical base. It is a multi-dimensional process which is ultimately rooted in self-awareness, self-realization, and the consciousness of kind in the universal community of African peoples." See P. Chike Onuwauchi, "Africanism: Toward a New Definition," *African Heritage Newsletter* 2, 1–2 (January–February 1971): 3.

36. Hollie West and Herbert Denton, "A Black Reappraisal," *The Washington Post*, May 4, D1.

37. As previously indicated, Kawaida became the basis of the Congress of African People, which expanded into a national organization co-headed by Amiri Baraka.

38. Molefi Kete Asante, *Afrocentricity: The Theory of Social Change* (Buffalo: Amulefi Publishing Co., 1980), 26–27.

39. Ibid., 56.

40. Ibid., 69.

41. "Zeta Phi Beta Sorrority, Inc., Delta Zeta Zeta chapter presents 17 Debs," *The Afro-American*, Section B, Saturday, October 13, 1990, B1. See also Pemela Reynolds, "Making Names for Themselves," *The Boston Globe*, April 7, 1989, 33, 44. The articles refer to a similar discussion in the April 1989 issue of *Essence* magazine, but also allude to the research of Annette Kashif, a Howard University doctoral student who says: "certain common suffixes in black names—'isha,' 'wana,' 'illa,' for instance—can be traced back to African or Arabic names. In fact, Reynolds says, other linguists maintain that in naming their children parents are not necessarily looking for their ancestral roots, but many of these names are actually reconstituted African and Arabic names with a definite rhythmic and syllabic pattern.

42. Michael Specter, "Shift to 'African American' May Prove There is Much in a Name," *The Washington Post*, October 16, 1990, A3.

43. "Rules of An Early Negro Society, 1796," in Herbert Aptheker, ed., *A Documentary History of the Negro People in the United States*, vol. 1, (New York: Citadel Press, 1967), 38. However, a masterful account of the name controversy as an expression of African-American culture appears in "Identity and Ideology," a chapter in Sterling Stucky's impressive work, *Slave Culture: Nationalist Theory and the Foundations of Black America* (New York: Oxford University Press, 1987), 193–244. He agrees that the difficulty of making out of many different peoples one, in terms of their conscious identity—or the process of "panafricanization"—"had an important bearing not only on the status of the Afro-American but on the question of African liberation everywhere." He thought that, even though it was "imperfectly understood," the fact that "the pull of Africa profoundly influenced the thought and feeling of millions of Blacks" was an essential fact that underlay the periodic discussions about the name. (243)

44. "All Things Considered," National Public Radio, Monday, October 15, 1990. David Duke lost the November 16, 1991, governor's race in Louisiana by 61 to 39 percent to former governor Edwin Edwards, with a massive turnout of the Black vote.

45. John Henrik Clarke has a substantive review of the history of the Black naming process in "Can African People Save Themselves," part four, *The City Sun*, October 10–16, 1990, 5. He says that as late as the turn of the century, George Washington Williams, in his *History of the Negro Race*, was still alternating between the use of the

term "African" and "Negro." But that the term "Negro" was more frequently used confirms Stucky's observation of the building reluctance of Blacks to use this term, because it had become a term of derision and one which severely separated them from their American patrimony. Where Stucky and Clarke would part is clearly in Clarke's assertion that "after the middle of the nineteenth century in the United States Black Americans were no longer considered Africans."

46. "Pan-Africanism: Land and Power," in Robert Chrisman and Nathan Hare, *Pan-Africanism* (New York: Bobbs-Merrill, 1974), 10.
47. Stokely Carmichael, *Stokely Speaks* (New York: Vintage/Random House, 1971), 84–87.
48. V.P. Franklin, *Black Self-determination: A Cultural History of the Faith of our Fathers* (Lawrence Hill and Co., 1984).
49. Statement on his resignation from the American Political Science Association, 1971.

Bibliography

African Culture: Algiers Symposium, July 21–August 1, 1969. Alger: Societe Nationale d'Edition et de Diffision, 1969.

Ajala, Adekunle. *Pan-Africanism: Evolution, Progress and Prospects.* London: Andre Deutsch, 1973.

Ake, Claude. *Revolutionary Pressures in Africa.* London: Zed Press, 1978.

Alpers, Edward A., and Pierre-Michel Fontaine, eds. *Walter Rodney: Revolutionary and Scholar: A Tribute.* Los Angeles: Center For Afro-American Studies and African Studies Center, University of California, 1982.

American Society of African Culture, ed. *Pan-Africanism Reconsidered.* Berkeley: University of California Press, 1962.

Appolus, Emil, ed. *The Resurgence of Pan-Africanism.* London: Freedman Brothers, 1974.

Arnold, Millard, ed. *Steve Biko: Black Consciousness in South Africa.* New York: Random House, 1978.

Asante, Molefi Kete. *Afrocentricity: The Theory of Social Change.* Buffalo, New York: Amulefi Publishing, 1980.

Babu, Abdul Rahman Mohamed, *African Socialism or Socialist Africa?,* London: Zed Press, 1981.

Baraka, Amiri, ed. *African Congress: A Documentary of the First Modern Pan-African Congress.* New York: William Morrow, 1972.

431

Cabral, Amilcar. *Revolution In Guinea: An African People's Struggle.* London: Love and Malcomson, 1969.

Campbell, Horace. *Rasta and Resistance: From Marcus Garvey to Walter Rodney.* Trenton: African World Press, 1987.

Carmichael, Stokely. *Stokely Speaks: Black Power Back to Pan Africanism.* New York: Vintage / Random House, 1971.

Carmichael, Stokely, and Charles Hamilton. *Black Power: The Politics Of Liberation in America.* New York: Vintage/Random House, 1967.

Chrisman, Robert, and Nathan Hare, eds. *Pan-Africanism.* New York: Bobbs-Merrill, 1974.

Counter, S. Allen, and David L. Evans. *I Sought My Brother.* Cambridge: MIT Press, 1981.

Cromwell, Adelaide M., ed. *Dynamics of the African Afro-American Connection: From Dependency to Self-Reliance.* Washington, D.C.: Howard University Press, 1987.

Drachler, Jacob, ed. *Black Homeland, Black Diaspora: Cross-Currents of the African Relationship.* Port Washington, N.Y.: Kennikat Press, 1975.

DuBois, Shirley Graham. *His Day Is Marching On: A Memoir of W.E.B. DuBois.* New York: J.B. Lippincott, 1971.

Egbuna, Obi. *Destroy This Temple: The Voice of Black Power in Britain.* London: MacGibbon and Kee, 1971.

Esedebe, P. Olisanwuche. *Pan-Africanism: The Idea and the Movement, 1776–1963.* Washington, D.C.: Howard University Press, 1982.

Fernandez, Florestan. *The Negro in Brazilian Society.* New York: Columbia University Press, 1969.

First World Festival of Negro Arts: Colloquium on Negro Art, Dakar, April 1– 24, 1966. Paris: Présence Africaine, 1968.

Fontaine, Pierre-Michel, ed. *Race, Class and Power in Brazil.* Los Angeles: Center for Afro-American Studies, University of California, 1987.

Gerhart, Gail. *Black Power in South Africa: The Evolution of An Ideology.* Berkeley: University of California Press, 1978.

Gibson, Richard. *African Liberation Movements.* New York: Oxford University Press, 1972.

Harris, Joseph E., ed. *Global Dimensions of the African Diaspora.* Washington, D.C.: Howard University Press, 1982.

Hill, Adelaide Cromwell, and Martin Kilson, eds. *Apropos of Africa: Sentiments of American Negro Leaders on Africa from the 1800s to the 1950s.* London: Frank Cass & Col., 1969.

Howard University, Black Diaspora Committee, Department of History, ed. *The African Diaspora: Africans and Their Descendants in the Wider World to 1800.* Lexington, Mass.: Ginn Press, 1986.

James, C.L.R. *At the Rendezvous of Victory.* London: Alison and Busby, 1984.

Jenkins, David. *Black Zion: Africa, Imagined and Real, As Seen by Today's Blacks*. New York: Harcourt, Brace and Janovich, 1975.

Kodjo, Edem. *Africa Tomorrow*. New York: Continuum, 1987.

Langley, J. Ayo, ed. *Ideologies of Liberation in Black Africa, 1856–1970*, London: Rex Collings, 1979.

Magubane, Bernard. *The Ties That Bind: African-American Consciousness of Africa*. Trenton: Africa World Press, 1987.

Marable, Manning. *African and Caribbean Politics: From Kwame Nkrumah to Maurice Bishop*. London: Verso Press, 1987.

Martin, Tony. *Race First: The Ideological and Organizational Struggles of Marcus Garvey and the Universal Negro Improvement Association*. Homewood: Greenwood Press, 1976.

———. *The Pan-African Connection: From Slavery to Garvey and Beyond*, Dover, Mass: The Majority Press, 1983.

———. *The Future in the Present: Selected Writings*. Westport, Conn.: Lawrence Hill, 1987.

Mazrui, Ali A. *World Culture and the Black Experience*. Seattle: University of Washington Press, 1974.

M'buyinga, Elinga. *Pan Africanism or Neo-Colonialism: The Bankruptcy of the O.A.U.* London: Zed Press, 1975.

do Nascimento, Abdias. *Racial Democracy in Brazil: Myth or Reality*. Ibadan: Sketch Publishing, 1977.

Nascimento, Elisa Larkin. *Pan-Africanism and South America: Emergence of a Black Rebellion*. Buffalo: Afrodiaspora, 1980.

Nkrumah, Kwame. *Africa Must Unite*. New York: International Publishers, 1963.

———. *The Autobiography of Kwame Nkrumah*. New York: International Publishers, 1957.

Nettleford, Rex. *Mirror, Mirror: Identity, Race and Protest in Jamaica*. Jamaica: Collins Sangster, 1970.

Ofuatey-Kodjoe, W., ed. *Pan-Africanism: New Directions in Strategy*. Lanham: University Press of America, 1986.

Padmore, George. *Pan Africanism or Communism? The Coming Struggle for Africa*. New York: Roy Press, 1956.

Resolutions and Speeches from the Sixth Pan African Congress. Dar es Salaam: Tanzania Publishing House, 1976.

Rose, E.J.B., and Associates. *Colour and Citizenship: A Report on British Race Relations*. London: Oxford University Press, 1969.

Scobie, Edward. *Black Britannia: A History of Blacks in Britain*. Chicago: Johnson Publishing Company, 1972.

Senghor, Léopold. *Négritude and Humanism*. Paris: Editions de Seuil, 1964.

Shapiro, Norman, ed. and trans. *Négritude: Black Poetry From Africa and the Caribbean*. Stonington, Conn.: October House, 1970.

Thompson, Vincent B. *Africa and Unity: The Evolution of Pan-Africanism.*
London: Longman, 1969.

Turner, James, ed. *The Next Decade: Theoretical and Research Issues in Africana Studies.* Ithaca: Africana Studies and Research, Cornell University, 1984.

"The World Dimension of the Community of Black Peoples." *First Pre-Colloquium of the 3rd World Festival of Negro Arts.* Paris: Présence Africaine, 1981.

Index

Books in the African American Life Series

Coleman Young and Detroit Politics: *From Social Activist to Power Broker,* by Wilbur Rich, 1988

Great Black Russian: *A Novel on the Life and Times of Alexander Pushkin,* by John Oliver Killens, 1989

Indignant Heart: *A Black Worker's Journal,* by Charles Denby, 1989 (reprint)

The Spook Who Sat by the Door, by Sam Greenlee, 1989 (reprint)

Roots of African American Drama: *An Anthology of Early Plays, 1858–1938,* edited by Leo Hamalian and James V. Hatch, 1990

Walls: *Essays, 1985–1990,* by Kenneth McClane, 1991

Voices of the Self: *A Study of Language Competence,* by Keith Gilyard, 1991

Say Amen, Brother! Old-Time Negro Preaching: *A Study in American Frustration,* by William H. Pipes, 1992 (reprint)

The Politics of Black Empowerment: *The Transformation of Black Activism in Urban America,* by James Jennings, 1992

Pan Africanism in the African Diaspora: *An Analysis of Modern Afrocentric Political Movements,* by Ronald W. Walters, 1993